D0271386

WHEN THE CLOUDS FELL FROM THE SKY

ROBERT
CARMICHAEL

WHEN THE CLOUDS FELL FROM THE SKY

A Daughter's Search for Her Father in the
Killing Fields of Cambodia

ROBINSON

ROBINSON

First published in Thailand in 2015 as *When Clouds Fell from the Sky*
by Asia Horizons Books Co. Ltd.

First published in Great Britain in 2019 by Robinson

Copyright © Robert Carmichael, 2015, 2019

1 3 5 7 9 10 8 6 4 2

The moral right of the author has been asserted.

All rights reserved.
No part of this publication may be reproduced, stored in a retrieval system,
or transmitted, in any form, or by any means, without the prior permission in
writing of the publisher, nor be otherwise circulated in any form of binding or
cover other than that in which it is published and without a similar condition
including this condition being imposed on the subsequent purchaser.

A CIP catalogue record for this book is available from the British Library

ISBN: 978-1-47214-374-7 (hardback)
ISBN: 978-1-47214-375-4 (trade paperback)

Printed and bound in Great Britain by Clays Ltd, Elcograf S.p.A.

Papers used by Robinson are from well-managed forests
and other responsible sources

MIX
Paper from
responsible sources
FSC® C104740

Robinson
An imprint of
Little, Brown Book Group
Carmelite House
50 Victoria Embankment
London EC4Y 0DZ

An Hachette UK Company
www.hachette.co.uk

www.littlebrown.co.uk

FOR NEARY
who trusted me with her story

CONTENTS

*And everyone wants to know: Who? Why? Out of the sighing arises more
than the need for facts or the longing to get closure on someone's life.
The victims ask the hardest of all the questions: how is it possible that
the person I loved so much lit no spark of humanity in you?*

Antjie Krog, *Country of My Skull*

*No man is an island, entire of itself; every man is a piece of the
continent, a part of the main. If a clod be washed away by the sea,
Europe is the less, as well as if a promontory were, as well as if a manor
of thy friend's or of thine own were; any man's death diminishes me,
because I am involved in mankind, and therefore never send
to know for whom the bell tolls; it tolls for thee.*

John Donne, *Meditation XVII* (1624)

MAP OF PRESENT-DAY CAMBODIA

This map, using the country's 2015 provincial boundaries, illustrates the locations of all places referred to in the book.

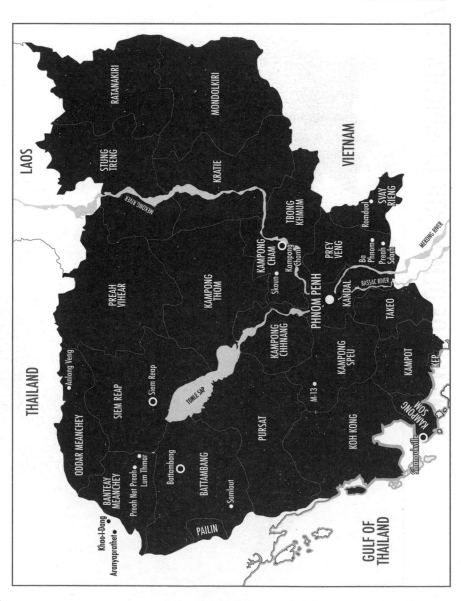

x

ZONE MAP OF DEMOCRATIC KAMPUCHEA (1975–79)

Under the Khmer Rouge, Cambodia was renamed Democratic Kampuchea and divided into geographical zones. Among those was the North-west Zone, which is where most of Ouk Ket's family was sent in 1975.

The map's arrows show the paths taken by Ouk Ket's relatives.

1. Journey of Ouk Saron, Ket's brother, to Svay Rieng in 1975.

2. Journey of Sam Sady, Ket's cousin, and her family in 1975, first to Ba Phnom and from there to Preah Sdach.

3. Journey of Sam Sady and her family to Pursat in 1977.

4. Journey of the members of Ket's family
   – his parents and most of his siblings
   – to Lum Thmar in 1975.

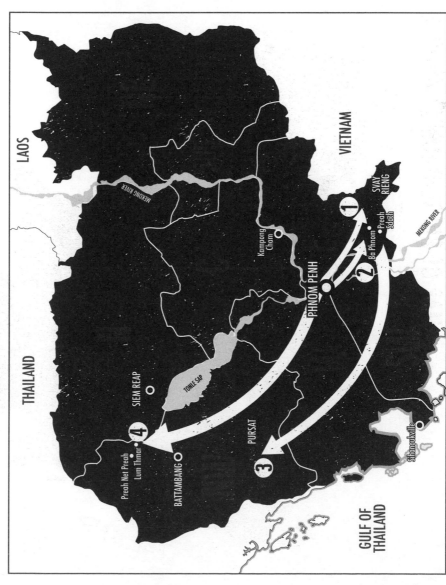

xi

PREFACE

CAMBODIA HAS TAKEN UP far more of my life than I dreamed it would. When I first arrived in 2001, I expected to spend a year, perhaps two, working in Phnom Penh as a journalist. As it turned out, I did leave after two years but I returned in early 2009 to cover the trial of Comrade Duch, the former head of the Khmer Rouge's brutal torture and execution centre codenamed S-21, and one of the people at the heart of this book. By the time I left in 2017, I had lived there for a decade.

My fascination with the country stems in part from my keen interest in how humans survive the most punishing experiences – from the First World War to the Holocaust to the siege of Stalingrad. Although I don't recall when I became aware of humankind's remarkable capacity to endure, it might well have had something to do with the fact that my grandfather survived months in the trenches of France and Belgium during the First World War.

My linked interest in the injustices that humans feel permitted to inflict on others was surely the product of growing up in South Africa: I was at school in the 1980s as apartheid was driven to collapse, and I was struck by what was taking place outside the privileged suburbs of my youth.

It goes almost without saying that there are numerous and profound differences between South Africa and Cambodia, yet one element they have in common is a post-atrocity reckoning of sorts for the suffering meted out to the majority of their peoples. South Africa's effort, the Truth and Reconciliation Commission (TRC), began its hearings in 1996. This was explicitly not a judicial process; its mission was to promote healing and understanding. Perpetrators who told the truth about their acts of political criminality were effectively guaranteed an amnesty. Although I was living in London during the two-year-long TRC process, I made sure to attend hearings on my rare trips back to Cape Town.

A decade later the tribunal to judge the crimes of the Khmer Rouge, the communist rulers of Cambodia between 1975–79, started its work. The model chosen was a hybrid court, part United Nations, part Cambodian, whose mixed nature is reflected in its unwieldy name: the Extraordinary Chambers in the Courts of Cambodia (ECCC). It is more commonly known as the Khmer Rouge tribunal. Its mission was to judge the surviving senior leaders of the Khmer Rouge as well as those thought 'most responsible' for the crimes of the period – a huge task given that two million people, or one in four Cambodians, are believed to have died from execution, starvation, illness or overwork in less than four years.

I felt then about the TRC as I do now about the Khmer Rouge tribunal: that witnessing such events is a rare privilege. I am extraordinarily fortunate to have been able to follow Cambodia's experience at such close quarters.

The topic of post-atrocity justice is both complex and fascinating, and the different paths chosen by South Africa and Cambodia are instructive. Neither is perfect, and nor could they be given that they are dealing with crimes against humanity, yet they went their different ways on the logical ground that doing something is surely better than doing nothing.

Rights advocates disagree with a TRC process that offers immunity in exchange for the truth. Critics of the court model, on the other hand, say it is slow, costly and – particularly when held outside the country where the crimes took place – of limited value for those whom it is meant to represent. A judicial process focuses less on truth, more on evidence and procedure, and is little concerned with reconciliation. Who is to say which of these – truth, justice or reconciliation – is the most important?

And yet, while the ECCC's hybrid model had the benefit of conducting its hearings inside Cambodia and in Khmer, the local language, its major flaw was that locating it in-country left it open to political interference. Such meddling is, perhaps, no surprise; after all, these are formal mechanisms to deal with crimes that are inherently political. What counts is who takes the decision on how to proceed.

In South Africa, the African National Congress won the democratic vote in 1994, ousting the apartheid-era National Party. In Rwanda, where 800,000 people were murdered in three months that year, Paul Kagame's Rwandan Patriotic Front expelled its genocidal predecessor. In both cases the incumbents lost power; the winners, untainted by the crimes of the previous regime, chose the path.

Cambodia was different: its current government was installed by Hanoi in 1979, and many of those in power today, including the two men still (as of 2019) at the top of the ruling Cambodian People's Party (CPP), were Khmer Rouge officials who defected prior to the January 1979 overthrow of Pol Pot's Democratic Kampuchea. That meant this new government was no 'out with the old' but something much more subtle, and the choice of a tribunal rather than a TRC was a direct consequence; the opaque balance of political power meant Prime Minister Hun Sen had little to gain from a TRC process. On the other hand a multi-million-dollar hybrid court where Cambodian judges were in the majority, despite the checks and balances designed by the United Nations to stop political interference, was more appealing.

The scale of Cambodia's experience also precluded a fair solution. With the best will in the world, no country could tackle the criminal neglect and cruel actions that led to the deaths of so many men, women and children, a near four-year period of catastrophe that many Cambodians refer to as *neuv pel del porpok thlak pi leu mek*, or 'the time when the clouds fell from the sky'. The cost would be staggering and the tribunal would drag on unworkably for decades. And so justice must be limited and whether one chooses a TRC or a judicial process, most of the guilty will get away with murder.

The advantage of both systems is that some truths will emerge, some victims will be heard, and citizens and outsiders alike will get the opportunity to learn what happened. South Africa's TRC was designed to promote healing and foster reconciliation and, in choosing that route, it elevated truth over justice. The ECCC, on the other hand, represents a judicial process (albeit one that incongruously has reconciliation as an additional goal).

At the time of writing, the ECCC has not been a shining success and it is highly unlikely to become one. The tribunal has numerous critics, some of whom have put forward well-founded arguments about serious flaws in its conception and structure, to say nothing of its ponderous and at times mismanaged operation; these are particularly egregious issues given the crimes before it, and the advanced age and poor health of the few accused and many of the survivors.

And yet I would argue that the fact that it is taking place at all is a triumph of sorts, and I believe some form of justice delivered (admittedly imperfectly and very late) is better than none, and that the public airing of the crimes of the Khmer Rouge will prove beneficial and informative – certainly not for everyone, but for some people now and for more people in future years.

Already the ECCC has inadvertently generated what I feel will one day be seen as its most important legacy: a curriculum that teaches the rule of Pol Pot's Khmer Rouge in schools so that those Cambodians fortunate enough not to have experienced that period can learn the bitter truths of those times. Ten years ago the treatment in students' textbooks of the Khmer Rouge's reign was limited to a few paragraphs; today pupils have a well-researched 100-page book – courtesy of foreign donors and the Documentation Center of Cambodia (DC-Cam), a redoubtable local research organisation – that accurately portrays the causes and effects of Democratic Kampuchea. That textbook was not a direct consequence of the ECCC, yet it is hard to imagine it would have seen the light of day had the tribunal not been established.

Three final points. The first is that this book, although containing its fair share of history, is at heart an account of one family's search for justice. At least 1.7 million people died or disappeared during the Khmer Rouge regime, but numbers of that magnitude are so vast that we cannot meaningfully comprehend them. The best way, then, to grasp the scale of what happened is by focusing on individual accounts, and it is the story of Ouk Ket, his wife Martine and their daughter Neary that has allowed me to do that. The second regards the term 'Khmer Rouge' ('Red Cambodians'), which denotes Cambodia's communists. Grammatically the term ought to be 'Khmers Rouges', but that plural form is rarely used in English. Consequently, I have followed the convention of the singular form while using it as a plural noun. So you will read that 'the Khmer Rouge were' rather than 'the Khmer Rouge was'.

The third refers to the use of tenses. The bulk of the book is written in the past tense, but I have chosen to portray the sections of Duch's trial in the present tense to ensure it remains as current in the reader's mind as it was in mine at the time.

It hardly bears saying that any errors or omissions in this book are mine.

ROBERT CARMICHAEL

ACKNOWLEDGEMENTS

ALTHOUGH THE ACT OF WRITING is a solitary effort, a book such as this is inevitably the result of the combined labours of many people. First and foremost, I must thank Neary Ouk for allowing me to use the story of her life as one of its key elements. Neary has been honest to the point of pain, and I can only guess at the emotional effort of the past few years. I also owe Neary's mother, Martine Lefeuvre, an extraordinary debt of gratitude.

Neary's aunt in Phnom Penh, the always-charming Sam Sady, was a fount of information about her cousin Ket – Neary's father – and was kind enough to spend hours telling me about life before, during and after the Khmer Rouge. Her motivation is simple: Sady, a teacher, feels that widening the pool of knowledge about those years could preclude something similar happening elsewhere. My thanks also to Sady's husband, Lim Sophon.

This book draws on the work of many researchers and academics, but I must single out David Chandler for his generous efforts. He has been unfailingly encouraging, eager to see it get to print, and provided valuable feedback with two comprehensive reviews of the draft.

I am also grateful to my other reviewers: Andrew Carmichael, Daniel Mehta, Ellie Dyer, Abby Seiff and Anne Heindel.

Among the researchers and academics whose work helped me better understand facets of the Khmer Rouge are: Youk Chhang, Stephen Heder, Craig Etcheson, Bernd Schaefer, Mychelle Balthazard, Leakhena Nou, Ben Kiernan, Alexander Hinton, Philip Short and Peter Maguire.

I would like to thank Ong Thong Hoeung and his wife Bounnie for their assistance. Special thanks also to film- and documentary-maker Rithy Panh.

Many of the Khmer Rouge-era proverbs I have used come from Henri Locard's insightful publication *Pol Pot's Little Red Book, The Sayings of Angkar*.

Among the Cambodian interviewees, I wish to thank: S-21 survivors Bou Meng and Chum Mey; the late Roth Marany, whose three children died during the time of the 'fire without smoke'; Uch Sorn, one of the few survivors of Duch's first prison M-13A; and village chief Nai Kong.

Others who have directly or indirectly contributed include: Rob Hamill, Tanja Schunert, Fabienne Luco, Laura McGrew, Alexandra Kent, Gregory Stanton, Julio Jeldres, Helen Jarvis, Michael Vickery, Theary Seng and Naly Pilorge; also Tim Minea, Rothany Srun and Sonja Meyer from the reconciliation NGO Kdei Karuna; and Chhim Sotheara and Judith Strasser from mental health services organisation TPO Cambodia. DC-Cam's Anne Heindel along with Clair Duffy and Heather Ryan from the Open Society Justice Initiative were consistent and generous voices of legal common sense.

I am indebted to Christophe Peschoux for allowing me to cite from his lengthy interview with Duch, conducted in 1999 shortly before the former head of S-21 was arrested. Also to Olivier Bonifacio for his help in rendering key moments in Duch's trial from their original French into English.

Staff at the Khmer Rouge tribunal who provided assistance over the years include Lars Olsen, Andrew Cayley, Silke Studzinsky, Rowan Downing, Bill Smith, Michael Karnavas and the late Reach Sambath.

For permission to access the archives at the Tuol Sleng Genocide Museum, thanks to the former Minister of Culture Him Chhem and his staff. At the archive, thanks to museum director Ke Soponnaka and staff Yin Nean and Lach Voleak Kalyann.

Within the field of journalism in Cambodia, one person stands out: Michael Hayes, the founder and former publisher of the *Phnom Penh Post*, who, based on little more than a hunch, employed me as its managing editor between 2001 and 2003. Thus began my interest with Cambodia's bleakest years.

Others from those early Cambodia days include Luke Hunt, Vong Sokheng, Lon Nara, Bill Bainbridge, Patrick Falby, Rajesh Kumar, Caroline Green, Charlotte McDonald-Gibson and – across town at our great rival the *Cambodia Daily* – Kevin Doyle.

After I returned to Cambodia in 2009 many journalists were helpful in various ways, particularly Brian Calvert with whom I spent numerous hours on the book's structure and content. Others who provided valuable assistance along the way include Elizabeth Becker, Nic Dunlop, Hurley Scroggins, Stephanie Gée, Mary Kozlovski, Anne-Laure Porée, Sebastian Strangio, Irwin Loy, Jared Ferrie, Laura Villadiego (especially for her efforts in trying to drum into my head the history of left-wing thought), Michelle Fitzpatrick, Nate Thayer, Greg Lowe, Douglas Gillison and Kate Bartlett.

Special thanks to photographer John Vink for the author photograph and for one of the display images used. Also to Charles Fox of the Found-Cambodia Project, as well as Daniel Mehta and Rachel Foo for permission to reproduce other photographs.

My gratitude to Roland Neveu and also to the very talented Erika Piñeros for her help in numerous creative areas including the final map lay-out and design.

At Little, Brown, thanks to Duncan Proudfoot, Rebecca Sheppard and Lucian Randall.

Many of the photographs in the book come from DC-Cam's archive. Thanks there to Sophat Morm, Socheat Nhean and Dara Vanthan.

I am indebted to journalists Sonny Chhuon and the late Dave Walker for introducing me to the story of 'the good village chief' Van Chhuon. Also to journalists Brian Calvert (again) and Kay Kimsong for *The Ghosts of Svay Rieng*, their story about the rise of the Khmer Rouge in south-east Cambodia, and for allowing me to access the documents behind it.

For translation work, thanks to Thor Sina in Phnom Penh and to Sam Sona in Siem Reap. Early versions of the book's maps were by Amy Martin. A special hat-tip to Paul and Mila Holloway, and another to Dave Potter and Hong Sotheary at the office in Phnom Penh.

Very special thanks to Dar Seng, a generous spirit and good friend who proved one of the book's staunchest supporters and whose influence runs through it. Thanks, too, to his former colleagues at the Center for Justice and Reconciliation, particularly Im Sophea and Jennifer McNulty. And to Sam Sothy and Heng Sovichet for their efforts in unravelling the meaning behind *The Song of Suffering*.

Assistance by email came from Gunnar Bergström.

I am acutely aware that we are but little without our families, and I am very fortunate for mine: to my late father, Duncan, who would have read this book keenly; to my mother Glenda, a consistent source of love and encouragement throughout our lives; and to my supremely talented siblings: my sister Jennifer and her family; my older brother Duncan and his family; and my younger brother Andrew and his family.

Last, and by no means least, I would like to acknowledge the love and support of my wonderful wife Beáta, who has unfailingly supported the multi-year effort that this book became – and our delightful son, Daniel, who brightens our world each day.

LEAVING S-21 PRISON: JANUARY 7, 1979

IT IS EARLY JANUARY, the height of the cool season, and the monsoon rains have ceased. In Cambodia these are traditionally the months of bounty when farmers harvest the last of the season's crop, and diesel-powered mills strip the rough outer husks from the grain, in the process producing pure, white rice. Brute force to generate a nation's most basic need.

In the courtyard of an old school in the capital Phnom Penh, the bony fronds on the coconut palms rustle in the breeze. If you and I could soar on this day, we would see below us four school buildings laid out in a half rectangle and, nearby, a wooden office between the entrance gate and these three-storey blocks. Uniformed figures move between them with a sense of urgency.

Inside the compound stands a man who is the very model of efficiency. Little more than a decade ago he was a humble and respected mathematics teacher, but for the past eight years he has inspired only terror, and this former school surrounded by a double-layered fence of corrugated iron fringed with barbed wire is his domain. More than that, this place, the Khmer Rouge's most secret prison, known by its codename S-21, is largely his creation.

Comrade Duch barks orders.[1] Thin-hipped, his features are striking: not the rounded Cambodian face seen in the stone colossi of the 800-year-old Bayon temple in the distant north-west, but long, narrow, pale; evidence of his Chinese heritage.

In a photograph taken at this place, Duch, his neatly pressed shirt shorn of insignia, is seen walking into a room. Two pens in his top pocket and the pistol on his belt mark him out as a man of rank, yet although Duch is in absolute control of his surroundings, he seems not entirely comfortable. His smile is awkward, even shy and ingratiating.

---

1. Duch's name is pronounced 'Doik', with the stress at the beginning of the word.

Duch usually speaks softly to his staff, yet they are terrified of him. They have good reason. As head of the Khmer Rouge's secret police, or *santebal,* Duch wields awesome power. He reports directly to the senior leaders of the Khmer Rouge, and his job is simple: to process those deemed to be enemies of the revolution, so-called traitors who have burrowed into the movement on behalf of the CIA or the KGB or the treacherous Vietnamese; to draw out their complicity through torture; and, once their confessions are written down and approved and their purported accomplices named, to authorise their executions.

This is a battle without end and there have been no half measures. Indeed it has only intensified since Pol Pot's Khmer Rouge forces won the civil war in 1975. To be brought to this machine that Duch has helped build is to be guilty by default since the movement's faceless leaders – known as *Angkar,* or the organisation – have, in the saying of the time, the eyes of a pineapple. That means *Angkar* is all seeing and infallible, vested with super-natural powers. As such *Angkar* is judge and jury, and Duch its executioner.

At least 14,000 men, women and children have been brought to S-21 during its three-and-a-half-year existence, and almost without exception their fate, and that of their families, was execution, preferably once their confessions laid bare their supposedly subversive activities.[2] Most, it should be said, were guilty of no such thing. It made no difference. Those named as accomplices would in turn often be arrested, brought here and processed by means of whips, electrocution and any number of tortures to serve *Angkar's* most basic need: the success and purity of the revolution.

This task is straightforward and mechanical, and contains no grey areas. That appeals immensely to Duch, a rigid man who prides himself on logic and efficiency, the virtue of certainties, the acknowledgement of a job well done and the satisfying symmetry of an order received and flawlessly carried out. But for the past few months the pitiless harmony that has characterised Duch's life for nearly a decade has been undone.

Despite Duch's best efforts – and they have been extraordinary – the revolution's foes seem only to have multiplied over the years. First there were the remnants of the Lon Nol regime that Pol Pot's Khmer Rouge overthrew in 1975, and then there were those in the population who did not support the revolution. These two groups were the first to be targeted by the new

---

2. The true number of victims of S-21 will never be known, but most estimates begin at 14,000 and range as high as 30,000. Part of the challenge is that many victims were not documented; another is that the records of many of those who were documented have since disappeared.

Khmer Rouge rulers. Yet even before the Khmer Rouge took power it was apparent that other enemies lurked far closer to the movement's heart. Some of the most senior cadres have been accused of treachery and, since taking power, Duch's top-secret security prison has elicited confessions that prove these strings of traitors reached the very top.

This messianic fervour to rid the country of its enemies and the twin obsession with secrecy ought to have made the movement invincible and brought order to its rule, yet the opposite holds true. Away from Duch's domain all is chaos and that tumult has now seeped into his creation. Tens of thousands of Vietnamese troops and thousands of Cambodian rebels who invaded the country a fortnight ago from the east have overwhelmed the Khmer Rouge soldiers. By now they have reached the outskirts of Phnom Penh. The capital is about to fall and the Khmer Rouge's leaders have begun to flee west.

Days earlier Duch's boss instructed him to kill the remaining prisoners and leave. And so the Chinese trucks holding the last emaciated inmates, perhaps as many as 500 people, stole out of S-21's gate at night and clawed their way down rutted roads eight miles south to a place called Chhoeung Ek, a former Chinese cemetery surrounded by rice fields. There, like thousands before them, blindfolded and handcuffed, the condemned were led one by one, stumbling exhausted across the uneven ground. Thin fluorescent tubes leached a pale light across a large pit where they were made to kneel. In a practised routine, the executioners employed by S-21 smashed a metal bar across the back of each prisoner's neck. Before they toppled into the grave filled with still-warm corpses, another Khmer Rouge cadre tore a knife across their throat, or thrust it into their stomach. The handcuffs were removed and their clothes were stripped. Then they were kicked, lifeless, into the pit.

One by one they fell, fresh, like tears, and slowly the ground welled up with the bodies of those deemed enemies of the revolution. Then the trucks turned, lighter now and quieter, their diesel engines rumbling, and bumped back up the well-travelled road to the city that would soon empty for the second time in less than four years.

WITH SO MUCH GOING WRONG in these final weeks, Duch has struggled to concentrate. He has become unmotivated, sleeping long hours and reading novels to pass the time. This is out of character, but these are strange, disordered days. Rumours swirl through the ranks of the Party like eddies on the Mekong, the great river that runs past the capital just a mile away. The latest is that the country's leader Pol Pot, known as Brother Number One, has fled the city.

Tired, unable to focus, sleeping too much: these are classic signs of depression and Duch's is stoked by the belief that he will soon be arrested and executed, consumed by this monstrous machine he has helped to create and maintain. Already his protector and former boss, the defence minister Son Sen, has been implicated. And just two months ago one of the most senior leaders in the Communist Party of Kampuchea (CPK), Vorn Vet, was brought to S-21 as an enemy and executed. Duch had known Vorn Vet, his former mentor, for years.

So many have been brought here in recent months that Duch is convinced the all-seeing *Angkar* now has him in its sights. For weeks he has operated in a funk, sometimes passing time in a room where a few fortunate prisoners, temporarily reprieved on account of their artistic skills, paint portraits of Pol Pot. Seated on a chair, Duch has watched these wretched men carefully apply paint to canvas, building up image after image of Brother Number One. This creative process in the midst of so much choreographed destruction soothes the former mathematician. His presence, on the other hand, terrifies these artists who are alive solely because Duch has decided they have something to offer. At any point he could have them executed.

Although Duch has run out of time to finish everything to his satisfaction, and despite his depression, there are numerous efficiencies: prisoners are tortured until these last days – after all, who knows what secrets they are hiding? But as January 6 becomes the early morning of January 7, 1979, the sound of artillery fire draws close. The invading army has reached the outskirts of Phnom Penh, and Duch is out of time.

As the sun tracks higher in the sky, the assurances he received from his boss – Brother Number Two, Nuon Chea – only days earlier that the invaders would be repelled are revealed as worthless. In Building A, once a classroom for eager schoolchildren, the final 14 prisoners in that section are murdered with a bayonet. Their corpses stay shackled to the rusting iron bedsteads, blood congeals on the floor and the green flies settle. Only those two-dozen or so detainees who have been put to work – the artists, the sculptors and the mechanics – are permitted to live for now.[3]

In the frenzy of exit there is no time to load S-21's copious archive that

---

3. By 2019, almost all of the survivors had disappeared or had died.

holds thousands of minutely detailed confessions, numerous administrative documents, and the lists and photographs that are stored here. The regime's paranoia and its related obsession with secrecy mean even Duch was not told about the evacuation until two days ago.

He cannot take the archive with him, but he does not destroy it either. Perhaps he fears that setting it on fire will draw attention, or maybe he believes this retreat from Phnom Penh is temporary. Or possibly the creative spark within Duch cannot allow him to undo what he has spent so many years laboriously crafting. S-21's archive is after all the defining work of Duch's 36 years.

The upstairs holding cells, the former classrooms into which dozens of shackled prisoners at a time were crammed between torture sessions, and the nearby rooms where interrogations were carried out, contain the detritus of oppression and blunt brutality: handcuffs, whips, chains and shackles sit near ammunition boxes of human excrement. In the wooden office building, papers lie scattered, the by-products of excruciating savagery, ruffled now by a gentle breeze.

For nearly three years the screams of prisoners being tortured ruptured the atmosphere day and night. Now the sound of shelling tears the fabric of the morning air. Enemy troops are moving down the nearby boulevards of Phnom Penh, closing in. To stay longer is to risk being captured and killed. Duch, doubtless angered by this sloppy ending to an otherwise meticulous operation, orders his staff and the handful of useful detainees to join the exodus.

Dressed in black and with his pistol strapped to his hip, Duch walks across the dusty compound towards a signboard that hangs above the entrance. Yellow letters on a red background exhort cadres to: 'Fortify the spirit of the revolution! Be on your guard against the strategy and tactics of the enemy so as to defend the country, the people and the Party.'

But the country is beyond defending, the revolution has imploded, and the believers are fleeing. Despite his vigilance against the enemy's strategies and tactics, and all the support given to him by the leaders, Duch, the key person tasked with security, has failed to protect the revolution.

With that on his shoulders, the commandant and his charges pass through the main gate of S-21. The few surviving prisoners, who have spent months in a state of unending fear, are ordered to walk in single file, and told they will be shot should they put one foot wrong.

This motley group slips like thieves through deserted backstreets, the midday sun beating down, south towards the killing field of Chhoeung Ek. Before dusk they have escaped the city, and S-21 recedes, a scatter of leprous buildings on a quiet backstreet where corpses draw the flies and papers ghost across a dusty courtyard. As the sun dips below the horizon, the evening's rich colours drain to grey. Then the night's cloak is laid across the skin of this fraught land and Comrade Duch vanishes into its protective folds.

The enemy will carry out activities against us and against our revolution in various forms. This is a continual struggle between revolution and counter-revolution; it will not stop. Arm yourselves with the stance that the enemy will exist for 10, 20, 30 more years.

Enemies still continue their activities. The enemy inside is like that; the enemy outside is the same. Outside, the imperialists and all the other enemies have not stopped; they attack us in every form ... We must be constantly vigilant.

— From 'The Enemy Situation', *Revolutionary Flag* magazine, June 1976

Revolutionary Flag was the Khmer Rouge's monthly magazine for cadres. It was written anonymously by Brother Number One, Pol Pot, and his deputy Nuon Chea, Brother Number Two.

CHAPTER ONE

THE HOMECOMING

THE TERMINAL AT Phnom Penh's airport is pale and low-slung and clings to the edge of the concrete apron as though trying to escape the relentless heat that lies heavy on this wretched land. It is June 1977 in Democratic Kampuchea, the name Pol Pot's revolutionary government has given Cambodia after seizing control two years earlier, and black-clad Khmer Rouge soldiers await the arrival of the weekly flight from Beijing.

From the north a dark speck draws closer through the heat haze and takes familiar shape. This plane is Democratic Kampuchea's only formal link with the outside world.

Among those on board is 30-year-old Ouk Ket, a handsome junior diplomat who for the past five years has been based at the Cambodian embassy in the West African state of Senegal.[1]

Some months earlier Ket had received a typewritten letter, a soothing demand to return home.

'To Beloved Comrade working at the Embassy of Democratic Kampuchea in Senegal,' it began, 'per the advice of the Ministry of Foreign Affairs of Democratic Kampuchea, I would like to inform you as follows:

1. The ministry has decided to ask you to come back to Cambodia. Please make arrangements for the trip upon receipt of this letter.

2. As for your family, please ask them to wait for a while. They can stay with their parents.

3. As for the embassy building, we have asked the Chinese embassy to look after it. Please also confirm with the Chinese embassy.

---

1. Cambodian custom is for a person's family name to precede their given name, and to refer to the person by their given name.

4. The government requests you to come to Cambodia to get educated to better fulfil your responsibilities.

With warmest revolutionary fraternity, Beijing, April 11, 1977, Democratic Kampuchea Embassy.'

The letter was signed by Democratic Kampuchea's ambassador to China, Pich Cheang, a short, animated man in his thirties. Pich Cheang, who favoured peasant garb, gold teeth gleaming beneath a crew cut, was a fervent believer in Cambodia's revolution. It was, he held, perfect in every way and had nothing to learn from others, not even from Democratic Kampuchea's friends. An Australian diplomatic memo written around that time described Pich Cheang as a smiling, burgeoning presence on the diplomatic circuit despite his apparent lack of Chinese, French or English, the *lingua francas* of the Beijing ambassadorial corps.

China and Cambodia were, as the saying goes, 'as close as lips and teeth' but this was largely a one-way relationship. China was the regime's key backer, supplying arms and food, diesel fuel and farming implements, as well as thousands of advisers to help the revolution succeed.

The letter sent to Ket was one of hundreds that went to Cambodian diplomats and intellectuals around the world calling them home to rebuild a nation that had suffered greatly during five years of civil war. Although the letters seemed benign, in truth they were a ruse. The leaders of Democratic Kampuchea had become increasingly convinced that their enemies were everywhere, even and especially hidden within the ultra-Maoist movement's own ranks. Tens of thousands had been murdered in purges that obliterated the ranks of the previous government. Now these purges were sweeping through the new ruling class.

For Democratic Kampuchea's leaders, men like Ket are quite simply not to be trusted. Ket is a royalist, not a communist; moreover he is educated, which counts further against him. Worse still he is foreign-educated. But Ket has little inkling of these dangers as the jet descends after its five-hour flight. Other than refugee tales there has been no news out of Cambodia since her rulers closed the borders in April 1975. There is no mail service and, other than the weekly plane from Beijing, nobody is allowed in or out. Away from the eyes of the world, the movement has restructured society to its bleak and brutal vision.

No doubt Ket peers out of the plane's oval window as the rice fields and sugar-palm trees of his beloved homeland rise up in greeting. Below him like mirrors are the vast, water-filled craters pitted in the soft skin of the land, a glimmering record of the years-long destruction wrought by thousands of B-52 sorties by the United States' air force until 1973. Carving north to south through this tarnished scene are the pale, tea-coloured, silt-heavy waters of the Mekong River that flow past Phnom Penh before turning for Vietnam and the coast.

Ket has been gone nearly a decade, first studying in Paris and then working at the Cambodian embassy in Senegal. Now he is almost home, and with that, you would think, will come the chance to see his parents, siblings and extended family – the cousins, aunts and uncles who are such an integral part of Cambodian life – to enjoy once again Phnom Penh now unfolding ahead of him, to eat the mild coconut fish curry called *trei amok*, to drink sugarcane juice, to pray at the Buddhist *wat* near his parents' house. Who could not be filled with excitement at such a homecoming?

Ket surely experienced the same feelings as another friend from his Paris days, a young Cambodian intellectual who had returned to Phnom Penh in July 1976. Like Ket, this friend was excited to be coming home to rebuild the country, and was similarly disbelieving of refugee stories of massacres and slave labour. The leaders were patriots, hard-working people, this young man thought. Cambodians would not kill Cambodians. He dismissed, too, the tales of starvation because, having grown up in a village, he knew this was a nation of abundance: fish, fruits and vegetables had always been plentiful.

For this softly spoken, pro-revolutionary man, disillusion came quickly. Ong Thong Hoeung[2] expected to see his family and friends at the airport, but on landing there were only child soldiers, angry-faced and dressed head to toe in black. He was seized by 'a strange and terrible sensation' as though he had landed on another planet. He wrote in his memoir:[3]

> Just a few minutes earlier, up in the sky, we had been laughing, trying to make out the patterns of the rice paddies on the ground, the canals, dykes and dams. We had been trying to admire the achievements of the revolution so frequently reported in the bulletins of the [Cambodian] mission in Paris. Cambodia was, we knew, a work site where everyone was labouring with joy.

---

2. Pronounced 'Ong Tong HOO-eng'. His family name is Ong, and his given name – by which Cambodians are customarily addressed – is Hoeung.

3. His full experience is recounted in his book J'ai cru aux Khmers rouges: Retour sur une Illusion, Ong Thong Hoeung (Paris, Buchet-Chastel, 2003).

But there were no welcoming smiles and no words of kindness, only a sullen mood that hung thick in the air. Hoeung grew fearful, even more so when the cadre at the immigration desk took his passport and threw it in a bin that was already half-full with others.

'People told me I could get it back later, but in my heart I knew this was over,' Hoeung told me years later.

It was a day of rude awakenings in the realities of the new Cambodia. From the airport, Hoeung and the others were taken in a clapped-out mini-bus through an empty, shattered city and offloaded at a training college that was now a re-education centre called K-15. There they were to 'rebuild' themselves by breaking rocks, growing rice and, most importantly, by producing 'fertiliser number one' – mixing human faeces with urine, a central task of the revolution's drive for self-sufficiency. There were self-criticism sessions too whose overt purpose was to ensure they forgot everything that had gone before, stripping these 'imperialist lackeys' of their individuality and subsuming them utterly to *Angkar*.

On arrival at K-15, Hoeung met friends who had left Paris three months before. He barely recognised them. He wrote:

> It was beyond belief! They were skin and bones, skeletal. We had only been apart for three months. They were all dressed in black, like the people we had seen at [the airport]. The difference was that here they were wearing the clothes they had brought from France, but they had been soaked in mud to give them the required colour. And they weren't just thin, they were dirty, and covered in sores and boils. When they smiled at us, we could see that their teeth were black. Some of them had lost nearly all their teeth. They looked as if they had come out of the Buddhist hell or a Nazi concentration camp.

In short order Hoeung's dream, that he had come home to a socialist utopia, was shattered. Eventually *Angkar* sent him to a labour camp where the optimism he had once held was crushed by a revolution that demolished humanity with lies, distortions and inversions of reason. The main enemies of the revolution, the returnees were told, lay within each one of them and it was their sacred duty to uncover that hidden foe.

CAMBODIA HAD CHANGED beyond recognition between 1968, the year Ket had left for Paris with a scholarship to study statistical engineering, and that hot June day nine years later when his plane landed in Phnom

Penh. In 1968 the head of state was Prince Norodom Sihanouk who had abdicated as monarch 13 years earlier to pursue politics.[4] Sihanouk was sly, ruthless, charming and divisive, a combination that ultimately isolated people on the left and polarised the country. Yet even in 1968 the Khmer Rouge, at that time Sihanouk's sworn enemy, were an annoyance more than a consequential danger, and Cambodia had not plunged into the abyss of civil war. Yet it was starting to teeter and many people were worried.

Among those was Ket's father, Ouk Chhor. In his privileged capacity as major-domo at the Royal Palace in Phnom Penh, Chhor ran the royal residence for Sihanouk. In that position he accompanied the Francophile prince on trips around the country and abroad. Chhor's role was to attend discreetly to Sihanouk's needs. He tasted the prince's food, waited on him at banquets and helped him to dress. A photograph of a state banquet from that time shows Chhor, white-clad and hovering like a moth near the flame that was Sihanouk, ready to fetch, carry and tidy away. In the 1950s and 1960s a steady stream of minor dignitaries and a few significant ones visited Phnom Penh, then a quiet, low-rise city of 500,000 people. In 1966 France's President Charles de Gaulle came; the following year it was the turn of Jackie Kennedy, the glamorous widow of US President John F. Kennedy. Sihanouk, charmed by Jackie, wrote jazz compositions in her honour.

As the first-born, Ket was always going to be his father's favourite, but he was also intelligent and hard-working, characteristics that pleased Chhor tremendously. The couple had another eight children after Ket was born in 1946, but he remained the golden child. The family was not rich but they were comfortable, and Chhor had enough land on his small plot in Phnom Penh's undeveloped southern sector to give a portion to his wife's brother in 1966. Ket's uncle had moved back to the capital after struggling to make a living in Prey Veng, a south-eastern province along the Vietnam border. The brood of cousins became the family next door. Among them was 13-year-old Sady.[5]

When I met her, Sady was a teacher, a diminutive lady with sparkling eyes and a gap-toothed smile under a fringe of cropped hair, and she lived with her husband and their children in a wooden house just yards from where the two families grew up all those years ago. The sound of monks

4. Sihanouk, Cambodia's pre-eminent twentieth-century politician, died in October 2012, shortly before his 90th birthday.

5. Cambodian names usually take the stress on the last syllable, so her name is pronounced Sa-DEE.

chanting prayers at the nearby *wat* drifted down the dusty alleyway, mixing with rooster calls, the chatter and shrieks of children playing, and the puttering of motorbikes along the narrow pathway that runs outside her gate. It is typical Cambodia – religion, wooden homes, children, dust – and in Sady's house an alert dog, a television that was always on, and an occupied hammock swinging as regularly as a metronome in the morning air.

Sady has fond memories of Ket, who was seven years her senior. Ket was bright yet he would nervously chew his nails while revising for his exams. As we talked, a long-forgotten memory sprang into Sady's mind: how Ket would use his foot to sketch the solutions to maths puzzles in the beaten-earth of the family compound before committing the answers to paper.

'He always drew with his foot,' Sady mused decades later.

Ket's studiousness won him a scholarship from France's foreign ministry to study in Paris, and though it would hardly have hurt his chances that his father worked for Sihanouk, he certainly had talent: Japan had offered him a scholarship too. His fluency in French likely decided the contest.

Sady's abiding memory of the young Ket was a young man who was obsessed with self-improvement. He exhorted his siblings and cousins to do better at school, bought books for Sady to improve her grades, and helped her brothers with their studies. In the evenings he strummed his guitar, and on weekends he and Sady ventured to nearby fields, now the dusty outer suburbs of Phnom Penh along Route 1, where he taught her how to catch *changrit* – a cricket-like local delicacy when fried. Sady poured water into the holes, and the *changrit* scrambled out in a frenzy into Ket's determined grasp.

In short, life in 1960s Phnom Penh was good. The children went to school, their fathers had jobs – Sady's worked as a guard at the grim, French-built prison known as T3 – and they lived comfortably. Behind the two simple, stilted wooden homes was a large pond where the children went regularly to beat the year-round sticky heat by swimming or by boating across it in a two-metre-long wooden canoe propelled with a pole.

Today many Cambodians remember the 1950s and 1960s as a golden age. Sady does too. Good though those years were, however, the country's increasingly fraught politics meant the burgeoning tensions were obvious even to a teenager.

'People couldn't talk about politics at all,' she recalled. 'It was very dangerous before the war happened, so nobody dared to.'

TWO EVENTS STOOD OUT from those days. One was the time Ket took the children to nearby Nary Island. They played catch in the river, the big fish trying to trap these smaller human fish who tumbled in the shallows, a skinny-limbed jumble, squealing and splashing their way to freedom. When it came time to leave, Ket realised that a ring his father had given him had slipped from his finger. This was no ordinary ring: the gold band crowned with a diamond had been a gift from the king of Thailand to Chhor on one of his trips accompanying Sihanouk. Chhor had passed it on to his favourite child.

'You see, from when he was born Ket always wore jewellery, which is why Uncle Chhor gave him the ring,' Sady said. 'And Ket loved diamonds – if he had a watch, there would be a diamond. That is what Ket liked.'

Chhor bought the other children jewellery too, but for them it would be of gold or silver.

'For Ket mostly he bought diamonds, because he was a good student, the smartest.'

The loss worried Ket so much that he stayed away for hours.

'He dared not return, and just stood under a tree,' she said. 'He was afraid he would be beaten, but his father came to take him home and spoke gently to him. Uncle Chhor wasn't angry and he told Ket: "Don't be sorry – we will buy you another."'

In an effort to recover the ring Chhor hired several villagers to dive the river's muddy reaches. But the ring had disappeared, swept away and settled in the silt out of the grasp of human hands.

A far darker cloud loomed in late 1968 during Pchum Ben, the 15-day Buddhist festival when Cambodians remember their deceased relatives, and take offerings and food for the ancestral spirits to the *wats* that have for centuries formed the hub of village life.

Sady had just returned from a visit to extended family outside Phnom Penh and was sleeping under the house with her youngest brother and one of her younger sisters. Ket was next door reading a book. Around two o'clock on that warm afternoon she woke to a commotion. People were running and shouting, their voices brittle with panic. Sady and Ket rushed to the large pond near the house and saw villagers frantically searching for Sady's younger brother Saroeun.

Earlier Ket had spoken to his father and advised against the children using the boat on this baking day. But little Saroeun had gone with his two teenage cousins – Ket's younger brothers, who were 17 and 18 – as well as two of his sisters aged 10 and 12. Halfway across the lake one of the girls jokingly threw out the bailing bucket. But the wooden boat had a leak and they needed the bucket to stop it filling with water. One brother stood up to try and retrieve it, the boat capsized, and the five were pitched overboard.

'A lot of people came to help, and some jumped in including my father,' Sady said. 'But the lake was very deep.'

Unable to swim well, Ket stood powerlessly on the shore watching his four flailing relatives, scanning the disturbed waters. Before long the four were back on shore with the boat and the punting pole, but Saroeun was nowhere to be seen.

'Ket grabbed the pole to beat his brothers, but my father restrained him saying: "Please don't do that. Your brothers had not meant for Saroeun to die,"' Sady said.

Saroeun's body surfaced the following day. He was just seven, and his death hit Ket hard.

'We held the funeral ceremony at Russey Srok pagoda. Ket felt terrible throughout the service,' she said. 'Ket said he should have prevented them from going to the pond or at the very least should have followed them, but he hadn't done so. He was terribly angry with his brothers.'

Two weeks later Ket left for France to take up his scholarship studying statistical engineering. That day he had a long conversation with his father, and then both families crammed into a van that Chhor had hired for the 15-kilometre drive across town to the airport on the city's western edge so that they could see Ket onto the Air France flight.

'Ket was very upset the day he left,' Sady said. 'He cried and told us please to study hard and not to forget our education. He wanted his brothers to have a lot of knowledge. I will never forget those words of his: "You must study hard."'

As was Ket's custom he continued to send books to Sady. He wrote regularly too, to her and to the rest of the family but, as it turned out, that November day in 1968 was the last time Sady saw her beloved cousin.

PARIS AT THE END of the 1960s would have been magical for a young man fresh from the languor, heat and dust of Cambodia's capital. The low-rise architecture of his hometown had little in common with the imposing stone edifices of Paris, but Phnom Penh's government buildings of stucco and plaster, pillars, iron railings and high ceilings did echo those of France's provincial towns.

Ket spoke fluent French, which was still Cambodia's official language despite the country having won her independence 15 years earlier, and was familiar with the literature and music of the West. By 1968 the rock'n'roll sounds of the US and Europe had infiltrated Cambodia, as had fashion, hairstyles and magazines – at least in urban areas – so although France was a foreign nation, it was far from alien.

The year Ket arrived in Paris had been a time of significant change, a ferment of activism. The strikes and student riots that had convulsed France in May shaking the establishment were over, yet the political ideologies that motivated them were uppermost in the minds of many students. But not, it seems, in Ket's. The 22-year-old was serious about his studies, and as the first-born son he had responsibilities that he was determined to fulfil. He wrote regularly to his family in Phnom Penh, and worked hard. It paid off: a year on he was admitted to the second and final year of his diploma with a score above 80 per cent.

There were many Cambodians in Paris, a legacy of France's 90-year rule until its granting of independence in 1953. For decades France had awarded scholarships to bright Cambodians, and it was in Paris that several of these men and women were introduced to the seductive visions of Marx, Lenin, Mao and Stalin. Two decades before Ket arrived, some of those who would become the leaders of the Khmer Rouge, including Pol Pot, had studied in France; as the 1960s wore on and Cambodia's politics drove adherents towards one extreme or another, a new generation of students in Paris would fracture along the polarised lines of home.

Some who had returned to Phnom Penh in earlier years to engage in politics fell foul of Sihanouk as he kept a rigid hand on the reins of power. Some opponents were executed, others were jailed and tortured. As repression increased in the 1960s many fled to the *maquis*, the rural areas where the Khmer Rouge had based themselves and joined the communist movement. Sihanouk christened them *les Khmers rouges* or Red Cambodians. By 1968, the leftist Cambodian students in Paris regarded Sihanouk as the enemy; given his father's post, that must have put Ket in a tricky position.

Explaining the wave of tumult that enveloped Cambodia from the late 1960s will come later, but suffice it to say that after 1966 Sihanouk lost the confidence of his increasingly independently minded government.

In March 1970, his former colleagues – including his prime minister, Lon Nol – ousted Sihanouk in a bloodless coup while he was out of the country. Sihanouk, furious, travelled to Beijing where he was persuaded to join with his former enemies: the Khmer Rouge and their backer, North Vietnam.

As political turnarounds go, it was one of the most remarkable of the twentieth century. For Sihanouk, who wanted to return to power, the temptations of such an alliance were irresistible. For Cambodia it proved to be of profound significance as Sihanouk exhorted his 'children', as he called the population, in tape-recorded messages to join with him and the Khmer Rouge in fighting the usurping pro-American regime. Thousands heeded the prince's words, and the Khmer Rouge exploded from just a few thousand fighters to tens of thousands.[6] Backed by China and North Vietnam, the Khmer Rouge forces would eventually become unstoppable.

After allying himself with the Khmer Rouge, Sihanouk established a government-in-exile in Beijing: the Royal Government of National Union of Kampuchea, known by its French acronym GRUNK. Sihanouk became head of state, and established the Front Uni National du Kampuchea, or FUNK, as the political party for non-communists who wished to support what he now regarded as his revolution. The Khmer Rouge were to operate as GRUNK's army on the ground.

In the alphabet soup of the time, GRUNK was a composite of the Khmer Rouge and FUNK but as Sihanouk ought to have known, he who controls the guns has his hands on the levers of power, and that person was Pol Pot. As Brother Number Two Nuon Chea told the head of a visiting Danish Maoist delegation in 1978, allowing Sihanouk to become the nominal head of the resistance 'meant nothing because we were the masters of the situation'.[7]

---

6. Among those who joined the Khmer Rouge was Hun Sen who, as of 2019, is still Cambodia's prime minister, an authoritarian and one of the longest-standing political leaders in the world. In 1977 Hun Sen defected from the Khmer Rouge and fled to Vietnam. In late 1978 he returned to Cambodia as part of the invading force that overthrew Pol Pot's government. It remains unclear in what year Hun Sen joined the Khmer Rouge. Ben Kiernan [*The Pol Pot Regime* (Yale University Press, 3rd edition, 2008, p. 370)] states he joined the CPK – the political party of the Khmer Rouge – in 1971 but that does not preclude him having joined the revolution before that. In Kiernan's *How Pol Pot Came to Power: Colonialism, Nationalism and Communism in Cambodia: 1930–1975* (New Haven & London, Yale University Press, 2004, p. 254) he writes that Hun Sen fled Phnom Penh in 1967 and worked as a courier for the local leader of the communists. Mehta [*Hun Sen: Strongman of Cambodia*, Harish C. Mehta and Julie B. Mehta (Graham Brash (Pte.) Ltd, 1999)] says Hun Sen joined the revolution in 1970 (pp. 11, 21) in response to Sihanouk's call. Assuming Kiernan is right, and there is little reason to suppose otherwise, Hun Sen probably joined the communists several years prior to Sihanouk's overthrow and for reasons other than those he has subsequently claimed.

7. 'Statement of the Communist Party of Kampuchea to the Communist Workers' Party of

These, broadly painted, were the changes that had overtaken Cambodia in the few years since Ket had left the country in November 1968. On that day Ket and his father had a long talk during which Chhor reminded his eldest how much the family owed Sihanouk, and told him: 'You must never betray the Prince.' That instruction would later have profound consequences.

During his first year of study in Paris, Ket had managed to stay out of politics but the coup and Sihanouk's dramatic realignment with his former enemies meant neutrality was no longer possible. Ket made his loyalties known, driven no doubt in part by his father's words. When Ket's second and final year of study came to an end, supporting Sihanouk meant he could not return to Phnom Penh. The capital, like most of the country in 1970, was under the control of a new, anti-Sihanouk government. For Ket, going home was not an option.

THE YEAR 1970 WAS MOMENTOUS for Ket on a number of grounds. It was his last year of study, which would be significant for any promising student, and his country's tortured politics meant that he had been compelled to choose sides when he would rather have avoided doing so. It was also the year he met 18-year-old Martine Lefeuvre. It happened at a campsite favoured by students on the French coast where Martine, an only child, was holidaying with her parents and a friend. At the camp, the guitar-playing Ket won a music competition playing Beatles' songs – 'Ticket to Ride' and 'Hey Jude'. Martine took one look at him and thought: this is the man for me.

They fell in love and a few months later Martine moved in with Ket at the Pavillon du Cambodge, the halls of residence for Cambodian students at the Cité Universitaire on the southern edge of Paris. Politics made residence life tense and at times dangerous, with older Cambodian students espousing the Soviet-influenced Communism of the French Communist Party battling their younger colleagues who preferred Mao's version. In one incident the couple were caught between two groups of fighting students; Ket grabbed his books and his girlfriend and they fled their room.

They married the following year at the Hotel de Ville in Martine's home city of Le Mans. Ket was 25, fresh-faced and beaming, and wore a white carnation in the buttonhole of his navy blue suit. Martine, in a simple white

Denmark', July 1978, by Nuon Chea, Deputy Secretary, CPK. Nuon Chea's speech was reproduced in *Searching for the Truth*, a magazine published by research organisation the Documentation Center of Cambodia (August 2001, p. 8).

dress, her brown hair swept back and a bouquet in hand, looked exultant. In one image Ket stands behind Martine's seated grandparents, his thin, dark tie with white polka dots matching the one worn by Martine's beret-clad grandfather. Even the weather played its part, with the wedding party on the terrace bathed in autumnal sunshine.

Two months later, Ket's loyalty to Sihanouk was repaid when he was posted to Senegal as third secretary at GRUNK's embassy in Dakar. Senegal was one of many countries that refused to recognise Lon Nol's government that had overthrown Sihanouk, insisting instead on the legitimacy of his exiled GRUNK movement with its Khmer Rouge ally.

Martine joined him there in January and the following year their son Mackara (meaning 'January' in Khmer) was born. They were still in Senegal when their daughter Neary, which means 'Lady', was born in July 1975, three months after the Khmer Rouge had taken power.

Those years in Senegal, said Martine, were the happiest of her life.

'We were a Franco-Khmer couple whose children were born of African soil, and this tri-continental contribution was the wealth of our family: a family that was open to the world without any kind of prejudice regarding race or religion or regarding lifestyle,' she said.

Her parents in France loved Ket as a son, and Martine learned to read, write and speak Khmer, the language of Cambodia with its simple structure, its vast vocabulary and its intricate Indian-derived alphabet. Ket had impressed her with his guitar playing, yet he also played the mandolin, the harmonica and the Cambodian flute despite having no formal training. He was a dab hand at volleyball and at preparing food too, whether Cambodian or French, Lebanese or Indian.

'He would just step out of his diplomat suit and dress up in his Khmer sarong and start cooking for us,' she said. 'Life with him was pure happiness.'

He wrote home often and travelled in the region too. There is a picture of him sitting barefoot on a reed mat in a Tuareg tent, smiling, holding on to a wriggling baby goat while the tent's owner and family face the camera with him. He looks relaxed, a man every bit at ease in the tent of a Tuareg nomad as at the formality of a diplomatic reception.

It was not to last. In 1976 Sihanouk, who had returned to Phnom Penh after the Khmer Rouge's victory the previous year and been installed as head of state, realised he had been duped and wielded no power. The Khmer Rouge leaders soon forced him to resign. Sihanouk was not allowed to leave but, probably at China's insistence, the Khmer Rouge let him live despite murdering several of his children and grandchildren. For the next three years Sihanouk was a prisoner in the capital.[8]

The effects rippled across the globe to Senegal. Although Pol Pot's Democratic Kampuchea had maintained the GRUNK positions at overseas embassies, Cambodia was a closed country that earned almost no money from trade. Ket had not been paid in more than a year and the couple had little left in the way of savings. The pressure was already building when, in April 1977, the letter arrived recalling him.

The following month the couple returned to France and decided that for the time being Martine and the children would stay with her parents. Initially Ket contemplated taking Mackara, who was nearly five, but at the last minute he changed his mind.

Going home to help rebuild his homeland, which had been ravaged by more than a decade of war, was a heady prospect for Ket.

'He wanted to teach,' said Martine, 'because he would say that there is nothing worse than ignorance.'

They shopped in town for the items Ket would need: a raincoat, shoes, a suitcase and sunglasses. On the bus they stood holding on to the leather straps. Martine, feeling uneasy, looked at his face – 'very handsome' – knowing that she would not see him for months then blurted out an odd sentence: 'If one day I were to learn that you are dead, I will never believe you died a natural death. You will have been murdered.'

Ket turned to Martine, tapping her gently on the cheek.

'But, honey, Cambodians are not savages,' he told her with a smile.

'And he was so sure of himself, so when I heard that I trusted him,' she recalled.

The lack of news from his family over the past two years concerned Ket, but the trip represented a chance both to reunite with them and to prepare for a new life in a land Martine had never seen but to which she was happy to move. Ket packed passport photographs of Martine and the children, and promised to send a Cambodian passport in due course.

There would be plenty for Ket to do before then. For a start he would need to find a home for his family in Phnom Penh, unless of course the foreign ministry chose to send him abroad again.

---

8. A period that Sihanouk covered in his memoir of the time: *Prisonnier des Khmers rouges* (Paris, Hachette littérature générale, 1986).

His only doubts were what sort of work the regime would allocate to him. The final sentence in the letter seems to have unsettled him: 'Come to Cambodia to get educated to better fulfil your responsibilities.' What could that mean?

'Perhaps,' he told Martine of his worst fears, 'I'll have to do some agricultural work.'

'So he went back in that state of mind, in full confidence,' she said.

THERE IS A PHOTOGRAPH taken on the day Ket left France. It is June 1977, a fine summer's day, and he is standing in his in-laws' garden in Le Mans with Martine. She holds Mackara, Ket holds Neary, who looks at the camera with a two-year-old's puzzled expression. Behind them is a trellis fence with a creeper, and in the flowerbed are white arum lilies. The scene is pure 1970s suburbia: Martine, 24, in a red jersey and beige trousers; Ket, 30, dressed as for a business trip: hair neatly combed, a blue shirt and tie under a buttoned-up navy cardigan, pressed dark trousers and polished black shoes. Ket looks at the camera through his new sunglasses with the hint of a smile, or perhaps his mouth was caught in a moment of banter with his father-in-law. The image is ordinary, but the moment it represents is profound: of a man setting off for his homeland after nearly a decade away.

AT THE AIRPORT IN PARIS, Martine and the two children said their farewells. Ket walked through passport control with his diplomatic passport and on to the plane that took off for Pakistan and then China, the weekly flight from Beijing being the only way to reach Phnom Penh.

From Karachi he sent a postcard to the family in Le Mans, scribbled quickly between flights. It showed a woman sitting on a camel bedecked in its finery, its lips turned back in a half-grin, half sneer. It is a comical image doubtless chosen to make the children laugh during their father's absence. The date was June 9, 1977, the card written and franked that day. His message told them how much he loved them, and added in typical fashion: 'You must study hard.'

The next postcard was from Beijing. There was little for the children to enjoy in this austere image. In Maoist style it was a dull photograph of the orange-bricked Overseas Chinese Hotel where Ket was instructed to stay. Even the two stamps convey revolutionary fervour – a red, caterpillar-track tractor is hoisted across the face of one stamp to join a uniform line of red tractors. The other, placed upside down, portrays a heroic-looking worker with a hoe over his shoulder being applauded by another.

The postcard was signed by a fellow Cambodian, Loeung Hong Sour, a friend of the couple. Sour had worked at the GRUNK embassy in Tanzania as third secretary and had received a similar letter recalling him to Cambodia. In the postcard Ket told Martine and the children: 'On June 11, 1977 I will be in Phnom Penh.' In Khmer he repeated his love for them, again telling the children that they 'must study hard'.

On June 11, a Saturday, the weekly flight from Beijing took off with Ket and Sour on board. Several hours later it touched down in Cambodia's swelter and the two men disembarked.

In Le Mans the days slipped long and dry through high summer, and Martine held on to the two postcards and waited for further news. The couple had agreed that once Ket was settled in Phnom Penh and knew what the foreign ministry had planned, he would mail another postcard calling the family to Cambodia.

And so Martine, Mackara and Neary waited. As the weeks passed, the summer heat cooled to autumn. Still there was no word from Ket.

In September, Martine took the children to the Chinese embassy, which was housed in a grand building on Paris's Avenue George V. As Beijing was Ket's last known stop and as China was Democratic Kampuchea's staunchest ally, it was logical to see whether the embassy could assist.

The official to whom she handed Ket's image showed it to Mackara, who was not yet five, and asked the boy: 'Do you know the person in the picture?'

'Yes, of course,' Mackara replied. 'It's Daddy.'

But the Chinese embassy refused to help.

Martine returned home empty-handed and the family continued living in this strange, suspended state. Autumn became winter, and in Le Mans the pale petals of the arum lilies were crushed by the cold and became one with the freezing soil. Christmas was a mute affair. As 1978 began, there was still no news.

Ouk Ket had disappeared.

One hand for production, the other for striking the enemy.

— Khmer Rouge slogan

If you wish to destroy the enemy,
you must destroy the enemy within your own person.

— Khmer Rouge slogan used during re-education sessions

CHAPTER TWO

GONE AND LOST

THREE MONTHS BEFORE NEARY was born in Senegal, the Khmer Rouge captured Phnom Penh. The fall of the capital, on April 17, 1975, was by then inevitable. A decade earlier it would have been incomprehensible.

On April 1, 1975, the usurping prime minister, Lon Nol, a former general who had proven himself a hopeless leader and a woeful military tactician, fled Cambodia for Hawaii having been awarded one million US dollars by his government colleagues. On April 12 the US, which had been supplying Lon Nol's forces for the past five years as well as ferrying food to the capital, closed its embassy and evacuated its staff by helicopter. Earlier that year the Khmer Rouge had cut the supply route along the Mekong River, one of Phnom Penh's two lifelines. With the capital surrounded, the airport being shelled and the US pulling out, the city stood no chance of survival.

Over the preceding years hundreds of thousands of people had sought refuge in Phnom Penh, some driven there by the pervasive US bombing that lasted until September 1973, others fleeing the Khmer Rouge who controlled ever-larger tracts of the country. As a result the city's population had risen from 500,000 to two million. Many of these newcomers slept on the pavements or lived in huge slums on the city's outskirts.

The Khmer Rouge's leaders approved the final push on the capital in December 1974, and during the first months of 1975 conditions in Phnom Penh deteriorated rapidly. The fringes of the city had long been unsafe with night-time shelling and Khmer Rouge cadres kidnapping people and taking them to the 'liberated areas' that the movement controlled. Now with supply lines squeezed there was seldom enough food, and thousands starved. Rockets punctuated daily life, an indiscriminate terror that hit homes, schools and hospitals.

By this time Ket's cousin, Sady, was 21 and living with her family in the centre of town. Ket's parents and siblings had also left their home in the south-east sector and moved to staff housing on the grounds of the Royal Palace where Chhor, who had little interest in politics, was kept in his post after Lon Nol's 1970 coup. Chhor's role during Lon Nol's five-year Khmer Republic had been to ensure that the buildings and grounds were properly managed.

Phnom Penh fell during Khmer New Year, a key holiday that comes during the hottest time of the year. The three-day celebration in this largely agricultural nation marks the start of the rice-planting season. For centuries the New Year has been a time of celebration, and the end of fighting meant further cause for joy. Surely now life would improve?

It certainly looked promising, Sady said years later. The Khmer Rouge had commandeered an army truck from Lon Nol's defeated forces and it trundled through the streets flying a white flag and broadcasting a message of peace.

'They were telling people to come out onto the streets and cheer, because *Samdech* Sihanouk would be coming later that day,' said Sady, using the honorific term for the revered former king and head of state. 'Our country would not fight with each other again, and they said those families with guns should hand them over.'

At 3pm Sady was one of thousands lining the streets shouting *chaiyo* ('victory') in anticipation of Sihanouk's arrival.

'All the people had come outside onto the streets to cheer,' she recalled, 'but we didn't see *Samdech* Sihanouk. We only saw the Khmer Rouge.'

The residents believed that with Sihanouk back 'we won't have war, we won't be driven away, we can go back to doing business as we used to do'. Within hours those hopes were shattered.

'By now the truck was broadcasting a new message: they told people that the US was preparing to bomb the city, so they said they wanted us to leave by midnight, but only for a few days,' she recalled. 'We were told we must take provisions for those days. When we heard that, we left to pack some belongings and make preparations.'

Sady first tried to reach the Royal Palace to find her uncle and cousins but the Khmer Rouge cadres, mostly teenage peasants, barred the way and threatened to kill anyone who persisted. Instead she headed for the family home in the south-east quarter across the Monivong Bridge. On the way she watched horrified as Khmer Rouge soldiers shot and killed several people.

The evacuation of Phnom Penh proceeded unevenly, in part because Khmer Rouge troops from at least four regions controlled different parts of the capital. So many people were on the move that it took Sady nearly a day to travel the eight kilometres from the city centre to the family home. It took Chhor 12 hours to cross the Monivong Bridge, which is just a few hundred yards long.

The two families spent the following day readying provisions – rice, soy sauce and *prahok*, the fermented fish paste that is a staple of Cambodian food. While they were packing, a Khmer Rouge soldier came up and asked her father for a drink of water, then warned him to be careful.

'He whispered: "Don't tell the truth – if you worked for the former king or the government don't say anything or the cadres will kill you",' Sady recalled.

Sady's family was fortunate to have a pushcart in which they could pack their food, pots and clothing. Chhor's had a motorbike and a bicycle and had to balance the load in a manner that Sady recalled was 'untidy'. Given what was to come, the pushcart was by far the better option.

And then they waited, first for one day then for another and then another, unwilling to leave as tens of thousands of people moved slowly down Route 1, the national highway that lay just 200 yards from their front door. The refugees were packed so tightly that they walked with their arms jammed to their sides like penguins, a mass of humanity trudging treacle-slowly in the dust and the heat into the unknown.

On the fourth morning as the sky paled from black, a truck drove into their area with a blunt warning to 'get out of your houses'.

'You are not permitted to stay in your own homes or in the city,' the loudspeaker crackled. 'If you go to the countryside there is food to eat there. There are community workers waiting for you. If you don't want to go and you stay here without food then we won't be responsible for you.'

A neighbour, a former corporal in the defeated army, pleaded with the cadres to be allowed to stay a day or two longer hoping that by then his wife and children would have made it home.

'They shot him quickly: *pom-pom*,' Sady said, echoing the soft-sharp sound of the bullets. 'We were terrified and knew we had to leave.'

Chhor told the two families they should not wait for each other.

'It will be a very difficult trip,' he told them. 'If they ask you any questions, don't tell them your background because they will arrest you. Say that you sold vegetables or were farmers. And do whatever they tell you.'

Around 5am Chhor's family left, the bicycle and motorbike laden awkwardly, his wife with provisions perched on her head, their children with food gathered in *kramas*, the ubiquitous cotton scarves of Cambodia, wrapped around their waists and slung over their shoulders. Sady found it hard to watch as her cousins and the last of their neighbours trudged down the unpaved street to join the exodus.

'And Uncle Chhor was very fat so he walked slowly-slowly,' she said. 'He walked a little way, then he took a rest, then he walked a little further, then he rested again.'

By the time Sady's family left just 15 minutes later the sun was rising rapidly over the flat landscape and Chhor's family had been swallowed in the slow-rolling river of humanity, their motorbike and bicycle joining countless pushcarts, bicycles, cars and cyclos on the national road to the south-east. It was a scene replicated along the narrow web of roads emanating from every city and town, a nation on the move, millions cast out with just the possessions they could carry.

BEFORE ENTERING THE CITY the Khmer Rouge had warned they would execute the seven 'super traitors' of Lon Nol's defeated government, but would spare everyone else. Sady watched that lie unravel during the first days of Pol Pot's rule as the Khmer Rouge murdered many through a mix of cunning and duplicity.

'The Khmer Rouge would call out on the loudspeaker: "If you had a government job then please return and take up that job to help our country, because we don't have many skilled people,"' Sady said. 'And some people who were officers or doctors, well, the conditions on the road were so difficult and they didn't know where they could get water or rice for their wives or children, so they went over to the cadres and told them: "I worked in this place or that place." And Pol Pot's soldiers said: "Please, get in the trucks."'

'So they went with the cadres, and left their wives and children here near Wat Nearoth, and the families just stayed there by the side of the road,' she said. 'They told their families: "Please wait four or five days and I will come back and fetch you." But they were gone and lost, gone and lost.'

If the cadres suspected that you had worked in government or were educated, they would call you over for questioning. A garbled answer was reason enough to be taken away for execution. They summoned Sady's father, who worked as a prison guard, but he convinced them he was a farmer and that he drove a *cyclo*, the three-wheeled pedicabs that ply Phnom Penh's streets. Her father's siblings, who were also civil servants, decided it was safer to split up.

The degree of cruelty meted out varied depending on which Khmer Rouge army manned which route out of the city. Troops from the Northern Zone were implacably hostile; those from the Eastern Zone were more accommodating. Australian historian Ben Kiernan wrote that one evacuee travelling for two weeks along Route 3 did not see anyone killed although he did hear that some women had died in childbirth. Others on different roads recalled dozens dead. Kiernan estimates 20,000 died in the evacuation of the capital alone.[1]

Across the country thousands more were murdered. In Battambang, the country's second city, the Khmer Rouge ordered all officers and soldiers from the defeated regime to assemble at military headquarters. They were driven away in trucks and executed. Hundreds of soldiers who had surrendered in Siem Reap were also killed. It was the same story in the towns of Kampong Chhnang, Pursat and Pailin, with civilians and former regime officials shot in large numbers.

Sady and her family survived this gauntlet, and their minds soon focused on other challenges. April is the peak of the hot season when temperatures can climb above 40 degrees Celsius and it also marks the turn into the wet season when drenching tropical rains drift across the land like curtains the colour of lead. By now the conditions were intolerable: there were too many people competing for firewood, and the water level in the Mekong was low despite the start of the rains.

'It was a 10-metre climb from the top of the bank down to the river, and that made it very difficult to get down and bring back water,' Sady said of the steep, slick banks. 'There was so much suffering.'

As they headed down Route 1, which carves its way along the west bank of the Mekong, the living passed the dead and the dying discarded by the roadside. The line between life and death was tenuous: you could be killed if the cadres simply did not like the look of you.

---

1. *The Pol Pot Regime: Race, Power and Genocide in Cambodia under the Khmer Rouge, 1975–79*, by Ben Kiernan (Yale University Press, 3rd edition, 2008), p. 49.

'On one of those days a pregnant woman fell ill and nobody went to help. We weren't allowed to help anyone. We had to keep walking,' Sady said. 'She died there on the road, and the Khmer Rouge kicked her to the side and trampled on her body.'

Decades later the casual brutality meted out to that woman remained vivid as Sady recalled the wretchedness, the press of the crowds and the inescapable heat.

Her family decided it would be easier to travel between midnight and sunrise when it was cooler, yet it was no quicker and they struggled to cover more than a few kilometres a day as they pushed on to their destination: the south-eastern province of Prey Veng where they had lived until 1966 before moving to Phnom Penh. Each morning they erected a sheet of canvas, a patchwork of smaller pieces sewn together, then cooked rice and waited out the heat and the rain under this rough shelter that was too small to cover them.

A fortnight after leaving Phnom Penh, her parents and nine siblings reached Neak Leung, the ferry port on the Mekong 60 kilometres from the capital. Prey Veng province lay on the opposite bank. After spending five fruitless days waiting for Chhor and his family they decided to cross the river. There was no ferry so they were forced to pay a boatman to get to the other bank. His price was the family's two dogs.

'I don't know what happened to the dogs,' she said. 'Perhaps they ate them, but at any rate the boatman was very happy to see them.'

It was years before Sady found out why her cousins had not come: en route they had reached a village with too little food and too many people, and by now Chhor was exhausted. When the cadres announced that those born in Battambang province, Cambodia's rice basket, could hitch a ride there on trucks and boats, Chhor decided their best bet was to lie about their origin.

'Uncle Chhor hoped his family would survive there, because he knew Battambang had a lot of rice,' Sady said of her uncle's choice. 'He hoped that in Battambang there would not be too much suffering.'

THE LEADERS OF THE KHMER ROUGE had no shortage of reasons to empty every city and town. One purpose was to turn the country into a vast labour camp, a nationwide gulag focused on agriculture where – in a direct echo of Mao's call a quarter-century earlier that he would 'force them to work with their hands in order to become new men' – the supposedly decadent urbanites would learn from the pure peasants who comprised 85 per cent of the population. The Party line deemed that those who had lived in towns and cities were lazy, exploitative and lacked morality. The rural majority, on the other hand, knew the value of hard work. And so for ideological reasons – to become self-sufficient and to recover their original Khmer-ness – those in urban areas would be forced into the fields.[2]

While it is also true that the Khmer Rouge could not have fed and administered Phnom Penh's two million people, there was much more to it than that. Kiernan noted that the war in neighbouring Vietnam was nearly over by the time Phnom Penh fell on April 17.[3] Two weeks later the South Vietnamese capital Saigon was captured by the North's communist forces. The Khmer Rouge wanted to wrest back some of the land known as Kampuchea Krom, an area in southern Vietnam lost by Cambodia in the late seventeenth century. The strategy to empty Cambodia's urban areas was devised when it seemed the war in Vietnam would drag on through 1975, and the Khmer Rouge leaders calculated that they could annex land during the confusion of their neighbour's civil war. Emptying built-up areas would deprive a retaliating Vietnam of military targets.

The renowned film-maker Rithy Panh, who was 11 when he and his family were forced out of Phnom Penh, saw it differently. The Khmer Rouge's reasoning, he concluded, had nothing to do with problems of feeding the urban population or with fears of an American bombardment. Instead the forced evacuation was far more sinister, 'the beginning of the extermination of the "new people", namely … capitalists, landlords, civil servants, members of the middle class, intellectuals, professors, students'.[4]

The leaders certainly had an ideological eye on Democratic Kampuchea's place in the global revolutionary firmament. They felt other countries had failed in their approach to class war, and that was a mistake Pol Pot and Nuon Chea were determined not to make. As far as the Khmer Rouge were

---

2. Father François Ponchaud, a long-time Cambodia resident and author of *Cambodia: Year Zero*, (published originally in French as *Cambodge année zéro*, Editions Renée Julliard, 1977) felt this was the true reason for the evacuation. See his testimony to the UN-backed Khmer Rouge Tribunal, known formally as the Extraordinary Chambers in the Courts of Cambodia (ECCC), on April 9, 2013.

3. Kiernan, op. cit., p. 63.

4. *The Elimination: A Survivor of the Khmer Rouge Confronts His Past and the Commandant of the Killing Fields*, Rithy Panh with Christophe Bataille, translated by John Cullen (The Clerkenwell Press, 2013), p. 40. (Originally published in French in 2012 as *L'élimination* by Éditions Grasset & Fasquelle.)

concerned, there were loyal cadres and there was everyone else, with the latter constituting a nest of spies and enemies squarely obstructing the path to pure socialism. Revolutions in other countries had sown the seeds of their own destruction by neglecting to destroy these 'oppressor classes'. In Pol Pot's unyielding vision, emptying the cities and towns would eliminate these feudalists and capitalists at a stroke.

As a Party document later crowed, the evacuation had 'swept away' private property and 'extricated [intellectuals and students] from the filth of imperialist and colonialist culture'. It had also limited any chance of resistance by dispersing potential threats, which was a key reason Buddhism was banned. A final benefit that fitted Pol Pot's pro-Khmer ideology was that this would 'Khmerize' the capital, which in the previous decade was nearly 60 per cent ethnically Vietnamese and Chinese.

It was for all these reasons then that millions of Cambodians found themselves trudging into the dangerous unknown by the time Pol Pot arrived in Phnom Penh in late April, his first time back since fleeing to the *maquis* 12 years earlier. A meeting of the leaders that month ruled that Sihanouk would remain head of state, and emphasised that the real victors of the revolution were 'the people', a conclusion that would surely have surprised Sady and many of her fellow Cambodians had they known of it.

In May a five-day meeting addressed by Pol Pot and Nuon Chea handed down the regime's social, economic and political policies to a bevy of military and civilian cadres who had been summoned to the capital. These policies dictated that the cities and towns would remain empty. The cadres were told to execute surviving senior members of the Lon Nol regime, to defrock all Buddhist monks (who were disparaged as 'tapeworms gnawing at the bowels of society') and to put them to work in the fields. The purifying flame of revolution would see the country remade: there would be no private property, no money, no schools, no organised religion and no markets. For city people particularly, it was the antithesis of all that had come before.

Instead the people were to be herded into collectives, where they were enslaved to grow rice and to build dams and irrigation channels. Agriculture and self-sufficiency were the new watchwords of Democratic Kampuchea with 'three tons per hectare' demanded from rice production. Each area was ordered to remit a fixed tonnage of rice based on a simple calculation: take the number of hectares under cultivation and multiply that by three to get the expected harvest; then deduct what was needed to feed people at the local level. The rest was to be sent to the centre. Local conditions were deemed irrelevant, and the slogan was not an exhortation but an order with no account taken of the fact that – in a nation of often-poor soil and with limited irrigation, to say nothing of the effects of years of civil war – few areas could generate three tons per hectare in the first place. The leaders would instead conclude that regions that failed to send their quota had been infiltrated by enemies subverting the revolution and would need to be purged. Local cadres, well aware of the consequences of that, simply cut the amount of rice they kept back for the people in their areas. As the coming years would show, famine was the inevitable result.

The leaders also decided Democratic Kampuchea would be ethnically pure Khmer with an exception made for the minority peoples in whose northern and north-eastern redoubts Pol Pot and his comrades had spent years fomenting revolution, admiring them as unsullied by modern decadent ways. To that end the Khmer Rouge murdered or forced across the border all ethnic Vietnamese, whom they regarded as inherently untrustworthy. In their bid to create a uniform nation, they also unleashed a wave of repression against Cambodia's indigenous Muslims, the Cham people.

As the families of Ket and Sady would soon learn, the dispossessed urban population was to be treated with revolutionary harshness. Evacuees were branded 'new people', '17 April people' or 'deportees', all terms that broadcast their unfamiliarity with the Party line, with the revolution and with the new political reality. Until purified, all 'new people' would remain firmly under suspicion and at the bottom of Democratic Kampuchea's new caste system. At the top were the poor peasants, known as 'base people' or 'full rights people'; in between were so-called 'candidate' members, many of whom were peasants who were unfortunate enough to have deportee relatives.[5]

With that, society was upended and a nation was enslaved. Cambodia would remain under Pol Pot's yoke for three years, eight months and 20 days.

AFTER THE FAMILIES WERE DRIVEN OUT of the capital, Chhor's third son Saron went his own way, heading south-east with his wife Ra and their young son to her home province of Svay Rieng, which borders Vietnam. Saron expected there would be enough food there and that the work would be manageable. Saron's uncle went with them too. He was married to Ra's aunt who was also from Svay Rieng.

5. Kiernan, op. cit., p. 184.

The rest of the family – Chhor, his wife and their remaining seven children, aged from six to 26 – journeyed by truck, boat and train for 350 kilometres in the opposite direction to Battambang province. As it turned out some parts of Battambang did have enough food at that time, but the area where Ket's parents and siblings arrived in May 1975 was not one of those. The Khmer Rouge had done away with the old system of provinces. Democratic Kampuchea, as the new regime named itself the following year, was divided into seven zones, each of which comprised several regions. Below the level of regions were districts, and below them were communes and then villages.

The North-west Zone, into which Battambang fell, had seven regions, and Chhor's family was sent to a village called Lum Thmar in Region 5. Prior to the evacuation of the towns and cities 170,000 people lived in Region 5, but that number more than doubled in the months after April 1975 with an additional 200,000 evacuees dumped there. The result was a catastrophic shortage of food as supplies dwindled ahead of the year-end harvest, which in any event would not have provided enough rice.

The situation in Region 5, although bad, was made even worse by the decision of its local leaders to push ahead with irrigation projects rather than putting the new arrivals to work growing food. This was a direct consequence of Nuon Chea's order at the May meeting that cadres must fulfil the Party's plan to build socialism by modernising agriculture through constructing dams and canals. This work was done by *chalat*, mobile work brigades of teenagers and young adults who laboured from dawn until late at night, toiling under the constant threat of execution by the 'black crows' as the cadres were known. Workers who met their target for the day – moving, say, three cubic metres of earth by hand – would be fed, though even then it was rarely enough. Those who failed would receive half rations or nothing at all, and they had to make up their work shortfall the following day. Should they fail again they risked execution. In such circumstances illness or disease, for which there were no medicines, quickly carried off countless people.

After Chhor's family reached Lum Thmar his four eldest offspring were ordered to join a *chalat*, while the three youngest were taken elsewhere. Chhor and his wife stayed behind in the village and were put to work in the rice fields. To see their youngest children they needed permission from the commune chief. It was a torrid time for evacuees and even worse for families such as Ket's, unused to manual labour.

'Because Ouk Chhor's family used to work for [Sihanouk], none of the children had any experience of such hard work,' said Sady, whose family at least had some farming background. 'They had lived in a nice house and they had eaten nice food, so when they encountered this they suffered terribly.'

As 1975 wore on, problems mounted for the Chhor family. The Khmer Rouge had outlawed money, which meant their cash was worthless. As food shortages worsened, the family traded most of their small stash of gold and jewellery for extra rations of rice porridge. That got them through the first months but when the rains came the following year Chhor, who had picked up a leg infection, fell ill with diarrhoea. He was now at serious risk of execution, because the Khmer Rouge regarded the sick as malingerers, 'victims of their own imagination' who had failed to re-educate themselves and therefore deserved to be killed.

In desperation Chhor's wife gave the commune cook 100 grams of gold for a spoonful of palm sugar.

'She wanted to combine it with palm wine, but there wasn't any to be had,' Sady said. 'It was useless, and she couldn't cure Ouk Chhor's illness.'

Not long afterwards, Chhor died. A decade earlier he had been at the side of Sihanouk attending to his luxurious needs. Now his widow, Saray, was forced to drag his emaciated body to the village cemetery, where she buried him on her own. The village chief forbade her to weep.

Her troubles were not over. Days later a truck offloaded the wasted corpses of two of her sons: Chhon – whose wife and four children died later – and Sarin. Both had starved to death while working in the *chalat*. Saray hauled their bodies to the village cemetery and buried them on her own. Once again the village chief forbade her to weep.

Within a month Saray had buried two more children: Sarath, who died of malaria – 'he was clever, like Ket,' Sady said – and her eldest daughter Vanny. All four had been in the same *chalat*.

'They had worked together digging irrigation canals,' Sady said. 'But if one got sick, they could not help each other. The Khmer Rouge would not allow that.'

The deaths of her husband and four children within weeks devastated Saray. Worse still the Khmer Rouge would not allow her to mourn. In Democratic Kampuchea, the only loyalty permitted was to the Party, and the only love possible was for *Angkar*. Those who felt differently were told that they lacked sufficient revolutionary zeal, and risked execution.

'She felt she was going nearly crazy, but she didn't dare to cry because she feared the Khmer Rouge cadres would kill her if she did,' Sady told me.

After returning to Phnom Penh in 1979, Saray learned that her son Saron, who had gone to Svay Rieng, was also dead. Within days of reaching his wife's village, the local cadres had thrown him in jail where he was beaten and starved. He eventually choked to death on a handful of rice. Saron, who had worked as an aircraft engineer for the Lon Nol regime, believed he would stand a better chance under the protection of his in-laws, who had become Khmer Rouge functionaries. Sady is convinced someone betrayed Saron and his uncle, who was also jailed and killed.

And so by mid-1976, just a year after the Khmer Rouge had taken power, more than half of Ket's immediate family was dead. Ket, at this stage in Senegal with his wife and two young children, had no inkling of the agony that had enveloped his country. He would remain unaware of it until he returned a year later.

ALTHOUGH THE EXACT NUMBER of deaths under the Khmer Rouge will never be known, it is believed that between 1.7 million and 2.2 million people died, one in four of Cambodia's population alive in April 1975. Around half were executed; the rest succumbed to overwork, illness or starvation before the Khmer Rouge were driven from power.

Cambodians who lived through this period refer to it in different ways and, not uncommonly, use the physically impossible to emphasise the scale of the catastrophe. One such phrase is *neuv pel del porpok thlak pi leu mek*, or 'the time when the clouds fell from the sky'. The words have added resonance in this agricultural land, said Youk Chhang, a survivor of those years and today the director of the Documentation Center of Cambodia, or DC-Cam, the country's key research organisation that focuses on the crimes of Democratic Kampuchea. For many Cambodians clouds evoke beauty, freedom and spirituality, and in that way they stand as the epitome of all that humans should aspire to be. But to the Khmer Rouge, with their harsh, collective beliefs, he said, such individuality was anathema; to them, clouds were arrogant. And so, 'clouds' became a denigrating label for city dwellers like Youk Chhang: people who, the cadres claimed, regarded themselves as superior to the rural population in the same way as the clouds sit above the land. The Khmer Rouge would make sure to bring these 'arrogant' urbanites down to earth and into a hellish existence.

Discussion of the circumstances surrounding the Khmer Rouge's demise and of the decision by China, Thailand and the West to sustain Pol Pot's forces through the 1980s and into the 1990s is beyond the scope of this book. Suffice it to say that by January 1979, when the Khmer Rouge leaders and forces were driven west to the Thai border by an invading force of Vietnamese troops and Cambodian rebels, hardly a family was left unscathed. As Cambodia's fourth government in a decade cemented its hold on power, millions of traumatised people began to make their way home. For the second time in four years a nation was on the move.

It took Sady until June 1979 to reach the house where she had stood on that hot April morning four years earlier, watching Aunt Saray fleeing into the unknown with Uncle Chhor and their children, the family laden down so untidily with their provisions. Now Aunt Saray was back, and over meagre evening meals she told Sady what had happened: somehow the cadres in Region 5 had learned that Chhor had worked for Sihanouk and that his children were educated.

'And so the family suffered more than others,' Sady explained. 'That's why they didn't like them, and it's why they put extra pressure on them, forcing them to work harder and not giving them enough food.'

At times food was in such short supply that Aunt Saray scavenged geckos from the wall and ate them raw. When the Khmer Rouge retreated, she fled with her three surviving children.

'She still had a little gold left so she hired a boat,' said Sady. 'She didn't care about the money. She spent the last of it to come home to Phnom Penh.'

The country was devastated. Like most families, Sady's returned with nothing and scrabbled a living.

'After we came back my husband gathered detergent bottles and decanted the liquid into smaller bottles, which we swapped for food,' she said.

Sady's family had endured a torrid time, but at least most had survived. The Ouk family had been decimated. By 1979 Chhor was dead, as were four of his sons and one daughter. A daughter-in-law had perished too, as had her four children. Chhor's father was also dead.

But Aunt Saray and the three youngest children were alive, and she took consolation in knowing that her eldest son Ket, the golden child – and, since his father's death, the head of the family – had been overseas when the Khmer Rouge took power. He surely would not have returned to this holocaust.

BY EARLY 1979, half a world away in France, Martine had spent 18 months on an increasingly desperate search for word of Ket, while at the same time looking after their children. By now Mackara was six, Neary was three and a half, and the little girl cried every day for her missing father.

The stories of terror and destruction emanating from the hermit nation that had been Democratic Kampuchea chilled Martine. Tens of thousands of exhausted refugees streaming into camps in Thailand told of executions, starvation, extraordinary cruelty and vast gulags where people were worked to death, all of this overseen by the invisible *Angkar*. It was clear Cambodia had gone through hell. The ongoing lack of information about Ket only added to Martine's fears. She wrote letters to anyone she thought might have news, including to his former boss, a man called Chan Youran.

In the early 1970s Chan Youran, a non-communist and a supporter of Sihanouk, had been the GRUNK ambassador to Senegal where Ket was posted. He and Ket seemed to get on well: when Neary was born in 1975, Chan Youran had sent a card to the couple congratulating them on the arrival of their second child. By 1979 Chan Youran, who had spent the years during Democratic Kampuchea working for the foreign ministry in Phnom Penh, was one of the few former moderates still alive.

Even after the Khmer Rouge's ouster, Chan Youran chose to remain with the movement. Early in 1979 he was sent to Switzerland, part of a delegation despatched by Pol Pot as he sought to secure international condemnation of the Vietnamese-installed government in Phnom Penh. Despite widespread knowledge of the Khmer Rouge's crimes, the shoddiness of big power politics during the Cold War meant Pol Pot succeeded in retaining Cambodia's UN seat for more than another decade.

And so, after more than a year of fruitless effort, you can imagine Martine's elation when she received a letter from Chan Youran, mailed from the Hôtel d'Auteuil in Geneva on March 20, 1979. Chan Youran, who wrote to Martine in French, began by acknowledging that he had received a letter she had written to him in Beijing two months earlier, seeking news of Ket.

'I wanted to reply right away,' Chan Youran explained, his neat script slanting across the hotel's writing paper, 'but as you are doubtless aware, we have much to do in our fight against the Vietnamese, for we must at all costs liberate our homeland.'

After thanking Martine for her 'noble sentiments' about Cambodia's plight, Chan Youran penned the following lines:

'I know [Ket] was fine before the Vietnamese invasion. I therefore hope he will continue to enjoy good health,' he wrote. 'Ket, as we both know, would never accept losing our homeland, and he is currently fighting our enemies. We all wish him much success in our people's struggle … Permit me to say that, whatever happens, Ket will remain faithful and attached to you and the children. Kiss the children and send my regards to your beloved parents.'

Martine, clutching the two-page letter, was astounded. After so long without any news, she had finally heard – from Ket's former boss, no less – that her husband was, as recently as January, alive and well. Desperate to know more she bundled her children onto a train and headed for Switzerland.

Three decades later, when Neary told me about it, the trip was still vivid in her mind. Martine dressed them in the drab clothing favoured by the movement: black pyjamas for the three-year-old Neary; a khaki jacket and the chequered *krama* worn around the neck for Mackara. Martine cut her hair in a bob and wore a white cotton shirt and the *sampot Khmer*, the traditional ankle-length silk skirt with gold thread.

'She got dressed like a real Khmer woman and I remember she cut her hair to go and see them because at the time all the women in Cambodia had to cut their hair. No one was supposed to be elegant, so to please them …' Neary trailed off. 'She wanted them to feel they had nothing to fear from her. And I was wondering: Why is she cutting her hair? And why have I got these black pyjamas? And why is everything so black?'

Martine and the children met Chan Youran and three other members of the delegation in a landscaped park in Geneva. Martine managed to take a few photographs of the four besuited men, their polished shoes reflecting bright sunshine. In one, the four are sat on a bench, Neary between them. Two look squarely at Martine's camera, while a third glances away. Chan Youran, in the only photograph in which he appears, took that moment to bend forward, obscuring his face, as he dislodged a stone from Neary's sandal.

Chan Youran was far vaguer in person than he had been in his letter. He was, in a word, evasive, unable to offer even the most basic information: what work Ket had been doing, where he had been living or the state of his health. Agonised, Martine realised that Chan Youran had lied in his letter and had not seen her husband. It was a desperate blow, and she returned to Le Mans distraught, Mackara and Neary in tow.

Through the rest of that year Martine reconnected with old Cambodian friends, former students from her days with Ket in Paris. Like Ket, they had returned to Democratic Kampuchea during those dark years but were now back in France. None had news of him, but their accounts of being interned in re-education centres and camps and the experiences they had lived through horrified her.

One handed her a sheaf of papers written by a man called Hu Nim, the Khmer Rouge's information minister. Hu Nim, who had spoken out against some of the movement's most egregious policies, was arrested in April 1977, the day before the foreign affairs ministry sent Ket his recall letter. This bundle of papers, Martine later learned, was the seventh and final draft of Hu Nim's so-called 'confession', obtained after beatings, whippings and water torture, the product of a broken man. In it Hu Nim confessed to being a CIA spy – which was untrue – who had worked for decades to undermine the revolution, telling his torturers: 'I am not a human being, I am an animal.' He was executed on July 6, 1977, along with 126 other 'enemies' of the revolution.

The document left Martine aghast.

'And that's when I started thinking that something very serious might have happened to my husband,' she said.

With her fears burgeoning, Martine wrote to Sihanouk, whom she had met in 1973 at the embassy in Senegal when he had toured Africa as GRUNK head of state. In 1979 Sihanouk was still in the arms of the Khmer Rouge despite their loss of power and, more remarkably, despite the movement having killed five of his children and 14 of his grandchildren.[6] He telegrammed his suggestion: contact Chan Youran. This circle of futility left Martine frustrated at every turn, yet there was no way forward. Under the Khmer Rouge, Cambodia had been closed to outsiders for nearly four years. The Vietnamese-backed government now in power saw no reason to change that.

In December 1979 Sihanouk held a press conference near Paris to drum up support for the ousted Khmer Rouge. Martine gatecrashed the event and asked Sihanouk if he knew Ket's whereabouts. He told her he had no idea, so she put the question to a man called Thiounn Prasith, who at the time was Democratic Kampuchea's ambassador to the UN and who was seated alongside Sihanouk. In an extraordinary outburst Prasith, one

6. See, for example, RETIRED KING SAYS KR MURDERED HIS CHILDREN, GRANDCHILDREN, Douglas Gillison, *The Cambodia Daily*, April 22, 2008.

of the regime's most notorious apologists, snapped at Martine: 'Don't put your life on hold for him!'

Martine left the press conference in a daze.

Later that month a women's organisation in France bought her a ticket to Thailand, which was host to tens of thousands of Cambodian refugees. Martine hoped to find Ket or members of his family in camps just inside the Thai border. She left the children with her mother and, on Christmas Day 1979, reached Khao-I-Dang camp. Two months after opening it was already home to 80,000 people with 1,600 more arriving each day. It was raining heavily and the camp was a slick, sticky sea of mud.

'I am going to discover in these camps the sheer horror that the people I had known, and that all Cambodians, had endured,' Martine said of the experience that ended up convincing her to study nursing on her return to France. 'Every day we brought five or six children, young children, five or six months old, who were dying from lack of food or from dehydration, and I would do whatever I could to help all of these people.'

As the weeks went by she encountered a few familiar faces. One of those was Ong Thong Hoeung, the intellectual who had returned to Cambodia the year before Ket, and who had been imprisoned in a camp for returnees. He assumed Martine had come to Khao-I-Dang after receiving a letter he had recently sent her. No, she replied, I didn't get a letter.

And so Hoeung explained that in the months after the Khmer Rouge were overthrown he had worked at Tuol Sleng, as S-21 had been renamed, helping the country's new Vietnam-backed rulers to sort through Duch's archive of abandoned documents, organising the confessions and drafting a list of prisoners who had been executed. The reason Hoeung went to work there in mid-1979, he told her, was to find out whether any of his missing friends had been taken there. He recognised hundreds of names.

The name 'Tuol Sleng' meant nothing to Martine, so amid the mud and the rain and the heat of the refugee camp, Hoeung explained its function.

'It was an extermination camp,' he told her. 'I found your husband's name in the Tuol Sleng files.'

SHORTLY AFTER SHE MET with Hoeung, Martine returned to France. 'Up until that point, I had believed I would find my husband,' she said. 'I was utterly devastated.'

Hoeung's letter was waiting for her, a few words jotted on a scrap of newsprint: 'Martine, Ouk Ket was exterminated at Tuol Sleng.'

For a week the children asked constantly for information about their father. One evening she took them into her arms.

'So they are four-and-a-half years old and seven years old, and both my son and my little daughter ask me every day: "Have you seen Daddy?"' Martine said as her voice trembled on the abyss and the tears welled.

'Are we going to see Daddy?'

They were the same two questions that Mackara and Neary had been asking since Ket had disappeared nearly three years earlier. And as difficult as it was, Martine knew she had to be honest with them.

'And I must tell them: no, they will never see their daddy again.'

LIFE INSIDE S-21

'The conditions were so inhumane and the food was so little. There was a big pot of gruel to be distributed between 50 or 60 of us, so we only had three spoons of gruel for each meal, and the spoon was like a coffee spoon, so little. It's not like a normal rice spoon. And the spoons would be collected and if any prisoner hid or concealed a spoon and if [the guards] found it out, then they would beat them up or kick them.

I lost my dignity because the condition of the prisoners [compared with] the guards was so distant. It's like humans compared with animals. Even to animals they would give enough food.

I arrived on 7 January 1978 … and stayed in that room for one month and a few days. [We] were only allowed to lie down, and we would not be allowed to sit up unless we sought permission from the guards. Otherwise we would be beaten up. On the whiteboard there were regulations, internal regulations. For example, we would be warned not to make [any] noise or communicate with one another. We had to listen to the guards and not be liberal, and so on and so forth. So we could not do anything without any permission.

We received a bowl of gruel at eight o'clock in the morning and we got another one at eight in the evening. We were allowed to do exercise in the morning but while we were still shackled. In our room, we slept there and ate there and relieved ourselves inside the same room, and we were not allowed to move even an inch from where we belonged, where we [were] put.

And when we were allowed to do exercise, our legs were still shackled to the metal bars and we could hop to do exercise. If we didn't hop then they would beat us also. We were so weak, and how could we hop? But we just did it against our will to avoid being whipped. And while doing the exercise, we could only stop hopping after we received an order or permission from the guards. Otherwise we would hop until we died.

And they allowed us to have a bath and a young guard would use a hose, a water hose, and spray the water on approximately 50 prisoners all at once and after five minutes they would stop spraying the water.

We were never washed or had a bath for quite some time, so we developed some kinds of skin rashes and we felt so itchy and the floor was wet and we couldn't sleep after the bath. So we had to remove our clothes to dry the wet floor ... so that we could sit up ... [We] had to remove our clothes while still being shackled. You could imagine how difficult it was.

And we were so hungry that we ate insects, the insects that dropped from the ceiling. We would immediately grab them and eat, and when we were eating those insects and were spotted by the guards then we would lie to them [saying] that we had not done anything. If they found out that we were eating insects we would be beaten also, so we could do that only if we avoided being seen by the guards.

So death was imminent and people died one after another, and at about 10 or 11pm the corpse would be removed, and we ate our meal next to the dead body, and anyway we did not care because we were like animals.'

— Vann Nath, an artist and S-21 survivor, speaking at the UN war crimes tribunal in Phnom Penh in June 2009. Vann Nath survived a year in S-21, spared by Duch after he learned that this prisoner had skills. In the prisoner ledger Duch wrote 'keep for use' next to Vann Nath's name, and put him to work painting portraits of Pol Pot. Vann Nath's book – *A Cambodian Prison Portrait. One Year in the Khmer Rouge's S-21* (White Lotus, 1998) – tells his story.

CHAPTER THREE

A RARE VIOLENCE

BY JANUARY 1980 Martine at least knew why Ket had disappeared but little else was settled: there was no body, there were no papers, there was no death certificate and, under its new government, Cambodia remained closed, which meant that Martine could not visit to find out more. On top of that she had the word of just one person who had seen Ket's name in S-21's archives. In such a situation who would not hold out hope?[1]

Neary certainly did. Buoyed in part by the optimism of youth she grew up believing her father was alive. As the 1980s rolled by she heard talk of Ket and a prison camp, but she was still a child and did not understand how the two were connected. Her father's absence was normal, but there were extraordinary reminders. There was the time a teacher asked about Ket's occupation. She could not answer, and that evening she asked Martine. 'Deceased diplomat,' her mother replied. Diplomat, thought the young Neary, well that I can understand as a job. But "deceased"? How do they go together?'

'I had to explain. It's like I had to justify myself all the time,' she said. 'I couldn't write "deceased" only, and I couldn't write down "diplomat", because he was dead.

In the end the teacher wrote down "deceased diplomat", and Neary left it at that.

'I didn't question it much when I was a kid because you know, you go to school, you have your friends, and you have your life when you're a kid.

---

1. Psychologists call this 'ambiguous loss', a term used to describe situations such as this in which someone disappears. With no proof of death, it is common for their loved ones to hold on to the hope that the missing person is still alive. The uncertainty surrounding the fate of the missing means those left behind are unable to mourn properly. Ambiguous loss 'is the most devastating [of all losses in personal relationships] because it remains unclear, indeterminate.' *Ambiguous Loss: Learning to Live With Unresolved Grief,* Pauline Boss (Harvard University Press, 1999), p. 5.

And politics is not for kids. It's an adult story so I wasn't wondering more than that,' she said. 'When I was asked, I said that my father disappeared in Cambodia and that was all, because I didn't know what to say.'

On occasion she would listen to audiotapes that her parents had made in Senegal of Ket talking to the children during the seemingly insignificant day-to-day tasks like feeding Neary. The memory makes her smile: hearing the disembodied voice of a man she barely remembers, a doting father chirruping to his infant daughter in French 'with a little Khmer accent'.

Neary lived in a 10th-floor apartment in Le Mans with her mother, who worked in a local hospital, and her maternal grandmother ('they were like a married couple'). Years later some of Neary's friends told her that they always felt there was something missing in her life, though they struggled to say quite what that was. For Neary the void simply grew: one person was missing while everyone else in her life – her grandmother, her mother and her brother – served as a constant reminder of him. As the years passed, Ket's absence became Neary's most constant presence and her behaviour reflected that. The teenage Neary was a tearaway, partying to excess. As she grew older the gap between her and Martine widened.

THE END OF THE COLD WAR in 1988-89 shook up the global order. Its effects were felt around the world, even by this fractured family muddling through life in central France, because among its consequences was the fact that Cambodia could no longer rely on Vietnam. For a decade the government in Phnom Penh had been propped up by Hanoi as it battled the Khmer Rouge remnants and the non-communist resistance. The decline of the Soviet Union, long a sponsor of Vietnam, meant Hanoi's support was no longer feasible.

In September 1989 the last Vietnamese soldiers left and Cambodia began to open up. By chance one of the earliest visitors was an agricultural expert from Le Mans, whose pending trip was reported in Martine's local newspaper. Martine contacted the woman who promised to try and track down Ket's family.

A month after the woman left, the 15-year-old Neary brought up the post on her way in from school. One letter bore a Cambodian stamp. Her heart leapt at the thought that this letter could be – must be – from her father after so many years of silence but it was written in Khmer, which Neary could not read, so she phoned her mother. Ket had taught Martine to read and write Khmer, and she rushed home from work. When Martine emptied the envelope, a photograph of Ket fell to the floor.

'Can you imagine, after 13 years missing? And Mum thinks: It's your dad writing this.'

Martine, trembling, started to read aloud, translating as she went. Yet as she mouthed those first, slow words the door slammed shut on their hope.

'Oh, my beloved son,' the letter began. 'How are you?'

Martine's efforts to reach Ket's family had succeeded but the message had become garbled in the process. His mother, Saray, thought her eldest son was alive and living in France.

'My Khmer grandmother was talking to him,' said Neary. 'This is how we learned that she didn't know he had gone back to Cambodia.'

Martine decided it was time to visit Phnom Penh, and for a year the family scrimped and saved. The children made trinkets and sold them to their classmates to raise extra cash.

Martine, Mackara and Neary landed in Phnom Penh on July 16, 1991. It was Neary's 16th birthday. For Neary the trip had a number of purposes: to meet her Cambodian family, to find out about the country's culture, and 'just to know who we are'.

'I came here with the idea that my dad is not dead, and maybe I will know what has happened,' Neary told me years later. 'In my head he has disappeared, but that doesn't mean anything concerning the end. Has he gone crazy? Has he gone to Vietnam? Has he got another life? You know it's like a quest; you don't have answers so you look for it all your life. And the less you have elements, the more you're looking.'

During their three-week stay all three fell ill; Mackara nearly died from dysentery. They stayed at Ket's family home, the same wooden house on stilts in which he had grown up in the south-east of the capital. Saray, Ket's mother, was still a dignified woman despite the trauma of losing most of her family and the grinding poverty into which they had been forced.

'She had this, it was in her,' Neary said in her French-accented, lilting English. 'She was poor, she had nothing left, she had lost many kids under the Khmer Rouge, and she was skinny and smoking all the time, but she was still naturally noble.'

Her grandmother's house was the most beautiful on this dusty street, the tallest, 'the most Khmer-like', as Neary put it. Behind it a cluster of banana and papaya trees ran down to a pond. The front yard was postcard

Cambodia: a beaten-earth compound swept clean of leaves each day, hens kicking up puffs of dust in the low morning light, and a mango tree into whose branches the ragged neighbourhood children clambered and sat and stared wide-eyed at these strange, pale visitors. The year Neary visited, the mango tree was laden with fruit and curious children in equal measure.

THE MAIN REASON for the visit was, of course, to learn what they could about Ket and about S-21. Aside from snippets they had gleaned about the Khmer Rouge's most secret prison – what Martine called 'fragments of this murderous madness' – they knew very little.

It turned out Ket's family had known for years that he had been taken to S-21. In 1979 Sady had visited the former prison after a government radio broadcast advised anyone who was missing relatives to go there and check against a list of names written up in a book. For Sady, seeing the name of her beloved older cousin with whom she had been so close was a bewildering experience.

'Ket lived overseas, so I didn't expect his name to be there,' Sady told me. 'I went there because I had other relations we had lost at that time and I was looking for other names. When I saw Ouk Ket's name on the last sheet of that book I felt very shocked and afraid.'

At first Sady's relatives dismissed the notion that Ket had been taken to S-21, so she went back to check again a few days later. In the end her younger relatives were convinced but for more than a decade Ket's mother, Saray, was not.

'And she refused to believe her son was dead until she met Martine in 1991,' Sady said. 'Only then did she accept it.'

A FEW DAYS AFTER ARRIVING in Cambodia, Neary, Martine and Mackara went with Sady to S-21, which had been renamed the Tuol Sleng Genocide Museum. They entered the courtyard through the same gate Duch had used to flee 12 years earlier, and encountered first-hand its full horror. The sign exhorting the cadres to be strong and defend the revolution against its enemies had gone, but much else remained. A corrugated-iron fence topped with barbed wire surrounded the complex. The four of them stood in the courtyard in the dust and the heat facing the three-storey buildings that had comprised S-21's main block. To their left was Building A. Buildings B and C were in front, and Building D was to their right.

The rooms on the ground floor of Building A were used for the most important prisoners, people such as Hu Nim, the former information minister. Other prisoners, hundreds of whom were held here at any one time, were either shackled in rows on the floors of the former classrooms or chained alone in tiny cells made of wood or rough brick. Nearby were the buildings where interrogators practised their craft, extracting confessions through torture in order to prove to the Party's satisfaction that these men and women were enemies of the revolution. The operation was straightforward. Prisoners had to confess to their treasonous activities. Once they had done so their confessions were written up and passed to Duch for review. Those of the most important prisoners were sent to *Angkar* for feedback and guidance. Less important prisoners fell entirely within Duch's purview and it was up to him to determine whether their confessions were sufficient to warrant immediate execution or whether further interrogation and torture were needed to produce a more compelling truth. It made no difference to the prisoners – they were always executed – but it was important to the Party and to Duch that this process be properly managed.

Soon enough S-21's Kafkaesque nature would become familiar to Neary: that to be brought here was to be condemned to death and that there was no escape. But for now the experience of seeing this place where she had been told her father had been taken was simply harrowing.

'My brother and I went into one of the two buildings on the left-hand side, and that for me was the shock of my life,' Neary said. 'And I say "shock", because when I walked into the first room and then visited the others, I understood that this first room was the most murderous where the truth was at its most glaring.'

It was here that Duch's team had killed the last prisoners, leaving the corpses shackled to the beds. A large black-and-white photograph on the wall of each room showed the gory scene that the Vietnamese forces found just a few days later. In many rooms Neary saw rusting metal bars with shackles, used to bind the prisoners' ankles, scattered on the tiled floor. In some were sculpted moulds, crafted to produce busts of Pol Pot.

On the wall in another building was a huge monochrome photograph of the mass graves at Chhoeung Ek, the killing field where thousands of S-21's inmates were executed.

'And on the wall there were more black-and-white photographs and – I'm weighing my words carefully here – black-and-white photographs of a rare violence, because just imagine how much more violent these images would have been had they been in colour,' Neary said.

Even in monochrome they are shocking: broken bodies on stretchers, rough bandages on wounded limbs, black blood seeping across pale tiles, the consequences of uninhibited power unleashed on the powerless.

'[There were] emaciated faces, caved-in skulls, and a detainee with his legs still shackled, and who had been beaten, lying in a pool of blood, and you think he is dead, and with leaves thrown on his face and in that same pool of blood,' Neary said. 'It is not so. Two photographs later, the same image but the detainee isn't dead. He raises his hand and he tries to get up on his elbow, with his beaten-in face, and I asked myself: From whom is he asking help?'

Neary and Mackara entered Building B where the former classrooms, divided into dozens of cells, had been linked by punching rough doorways through the adjacent walls.

'We go through a door that plunges us into the most surreal world. In this second room ID photographs covered every wall, and these faces stared at us, drawing us in, one by one, passing us from one to the other,' she said.

Most prisoners brought to S-21 were photographed on arrival. As with the confessions, many images have disappeared, but many others survived even though their subjects did not. The two teenagers scoured the walls of these monochromatic faces, each with a number pinned to their clothing, and this anonymous, long-dead army stared blankly back. Neary struggled to calculate the greater horror: that so many men, women and children had passed through S-21, or that the images of an unknown number of forgotten others were no longer in existence.

'I continued through this room and I saw another door which brought me to a third room with just as many pictures on the walls and just as many people staring back at me,' she said. 'And I said to my brother: "We have to start again and look at them one by one because our father might be in there. And if he is, we cannot miss him.'

Slowly, methodically, Neary and Mackara started over trying to locate Ket's face, scanning the hundreds of images, desperate to find him. But eventually they were forced to admit defeat and left the last room into the thick midday heat with no photograph to prove that Ket had ever been here. Equally troubling, there was no shortage of evidence to illustrate what sort of place S-21 had been.

'And I was thinking about all of these victims who waited for someone to come and help them, and who tried to hold out for as long as they could, when in fact nobody ever came,' Neary said. 'That is the day a seed of poison landed in my body, and since then I have not stopped trying to find out what happened.'

Later on that muggy July day the family got access to a dusty archive room, but only after the member of staff who had the key extorted a bribe for opening the door. In that room, heaped with stacks of dust-ridden folders of documents and photographs, they found the entry register for June 1977 and the execution register for December. Among the hundreds of names on the latter was Ket's. Next to that was his job as a diplomat and three dates: his birth date, August 1, 1946; the date he was brought to S-21, June 15, 1977, just four days after returning home; and the date of his execution, December 9, 1977, nearly six months later. The last date bore Duch's signature.

And that was all there was to see. There was no file, no photograph and no confession; just a few lines on some worn pages. Whatever the torturers managed to extract from Ket in that time remains lost, but it is likely that he eventually confessed to working for the CIA or the KGB or the Vietnamese, and it is likely too that he named names, as nearly all of the prisoners did. The process, after all, required a confession and 'strings' of fellow traitors. In Ket's case, as for many of those brought here, its 'incriminating' contents would surely have been a fabrication given up in desperation to stop the pain. Like most of the prisoners at S-21, Ket was not guilty of trying to undermine the revolution. But finding his file would have provided Neary some strange peace of mind, proof that her father was indeed dead. In 1991 what she did manage to find was not enough to persuade her he had been brought here, tortured and then 'smashed', as the Khmer Rouge parlance had it.

'I never took the content of those documents at face value,' Neary said of the prison ledgers. 'I always told myself that they were not representative and that perhaps I could find something, and I needed to find something, to better prove this.'

THERE WERE TWO OTHER MOMENTS that stood out that day. One was when Neary found Martine standing in front of a board of images, crying and pointing out Cambodian friends she and Ket had known in Paris. The other was when Sady showed Neary a photograph of Duch and told her:

'This is the man who used to run S-21.' It was the first time Neary had seen the face of the man who had signed her father's execution order, but Duch's picture did not register in her mind. Having spent hours absorbing the faces on hundreds of black-and-white images, that was hardly surprising.

'His was just one more face,' she said. 'I remember that I told myself that this man was the guardian of the school and, I mean it sounds stupid, but at the time I didn't even know if my dad had come here.'

THE FOLLOWING DAY Sady took them to Chhoeung Ek, the killing field south of Phnom Penh where most of the prisoners from S-21 were taken to be executed. The Khmer Rouge believed in 'pulling out the grass by the roots', which meant killing entire families. And so the children of S-21's prisoners were murdered here too, the babies held by the legs and smashed against a gnarled tree and their bodies dumped in nearby pits.

While Neary was flying in from Bangkok she had looked out of the window at the flooded fields that glinted beneath her like shards. Now on the bumpy road to Chhoeung Ek she was for the first time enveloped in the countryside, juddering through a rural idyll of rice fields, sugar-palm trees and skinny white cattle, with the bright sun beating down.

'We arrived in a secluded place, which was very quiet, and there was the mausoleum of Chhoeung Ek with 18 layers of skulls,' she said.

Today Chhoeung Ek is hardly secluded. The city's sprawl has nearly caught up, the nation's newest brewery stands close by, and many of the rice paddies that once mirrored the sky are walled off, drab plots awaiting the urban creep of concrete and brick. Chhoeung Ek is a staple on the tourism circuit, known to tens of thousands of visitors as The Killing Field, as if in Democratic Kampuchea there had been only one.

The mausoleum was built at Vietnam's insistence in the 1980s to house thousands of skulls, the last remains of S-21's inmates. Most of the pits from which they were excavated are now depressions in the ground. In front of them a verdant lawn links the bizarre, multi-storeyed tower packed with the skulls of hundreds of victims with a building that houses exhibits such as clothing, as well as bamboo staves and rough killing equipment.

Back then, said Neary, Chhoeung Ek was less sanitised.

'The first thing you see is not a hole and someone dead lying in it – no. Only you see that it is very green, and indeed you know that nature likes to be fed,' Neary said with bitter irony. 'And then suddenly you think: what's this hole for? And there are bones with ropes still attached. So then you get it – that the skulls over there in the mausoleum are the heads of the people who are inside these holes.'

The reality of Chhoeung Ek hit Neary while she and Mackara walked in slow shock between the pits, apart from each other yet not too distant.

'And after that I remember that we looked at each other and couldn't say a word to one another,' she told me two decades later.

Neary paused, a trailing-off that would become common to our many conversations. At these times it was easy to perceive the profound weariness that had settled on her, the cruel burden that circumstance had placed on her shoulders. These were the moments when she became lost in the maze of her own story, one that had provided few answers despite the years she had spent seeking them.

'And since that moment,' she said, 'we have been linked by something so traumatising that we have lost the capacity to talk to each other. I haven't even seen my brother in more than eight years.'

BEFORE THEY RETURNED TO FRANCE, the family held a Buddhist ceremony for Ket. In Cambodia such an event is not just for the extended family; it is for the district, and everyone helps. The preparations took place in the open area between the stilts under her grandmother's wooden house.

'So you find yourself with kilos of meat, kilos of herbs, kilos of flowers, and all the girls are participating,' Neary said, smiling at the rich flood of memories. 'I remember there was a girl called Srey and we were very close because maybe she was 20 and I was 16.'

The young women braided each other's hair with *champa*, a white, tubular flower with a heady fragrance.

'You take one hair, one long hair, and at the end of it you turn the flower around and it stays in the hair and then you put more in,' Neary said. 'And the atmosphere is not like in France where funerals are sad. The atmosphere was pleasant and joyful. It was very lovely.'

In the afternoon the orange-robed monks, shaven-headed and barefoot, came from the nearby pagoda and offered prayers for Ket and for all those in his family who had perished. The rhythmic, monotone chants swirled around the framed photograph of Ket that Martine had brought from France, then rose into the dusty air.

'The ceremony took something like two hours – the monks stayed in the lotus position and they were saying the Sanskrit words and they don't stop. It's a big energy and makes you very dizzy because there is lots of incense,' Neary recalled. 'And there were flowers *everywhere*.'

Relatives came from across Phnom Penh; a few even travelled from the other side of the country. As night descended, the candles were lit and the guests feasted on noodles, spicy soup, rice and vegetables.

'But it was very strange for me because we had this picture of my dad and actually we had no body. So at that time I was wondering: why are we doing this ceremony and whom are we putting in the grave? Am I putting in the grave someone who is not dead?' Neary said slowly.

In the absence of a body, this ceremony was as much as the family could do. But as Neary returned to France, none of it was enough to convince her that her father was dead.

In the course of this struggle I call on all those of my children, military and civilian, who can no longer endure the unjust oppression by the traitors and who have the courage and patriotic spirit needed for liberating the motherland, to engage in guerrilla warfare in the jungle against our enemies.

If you are armed and have already mastered military skills, I will provide you at the opportune time with munitions and new arms. If you do not yet have arms but wish to acquire military skills, I will take necessary measures to send you to the military school of the National United Front of our Kampuchea which is being established way out from your barracks and villages, and this is in order that the enemy will not be able to reach or locate it.

Those of my children who live in and around Europe and wish to serve the motherland and the people by joining the Liberation Army or the National United Front of Kampuchea, please come to see me in Moscow or Peking. Long live Cambodia!

— Sihanouk's radio address – made five days after the March 1970 coup that removed him from power – calling on Cambodians to head to the *maquis* and join the National United Front of Kampuchea, better known by its French acronym FUNK, against Lon Nol's Khmer Republic. (Taken from *Shadow Over Angkor*, volume one of Norodom Sihanouk's memoirs by his official biographer Julio Jeldres.)

CHAPTER FOUR

SEEDS OF A BITTER HARVEST

THE KHMER ROUGE'S TAKEOVER of Cambodia in 1975 emerged as the consequence of a series of unusual and even unique events that took place in the country and the region over the preceding decades. The roots of the Khmer Rouge's victory lie in the years before 1975, so it is worth trying to unravel the skein of causes, effects and personalities involved.

Although picking a starting date is something of a random exercise, 1949 seems as good as any. This was the year that the young Pol Pot left Cambodia for Paris, ostensibly to study radio engineering. Pol Pot went there under his real name, Saloth Sar, and was the beneficiary of the French-funded scholarship programme that allowed promising Cambodians to study overseas.[1] But Pol Pot, though well connected, was an unpromising student and after repeatedly failing his course, his scholarship was withdrawn.

Paris, where Pol Pot lived until the end of 1952, was a city awash with the seductive revolutionary rhetoric that resonated with many Cambodian students in the closing years of the colonial era. At the time Cambodia was still part of France's empire, and her youth studying in Paris could see in the arguments of the day a future beyond the corruption of their country's elite and what they perceived as French 'oppression' at home. Post-war France was alive with left-wing ideology, and many Cambodian students had their minds opened to communist political theory and talk of revolution that would have been regarded as seditious back home.[2]

---

1. Although he did not take the name 'Pol Pot' until many years later, I have chosen to refer to Saloth Sar by his revolutionary name throughout to avoid any confusion.

2. Pol Pot was in France at a fascinating time in the international communist movement. He arrived in Paris on October 1, 1949, the very day Chairman Mao proclaimed the founding of the People's Republic of China. Pol Pot reached Cambodia again in January 1953, two months before the death of

Pol Pot's real education in France lay not in engineering but in the -isms of left-wing thought: communism, Marxism-Leninism and Stalinism. In Paris he met or reconnected with those fellow students with whom he would foment revolution and who, as the years passed, would become key power brokers in the Khmer Rouge: men like Thiounn Mumm, Ieng Sary, Son Sen and Hou Youn. All of them joined the French Communist Party (known by its French acronym as the PCF), which was the most Stalinist of the communist parties in Western Europe. Stalin's writings were of particular influence at the time and were required reading for communists in France. Given Cambodia's later history it is worth considering how deeply the Soviet leader's unyielding views resonated with these newborn communists.

In an essay written in 1938, around the end of the USSR's Great Terror when between one million and two million people were executed (including two-thirds of the Communist Party's 139-strong Central Committee), the Soviet leader wrote that victory had required the party to purge itself of 'capitulationists, deserters, criminals and traitors'. Stalin railed that these 'dregs of humanity' and 'insects' were to blame for 20 years of criminality perpetrated at the behest of 'the espionage services of foreign states'.[3]

'[But] these contemptible lackeys of the fascists forgot that the Soviet people had only to move a finger, and not a trace of them would be left,' Stalin wrote.

He lashed out too at the intelligentsia, claiming the 'old class dividing lines between the working people of the USSR were being obliterated [and] the old class exclusiveness was disappearing', thereby laying the foundations for a new society.[4]

Such rhetoric went down well in post-war France. As Philip Short wrote in his biography of Pol Pot, the PCF was 'viscerally anti-intellectual' by the time Pol Pot joined it, which meant his failure to graduate may have worked to his advantage.[5] Although a few in the Paris-based Marxist

---

Joseph Stalin, who was at the time the undisputed elder statesman of international communism. The subsequent ructions between the revisionists in the Communist Party of the Soviet Union (led by Nikita Khrushchev, who advocated the evolution of socialism through the ballot in non-USSR nations rather than through violent revolution) and the Communist Party of China (Mao felt violence was the only way to overthrow imperialism and capitalism), poisoned relations in international communism for decades. The leaders of Cambodia's communist movement, as events later proved, came to espouse Mao's view.

3. *The History of the Communist Party of the Soviet Union (Bolsheviks) of the USSR*, Josef V. Stalin, 1938, p. 347 (English version published 1939).

4. Ibid., p. 343.

5. *Pol Pot: History of a Nightmare*, Philip Short (John Murray, 2004), p. 66.

circle of Cambodian students fitted the category of 'intellectual', most were unable or unwilling to grasp the complexities of left-wing political theory or, for that matter, communism's international obligations. Instead they viewed it as a simple palette whose most attractive concepts were to be applied in broad strokes to Cambodia alone.

While Pol Pot and his fellow Cambodian students spent their evenings in Paris debating how communism could solve their nation's ills, France's grip on its former colonies in Indochina – Vietnam, Cambodia and Laos – was loosening and the struggle for control of the spoils was underway. In 1951, while Pol Pot was still in Paris, the Vietnamese divided the Indochinese Communist Party (ICP) into three, one for each of Indochina's constituent nations. The Cambodian arm was named the Khmer People's Revolutionary Party (KPRP). It was this that eventually became the Communist Party of Kampuchea (CPK), the Khmer Rouge's political arm.

The decision to separate the ICP into three national parties, though having nothing to do with Pol Pot, surely pleased the evolving nationalist. Pol Pot was likely glad, too, when Cambodia gained her independence in November 1953, several months after he had returned from France. By the time the year ended, Pol Pot had spent some months in the *maquis* in the Vietnamese-backed Cambodian communist resistance. As the years passed he gained the valuable trust of Hanoi, which dominated the movement. In 1955 the young King Norodom Sihanouk abdicated the throne and plunged into his political career. These two men from opposite poles of the social spectrum would eventually become unlikely allies.

In time, many Cambodians would look back on that first decade of independence as something of a golden age: a time of peace, optimism and relative prosperity. Independence was a source of immense pride, the nation was politically stable and its borders relatively secure. And while life was not easy for the rural majority, most of whom continued to scratch a living from their rice fields, the period was better for many and no worse for most than the years that had preceded it. For urban residents these really were the best of times. Phnom Penh, for instance, boasted good schools, plentiful markets and a surge of public buildings designed in a vibrant Khmer style. There were cinemas, theatres and music, and there was money to be made in this small city of tree-lined boulevards, home to a relatively cosmopolitan mix of Khmer, Chinese, Vietnamese and other foreigners.

Astride the political stage stood Sihanouk, who by 1955 had been elected prime minister and who later became head of state. Sihanouk was well liked at home, particularly in rural areas, and had boosted the country's international image in a way that no one had done before or has done since. In a bid to keep his weak nation safe from the Cold War whirlwind that tore across the globe after the Second World War, Sihanouk pursued a foreign policy of non-alignment, placing Cambodia in neither the US-led camp of the West nor the Soviet-led camp of the East.

Domestically Sihanouk kept a tight hold on the reins of power and refused to leave elections to chance. His 'national movement' that promoted Buddhist socialism – the Sangkum Reastr Niyum, which was effectively Sihanouk's party – won every seat in the elections of 1955, 1958, 1962 and 1966 by employing, when needed, a mix of violence, repression and co-option. In 1958, for example, his party won more than 1.6 million votes; its sole opponent, the left-wing People's Party (which was the KPRP's public front), reportedly won a mere 409 votes. The ballots of 1962 and 1966 were contested by Sihanouk's party alone.

By 1960, Pol Pot had become a significant figure in Cambodia's tiny, secretive communist movement. Some of the older leftists had decamped years earlier to Hanoi where they forged close links with Ho Chi Minh's communists. But many of the French-educated returnees like Pol Pot, Ieng Sary and others were based in Phnom Penh, and their presence in-country meant they exerted increasing control over the Party. Nuon Chea, who had not studied in France, also remained in the capital, hiding in plain sight as a portly businessman selling building materials. Short described Nuon Chea, who never came under the suspicion of Sihanouk's security police, as 'a master of disguise'.[6]

In September 1960 a group of around two dozen communists that included Pol Pot, Nuon Chea, Tou Samouth, Vorn Vet and Ieng Sary met secretly for three days on the grounds of Phnom Penh's railway station to thrash out a revolutionary agenda.[7] They held that life had become worse for most Cambodians since the elections of 1955 – a debatable contention

6. A decade later many of these exiles began to return to Cambodia from Hanoi. Initially they were welcomed, but before long they fell foul of Pol Pot's mistrust of Vietnam's influence on them. Some were killed by their fellow revolutionaries, while others escaped back across the border. After 1973 any who remained in Cambodia were executed on the grounds that they had become tainted by Hanoi.

7. At this meeting, the KPRP appointed new leaders: the first four posts were filled by Tou Samouth, Nuon Chea, Pol Pot and Ieng Sary respectively. By now Pol Pot and Ieng Sary were brothers-in-law, having married sisters Khieu Ponnary and Khieu Thirith respectively in the 1950s.

– and felt the solution was to 'annihilate' the regime of Sihanouk, who had run the country since 1953 and who appeared determined to remain in power for the rest of his life. Should peaceful methods fail, they would wage armed struggle from the rural areas on the grounds that the cities were host to 'the ruling class and the imperialists'.[8]

By this stage it was clear to the communists that they could not take control through the ballot box, assuming they had ever entertained such a course of action. In part their decision stemmed from Sihanouk's egregious electoral methods but it also reflected the fact that the communists had almost no popular support. They were not dissuaded, and to improve their position they began recruiting members and improving the Party structure. In the former they were helped by the fact that some of the senior Party members held jobs as teachers in the capital, which gave them access to malleable students.

Yet a successful revolution required far more than righteous indignation, and the powerless group that gathered in secret near the railway station must have wondered how they would ever triumph. These were difficult times, and they had little more than the distant support of their 'older brothers' in Hanoi and a near-religious determination to overturn society and start anew. The tumultuous events that overtook the region later in the decade would play a critical role in their march to power.

SIHANOUK, THOUGH UNWILLING to put too much trust in democracy, was genuinely popular, and that made the task of Cambodia's communists far harder. He was also intelligent, a workaholic, a skilful diplomat and a patriot, but was hindered by vanity, a sometimes erratic approach and his tolerance of corruption among some of his associates. As the 1960s increasingly showed, Sihanouk was capable too of authorising brutal methods when dealing with his opponents.

Some of Sihanouk's behaviour stemmed from his belief that he alone possessed the skills to navigate Cambodia through the challenges that were buffeting the region. His shrewd efforts while king to secure independence in 1953 using diplomacy and swagger proved he had considerable political talent: in sharp contrast to efforts elsewhere in South East Asia, Cambodia's independence was achieved in a relatively peaceful manner.

---

8. Short, op. cit., p. 137. (Citing *Falling out of Touch: A Study on Vietnamese Communist Policy Towards an Emerging Cambodian Communist Movement, 1930–1975*, Thomas Engelbert and Christopher E. Goscha, Monash University, 1995.)

Yet across Cambodia's borders, geography and the Cold War had collided with dangerous consequences. To the west was US-allied Thailand, a richer and more powerful nation than Cambodia and a traditional enemy. To the east was the kingdom's other long-established foe, Vietnam, which under the 1954 Geneva Accords had been partitioned between North Vietnam, soon to be backed by the Soviet Union and Mao's China, and South Vietnam, which was allied with France and increasingly with the US. In time, as we shall see, the civil war in Vietnam would spill across her borders into Cambodia with devastating consequences.

At home, Sihanouk's patronising but genuine affection for ordinary Cambodians – 'my children', as he often referred to them – resulted in measurable improvements in health and education. At independence in 1953, Cambodia had just eight high schools and no universities. By 1967 there were 200 high schools teaching 150,000 pupils, and another 11,000 students attended nine universities. By then more than a million young people had received an education. Sihanouk's laudable efforts marked a transformation in learning and generated a sea change in expectations among those who had been schooled. One of the youngsters who benefited from this explosion in education in the 1950s was a skinny village boy called Ong Thong Hoeung, the person who much later would later tell Martine that her husband had been taken to S-21.

Hoeung was born in 1945 – the year before Ket, and three years after Duch – in a village in Kandal province near Phnom Penh where his father had a small orchard. His Sino-Khmer parents were unusual among the villagers because they were determined that their children would receive the best schooling they could afford. His mother, 'an extraordinary saver', fed the family damaged fruit from their orchard, reserving the best to sell in the market.

Hoeung's parents instilled a love of reading and writing in their nine children, a passion for literature that has lasted a lifetime. When he was a boy, Hoeung told me with a smile, he took advantage of that to avoid extra chores: 'If I had a book in my hand when I was tending the fields, my mother wouldn't disturb me.'

I met Hoeung, who for many years has lived in Belgium, on the first-floor balcony of a restaurant on one of Phnom Penh's main boulevards during one of his visits to his homeland. He wore a beige baseball cap, beige trousers and a dark-blue T-shirt, a tourist staple with four Buddhist monks under umbrellas filing across his chest and 'CAMBODIA' emblazoned beneath them. The waiter brought a succession of small screw-top bottles of red wine that we drank in the post-rain cool of an April evening while traffic clattered past.

As he spoke, Hoeung, a slight, energetic, white-haired man then in his late sixties, rolled the red bottle tops around in his cupped hand, over and over. At times he would stare into the distance as though to focus his thoughts more precisely, and there were moments, unavoidable during interviews with Cambodians of a certain age, when his recounting of the abundant cruelties of the Khmer Rouge overwhelmed him – in his case the deaths of his father and of four of his brothers, their wives and their children. Throughout our conversation the bottle tops, revolving repeatedly in his palm, never left his grasp. When we left two hours later, Hoeung emptied them into a pale ceramic bowl on our table. They skittered in and lay still, crushed flat.

Hoeung was the fifth child and was bright and studious. When he was 11 he left the village to live in the capital with an older brother, a monk, at Wat Lanka, which is still a prominent Buddhist temple in Phnom Penh. In the ensuing years Hoeung's youthful certainties were undone, none more effectively than his belief that Sihanouk was the country's deserved leader, divinely ordained to steer Cambodia. Today Hoeung blames that impression on media brainwashing, which lavished extensive praise on Sihanouk. Yet those feelings were common enough at the time, particularly in rural areas: villagers would even claim to see the great man's image in the sun.[9]

Sihanouk had entered the political arena as the liberator of the nation: the man who had freed the Khmers from nearly a century of French control, and who had forged a common identity and a new sense of national pride. But what Hoeung saw during the three years he lived in Phnom Penh – 'a great turning point' – forced him to think beyond those achievements. Rural families such as his spent a small fortune sending their children to be educated in the capital, yet the students found that there were few openings when they left school.

'The only jobs were for teachers, police or government officials but no new posts were opening up and there was hardly any commerce,' he said. 'So that's when I began to suspect that things were different from what I had believed.'

---

9. After Sihanouk died in 2012, local media carried reports of Cambodians who claimed they had seen his face in the clouds, the sun, the moon or in swirls of candle smoke.

In 1965, after completing his schooling, Hoeung fulfilled a cherished dream when he left for France with a scholarship to study political economy. Living in Paris proved to be a profound experience, a place where a talented young man from a small village could stand equal with anyone – surely something the young Pol Pot had noticed nearly two decades earlier. That was not the case in Cambodia, where who you were was inextricably tied to your family, your class and how many hectares of land you owned.

'I realised in France that it's not so much about your family or what you do, it's about your appearance, your individuality,' he said. 'They don't care about those other things. The fact that I was exotic and somewhat cute, well, this was such a different world and such a different way of looking at things.'

It was an inspiration for Hoeung to find himself in a land where he could be whomever he wanted. In Paris he also found answers to his disillusionment with Cambodia's political and social problems: won over by the realignments promised by communism, he eventually became a staunch supporter of the egalitarian policies espoused by the Khmer Rouge.

It is a position he has long regretted yet at the time it was logical enough. The May 1968 student uprising across Europe resonated as strongly with Hoeung as it did with countless idealists who sought a younger and more equitable society. He started reading communist literature and attending student debates on Marxist thought, heady stuff amid exciting times. For this young man from a small village, here at last were the solutions to the most profound questions. Over the following years Hoeung's certainties only grew as Cambodia descended into a bitter civil war.

THAT DESCENT WAS LONG AND SLOW. During the 1950s and early 1960s, Sihanouk walked a fine line by promoting neutrality as both the best chance of avoiding the Cold War's destructive chill and ensuring that he held on to power. But after 1965, as the war in Vietnam heated up, Sihanouk foresaw that North Vietnam would defeat the US-backed government in the South. It meant Cambodia would one day have as her neighbour a unified, communist Vietnam, and that meant good relations with the North were of great long-term importance. Consequently, after 1965, Sihanouk allowed North Vietnam to use Cambodian territory as a transit route for arms and supplies, and to establish permanent bases there as rest areas for her troops and from where she could launch raids against the South.

These decisions lined the pockets of Sihanouk's cronies, who made money from the transit of supplies through Cambodia, and also fitted his strategic calculations. Sihanouk, to be sure, had little choice: Cambodia's army was no match for Ho Chi Minh's forces, which in any event could have come and gone at will. But it meant too that Sihanouk had effectively chosen one side over the other in the conflict unfolding next door, even if he pretended Cambodia was still neutral. This first element would prove an important miscalculation.

The second factor in the Cold War equation was Cambodia's relations with the US. Even before Sihanouk cut ties in 1965 that relationship had collapsed, poisoned by mistrust, apathy and not least by a failed effort by the US-backed rulers in South Vietnam to assassinate him in 1959.[10] It hardly helped that US troops and their South Vietnamese allies repeatedly crossed into Cambodia to attack some of North Vietnam's bases (whose existence Sihanouk had authorised but continued to deny), in the process killing Khmer civilians. In the eyes of the US Sihanouk was untrustworthy, and diplomatic relations did not resume – and then only at his request – until 1969. By that time the Khmer Rouge were openly at war with Sihanouk's regime.

Although these regional power plays were taxing for Sihanouk they were far more frustrating for Cambodia's communists as they tried unsuccessfully through the 1960s to get Hanoi and Beijing to back them against Sihanouk as they sought to move their revolution forward. In 1963 most of the communist leaders, Pol Pot included, had fled Phnom Penh for the *maquis* to escape Sihanouk's ruthless security forces, and for the next two years Pol Pot lived at Vietnamese-protected sites in eastern Cambodia or across the border in Vietnam. In 1966 he moved north to the forested, remote province of Ratanakiri, home to a large proportion of ethnic minority people whose way of life – untainted, in his eyes, by the corruption of the cities – would so influence the Khmer Rouge's view of a utopian society.

For most of that decade realpolitik forced Pol Pot and the other leaders of the Khmer Rouge to build their revolution with little help from their supposed fellow ideologists. In 1965, Pol Pot spent several months in North

---

10. *The Tragedy of Cambodian History: Politics, War and Revolution since 1945*, David Chandler (Silkworm Books, 1999), p. 107.

Vietnam where he received a humiliating message:[11] Hanoi's priority was to conquer the South and reunify the nation, and that task had grown tougher with tens of thousands of US troops landing there. The view from Mao's China was similar: revolutionary struggle in Cambodia was to wait. The logic was simple enough: by 1965 Sihanouk had cut ties with the US and was allowing North Vietnam free rein inside Cambodia, so there was no incentive for Hanoi to act against him and no reason for China – Hanoi's patron – to do so either.

The North Vietnamese leaders told Pol Pot he should view Cambodia's revolution less parochially. They told him Cambodia's communists were wrong to see the Cambodian revolution as a battle between feudal forces and their nation's oppressed masses. Instead the Khmer Rouge should see it as part of the global struggle between capitalism and socialism, and fall into line. In the same way that China's revolution had necessarily preceded Vietnam's, so too Cambodia's must wait until Vietnam's had succeeded with the US defeated and the nation reunited.[12]

For Pol Pot, with his focused but murky nationalist views, this was an offensive, irrelevant argument that was condescending and dangerous: if Cambodia's communists sat on their hands and waited until Hanoi agreed the time was right for his revolution, Pol Pot's inadequate forces would be wiped out. And while Sihanouk was useful to North Vietnam and was on good terms with China, in the eyes of the Khmer Rouge he remained the primary enemy. Yet Pol Pot also knew that Cambodia's communists were in a very weak position, and for now he toed the line.[13]

After leaving Hanoi, Pol Pot went on to China, which was then on the verge of the Cultural Revolution. Because China and North Vietnam were friendly with Sihanouk, both trips were made in secret. In Beijing, Pol Pot saw for himself what appeared to be the success of Mao's uncompromising discourse with its focus on permanent revolution, the importance of the peasantry and the responsibility that each person had to ensure the success of the revolution. All became elements of Democratic Kampuchea.

In China he found a communist revolution seemingly succeeding on an epic scale. Witnessing the fruits of Mao's victory in Beijing – where Pol Pot

---

11. *Brother Number One: A Political Biography of Pol Pot*, David Chandler (Silkworm Books, revised ed. 2000), pp. 69-71.

12. Short, op. cit., p. 157.

13. Chandler, *Brother Number One*, op. cit., p. 71.

received a warmer welcome than he had in North Vietnam, despite hearing a similar line with regard to Sihanouk – was surely more enticing than the plodding, painful and unfinished struggle against the US that was getting underway from Hanoi.[14]

WHILE THERE WERE REGIONAL TROUBLES aplenty to occupy Sihanouk as the 1960s wore on, he also faced significant challenges at home. By the time of the 1966 general election, Sihanouk had lost interest in electoral politics and for the first time did not hand-pick the candidates, preferring to focus his attention on the pending visit of France's President de Gaulle and on making films, a lifelong passion.

It proved an important error: the crop of new parliamentarians owed little to Sihanouk, while the urban population that had helped to elect the candidates on the left and on the right now regarded the former king as part of the problem.

Sihanouk's lack of interest in economics had led to his ill-fated decision in late 1963 to nationalise the import-export sector, damaging the economy and setting the urban elite against him. It was one of a number of factors that soon worsened Cambodia's position. The consequent slump in trade punched a hole in government finances, which were hit too by a drop in world prices for rubber, a key export crop.

Tax receipts on rice collapsed as well. The war in Vietnam drew in large numbers of soldiers, and the demand for Cambodian rice rocketed. On the surface that might appear to be good news, but because farmers and middlemen could make much more smuggling rice across the border, the exchequer's take fell sharply. In 1965 the Phnom Penh authorities taxed nearly 500,000 tons of rice exports. The following year, and with a similarly sized harvest, they taxed just 170,000 tons. In response the government compelled farmers to sell their rice to the authorities. In this largely rural nation that proved very unpopular.

The situation was made worse in the district of Samlaut in Battambang province, the nation's rice bowl, by grievances over land and indebtedness. In April 1967 two soldiers were killed there while forcibly collecting rice. In response the government sent in more troops, and the area erupted. By the time the uprising was quelled, hundreds of people, maybe more, had been killed and heads were placed on stakes to warn others. Trucks containing

---

14. Ibid., pp. 72–73.

severed heads were reportedly sent to Phnom Penh as proof that the army was dealing with the problem.[15]

Because the uprising failed, the Khmer Rouge denied responsibility for it at the time but later claimed that they had been behind what became known as the Samlaut Rebellion.[16] True or not, it encapsulated the Khmer Rouge's contention that they supported the rural majority against a venal government. More significantly, Pol Pot and the other leaders decided the time had now come for war, and in February 1968 the Khmer Rouge began attacking government posts.

The Samlaut Rebellion sparked smaller protests elsewhere, further enraging Sihanouk, who viewed such actions as a personal insult. In response he blamed left-wing parliamentarians Khieu Samphan, Hu Nim and Hou Youn. The three men fled in secret to the *maquis* where they disappeared from view, leading many to assume the security forces had killed them. Over the next three years the consequences of the Samlaut Rebellion exacerbated tensions among the key political players: Sihanouk, whose star went into decline; the urban elite, who were increasingly fed up with the plummeting economy; and the left, which was in the ascendant, boosted by domestic and regional events.

The rural uprisings brought out the worst in Sihanouk, and the last years of his rule were often marked by a sinister vindictiveness. In 1968, the year Ket went to Paris, Sihanouk ordered a number of suspected Khmer revolutionaries bound and thrown off a cliff.[17] He ordered other killings of revolutionaries, justifying himself in shrill fashion:

'I could not tolerate this and took stringent measures which resulted in the annihilation of 180 and the capture of 30 ringleaders, who were shot subsequently ... I do not care if I am sent to hell ... and I will submit the pertinent documents to the devil himself,' he raged. 'I will have them shot ... I will order the execution of those against whom we have evidence.'[18]

Flawed though Sihanouk was – even he recognised that – it is important to set his failures in context. He was leading a weak country that was

---

15. *Sihanouk: Prince of Light, Prince of Darkness*, Milton Osborne (Silkworm Books, 1994), p. 192.

16. Some academics hold that the uprising was spontaneous, and quote a statement by Pol Pot in 1977 for their position. Kiernan believes the Khmer Rouge were behind it, citing an internal history document drafted by the Party in 1967 (see *The Pol Pot Regime*, 3rd edition, p. 126, note 102).

17. *How Pol Pot Came to Power*, Kiernan, op. cit., p. 276.

18. *Peasants and Politics in Kampuchea (1942–1981)*, Ben Kiernan and Chanthou Boua (M.E. Sharpe, 1982), p. 195.

stuck in an unwinnable position between two far more powerful, hostile nations. His choices in regard to the war in Vietnam during the late 1960s were 'disastrous in the long run, perhaps, but rational at the time'.[19] Sihanouk also worked hard to secure international recognition for his country's borders and have its neutrality recognised. And, as history has shown, he saw the menace of the Khmer Rouge long before most.

It was the effects of the Vietnam War that proved the tipping point. Perhaps most damaging was the massive US bombing of Cambodia that killed tens of thousands of peasants, drove many more into urban areas, and was reportedly used by the Khmer Rouge as a potent recruiting tool. Research of the US bombing archives has shown that in 1965 the US began secretly targeting North Vietnam's bases inside Cambodia using airstrikes that, although limited, killed hundreds of Cambodian peasants in the first year alone.[20]

Ultimately the bombings failed to achieve their objective of forcing the North Vietnamese to withdraw from their bases in Cambodia, as the 1968 Tet Offensive proved, when tens of thousands of North Vietnamese troops and their Viet Cong allies attacked dozens of targets in South Vietnam in a coordinated action. Thousands had crossed into Vietnam from Cambodia having rested in bases whose existence Sihanouk had permitted and who had been supplied along lines he had known about and approved.

Had the Tet Offensive succeeded in sparking an uprising in the South and victory for the North, the US would have been forced out of Vietnam, and the Khmer Rouge, at this stage very weak, might well have become a footnote in the history of failed communist movements. As it turned out the Tet Offensive, while a propaganda victory for Hanoi, was a military failure for the North. Its most significant consequence was to help turn US public opinion against involvement in Vietnam.

By the time Richard Nixon entered the White House the following year, after pledging to end the Vietnam War under the slogan 'peace with honour', hundreds of American servicemen were dying each week and the US public was war-weary. In March 1969, Nixon unleashed the air force on Cambodia as he sought to grab the advantage against North Vietnam's military. Compared with the airstrikes of the previous three years, this was

19. Chandler, *Tragedy*, op. cit., p. 182.

20. 'Bombs Over Cambodia', Taylor Owen and Ben Kiernan (*The Walrus* magazine, October 2006).

a huge escalation: B-52s bombed Cambodia under the name Operation Menu with the targets known as Breakfast, Lunch, Supper, Dinner, Dessert and Snack.

Sihanouk had only recently re-established relations with the US, and Nixon's national security adviser, Henry Kissinger, later claimed that the Cambodian head of state had given the US a green light to bomb using B-52s. Many historians consider that unlikely: David Chandler surmised that Sihanouk had granted permission of a sort but said it was far more plausible that he had agreed to hot-pursuit actions of the type the US had undertaken from 1965, albeit more extensive and far-ranging.[21]

Nevertheless, starting in March 1969, the vast killing power of B-52s was deployed against North Vietnam's bases and the supply line known as the Ho Chi Minh Trail. Over the next four years Cambodia became the most bombed country in history.

As 1969 closed, Sihanouk's delicate balancing act was all but over.

ALL OF WHICH GOES some way to explaining why Cambodia's position had become so perilous when, in January 1970, Sihanouk flew to France, leaving behind a growing ferment of discontent among the urban elite. Publicly he was leaving for medical treatment, but in truth he was exhausted by the unending political wrangling that had characterised the past few years. Sharp-eyed observers at the airport noted that Sihanouk took much more luggage than expected and surmised that this would be a lengthy absence.[22]

After two months in France, Sihanouk left for Moscow, which was North Vietnam's key foreign backer. After that he planned to visit Beijing and then return to Phnom Penh.

It was not to be. On March 18, while he was in Moscow, Cambodia's parliament, which had slipped from Sihanouk's control, sacked him as head of state. Prime Minister Lon Nol and his deputy, Prince Sisowath Sirik Matak – a cousin of Sihanouk – took over. A few months later, the new government inaugurated the anti-communist, pro-US Khmer Republic.

Sihanouk was livid at this betrayal. When he arrived in Beijing he was quickly persuaded by Premier Zhou Enlai and others to throw in his lot with North Vietnam and the Khmer Rouge. To make the alliance more palatable,

---

21. Email correspondence with David Chandler, May 2013.

22. Chandler, *Tragedy*, op. cit., p. 191.

Pol Pot, who had come to Beijing in secret with the North Vietnamese prime minister Pham Van Dong, wheeled out the 'Three Ghosts' – Khieu Samphan, Hou Youn and Hu Nim – as the faces of the communist movement. Pol Pot remained in hiding and presumably felt that Sihanouk and the international community would welcome these well-known men, all former leftist ministers in Sihanouk's Sangkum government.

The coup and the alliance with Sihanouk provided a turning point for Pol Pot, who could now count on the open support of Hanoi and Beijing as he battled the Khmer Republic that, unlike Sihanouk, would not tolerate North Vietnam's presence in Cambodia. Behind the scenes, though, the Khmer Rouge leaders were annoyed that they had been strong-armed into a coalition government-in-exile with Sihanouk, their political and ideological foe. They felt that now was the time for all-out revolutionary struggle in Cambodia, and saw no reason to include Sihanouk in their pending victory.[23] China and North Vietnam, though, were insistent, and so for now the Khmer Rouge accepted this strange marriage to ensure they received arms, training and Vietnamese troops in their battle with Lon Nol.

To Pol Pot's frustration, what did not alter was Hanoi's position: its leaders were still far more interested in defeating the US and the South than in helping the Khmer Rouge come to power. Preventing Lon Nol's troops from threatening their forces was essential to North Vietnam's interests; overthrowing his government could wait. In its position, Hanoi failed to appreciate the change that had taken place within the leadership of the Communist Party of Kampuchea: the CPK was no longer the moderate, pro-Vietnamese organisation that it had been in 1954 or the acquiescent body it had seemed to be ever since. By 1970, as Kiernan has suggested, many of the Party's power-brokers were 'urban, French-educated, radical and anti-Vietnamese'.[24]

In radio broadcasts and tape-recorded messages distributed in Cambodia in the days after he was overthrown, Sihanouk called on people 'who can no longer endure the unjust oppression by the traitors' to head to the *maquis* and fight with him and the Khmer Rouge against Lon Nol's government. Many obeyed. Sihanouk was, after all, a god-king whose lineage stretched

---

23. From author's interview with Professor Bernd Schaefer, senior scholar at the Woodrow Wilson International Center's Cold War International History Project in Washington, DC. For a large part of his research, Schaefer has drawn on the archives of the German Democratic Republic (better known as East Germany), which was long an ally of Vietnam.

24. Kiernan, *Peasants and Politics*, op. cit., p. 14.

back more than a millennium. Out of loyalty to their former king, thousands swapped the cities and villages for the Khmer Rouge or stayed in their rural homes but gave support to Sihanouk's new ally.

Overnight the Khmer Rouge were significantly bolstered. Over the next few years these communist rebels, who were once little more than a ragtag militia, became an unstoppable force, professionalised by extensive military assistance from North Vietnam. It would take five more years before the movement captured Phnom Penh, but by 1970 its enemies had provided much of what was needed for victory.

AS MARTINE EXPLAINED, one consequence of the coup was that the students in Paris had to make a choice between supporting Sihanouk or backing Lon Nol's Khmer Republic. They were polarised further by a brief US-South Vietnamese invasion of Cambodia in April. Ket swiftly joined Sihanouk's *Front Uni National du Kampuchea*, or FUNK, the political party for non-communists who wished to back what the ousted head of state now regarded as his revolution.

Sihanouk's alliance demanded unnatural compromises from those who, like Ket, had never supported Cambodia's communists. But driven by his father's exhortation that he 'must never betray the Prince' and revolted by the atrocities in the burgeoning civil war, Ket was certain his choice was correct.

'Ket was horrified to see stories in *Paris-Match* magazine of Khmer Republic soldiers holding decapitated heads and eating the livers of their victims,' Martine had told Neary about that time. 'He couldn't imagine for a second that the Khmer Rouge were doing the same and worse to their compatriots.'

Ket's pro-FUNK stance saw his name added to a list of Sihanouk sympathisers and forwarded to Lon Nol's security apparatus. Back in Phnom Penh, Ouk Chhor was being watched closely by Lon Nol's people, and his letters to Ket were thick with the censor's black ink. Chhor warned his son that the Khmer Republic regarded Ket as a traitor for siding with Sihanouk, and told him to stay abroad.

For his part Ong Thong Hoeung, a member of the leftist Khmer Students Union and who would remain in France for another six years, also aligned himself with FUNK despite his antipathy for Sihanouk. He was swayed, he said, by FUNK's pledge to reunite the country and by its opposition to Lon Nol's regime.

Hoeung explained that all of the Cambodian students in France sought an equitable Cambodia; where they differed was how best to achieve it. Hoeung was not convinced by the arguments of his fellow leftists who espoused the Soviet model or by the reasoning of those who preferred Mao's approach. Instead he sought a third way by trying to combine elements of communism, humanism and science. Events later proved that his position was both idealistic and naive.

Yet the allure of being involved in creating an egalitarian society was understandable, and the intoxicating opportunity to fulfil that ambition – to be part of this great rebuilding – was what the silver-tongued Ieng Sary proffered these young Cambodians during his regular trips abroad in the early 1970s. As the travelling face of the Khmer Rouge, Ieng Sary, who was Pol Pot's brother-in-law and who would become foreign minister, had great influence among the students, and Hoeung recalled watching him speak in Paris on several occasions as the civil war raged across Cambodia.

Hoeung particularly recalled a visit by Ieng Sary after victory in 1975 when the Khmer Rouge foreign minister had appealed to the students and intellectuals to return to a reunited, peaceful and self-sufficient Cambodia. Those who had already done so, Ieng Sary assured them with honeyed words, were thriving in the struggle. It made them anxious to get back and over time hundreds applied to *Angkar* for permission. Hoeung estimated that over the next few years 1,700 Cambodian students and intellectuals – Ket among them – went home.

'[The intellectuals] were not looking to take advantage of the poor in order to become rich,' he said in reference to the exploitative behaviour that has for decades typified government officials in Cambodia. 'In fact they sold all their worldly possessions to come back and build a new Cambodia. Going home was exciting for those reasons.'

It surely was, yet for most it would prove fatal. By Hoeung's count just 200 would survive.

The Khmer people have suffered for more than 2,000 years under the yoke of oppression;

When the people rise up, the army cuts them down.

This is because of the damned spies that weasel their way into our midst to provoke us and harm us,

And so the people have firmly and resolutely decided to smash all spies.

CHORUS

Damned spies, you are the servants of the enemies;

We are determined not to let you deter us from our cause,

And we adopt a firm position to destroy you so completely that nothing, not even your bones, will remain.

— Song that Pol Pot ordered to be sung by children in areas controlled by the Khmer Rouge, 1970

From unpublished interview of Duch by Christophe Peschoux, 1999

CHAPTER FIVE

PEASANT HEROES, URBAN ENEMIES

IF THE SEEDS OF CAMBODIA'S DESTRUCTION were sown in part by regional conflict, economic problems and domestic political repression, its bleak fruition grew out of the Khmer Rouge's catastrophic social, economic and security policies. Some of that could be traced back to that 1960 meeting in Phnom Penh when the movement's leaders sought to solve a problem of pressing practical importance: how to inculcate socialist ideals in the minds of an uneducated peasant class and inspire them to rise up?

Had Karl Marx been alive, he would probably have suggested that they wait. Traditional Marxist theory, which was designed to undo the injustices of Europe's Industrial Revolution, holds that once the factory workers – the industrial proletariat – are organised and educated in Marxism, they will rise up and take over ownership of the means of production, overthrowing the exploitative capitalist class and benefiting from the fruits of their labour in a new society. Marx saw capitalism as a key stage between the backwardness of the European peasantry and the utopia of socialism – a necessary evil that contained the seeds of its own destruction and that had the potential to drag the peasant class into the ranks of the proletariat. Most importantly, the revolution, he insisted, would spring forth from the proletariat, not from the peasants. Marx's concerns about the peasant class, of whom he held a dim view, lay largely in whether they were natural allies on the road to socialism (he suspected many were not) or would emerge as counter-revolutionaries.

The challenge for quasi-Marxists in Cambodia and China was that there had been no Industrial Revolution, and hardly any of their citizens were factory workers. Cambodia had few factories and just a few thousand people employed in them; most of the rest of her six million people worked the land. Both communist parties needed to work out how to undertake a Marxist revolution without an industrial proletariat. With their profound cultural differences it is hardly surprising that Cambodia and China chose different routes.

China is a nation steeped in literacy and Confucian logic, and during two decades of civil war Mao's strategy involved telling the peasants that once the revolution had succeeded they would get their own land. It also meant showing them that the communists were more disciplined than their nationalist enemy. Mao knew the communists would fail if they pretended that they could emulate what Marx had said would hold true for European nations. Instead, said Mao, the approach must be tested and modified where necessary. Success meant being aware of the realities on the ground.

But if this sort of 'scientific' approach to communism in action made sense to Mao, it was of limited value to Pol Pot. The roots of the Khmer Empire of a thousand years ago were in India, not China. As a consequence Cambodia's Indian-influenced culture values the spiritual over the rational, and hierarchy above everything. Pol Pot insisted that Cambodia's approach to communism should follow its own path along lines that were Khmer and intuitive, requiring little input from traditional Marxism or its principles. Their approach to communism, Short wrote, was 'unschooled, almost mystical'.[1] This cultural difference was a key factor in the different approach. Khmer chauvinism played a part too, particularly the belief that, since the Cambodian people had constructed Angkor Wat, they could achieve any task they put their minds to.[2]

With no experience of a working-class existence, the leaders resolved the problem of Cambodia's missing proletariat by simply overlaying Marx's divisions onto the peasant class. In that way the poorest and the second-poorest ranks of peasants were deemed the revolutionary base, the so-called worker-peasants.

At their 1960 meeting in Phnom Penh the leaders decided that the key purpose of their struggle was a 'national people's democratic revolution'.[3]

---

1. *Pol Pot: History of a Nightmare*, Philip Short (John Murray, 2004), p. 148.

2. As Pol Pot put it in a speech in September 1977: 'If our people were capable of building Angkor [Wat], they can do anything.'

3. 'Communist Party of Kampuchea Policies on Class and on Dealing with Enemies Among the People and Within the Revolutionary Ranks, 1960–1979: Centre, Districts and Grassroots.' Paper written by Steve Heder, School of Oriental and African Studies (April 26, 2012).

With that in mind the Party divided society into five classes; the two most significant were the peasants and the 'feudal gentry', or landowners, who were a tiny minority. These two groups were felt to be in natural opposition to one another. The 'democratic' aspect of the revolution would see the peasants, who constituted the majority, rise up against the landowning class.

In a three-hour speech given in 1977, Pol Pot said the CPK leaders at the 1960 meeting, of whom he was one, had deemed that once the peasants threw their weight behind the revolution, the rest of society would naturally follow. Victory would inevitably ensue because their combined numbers would constitute more than 95 per cent of the population.

On the vexed question of who could take part, the CPK cast the net wide: anyone from the five classes, including the rich and titled, could help provided they had the right outlook or 'patriotic spirit', a quality that cut across class lines. Amid this talk of class, the subtext was who could and could not be trusted. As he recalled those early days, Pol Pot outlined ways to deal with those recalcitrants, those few per cent deemed unable or unwilling to accept the wisdom of the CPK's approach.

'First, win over any enemy who could be won over on some occasions,' Pol Pot said in 1977. 'Second, whenever possible, neutralise some of them in order to make them incapable of conducting any activities to attack us; third, isolate the contemptibly vicious ones in order to attack them.'

The revolution's second purpose was to rid the nation of the influence of 'imperialism', a term the Khmer Rouge's leaders defined as any external influence that subjected Cambodia to a semi-colonial position. 'Imperialists' were the one group that would always remain beyond the pale. In 2012, for instance, the Khmer Rouge's former chief ideologue Nuon Chea explained that 'lackeys of aggressive imperialism' were 'ultra-vicious in ill-treating the people and traitors to the nation'.[4] From early on this group could not be forgiven.

Yet the door was open to the rest, as Short noted, since what the CPK deemed important was not class but consciousness, and that was a concept that fitted neatly into Cambodia's dominant Theravada strand of Buddhism. It was not Marxism by any stretch, but it matched Cambodia's social and cultural belief system.

'The idea that "proletarian consciousness" could be forged, independent

---

4. Nuon Chea, speaking at the Extraordinary Chambers in the Courts of Cambodia (ECCC), January 31, 2012, as cited by Heder, ibid., p. 4.

of a person's class origins or economic status, became the central pillar of Khmer communism,' Short wrote.[5]

In those early days the CPK sought to bring on board as many people as possible. As the movement took control of larger areas, land confiscated from the 'feudal gentry' was given to landless peasants. By 1973 the Party had begun to institute harsh social policies in the areas it controlled. These included setting up farming collectives, forcibly moving people from one area to another, banning Buddhism and compelling everyone to wear black. Thousands fled to Vietnam. Many more either did not or could not.[6]

As the Khmer Rouge grew increasingly confident in the inevitability of their victory, the CPK began to move ruthlessly against its enemies. Over the coming years those enemies – some real, many imagined – would constitute an ever-growing category and would eventually consume some of the revolution's most ardent supporters.

IN LATE 2001 the *Cambodia Daily*, an English-language newspaper in Phnom Penh, received a phone call from a village chief in the south-eastern province of Svay Rieng. A man digging an irrigation ditch had found a rusted ammunition box full of documents, hundreds of pages of written and typed notes in cheap exercise books or jotted on scraps of torn paper, wrapped in plastic and secured with a banana leaf. Was the paper interested in seeing them? It was, and sent two journalists – American Brian Calvert and his Cambodian counterpart Kay Kimsong – down Route 1, the same road along which Sady and Chhor and countless thousands had travelled a quarter of a century earlier. Most foreign reporters in Cambodia did not speak much Khmer, so it was common practice at the *Cambodia Daily* and its rival, the *Phnom Penh Post*, where I worked, to team their expatriate journalists with their local colleagues. The expertise each brought to the table made for stronger stories.

A decade later Calvert was back in Cambodia after working abroad, and we met regularly on weekends at his flat overlooking Phnom Penh's red-roofed National Museum where, over coffee and doughnuts, we would discuss, structure and dissect the books we planned to write. On one of those days I asked him which piece from his time at the *Cambodia Daily* stood out for him ten years on. That was easy, he told me. That was how I

---

5. Short, op. cit., p. 150.

6. Chandler, *Brother Number One*, op. cit., p. 96.

heard about 'The Ghosts of Svay Rieng'.[7]

The cache of documents was dug up in a district called Romduol. If you lay down a ruler on a map between Phnom Penh and Ho Chi Minh City some 240 kilometres south-east, Romduol district lies at the centre of that line inside an area of Cambodia, known as the Parrot's Beak, that juts into Vietnam. This is flat terrain, part of the floodplain that drains into the South China Sea. In the early 1970s it was a war zone, where the US and their South Vietnamese allies fought the Viet Cong, and where the Khmer Rouge battled Lon Nol's forces, a place of B-52s, napalm, attack helicopters and death. Many of the ponds in Romduol today are bomb craters.

The scrappy collection of documents that the two journalists leafed through had once belonged to a Khmer Rouge security chief who lived in Romduol in the early 1970s. This rough mini-archive was still in journalist Kay Kimsong's hands and in 2011 I went to his office at the *Phnom Penh Post*, where he had moved, to examine it. There were minutes of meetings, reports from cadres to their superiors, instructions on how to treat people, biographies, lists of personal property, security orders, execution registers, lists of prisoners, assessments of village residents by age group ('young, mid-dle-aged, old, very old') and notes from confession sessions.

None of this was compiled randomly. Take the self-criticism documents, for example: the Khmer Rouge were obsessive about getting people to admit during group discussions to their unrevolutionary thoughts and failings. There was a cultural precedent – Buddhist monks do much the same – but this was insidious. Anyone laying out their innermost thoughts walked a dangerous tightrope: confess too much and you might be seen as an enemy and be executed; confess too little and you could end up accused of lying to *Angkar*, which would also prove fatal.

The documents covered the period after Lon Nol's coup and Sihanouk's call for people to side with him and the Khmer Rouge. Sihanouk's stance forced many to take sides and as the Khmer Rouge took control of parts of Svay Rieng province, for instance, their spies noted who spoke up for Lon Nol. Such people were 'lackeys of imperialism' and, as Nuon Chea pointed out decades later, imperialists were one category that could not be spared. They would be taken care of in due course.

Meantime it was important for the Khmer Rouge to know who owned

---

7. 'The Ghosts of Svay Rieng: Unearthed Documents Paint Picture of an Eastern Province Betrayed by Communism', Kay Kimsong and Brian Calvert, *The Cambodia Daily Weekend* magazine, February 9-10, 2002, pp. 6–14.

what. A document dated October 1973 is a property register of a place called Village Seven, with wealth marked in columns of buffaloes, cows, bicycles and rice fields. The Khmer Rouge eventually outlawed private property, so lists like this had an obvious utility, but they were also useful in determining what class peasants fell into, with the poorest regarded as the most trustworthy and the richest viewed with suspicion.

Other documents outlined the communists' unrelenting position on so-called crimes. One noted that villagers had been caught listening to the radio, presumably the broadcasts from Phnom Penh, a banned activity.

'Those whom we catch we educate two or three times, but if they still listen then we kill them,' it stated bluntly.

Another document written in 1973 contained the names of families that had run away, probably to Vietnam or Phnom Penh. A missive from the previous year named 10 people who had been arrested for protesting, and another for walking 'with no letter of permission'. Yet another told how cadres had interrogated villagers and beaten them for such infractions as 'drinking and walking around and cursing'. The revolutionaries' grumblings show the Khmer Rouge did not have everything their own way in Romduol.

'They do not respect the rules, and they do things freely such as visiting their friend's house without permission,' one cadre complained. 'They make decisions on their own … and are full of self-pride and they mock us.'

The documents were dug up at the former home of a man called Nam Saren. He had been a monk but in 1970, at the age of 18, he responded to Sihanouk's call to take up arms against Lon Nol. He was obviously soon trusted as a revolutionary: when the Khmer Rouge issued guns to 13 new cadres in Romduol district later that year, Nam Saren was one of those handed a weapon. He gave himself the *nom de guerre* Rithy (meaning 'Power'). Politics and revolution were new to him but the teenager took to his calling with religious devotion.

'After I joined the revolution there was no other job [for me],' he wrote in his autobiography, which was among the papers in the ammunition box.[8] 'I only worked and served the people and the revolution, which was against [those] who suck the blood and the bones of the poor people every day.'

Such fervour found reward. Within three years the Khmer Rouge had appointed Nam Saren district security chief. By then he had revised his reasons for joining the revolution.

'I found that the revolutionary struggle today was not about serving

---

8. Ibid., p. 6.

King Sihanouk,' he wrote. 'The revolution serves the lower classes and those at the base level like farmers and workers.'[9]

Whether through propaganda sessions, personal experience or more likely a combination of the two, Nam Saren's biography reveals an angry revolutionary. His bile for the rich – a relative term in a place like Svay Rieng – was obvious, as were his sociopathic tendencies.

'I say the worthless rich people and the worthless capitalists do nothing for the country. In one instance some of the worthless rich people drove a motorcycle past me and almost hit me. Then I said: "Hey! You are looking down on me!" Then I shot them five times because I was angry,' he wrote.[10]

Nam Saren explained this away on the grounds that he wanted to be rich and handsome and to eat good food, all aspects of life that in his view were reserved for the wealthy. To bolster his revolutionary credentials further, Nam Saren confessed some more unrevolutionary thoughts: he had killed and eaten a calf without permission, he had stolen mangoes and coconuts, he had dumped medicines, beaten prisoners unconscious, and neglected his comrades in their hour of need.

'When our co-workers were sick I just went and asked them how things were, and if they were going to die then to let me keep their shoes and other possessions,' he admitted, before stressing that these impurities were of him as an immature revolutionary. Now he was fully infused with the spirit of *Angkar*. 'I understand that only the proletariat and the utmost struggle can drive the welfare of the revolution.'[11]

It was men and women like Nam Saren who formed the vanguard of the Khmer Rouge's struggle and who enforced the policies handed down from on high. The new converts talked about the need 'to release all idealism, materialism and capitalism' and repudiated the old ways in which those who had power and wealth 'looked down' on those without. They were told that success required them to harden their hearts to stone, a notion deliberately counter to Buddhism: 'If our hearts are nourished neither by feelings nor compassion, then we can hold an unyielding position in our struggle.'[12]

---

9. Ibid.

10. Ibid.

11. Ibid., p. 8.

12. *Pol Pot's Little Red Book, The Sayings of Angkar*, Henri Locard (Silkworm Books, 2nd edition 2004), p. 151.

BY 1972 THE MOVEMENT'S SUCCESS could be depicted on a map by drawing a line from north-west Cambodia to the south-east dividing it roughly in two. Everything to the right of that line was under Khmer Rouge control, most (but not all) on the left was still in the hands of Lon Nol's Khmer Republic.

By then the Khmer Rouge had started setting up agricultural collectives and distributing land in areas under its control as part of the drive to eliminate markets, and with that to crush the property-owning classes. Not everyone was in favour of this move to socialist bliss, but that stance simply painted them as enemies belonging to the imperialist class.

'[Such enemies] were smashed ... one after the other,' the official CPK history noted with evident pride. Such diligence in smashing – *komtech* in Khmer, with the meaning 'to reduce to dust' – would see the revolution drive out 'the American imperialist aggressors and their lackeys and attack and smash the traitors to liberate the nation and class.'[13]

Yet the CPK's unyielding stance against its enemies did not stop it from telling cadres to treat errant villagers with some sort of understanding: to use politics and ideology to convince them of the error of their ways, rather than violence or intimidation. It was a schizophrenic approach that was a sign of what was to come: separating the merely misguided from those who were more profoundly flawed.

By 1973 the Khmer Rouge were speaking out against Sihanouk. They told local residents that Sihanouk's regime had worked against the interests of the poor and that the new society would put their concerns first. This new society was taking shape around them, with communal eating and collectives in place.

In Romduol the Khmer Rouge banned villagers from trading with areas under Lon Nol's control. As Nam Saren's spies spread out, reporting back on 'feelings, politics, culture and criticism', he wrote approvingly that the district's residents were now firmly against the Lon Nol regime and against Sihanouk too. Nam Saren's underlings, however, were dismayed at the lack of revolutionary vigour among some villagers.

'Some of them feel they want to follow [the Party's instructions], and some do not. Some believe the work should be carried out by their friends,

---

13. Others see an even greater nihilism in the word. Film director Rithy Panh wrote that *komtech* means 'to erase all trace' of someone, even of their death. 'Let nothing remain, no trace of life, no trace of death. Let the death itself be erased.' Panh, *The Elimination* (Other Press, 2013), p. 103.

and some are concerned about the poor,' one junior cadre, Comrade Korn, reported in August 1973.[14] 'Some are worried about the shortage of food. The reason [for these fears] is that they do not understand about their duty to the Party.'

There were other issues that worried the enthusiastic and disapproving Comrade Korn: villagers showed a lack of diligence in following the rules; farmers were speaking to the revolutionary cadres at a meeting 'as though they are giving the orders'; people grumbled about a lack of equipment; some villagers dressed like foreigners ('for example, men wearing tank tops and women wearing shirts that fit tightly to the body like a Vietnamese girl').[15]

On the plus side Comrade Korn was pleased to report that morality had shown some improvement, with those in the collective system dressing alike, eating communally and 'following *Angkar*'. The ongoing propaganda lessons seemed to be paying off too and a meeting earlier that month had educated villagers about class division and farming topics. This balancing of successes and problems was important for Comrade Korn. After all, too much of one or the other could lead to doubts about his revolutionary credentials.

By April 1974, exactly a year before Phnom Penh fell, his boss Nam Saren was exultant.

'Things have changed in the world. No other country could have forced the king and the monks and everyone to take part in the revolution,' he wrote.[16] 'The revolution struggled, and now we control 85 per cent of the territory and 95 per cent of the population.'

Nam Saren's figures were somewhat optimistic but his broader point was accurate enough. The Khmer Rouge were going to win. Some time after penning those gleeful thoughts, Nam Saren wrapped his notes in plastic, placed them in the ammunition box and buried them in his garden. The most likely reason is that Nam Saren had by then fallen under suspicion. The revolution had long been consuming its own and it is probable that Nam Saren was taken away and executed, his rage and revolutionary fervour turned to dust in Svay Rieng's rich earth.

In 2002 none of the villagers interviewed by the *Cambodia Daily* could recall Nam Saren's fate, but they did know that all of the early revolutionaries

---

14. 'Ghosts' op. cit., p. 10.

15. Ibid.

16. Ibid.

of Romduol district were removed from their posts after 1976. Throughout the 1970s men like Nam Saren had had extensive contacts with the Viet Cong, their supposed communist brethren, meeting to discuss prisoner exchanges, issues of taxation and improved communications. Romduol was, after all, on the border with Vietnam.

But unbeknown to the lower ranks, *Angkar* had already decided that Vietnam was an enemy that wanted to dominate Cambodia's revolution as Hanoi had done in neighbouring Laos, and put in place plans to purge cadres with such links. To be accused of having 'a Khmer body and a Vietnamese mind' by the mid-1970s was a contamination that guaranteed execution, and Nam Saren almost certainly fell victim to his own revolution. Perhaps it did not come entirely as a surprise: by then other cadres would have been taken away and killed for those very reasons, and Nam Saren's position meant he likely took some part in those murders.

Besides, as an ardent acolyte Nam Saren would have known Mao's oft-quoted phrase that revolution was not 'a dinner party ... but an act of violence by which one class overthrows another'.[17] The Khmer Rouge drummed their version of that into the minds of their cadres, as historian Henri Locard noted:

'Revolution's victory over imperialism is not about inviting guests to a dinner party,
Not about writing a text, not about embroidering flowers,
Not about having the right education, not about being soft,
Not about turning a blind eye and being indifferent,
Not about being well-mannered and polite,
Not about fearing the enemy;
The revolution is about seething with anger against one class,
About striking and destroying that class!'[18]

In that attitude lay the Khmer Rouge's logic towards their enemies, an inflexibility that Nam Saren had used to great effect in Svay Rieng. At some point in 1974 or 1975, Nam Saren realised he had crossed an invisible line, no doubt unwittingly, and had become the enemy. It was then that he dug a hole in the garden, wrapped his notes in plastic and buried them.

---

17. 'State Violence in Democratic Kampuchea (1975–1979) and Retribution (1979–2004)'. Henri Locard in *European Review of History*, Vol 12, No 1, March 2005, p. 122.

18. Locard, *Pol Pot's Little Red Book*, op. cit., pp. 155–156.

SALOTH SAR TOOK THE NAME 'POL POT'; Nam Saren took the name 'Rithy'; Comrade Korn's original name is lost to history. It was standard practice for cadres to operate under revolutionary names – the more names, the better, Pol Pot said, because it confused the enemy and that was half the battle. It also meant that those who were arrested would be unable to reveal the true names of their comrades even under torture, and it fitted the movement's obsession with secrecy.

The man in whom *Angkar* put its trust when dealing with its enemies was known as Comrade Duch. He proved an excellent choice. Duch's real name was Kaing Guek Eav, and he took his revolutionary name from two sources: Duch was a sculptor whom his grandfather had admired; he was also a character in a book that Kaing Guek Eav had liked when still a boy in primary school. In that book this fictional alter ego stood straight and read his words accurately and with a clear voice. That resonated with the person who, in Duch's own words years later, sought to be 'a well-disciplined boy who respected the teachers, who wanted to do good deeds'.

Duch joined the CPK in December 1967, an idealistic 25-year-old mathematics teacher who was greatly admired by his pupils for his simple lifestyle and welcoming approach. Two years before that he had graduated from a teaching institute that was a known hotbed of leftwing activism. Its head was a man called Son Sen, who had been in Paris with Pol Pot and who later became the Khmer Rouge's head of defence with overall responsibility for security centres like S-21.

In 1965 Duch had been sent to teach at a school in the small highway town of Skoun, north-east of Phnom Penh. Teaching was a highly respected profession, yet Duch cut an odd figure: he was a chain-smoker who dressed sloppily and rode a bicycle to class each day. In those days one would expect a person from a humble background to disguise his origins by dressing as best he could. Instead Duch seemed to celebrate his impoverished past. Convinced that this corrupt society needed to change and that the CPK was the route, Duch avidly read Mao, Marx and Engels, lectured his students on Maoism and screened Chinese propaganda films after classes.

Despite his enthusiasm, his start with the Party was hardly propitious. After the 1967 Samlaut Rebellion, Duch sent some of his most committed students to the nearest large town, Kampong Cham, to distribute leaflets calling on people to overthrow Sihanouk's 'fascist regime'. The students were arrested and Duch fled to a nearby Khmer Rouge base where he formally joined the CPK.[19] Weeks later he was arrested by Sihanouk's police and sentenced to 20 years' hard labour on charges of collaborating with foreign powers and attempting to break up the nation.

He served two years, and was one of hundreds of prisoners released by Lon Nol's new government after the March 1970 coup in what looked to be an attempt to curry favour with the left. Duch quickly joined the Khmer Rouge in the *maquis* where his intelligence, his dedication to the cause and his capacity to undertake any task meticulously marked him out to some of the senior leaders. For a time he was a political instructor at a Khmer Rouge military base, but by July 1971 his zeal and commitment saw him placed in charge of a prison called M-13 situated in a remote forested area 45 miles west of Phnom Penh. It was there that his transformation began.

M-13 was the collective name for two camps: M-13A, which Duch ran, and M-13B, which fell under his remit. M-13B seems to have been a transit camp, a holding pen for untrustworthy types being transferred by the Khmer Rouge between areas that the movement controlled. M-13A, on the other hand, was by any measure the precursor to S-21. Its main role, Duch said later, was to 'beat and interrogate and smash' the Party's enemies, tasks he was proud to carry out to 'protect the liberated zones, the people'.[20] Duch knew full well how important his job was to the success of the revolution in the eyes of the leaders.

At first those enemies were so-called spies who had crossed into the Khmer Rouge-liberated zone from government-held areas. Some were Lon Nol soldiers captured in clashes, others were genuine spies, but most of them were probably peasants simply going about their business as the civil war, where prisoners were routinely killed on both sides, swirled around them.

When Duch was appointed to run M-13A he was not yet versed in torture and interrogation, but he quickly developed those skills, honed them and imparted them to others. Most of those he selected to work for him were local teenage males aged 15–18, a group that he knew were malleable, gullible and eager to please.

One of its few survivors recalled that M-13A had a constant and

---

19. It was Vorn Vet, a senior member of the Party, who brought Duch into the CPK. Vorn Vet became Duch's boss when Duch ran the first of his prison camps – M-13A. In late 1978, Vorn Vet was imprisoned and killed at S-21 after falling under suspicion.

20. Duch in testimony to the ECCC (trial transcript, English, April 6, 2009, p. 66).

'terrifying atmosphere of fear and death'.[21] Prisoners were held in roofless two-metre deep pits in the ground, their legs shackled to a long iron bar. By 1974 food was in such short supply that detainees were fed only rice dust, kept alive solely to be interrogated. Those who survived torture, disease and starvation were executed. Just 10 were released during its four-year existence.

While M-13A and other execution centres continued their grim work, the leaders continued to refine their definition of precisely who constituted the revolution's enemies. By 1974 the CPK had decided that two factors should be taken into account: the first was the subject's economic criteria, which measured how poor they were; the second was their political attitude. Under the new system the poorest peasants were still regarded as the most trustworthy, but the fact they had laboured under a feudal system since time immemorial meant they might be 'slow of political understanding'. In this way the Khmer Rouge echoed Marx's unflattering opinion of peasants, likely after noticing – as Comrade Rithy and Comrade Korn had reported – that some in the areas they controlled were resistant to the revolution. For the CPK such people were not to be trusted: they required education and refashioning, and cadres were reminded to keep a watchful eye on them.

It was around this time, as the CPK prepared for victory, that it added another refinement that was to have profound significance, adding four 'special class' types that did not naturally fit within the five classes laid out years earlier. The four special classes were: Buddhist monks; soldiers and police in the Lon Nol regime; intellectuals; and members of minority tribal groups. Each group was seen as unreliable to differing degrees, but there was recognition that some could be educated in the ways of the revolution. Unsaid but understood was that each could constitute a centre of resistance to the Khmer Rouge.

It was all somewhat vague and subjective. After all one could surely be a Buddhist and an intellectual, or a member of the Lon Nol regime and a member of a minority group. As Nuon Chea had put it, those who were deemed enemies became that way through their conduct, not by virtue of their class origin. Yet at his trial in 2012 even Nuon Chea conceded this was a 'very complicated' subject and was unable to explain how it worked in practice. If the Khmer Rouge's chief ideologue could not make it clear then there was little chance that the indoctrinated and largely uneducated revolutionary youth gave it much thought when standing on the cusp of victory.

---

21. François Bizot, testimony to the ECCC (trial transcript, English, April 9, 2009, p. 46).

Then again, they were not meant to. The message hammered into them for years was that they were surrounded by enemies, and these were to be smashed without exception. In a clear echo of Mao's approach, the CPK's position was that it was better to smash 100 innocents than to let one guilty person go free.[22] The cadres absorbed the dehumanisation of the Party's enemies in terms that recalled Stalin's words about his foes: that they were criminals, traitors and insects working for foreign powers. Such people had to be purged 'one after another', even if they were found inside the Khmer Rouge's army or inside the Party machinery. Cadres were exhorted to be on the alert for enemies at all times.

Even as the Khmer Rouge prepared to take Phnom Penh in 1975, their forces were warned that enemies were disguised as civilians, traders and monks. *Revolutionary Flag* magazine made that much clear in an article titled 'Our People are Determined to Attack, Smash and Completely Eliminate the Enemy's Pacification Tricks and Activities during this Rainy Season'. The magazine, which was usually written by Pol Pot and Nuon Chea, ordered cadres to find enemies and smash them as a matter of urgency. The CPK's shrill approach in a climate of fear, suspicion and terror that it had whipped up over the years meant its followers were unlikely to give anyone the benefit of the doubt. After all, should *Angkar* later determine that cadres had allowed an enemy to escape, they would themselves be executed.

Victory brought no respite, with the CPK exhorting its followers to use 'absolute measures to attack and smash every last one', to stay alert for 'horrible elements' and 'no-good elements', to root out 'traitorous links', and to 'heighten the spirit of revolutionary vigilance'.

The forced evacuation of urban areas meant, among other things, that the CIA, KGB and Vietnamese spy groups that the CPK believed existed were dispersed and disorganised, but their members were still alive. In response, the cadres were ordered to find them and destroy them. The Party would continue to ensure that the people joined it 'most enthusiastically in making a revolution to smash the enemy'. At the same time the revolutionaries were told not to abuse their authority and kill people who simply made mistakes. 'Don't attack the forest,' they were warned. 'Attack the tiger.'

Years of double-speak, the unending talk of enemies and smashing, the seething paranoia, the exhortations to trust no one, and the 'constant

---

22. Or as Locard (in *Pol Pot's Little Red Book,* op. cit.) quotes the Khmer Rouge phrase current at that time: 'Better to kill an innocent by mistake than spare an enemy by mistake.'

heightening of revolutionary vigilance' in pursuit of the revolution must have been confusing and exhausting. The division of the nation into those who could be trusted and those who could not, and the blur between the two, ultimately meant that everyone was a potential enemy with the power to denounce and to be denounced. By 1975 the enslaved inhabitants had learned to trust no one and to say nothing as they worked and died in the labour camps. The phrase people used was *dam doeum kor*, which means 'to plant a kapok tree', the towering tropical tree that looms above some of Cambodia's most famous temples. Colloquially the phrase meant 'to say nothing', a pun on the double meaning of *kor* as both 'kapok' and 'silent'.

It was in those rural areas – the gulags, as Locard has called them – that the CPK now focused its efforts in striving for a socialist paradise. The sacred task of the revolution was to grow rice and everything was turned to that end. In Prey Veng, Sady and her family were put to work sowing rice, building dams and digging irrigation channels. On the other side of the country in Region 5, Ket's family were forced to do much the same. In pre-revolutionary Cambodia there had been little notion of class beyond that of the rich (the *neak mean* or 'people who have') and the poor. By the end of 1975 the class system had dissolved. Instead of five classes and four special classes, most people fell into one: the worker-peasant.

EVACUATING URBAN AREAS had eliminated the two classes regarded as exploitative: as the CPK's youth publication put it, the feudal class and the bourgeoisie were 'destroyed, reduced to naught and disintegrated as classes along with the political regime and economic foundations'. Also gone were the civil servants and small businesspeople who had comprised the petty bourgeoisie. Comrade Rithy would have approved. What was left from the original five classes were workers and peasants; along with the survivors of the other classes, these constituted the new worker-peasant class. The following year, in a publication titled *Hone Proletarian Ideology to Make it Most Sharp and Strong*, the Party leaders gloated that emptying the cities and towns had been a supremely successful act of class struggle.

The CPK had also dealt with at least three of the four special classes: Buddhist monks were forced to disrobe or were often shot for refusing to do so; Lon Nol officials were executed wherever they were unmasked while the rest tried to blend in, as Sady's father and uncles did; and the minority groups were now deemed part of the worker-peasant class. As 1975 drew to a close, the CPK trumpeted that 99 per cent of people were now worker peasants, all enjoyed equality and worked the land together, and Cambodia was fully democratic. The 'first steps of socialist revolution and the construction of socialism' were underway.

The rural peasants – the trusted 'base people' – were instructed to share what they had with the newcomers on the grounds that 95 per cent of the evacuees were 'good elements', but Pol Pot would later remind the nation that the remaining 5 per cent were saboteurs and spies determined to destroy the revolution. Cadres were ordered to uncover and smash the networks acting on behalf of foreign powers. As Sady remembered from her experience in Prey Veng, this was a cruel and terrifying time as the cadres sought any excuse to brand new people like her as enemies.

'If you did something wrong, they would call you and kill you,' she said.

Most enemies were dealt with locally, taken by cadres to the local security office before being executed. Others were simply shot or beaten to death. But the most important were taken to the capital. Shortly after Phnom Penh fell, *Angkar* ordered Duch to close M-13A and appointed him deputy head of a secret prison code-named S-21 that was based in the capital. His work at M-13A in ferreting out spies, traitors and enemies – or what passed for them – had pleased the leadership. In Duch they saw a man whom they could trust to continue the vital task of safeguarding the revolution.

For [the revolutionary], morality is everything which contributes to the triumph of the revolution. Immoral and criminal is everything that stands in his way.

— Sergei Nechaev (1847–1882), Russian revolutionary, *The Revolutionary Catechism*

The Party must protect the revolution as much as possible from any action conducted by enemy strategies in a direct way, as well as in an indirect way; in an open, as well as in a secret way … All Angkar *Party organisations and every Party member must always be good and clean and be pure politically, ideologically and organisationally by building on a permanent basis through their biography, by building a clear, clean and pure personal history consecutively and constantly.*

— From the statutes of the Communist Party of Kampuchea

The statutes were an internal Party document that every cadre was required to study, discuss and apply. Non-members of the CPK were not allowed to read it.

Report everything to the Angkar*!*

— Khmer Rouge slogan to ensure that the population spied on one other

CHAPTER SIX

NO MAN, NO PROBLEM

THE MEKONG SLIPS PAST PHNOM PENH in a slow swirl of rich sediment as it makes its way to its delta in southern Vietnam where it empties into the South China Sea. For most of the year this low-rise city and the largely flat terrain that surrounds it swelter under a humid shroud, but the advent of the dry season from November to February sees the temperature drop to 25 degrees Celsius, and tourists flow in to the north-west to marvel at the former capital of Angkor and its elegant Hindu and Buddhist temples built between the ninth and thirteenth centuries CE. Those years marked the apex of the Khmer Empire, a time of greatness to which Cambodia is still in thrall.

Eventually, as all must, the Khmer Empire crumbled, and the capital ended up here at the confluence of three rivers: the Mekong as it turns south-east on its ponderous run to the sea from its source in the Tibetan Plateau 4,000 kilometres away; the Bassac flowing south; and the Tonle Sap River, which connects the Mekong at Phnom Penh with the lake in the centre of the country. The Great Lake, or Tonle Sap, is the nation's beating heart and it undergoes two great pulses annually. Once a year, beginning in June, the volume of water in the monsoon-swollen Mekong overwhelms the Tonle Sap River and forces it to reverse course; now, instead of emptying its namesake lake, the Tonle Sap River is driven in the opposite direction in a months-long surge of water and silt. The Great Lake soon trebles in size and tracts of central Cambodia flood, bringing the gift of water to rice farmers and a bounty of fish, the most important protein source in this impoverished land, to all. By November the rains have ceased and, as the Mekong's water level drops, the great lake once more begins to drain. The flooded flatlands, now rich with the fierce green of countless rice fields, reappear, and the Tonle Sap River's south-easterly flow resumes past the capital.

Phnom Penh is far more developed than the rest of the country, her tarred streets increasingly dominated by the luxury vehicles of the elite. Most of the old riverside strip runs along the west bank of the Tonle Sap River with a promenade on one side of the road, and bars, shops and apartments on the other. During the day this road is busy with SUVs, motorbikes, trucks and the occasional *cyclo*, the bucket-seat bicycle-taxis that are being forced slowly into extinction. The promenade is largely empty, the people driven indoors by the heat, but as the sun sets, the air cools, the breeze picks up off the river and the area comes alive: small groups of people of all ages gyrate in the cool of the evening to disco sounds pumped out by energetic entrepreneurs vending a daily exercise routine. Other citizens walk and talk or play games of mini-football or *doeurt sai*, which involves a circle of people using their heel to kick a shuttlecock over the shoulder and high into the air, over and over again.

The passing stream of people on motorbikes and in cars, seeing and being seen, takes it all in, and as night falls fast the food carts become beacons, their cool fluorescent bulbs illuminating offerings of noodles, neatly stacked fruits or trays of fried insects.

This is a country of early to bed and early to rise and by 9pm most Cambodians have headed home. Now the tone turns, and where earlier there were families, couples and old people, these streets are host to foreign tongues as tourists patronise the restaurants and pubs, and Western men from 18 to 80 enjoy the all-night girlie bars whose neon lights line the narrow roads jutting west.

Come sunrise and, as the tourists sleep off the night's excesses, the promenade fills again as the Phnompenhois head to work or sit and watch the river roll past. The shadows of the palm trees lie long and slim in the low rays of the sun. Silver flagpoles bearing the banners of the countries of the world punctuate the view as fishermen's wooden boats beat their way along the river, and the shops, restaurants and cafes open again.

It was on one such morning in February 2009 that I pushed open the glass door of a bistro that boasted wifi, air-conditioning and good coffee. I had returned to Cambodia weeks earlier, drawn back by the opportunity to report on a landmark trial: Comrade Duch had become the first Khmer Rouge defendant to face charges at an international war crimes court.

During my first stint eight years earlier I had worked as the managing editor of the *Phnom Penh Post*, a newspaper with tabloid-sized pages that published in English once a fortnight and which made up with youthful enthusiasm what it lacked in money. Our competition was the *Cambodia Daily*, which published six days a week: 12 issues to every one of ours. After two years at the *Post*, I was ready for a change and in August 2003 I left Cambodia, headed home to South Africa and then to the United Kingdom, where I spent most of the next five years. As the plane took off from Phnom Penh, I remember peering out of the window at the rice fields glittering with monsoon rains, a mirrored quilt of mustard, green and silver checks that slid beneath the clouds, and puzzled at how a largely homogenous country of 14 million people could remain so impenetrable. After two years working as a journalist I felt none the wiser about this small nation's wretched history and why it had undergone such profound damage. But I had no plans to return and did not expect to learn the answers. Besides, the incomprehension was widely shared: most Cambodians could not fathom what had befallen their country, so what chance did an outsider have?

It was the news that Duch's trial would get underway that lured me back in those first weeks of 2009.[1] Other than its historic significance, I was drawn too by the hope that covering it would resolve at least some of my unanswered questions, and might explain why Cambodians had suffered such atrocious hardships three decades earlier.

That February morning the bistro was nearly empty: a woman sat alone at a table. She was in her early thirties with striking features – piercing dark eyes, olive skin and lustrous black hair. Behind her was the bar and a hissing espresso machine, the air a mix of coffee and bacon overlaid with a cloying mist of lemon-scented mosquito spray with which the friendly staff slowly poisoned themselves and their loyal clients. Avant-garde photographs of semi-naked Western women hung on the walls, faced discreetly away from the road.

I walked towards the rear, sat down and ordered my meal. Soon a second woman, older and with fairer skin, joined the first. Before long the three of us fell into conversation. It was then, quite by accident, that I first heard the story of Ket as, over coffee, Martine and Neary told me their family's terrible history in soft, French-accented English. They too had come for Duch's trial. Like a tragic double-act, one filling in the gaps when the other broke off

---

1. Duch's trial was the first to be held by the United Nations-backed war crimes tribunal known as the Extraordinary Chambers in the Courts of Cambodia (ECCC).

from their too-familiar tale, they outlined the elements: how Martine and Ket had met in France, fallen in love, then married and moved to Senegal where their two children were born; how Ket had been recalled in 1977 and disappeared; and how years of quiet desperation had culminated in Martine's visit to Khao-I-Dang refugee camp in 1980 and later the family's visit to Duch's former prison in 1991.

Neary asked whether I knew about S-21. I did, I replied. I had visited it many times during my earlier stint in Cambodia.

'They tortured Ket for six months!' Martine said sharply, her eyes flashing with anger and tears. 'Can you imagine? Six months!'

It was not a question I was expected to answer, yet it was what had occupied their minds for decades: the degradation and terror, the pain, the beatings and the spectre of death attached to the encounters with the men who wielded whips, fists and clubs, who put volts through weakened bodies, who forced pins under fingernails and held heads under water, dull men whose empathy was frozen by ideology.

Neary, soft-spoken, had little trouble conjuring the pleasure that the torturers took when inflicting pain on their charges nor the grotesque misery of those imprisoned.

'How you must miss a toothbrush, cleaning yourself, a blanket, a pillow, a coffee, or even some water,' she said. 'How frightened you must be when you only hear teenagers' voices, hear the shouts of others and don't know when it is going to be your turn to suffer being beaten, electrocuted, cut or burned.'

For Auschwitz survivor Jean Améry, torture was 'the most horrible event a human being can retain within himself', a practice that cruelly emphasised the fragility of life, that erased one's trust in the world, terminated one's hope and left the survivor with a perpetual fear.[2]

My many visits to the Tuol Sleng Genocide Museum, as S-21 had been renamed, had afforded me the luxury of distance from its ghosts. These corridors of story-less, monochrome images shared the bleak commonality that they had all been brought here and were dead. Each time I returned I found myself moving through the rooms in a bubble, the repetition of rows of faces merging into an anonymous mass. I would stop to study one or two, trying to retain their features and their details, a metal number pinned

---

2. *At the Mind's Limits: Contemplations by a Survivor on Auschwitz and Its Realities*, Jean Améry (Indiana University Press, 2009), p. 22.

to rough clothing, then move on knowing it would take days to study them all. Sheer volume overwhelms our natural compassion.

It was different for Martine and Neary: every picture reminded them of Ket. More than 30 years after Ket's disappearance, Martine was fragile, her loss raw and unrelieved, the unbroken cares of decades past etched upon her skin. Neary was the one in control, her youth radiating the strength that this injustice had cost her mother. They had already passed the moment when the child overtakes the parent, and it was clear that, now at least, Neary was the rock.

They had learned of Duch's pending trial the previous summer when Neary was clearing out her work locker ahead of her annual leave. Between the bills and flyers was a months-old newspaper story that a colleague, aware of her Cambodian links, had clipped for her. The article was about a French lawyer representing victims of the Khmer Rouge in Duch's trial. (Under Cambodia's civil law system, derived from France, people affected by crimes are allowed to take part in proceedings as civil parties.) Neary knew Duch had been arrested years earlier, but she did not know a trial was looming. She posted the article to Martine and went on holiday. By the time she returned, Martine had visited the lawyer and signed up as a civil party. Neary did too.

And so, Neary concluded, that was why they were in this brasserie on the banks of the Tonle Sap River in early 2009. Yet, although she was pessimistic about the worth of the judicial process, Neary did hope it would unveil some truths, no matter how small, about her father. When you are trying to find out what happened to someone you love, she explained, the merest sliver is like gold. I asked Neary what was at the top of her list. Ket's file, she replied. She wanted to see Ket's handwriting, to read his words, and to try and know his mind during his incarceration. He had been held there for months so his file must have been a weighty document but it was no longer in the archives. At some unknown point after January 1979 it had gone missing, as had thousands of files of other prisoners.[3] Some had probably been taken to Hanoi, others were removed by the new Cambodian government, while the rest were taken home by workers at the archive or used in the market to wrap food – paper was in short supply – or simply burned as rubbish.

As far as Neary was concerned, Ket's file had been purposely targeted and probably destroyed. The element of deliberateness seemed unlikely to

---

3. Today, fewer than half as many confessions as there were prisoners remain in existence. Most of the photographs taken of the prisoners when they were brought to S-21 have disappeared too.

me but Neary was adamant: some of the men Ket had known during those distant years as a diplomat were now well-connected, and his confession might contain compromising details. No matter the truth behind the file's disappearance, Neary had not given up hope of finding it.

Our long, fraught conversation was punctuated on occasion by what I soon learned was Neary's trademark laugh: a rare, rich burst that would light the room. There and then Martine told me not to be fooled, that it was to shroud the pain.

'Ah, *Maman*!' Neary replied in mock exasperation with a wide smile.

We finished coffee, swapped contact details, and I offered to help where I could, although I had few illusions about what that would be worth. I feared Neary might never find Ket's file or some of the truths she sought – and that in a quest in which she had put so much store. The two were wound tight as clocks and emotion was seldom far from the surface. Neary later told me that Martine had cried every morning during their stay in Cambodia, an outpouring she had previously managed to contain. The poison of S-21, forgotten when asleep, flooded Martine's mind when she awoke, her life 'made a nightmare by the intrusion'.

Later still, Neary told me she had wept each evening. The abundance of barbarous facts emanating from Duch's trial made the world harder for her to comprehend, not easier, and so she retreated into the necessity of silence and remembered those who had died. For both women, Duch's merciless creation constituted an unbreakable cycle, a burden that could not be set aside or escaped. As Neary later explained, paraphrasing the late US forensic anthropologist Clyde Snow – who had exhumed mass graves of people murdered in Argentina and the former Yugoslavia – what was hardest to bear was not that someone you loved was dead; that could be reconciled, eventually. What counted was the manner of their death.

IN APRIL 1976 DUCH moved S-21's operations to the former Chao Ponhea Yat high school in Phnom Penh. For the previous year much of its work – which in the words of historian David Chandler was 'to protect the Party centre' – was carried out at a prison and former psychiatric hospital south of the capital. *Angkar* put significant stock in the work of institutions such as S-21, as Nuon Chea made clear to a visiting Danish delegation in July 1978.

'The leadership apparatus must be defended at any price. If we lose members but retain the leadership, we can continue to win victories,' he told them. 'There can be no comparison between losing two or three leading cadres and 200–300 members. Rather the latter than the former. Otherwise the Party has no head and cannot lead the struggle.'[4]

Nuon Chea was a man of his word. He had two of his nieces and their husbands arrested and sent to S-21, where they were tortured and executed. Pol Pot's sister-in-law was also executed at the prison. Such revolutionary fervour in disregarding the bonds of family was regarded as a virtue in Democratic Kampuchea.

For the first few months of S-21's itinerant existence, Duch was its deputy head. By April 1976 his superior had been promoted – he was later arrested and executed – and Duch took control. The buildings were now entirely Duch's domain and the brutal methods used were his design. They were cruelly familiar to a diminutive artist-turned-revolutionary called Bou Meng, who was brought here in August 1977, just two months after Ket.

Bou Meng was born in 1941 to a peasant family in the eastern province of Kampong Cham, and was one of seven children. In those days the only way for a poor boy like him to get an education was to study at the pagoda where monks taught rudimentary literacy and mathematics. That was where, at the age of five, he discovered that he had artistic flair.[5]

In 1946 Cambodia was still part of French Indochina, along with Laos and what was to become Vietnam, but the post-war independence drive saw nationalists from the Khmer Issarak movement fighting French troops to oust the colonial power. Compared with Vietnam's effort, Cambodia's was low-level but it was occasionally bloody. Bou Meng once saw the head of an Issarak fighter mounted on a stake at a crossroads, placed there by French troops as a warning to others.

In the end France's efforts were for nothing, and Cambodia gained her independence in 1953. A decade later Bou Meng's creative talents allowed him to earn a living as a journeyman artist painting the billboards that advertised films shown in provincial cinemas. Those first years were good, but by 1968 the burgeoning civil war between Sihanouk's government and the Khmer Rouge made travel dangerous. Bou Meng returned to Kampong Cham and started a business painting black and white portraits.

Shortly after the coup against Sihanouk in March 1970, Viet Cong troops, who were supporting the Khmer Rouge, began appearing in the

---

4. As quoted in *Voices from S-21: Terror and History in Pol Pot's Secret Prison*, David Chandler (Silkworm Books, 2000), p. 16.

5. *Bou Meng: A Survivor from Khmer Rouge Prison S-21*, Huy Vannak (DC-Cam, 2010).

province in greater numbers. One night they executed one of Bou Meng's relatives, probably because they suspected he was helping the Lon Nol regime. But nobody knew for certain and in those tense times no one dared to ask. 'Silence is better than knowing more,' Bou Meng's cousin advised him. That viewpoint would become a feature of the next 10 years.

By now Sihanouk was appealing for his 'children' to join him and the Khmer Rouge in ridding the country of Lon Nol. Bou Meng watched as friends and acquaintances signed up. He was not political but he felt ashamed that he was doing so little for his nation. One day he heard Sihanouk's call on the radio 'to liberate the country, to search for independence and peace, and to bring development for the nation'.

'Once I heard Prince Sihanouk, there was no doubt in my mind,' Bou Meng wrote in his biography. 'I no longer hesitated to join the revolution.'[6]

Bou Meng and his wife, Ma Yoeun, made their way to the *maquis* and joined the resistance. Ma Yoeun worked as an actress putting on revolutionary plays; he painted portraits and flags. Every third day they sat through indoctrination and self-criticism sessions, and every tenth day married couples like Bou Meng and Ma Yoeun were permitted to spend the night together. Life as a revolutionary was thrilling yet difficult, a time that divided families and that was punctuated by countless forgotten tragedies. Bou Meng learned the following year that his younger brother, a captain in the Lon Nol army, had been killed fighting the Khmer Rouge.

In 1973 Bou Meng narrowly avoided death when a US B-52 bombed the area where he was working, leaving holes 'as big as ponds'. Schools in the Khmer Rouge-controlled areas were closed and the children were taught to hate 'American imperialists, feudalists and capitalists who oppress the poor'. That was also the year that the Khmer Rouge's relationship with their communist brethren in North Vietnam went into terminal decline. Bou Meng remembered seeing Vietnamese soldiers returning home and ethnic Vietnamese civilians fleeing across the border. What he did not know was that *Angkar* was also moving against its perceived enemies within its own ranks. Key among them were the Hanoi-trained Cambodian communists, who were accused of having 'Khmer bodies with Vietnamese minds'. The first significant purges of senior cadres began in earnest.

In 1974 Bou Meng noticed the tone of the indoctrination sessions was becoming increasingly anti-Sihanouk. Given that he had joined the

6. Ibid.

revolution to help Sihanouk's cause, this made him profoundly uncomfortable yet there was nothing he could do about it. Wisely he kept his head down. By the following year the war was over, and within days Bou Meng, his wife and their two young children were ordered to Phnom Penh. On the way they passed thousands of dejected people trudging in the opposite direction. An old man sitting under a tree told Bou Meng the Khmer Rouge had ordered people to leave while they searched for enemies.

'They told us that we would be allowed to return home [after] three days, but it's [been] about a week now,' the old man said.

That was the moment Bou Meng's doubts crystallised.

'It was then that I realised that the revolution had cheated us,' he said.[7]

It was too late. Bou Meng's family was split up. He was sent to paint signs on boats that transported goods along the waterways, and later to a technical school to draw diagrams of machine parts. Ma Yoeun went to work at a hospital. The couple's young son and daughter were sent under *Angkar's* orders to a centre in the capital where dozens of children of Khmer Rouge cadres were looked after by two elderly women. Bou Meng was only occasionally able to see his children or to meet with Ma Yoeun. His young family occupied his thoughts constantly.

By 1976 the revolution had begun to consume its own, and one evening cadres came for them. Bou Meng and his wife were sent to a harsh collective outside Phnom Penh where they were put to work in the rice fields, then in a workshop and later to dig irrigation canals. Like the others, Bou Meng and his wife were forced to work from sun-up to sundown, seven days a week and received just two bowls of rice porridge a day. Three times a week they attended 'livelihood meetings', group sessions that mixed revolutionary talk and self-criticism where they walked the tightrope between not criticising themselves enough and being too harsh. People were encouraged to speak up against each another.

As the months went by, Bou Meng got skinnier, but he kept quiet. Around him people disappeared 'one by one' and were replaced by new arrivals.

'My wife and I tried to think what mistake we had made,' he said. 'We were so nervous since we had never committed any mistakes against the revolution.'[8]

---

7. Ibid.

8. Ibid.

Then, in August 1977, the clouds looked to have lifted: two cadres told Bou Meng that *Angkar* had assigned him to teach students at the art college in Phnom Penh. It meant the couple were free of this place of backbreaking labour, woeful conditions and insufficient food. Perhaps, he thought, they might even have a chance to visit their children, who were still in the centre in the capital. Instead the truck dumped the couple at a house in central Phnom Penh where four armed men handcuffed and blindfolded them. His wife pleaded with the guards saying they had done nothing wrong. The men with guns screamed back: '*Angkar* has never arrested the wrong person!'

By the time his blindfold was removed, Bou Meng was standing in the photographers' room at S-21. He was handed a metal plate with the number 570 on it, photographed and measured. After answering questions about his background, his blindfold was replaced and he was taken to a room and shackled with dozens of men. He never saw Ma Yoeun again.[9]

IN ORDER TO MAKE SENSE OF S-21, I arranged to speak with David Chandler, one of the foremost scholars on Cambodia and the Khmer Rouge. We met at a riverside restaurant on the first floor of a colonial building with one of the best views in the country, looking across to the peninsula where the Mekong meets the Tonle Sap River. During the rainy season the storms roll in from the east, dark clouds spark lightning from their bellies, and, as they close in, a sharp wind whips the flags lining the promenade and people rush for cover. It was mid-2011 and this was one of those afternoons.

It was hard to believe that Chandler, an American, was nearly 80. His build was that of a man 20 years younger and his mind was remarkably agile. He was at turns indiscreet and irreverent, capable of delivering a scathing jab with machine-gun delivery. Interviewing him was a little intimidating, but he was perfectly charming. It counted in my favour that Michael Hayes, the former publisher of the *Phnom Penh Post*, had put in a good word on my behalf.

Before Chandler became a professor of history at Monash University in Australia, he worked for the US Foreign Service where, in 1959, he volunteered for a posting to Phnom Penh. It was a time when nobody in the corps sought out Cambodia, and he spent the next two years as a junior diplomat in Phnom Penh. The country captivated him.

Decades of obsession have provided Chandler with a quite exceptional

---

9. The only tangible item Bou Meng still has of his wife is the photograph taken of her when she entered S-21. See Bou Meng's testimony to the ECCC (document E1_41.1_TR001, July 1, 2009, p. 11).

knowledge. His most recent book was about S-21, and it remains the definitive work, the result of years of research poring over confessions and documents to piece together what made the Khmer Rouge's top-secret prison tick.[10]

When Chandler started working on his book he assumed the confessions would show who within the Khmer Rouge had opposed the regime and what they had done wrong.

'Well I was very naive,' he told me. 'You can't tell. You get a feel for some things sounding a little truer than others after a long time if you know how things hang together. But you could never say: "That's right – this is a bad guy or that's a totally innocent guy."'

Chandler immediately disavowed the common misconception – the 'black-and-white way that most people approach this' – that all of the 14,000 or more people taken to S-21 were innocent.

'It's actuarially impossible that no one would oppose this regime and that none of those who opposed the regime would get caught. It's very likely they'd get caught,' he said.

Others would be hauled in for making a joke or for grumbling about conditions under the Khmer Rouge.

'But anyway it's all lies – who brought whom into what, and what happened to whom and where,' he said of the contents of the confessions, including the frequent claims of being inducted into the CIA or the KGB. 'There's one case where somebody says he was brought in [to the CIA] by Khieu Ponnary, by Mrs Pol Pot, and Duch writes: "What? What? Verify! Verify!" It's as if he's saying: "Move this piece of evidence off the record, please! This isn't going to suit us very well."'

There was, of course, no way that Duch could have passed up the line the accusation by a tortured prisoner that Pol Pot's wife was an enemy of the regime.

After months of research, what stood out for Chandler was how devoted Duch was to his task.

'I don't think they knew how good he was going to be,' he said, 'but he was brilliant at sorting all the documents and seeing what was coming up through this and that.'

Not once in all of the confessions written up by the cadres did Chandler find a typographical error.

---

10. Chandler, *Voices from S-21*, op. cit.

'Never a typo in the whole thing. Of course not — typos are deliberate, right?' he said, playing on the Khmer Rouge's paranoia. 'I always think how there were no typos in the Angkor Wat carvings either. That's a precision that you owe to your work.'

I wanted to return to the basics, so Chandler explained S-21's purpose.

'The function was to document the destruction of Cambodia's – e.g. the Party's – enemies to the satisfaction of the leaders,' he replied. 'So they come in, and they're destroyed. It's a process.'

S-21 provided the leaders with the assurance that their enemies had been dealt with in the most secure way possible, through interrogation and then execution. Some intellectuals who returned, like Ong Thong Hoeung, were lucky enough not to be killed immediately and were sent to work camps where there was at least a chance of survival. Ket, on the other hand, was a returning diplomat linked to Sihanouk's FUNK movement and stood no chance.

The pursuit of enemies was an elemental obsession with the leaders, who had much earlier determined that they were engaged in permanent revolution, generating lists of names to be purged. Nuon Chea said as much in May 1975, shortly after victory. The following year Pol Pot delivered a notorious speech in which he used a medical analogy to warn of internal enemies, whom he described as 'a sickness in the Party'.

'We cannot locate it precisely. The sickness must emerge to be examined,' Pol Pot had said, adding that the search for such 'germs' had failed due to a lack of revolutionary fervour. 'In the Party, the army, and among the people we can locate the ugly germs. They will be pushed out by the true nature of the socialist revolution.'[11]

In 1977 Pol Pot again warned of internal enemies who sought to bring down the revolution. Such people were a 'life and death' contradiction and had to be eliminated. Pol Pot was happy to rely on China to prevent attacks from the nation's external enemies – the imperialist powers such as the United States and later Vietnam – but internal enemies were the bigger problem. Fortunately there was one sure way to proceed: send them to centres such as S-21.

'So they're all dead and there's no question of these guys coming back,' said Chandler, who wheeled out a quote often attributed to Stalin and apt in terms of how the Khmer Rouge viewed matters. 'One man, one problem.

11. Ibid., p. 44.

No man, no problem. No problem any more, there's no re-education.'

The lack of re-education under the Khmer Rouge was unusual in the region. The communists in Vietnam and China were by no means averse to executing people, but those deemed guilty of less serious crimes might be sent to camps to be re-fashioned. Not so in Democratic Kampuchea where Cambodian culture dictated that one's enemies were unable to change. That meant re-education was pointless.

What puzzled Chandler more was why the Khmer Rouge bothered photographing the prisoners or extracting forced confessions. S-21 echoed a judicial procedure that simply was not taking place.

'This is the very mysterious thing about S-21,' he said. 'They don't resemble anything that happened in China, where people were just locked up full stop, or Vietnam. They resemble the forced confessions in Russia and Eastern Europe after the Second World War. The show trials of Stalin – they resemble those confessions.'

Chandler had wondered whether the Khmer Rouge had learned about Stalin's show trials. Full written confessions were not the norm in the old Cambodia, where police instead followed the manner of the French *passage à tabac* with suspects brought in and beaten up to elicit their involvement. If that failed they would be sent to the judge for questioning.

In *Voices from S-21* Chandler theorised that a man called K'ang Sheng, who headed Mao's secret police and whose nickname was Mao's Pistol, may have had a lot to do with it. During his lifetime K'ang, who died in 1975, a year before Mao, was extremely influential and widely feared. By 1980 his posthumous reputation was in tatters as the former secret policeman was blamed for some of the appalling excesses of Maoist China.

In the 1930s K'ang was living in the USSR and was responsible for helping the Soviets to arrest and execute a number of expatriate Chinese communists. In 1937 he returned to China and aligned himself with Mao. Chandler reckoned that K'ang introduced the techniques Mao used to get rid of his political opponents at a time when the Chinese communists had diverged from the USSR's Comintern. Over the following decades K'ang headed more purges, was deeply involved in the Cultural Revolution and was a trusted member of the Central Case Examination Group, a body established in 1966 to investigate and purge senior members of the Chinese Communist Party. In short, he was a key player in the repeated purges of China's communists.

A Chinese source told Chandler that K'ang had met Pol Pot in 1966 when the Cambodian revolutionary visited Beijing. Chandler believed the two men met again during Pol Pot's 1970 visit when K'ang actively but unsuccessfully opposed the Chinese foreign ministry's endorsement of Siha-nouk after Lon Nol's coup.[12] The two men may have met once more the following year. Although it is impossible to link S-21's brutality with K'ang, he and Pol Pot certainly bonded: after K'ang died in December 1975, Pol Pot visited the Chinese embassy in Phnom Penh to pay his respects.

THE CRUELTIES METED OUT at S-21 ranged from the petty to the obscene. Bou Meng soon encountered both. Moments after he was taken handcuffed and blindfolded from the photographers' room, he stumbled on the stairs leading to the first floor of Building C. The guard yelled out at his 'blindness', and once they reached the landing he forced Bou Meng, who is less than five-foot tall, to carry him on his back up the remaining two flights. There Bou Meng was shoved into a room packed with dozens of wretched men manacled together. After the guards shackled Bou Meng, they removed his blindfold and handcuffs and left him.

'My room smelled bad,' he recalled. 'I glanced around and saw approximately 50 other prisoners sleeping on the floor in two lines. All were men. Some looked skinny and weak; some had long beards and moustaches; some looked deathly pale; and some bore scars left from wounds. They looked like ghosts. It seemed to me that all the prisoners were waiting for death. That was hell on earth!'[13]

Between the shock of what had happened, fear for his wife, the gnawing hunger, the groans from the men in the cell, the cold and the mosquitoes, Bou Meng was unable to sleep. For two months he lay shackled in that room. The prisoners were fed twice a day – a ladle of rice gruel. Should they fail to ask permission to defecate in one of four ammunition boxes or urinate in a plastic bottle, they would be whipped dozens of times. Talking was strictly forbidden.

The cruelties were as senseless as they were capricious. One night Bou Meng watched as a teenage guard repeatedly stamped on the chest of an old man, killing him. Other prisoners were taken away and never returned. Prisoners called out for their mothers, their words cutting through the gloom. By the time the guards came for Bou Meng, he was thin and weak.

---

12. Ibid., p.127.

13. Vannak, op. cit., p. 36.

They took him blindfolded to a room where they beat him with a bamboo stick until he collapsed. When he came round, they yelled at him about his CIA, KGB and Vietnamese contacts with whom he was working to undermine the revolution. After he told them he had no idea what they were talking about, they asked which tools he would prefer they torture him with: whips, electric cables or metal bars?

'It's up to you, brother,' he replied, exhausted. His answer unleashed a frenzy of violence as a young interrogator attacked him with an electric cable, ordering him to keep count of the number of lashes. When Bou Meng failed to do that, he was beaten to a bloody mess. That evening they shoved him into a cell on his own where he was again shackled. Bou Meng was in tears for himself, his wife and his children. Despite his hunger he was unable to eat from the bowl of gruel the cadre left in his cell.

'I sat on my buttocks with my knees folded close to my chest and my arms clasped around my knees,' he recalled. 'I tried to think what mistake I had committed.'

The next day it started again: the kickings, the beatings, the yelling, and again and again the same question about his CIA, KGB and *Yuon* – a pejorative term for Vietnamese – contacts.

'*Angkar* has never arrested the wrong person!' they screamed at his denials. 'You're an artist so you clearly have CIA contacts.'

They jammed a bamboo stick into the injuries on his back, demanding answers that he could not give. That night he lay immobilised in pain in the small cell.

On the third day they took him to a house outside the prison compound that one of the interrogation groups used for torture. The three interrogators referred to Bou Meng as 'it' and promised to 'straighten' his 'crooked mind'. Despite repeated electric shocks, he had nothing to tell them. In return they warned him not to conceal his spy networks, yelling the well-worn phrase: 'To keep you is no gain; to destroy you is no loss.'

It was another four days before Bou Meng cracked. By then he had realised that the truth was irrelevant. The interrogators wanted answers that satisfied the needs of their superiors and they would keep torturing him until he provided them. And so he did, fabricating a lengthy story of his efforts with foreign powers to undermine the revolution, pages packed with nonsensical 'truths' that told of his induction into the CIA when he was still a boy at the pagoda.

They wanted his networks too, so Bou Meng gave them the names of 20 people he knew, 'some of whom I assumed had already been arrested'. Once he had confessed, the torture ended and Bou Meng was taken back to his cell where he waited for death, unable to fathom why he had ended up here.[14]

IT WAS NOT UNTIL 2009 that Neary and Martine managed to find the photograph of Ket that had been taken on his arrival at S-21 on June 15, 1977. They were at the office of the Documentation Center of Cambodia (DC-Cam), the leading organisation researching the crimes of the Khmer Rouge, trying to find out more about S-21 and about Ket from DC-Cam's director Youk Chhang.[15] As Neary leafed through folders of photographs taken at S-21, she saw Ket's face.

'Mum recognised Ket and had no doubt at all it was him,' Neary told me later.

Other than the two entries in S-21's registers, this black-and-white image was the only evidence that Ket had ever been in Duch's prison. Later that year Neary came across an image of a man lying dead on a stretcher at S-21. She thought it might be Ket but it was hard to be sure: the photograph was taken from an oblique angle, the head toward the camera and the feet facing away. His arms were pinioned behind his back, which means he was probably still handcuffed, and his body was skinny and battered.

She could not be certain but Neary felt there was a good chance that this man with his wavy hair and prominent cheekbones was her father. I was far less sure, largely because most prisoners were not photographed after execution. Neary told me about a line in a book by Nic Dunlop, the Irish photojournalist who located and unmasked Duch in 1999, in which Dunlop and S-21 interrogator Prak Khan had walked through a room at the prison filled with images of the dead.[16] Dunlop had asked Prak Khan whether he remembered any of these people. Prak Khan had waited until the tourists had left the room then pointed to one image, of a man lying dead on a stretcher.

'This one,' he had told Dunlop.

Neary thought there was a chance that Prak Khan was referring to this

14. Bou Meng was permitted to live after Duch learned of his artistic skills. He was put to work painting monochrome images of Pol Pot.

15. DC-Cam was set up in 1995 as a part of Yale University's Cambodian Genocide Programme. Two years later it became an independent non-governmental organisation.

16. *The Lost Executioner: A Journey to the Heart of the Killing Fields*, Nic Dunlop (Bloomsbury Publishing, 2005).

photograph, so I emailed the image to the book's author and asked him. Dunlop wrote back promptly.

'To be perfectly honest, it's so long ago – six or seven years – that the only person who could help with any degree of certainty is Prak Khan himself,' he replied.

Because Prak Khan lives in a village near Phnom Penh, the obvious solution was to ask him to come to the former prison and ask him myself. Dunlop warned that Prak Khan would expect 'a present' afterwards – 'cash, most likely, plus any travel expenses'. Paying interviewees is regarded as unethical for any journalist, but in this case it raised a more profound moral problem: Prak Khan had tortured people at S-21 and it seems obscene to reward someone for knowledge gained in such odious fashion. Then again, I reasoned with myself, this was no ordinary interview. If this image were of the man that Prak Khan had remembered, and if by some quirk of fate he could provide enough information to convince me that it was Ket, then surely that would override the moral dilemma of paying him? Neary was desperate for any knowledge of Ket, even something as dreadful as the confirmation that this was her father's body on a stretcher.

The topic had come up before between Neary and Rob Hamill, a New Zealander whose brother Kerry was seized from a yacht off the Cambodian coast in 1978 and taken to S-21. Kerry was tortured as a suspected CIA spy under Duch's authority and then executed and his body burned. Having such a meagre amount of knowledge about their loved ones had caused both of them agony and so, with some reluctance, I decided to see whether I could get Prak Khan to meet me.

Prak Khan had started working at S-21 in 1976, not long after it opened. For several months he was stationed at the guardhouse on a nearby street. Trucks dropped the prisoners at his building where they would be blindfolded and roped together by their necks and walked up the dusty road, beaten and cursed at, before entering the main gate to be processed – their photographs taken, and then shackled in holding rooms or cells.

S-21 was top secret, which was why the trucks delivered their human cargo on the adjacent street, and at first Prak Khan did not know what he was guarding. But the regular to-ing and fro-ing soon made it clear that this was a prison. Later that year Prak Khan was appointed to an interrogation unit. S-21 had three of these: the political unit, the hot unit, and the *angkiem*, or chewing, unit. The political unit used persuasion and lies to get prisoners to talk; the hot unit practised moderate torture; and the chewing unit had carte blanche to do whatever its members chose. The chewing unit – like a dog chews a bone, the explanation went – dealt with the stubborn prisoners, those who would not confess, and it was to this unit that Prak Khan was assigned. By the time Ket arrived at S-21, Prak Khan was an experienced interrogator. Given that he is alive today and that many of his fellow interrogators were consumed by S-21, it is no great stretch to assume that Prak Khan was good at what he did.

Dunlop told me that Prak Khan was 'very direct' and would likely be prepared to talk. He was right. A day after my translator, Sina, called him to request an interview, the three of us – Prak Khan, Sina and I – met at the Tuol Sleng Genocide Museum. He was less of a physical presence than I had expected: wiry, perhaps five-foot-six, with the dark skin and rough hands and feet of a farmer. When Dunlop had interviewed him, he was struck by Prak Khan's unwillingness to meet his eye. The years and the interviews with journalists since then had made him less reserved. Talking about that time, he told me, relieved the tensions he still felt.

He was nervous to speak at first. Many Cambodians detest him, he explained, now that they know he worked here. Prak Khan wanted to be sure he could not be overheard so we walked away from the entrance gate and stood in the shade of a coconut palm next to the white graves of the last 14 victims of this place, Prak Khan with a faded gold-plated pen in the top pocket of a fake Pierre Cardin shirt with its frayed white collar. As he talked, he smoked, and over the hours he got through the pack. When he ran out, he helped himself to Sina's cigarettes.

I had assumed that someone who had done the job Prak Khan had would possess a harsh voice to match, and was surprised to find him softly spoken. As the day went on and he relaxed, I had the impression that he was being reasonably honest. He claimed he did not kill anyone under interrogation and that might be true. Interrogators who killed prisoners before their confessions were extracted ran the risk of being executed for undermining the revolution, as had happened to a colleague of his who beat four prisoners to death. Prisoners could be executed only after Duch's approval and, even then, most executions were carried out by another unit at Chhoeung Ek, not by the interrogators.

Prak Khan was never told why he had been chosen as an interrogator but he felt that his Grade 8 literacy level and command of basic French were likely factors. At the time he was excited at the prospect of doing something more interesting than guarding a barrier, but he claims that changed when he entered S-21 and saw what was going on.

'I felt afraid, but I dared not refuse, because if I said no then I would be killed,' he said. 'We had to follow all the orders to stay alive, and we knew that if someone said no they would be taken away and executed.'

Had his own parents been brought to S-21, he said, he would have tortured them too.

I could well believe it from a man whose answers were light on intro-spection and loaded with a certain unthinking resignation. Almost certainly he had never heard of Jean Améry, who wrote of Prak Khan's trade that, 'the dominion of the torturer over his victim has nothing in common with the power exercised on the basis of social contracts, as we know it'.[17] This power, Améry wrote, was utterly different from that of the traffic police or officials from the tax department or even from our dealings with leaders who wield absolute power and who could be terrifying and yet merciful too.

'But the power of the torturer, under which the tortured moans, is nothing other than the triumph of the survivor over the one who is plunged from the world into agony and death,' Améry wrote.

THE FIRST TIME Prak Khan went to an interrogation session with the *angkiem* unit he was accompanied by an experienced interrogator. After all, he had to learn the ropes. One of his favourite techniques was ramming pins under the prisoner's fingernails, he told me, helpfully pointing out what that involved: pursing his thumb and forefinger together and jabbing them at the middle finger of his other hand. My toes curled involuntarily. There were also regular training sessions conducted by Duch, but mostly those involved polit-ical indoctrination to disseminate the CPK's policies, not torture methods.

Soon enough Prak Khan was heading his own three-man team. The routine was straightforward. Each morning the prisoner would be taken from their cell, blindfolded and handcuffed, one cadre on each side to make certain they did not commit suicide by diving over the balcony.

'We held them like this,' Prak Khan told me, unexpectedly pinioning his arm firmly through mine by way of explanation as we stood under a tree. 'Then we would take them to the interrogation house; mine was up the road over there.'

Prak Khan's day started early and ended late: a morning session, an

17. Améry, op. cit., p. 39.

afternoon session, and an evening session, with the same prisoner in the same room for as long as it took to get the confession. That could be days or even weeks. Factoring in the time Prak Khan claimed he spent in hospital between 1976 and 1979, he guessed he had tortured around 30 people, although when the research organisation DC-Cam assessed the number of extant confessions bearing Prak Khan's name, the total was nearly twice that. A total of 51 carried his signature as interrogator and he helped to rewrite two others. In 1976 he interrogated five prisoners; the following year, when Ket was imprisoned, 15; and in 1978 a further 35. Prak Khan found time to interrogate one more on January 4, 1979, as the invading forces closed in.

Yet if the sessions were terrifying for the prisoners they were often boring for Prak Khan, who spent more than 10 hours a day asking prisoners the same question – to confess their CIA or KGB networks – and fielding the same confused answers in return.

'My understanding is that most confessions were not true,' he said. 'Sometimes we tortured them too much, and when we questioned them again they would say yes because they were scared of being tortured even more.'

I pushed Prak Khan on this point: how many of the 30 that he recalled torturing did he think were genuine CIA spies? Perhaps three, he replied. His answer surprised me. It was far more likely that none was in the league of foreign powers. I thought he might have misunderstood the question, so I asked again: how many of those 30 do you think today – in 2012 – were actually CIA? Three, he said again.

By now we had moved through two rooms of photographs and were sitting outside on a stone bench under a jackfruit tree. Tourists filed past us in small groups. When we were in Building B earlier, I had asked him whether he recognised any of the images of the dead men on stretchers. I had deliberately not mentioned Ket's name, although I did point out a number of pictures including the one Neary thought was of Ket. But each time Prak Khan shook his head. Instead he called my attention to several other photographs, one of which showed a young woman lying dead after jumping from one of the balconies. He remembered her suicide, he said.

Now in the shade of the jackfruit tree I opened my laptop and called up the image of the dead man on the stretcher. Do you recognise this man?

'I don't know him,' he replied, adding: 'That picture was hanging on the wall inside.'

'Yes. But you don't know him?'

'I don't,' he said.

I opened another image of Ket, the one taken on the day he was brought to S-21. Ket stared out at Prak Khan, and Prak Khan looked back at him.

'I don't know him,' he said. I told him that this prisoner's name was Ouk Ket. There was no recognition.

'The prisoners that I interrogated, those I would recognise,' he explained. 'Those I didn't interrogate, I wouldn't.'

I showed him a final image of Ket taken in France in 1970. Ket was dressed in Western clothing, a guitar in his arms and a Cambodian friend standing behind him. Neary told me both men had been killed at S-21. Did Prak Khan recognise either man? He shook his head.

'I've never seen them,' he said.

I told him that Ket was held here for six months.

'Quite possibly,' he replied.

When I said both men were diplomats and returned in 1977, Prak Khan said in that case they were probably killed.

'At that time they recalled the people working at embassies overseas, and those who came back were killed. Nearly all of them,' he said.

Finally I asked him which interrogators would have been tasked with torturing returned diplomats like Ket. There were no specific teams, he said. Unless the prisoner was senior, perhaps a ministry head or a district chief, then anyone could have been assigned.

I HAD HOPED TO LEARN something useful for Neary and Martine, but it was not to be. Despite knowing that it was a long shot I was still disappointed. Later I asked Prak Khan how he felt about the revolution that he had so fervently supported. Well, he replied, on reflection it was a disaster. We talked about Nai Nan, the young woman he interrogated at S-21 and with whom he claims to have fallen in love. It was a story that Dunlop recounted in his book and that epitomises the futility and tragedy of this place and this time.

Nai Nan, who was 19, had worked in a hospital in Phnom Penh as a nurse, which in practice meant she had the most rudimentary medical skills. One day she was arrested and brought to S-21, finally ending up shackled in Prak Khan's interrogation room. Days of intimidation failed to generate the requisite confession, and eventually Prak Khan gave her three options: confess to being a spy for the CIA or for the KGB or for the Vietnamese.

It took several months to get Nai Nan to confess, but she finally broke. Her confession was heartbreaking and pathetic. She chose the CIA option, she told him. She was tasked with sabotaging the hospital and had been ordered by her CIA handler 'to shit on the rice and beans next to the toilets in buildings and in houses to ruin the reputation of the command-post hospital because it was a model hospital'. Her next mission was 'to shit in the operating room'. Nai Nan was illiterate, so Prak Khan wrote out her confession, which he knew was sheer fabrication given for fear of further torture. Duch signed off on it and she was executed.

Prak Khan told Dunlop he would have married Nai Nan had *Angkar* permitted it, but wisely he kept his feelings about her private. By 2012 he was still angry at the system that had destroyed this young woman, and he seemed embarrassed too at his actions during those years. It was a terrible time, he told me, and he regretted the 'many cruel things' he had done.

'Sometimes I worry that the spirits of the dead will return and do something bad to me,' he said. 'But each time I go to the pagoda, I make sure to do good deeds to help the spirits.'

He grumbled too about his present hardships, saying that none of the cadres had got anything from their roles, not even money.

'We still have the wounds on our bodies from that time, but we have nothing else,' he said.

I wondered whether Prak Khan felt sorrier for himself than for those he had tortured.

We took a break at a stall near the entrance gate and I bought some drinks. Sina and I had Cokes; Prak Khan swapped his for an energy drink, and then sat next to Chum Mey, one of the few survivors of S-21, at the table where the former prisoner sells an array of photocopied books about Cambodia and the prison. Prak Khan and Chum Mey talked in relaxed fashion. Prak Khan asked how his sales were going.

Physical contact among members of the same gender is common in Cambodia, and throughout their 10-minute chat Chum Mey rested his hand on Prak Khan's leg. At one point Prak Khan placed his hand on Chum Mey's shoulder, not for long, but the gesture was there. It seemed encouraging that two men connected in opposite ways to this place could decades later have a polite conversation, although I felt too that it was reasonably likely Prak Khan was doing this for my benefit. I noticed that when he crossed the path to greet Bou Meng, who sits at another table each day selling his book, the atmosphere was distinctly cooler; Prak Khan quickly cut short his time with Bou Meng.

OVER LUNCH AT A NEARBY KHMER RESTAURANT, I asked Prak Khan whether he would do it again. Knowing what he knows now, and speaking as a Buddhist – many former Khmer Rouge once again follow Buddhism, from surviving leaders to the rank and file – what decision would he make if he were told to start work in S-21's interrogation unit?

It is worth explaining that, in the Buddhist context, this life is of value but it is merely one in a cycle of numerous lifetimes. Your actions in this life determine your position in the next, which means someone like Duch, for instance, could look forward to a long period in Buddhist hell to expiate his sins before his spirit could be reborn as a lowly animate being, such as a worm, and then work its way back up the chain. Similarly, Prak Khan's acts mean he would be reborn into a lower station in the next life. This surely means that a reflective believer would see the logic in behaving differently: give up this life so as to protect your future lives.

Not so, said Prak Khan.

'If they had power and they used it like they did before then I would do the same again,' he said between slurps of soup as the wall fans pushed hot air across the room, 'because if I refused to do it I would die, and nobody wants to die.'

Earlier Prak Khan had told me it was his fate to work at S-21. I ran that past my translator, Sina, who had spent nearly a decade as a Buddhist monk. To me this talk of fate seems all too conveniently to remove our responsibility for our actions, as though everything were written in stone and immutable. It strayed close to claiming: 'I am not responsible for what I did.'

While Prak Khan fielded a call from his son, who was studying electrical engineering, Sina talked me through the concept. In Buddhism, he said, we do not rely on fate. Life is about the actions we take.

'If you sow rice on a rock, it won't grow,' Sina explained. 'So we have to be careful with our actions. Buddhism teaches us today is more important than tomorrow or the past. We should take the past as experience for today, and if today is good then the future will be good.'

I pushed the point with Sina: 'Surely then you should not fear for this life since there are many more lives to come? Surely the right thing is to say: "Kill me – because I'm not going to do this." If you are a good

Buddhist, you would rather die – you would not do these evil things. Is that right?'

Of course, Sina replied.

'If he believes strongly in Buddhism then he does not fear to die. No one escapes from dying, right?' Sina said.

THE DEFINING ACT that S-21's inmates undertook was to pen their confessions. Illiterates like Nai Nan would have theirs written or typed out for them. Often the prisoners would be told that they need only confess the error of their ways and *Angkar* would forgive them. It was, of course, a lie. There was no chance for redemption. Democratic Kampuchea was a nation of Manichean logic in which to be against the Party was to be the enemy, and as such to be marked for death. The black-and-white photographs reflect this reality, that there was no middle ground, and so hundreds of thousands were tortured and executed in the network of prisons like S-21 that lay scattered around the country like the cogs of a monstrous machine.

The Tuol Sleng Genocide Museum is as close as most tourists will get to this machine. It was the Vietnamese, keen to justify their 1979 invasion, who decided S-21 should be preserved as a memorial to the 'genocide' that Pol Pot had wrought. In the final decades of the millennium, S-21 joined the ranks of Auschwitz and Treblinka as monikers for mass murder. Hanoi could have chosen any one of dozens of pagodas, schools, rice fields and clearings to show how and where the Khmer Rouge murdered hundreds of thousands, yet S-21 was a compelling choice because of what Duch had left behind. Since we cannot meaningfully engage with large numbers of dead, S-21's photographs allow us to see some of the people behind the statistics. Focusing on the individual also runs counter to the Stalin-inspired notion of the Khmer Rouge that 'to keep you is no gain, to destroy you is no loss' – that the individual has no value and that the collective is all.

Small wonder that so many died, and that such a senseless waste still consumes people like Neary, Martine and Sady. Like a boulder cast into the sea of humanity, S-21 destroyed thousands and its waves continue to wreak havoc. In Martine's case that is in part through thinking about Ket's 'slow death' and the terrible, numberless uncertainties of how he suffered. Without answers the mind runs wild with the possibilities.

The next generation was also profoundly affected, whether they were in Cambodia or living abroad, as Neary found to her cost.

'Everyone was in my head. It was too many people, and yet you have to live with the everyday life, so you get a job and deal with the living, and then you also have to live with the dead,' Neary told me. 'It is very heavy, because you don't know what happened to them, you don't know how they feel. Are they at peace with themselves? No, they aren't you see. They aren't, because they are always coming back.'

Duch's trial had given Neary a reason to return to Cambodia and she was one of many who hoped it would provide some answers. Cambodians rightly ask: Why did the Khmer Rouge do this to us? Yet this was not the murder of the 'other' as the Nazis painted their mass murder of Jews and Gypsies and others, or the Hutus of the Tutsis, or the Turks of the Armenians a century ago. In Cambodia, one of the world's most homogenous societies, Khmer killed Khmer in vast numbers.

I hoped Duch's trial would answer my questions too, and not the least of those was to try and understand Duch himself. After all, what kind of person inflicts such pain on so many people over so many years, and what had motivated Duch to do so? Yet it was far more important that Duch's trial and the tribunal's subsequent case against the surviving Khmer Rouge leaders would help Neary in her search for what had happened to Ket, and millions of Cambodians on quests of their own.

In the lead-up to his trial Duch had promised to deliver the unvarnished truth. I wondered whether he would hold himself to that or if instead he would emerge as an unreconstructed follower, a man for whom the promised certainties of the revolution remained paramount and whom its religion of secrecy had rewarded by sparing him when it had crushed so many others. Days after I met Neary and Martine, Duch's trial began.

THE REGULATIONS OF S-21

1. You must answer according to my questions – don't turn them away.

2. Don't try to hide the facts by making pretexts about this and that. You are strictly prohibited to contest me.

3. Don't be a fool for you are a person who dares to thwart the revolution.

4. You must immediately answer my questions without wasting time to reflect.

5. Don't tell me about either your immoralities or the essence of the revolution.

6. While getting lashes or electrification, you must not cry at all.

7. Do nothing, sit still and wait for my orders. If there is no order, keep quiet. When I ask you to do something, you must do it right away without protesting.

8. Don't make pretexts about Kampuchea Krom in order to hide your secrets or traitorous activities.

9. If you don't follow all of the above rules, you shall get many lashes of electric wire.

10. If you disobey any point of my regulations you shall get either ten lashes or five shocks of electric discharge.

— The rules for prisoners at S-21, which today are replicated in three languages on a large board at the former prison. During his trial Duch denied these rules existed and claimed they were 'fabricated by Vietnamese troops'. Other witnesses, including former staff, testified that the rules were accurate and were read out to prisoners prior to interrogation. Kampuchea Krom is today an area of southern Vietnam that once belonged to Cambodia.

CHAPTER SEVEN

THE FOUR 'NOTS'

KAING GUEK EAV, ALIAS DUCH, is a man who likes proverbs. Given his background as the head of the security police for one of history's most secretive political movements, his choices bear the stamp of decades of survival.

'The more secrets you can keep, the longer you will survive.'

'If you can keep what you are doing secret, then you are halfway to success.'

Or this one, known as The Four 'Nots': 'Not to speak, not to know, not to see and not to hear.'

These sayings, which he told to the judges during his trial, are freighted with a heavy irony given his function as the regime's key person entrusted with extracting secrets, a job made more difficult given that most people taken to S-21 were innocent of plotting against the revolution. Perhaps it escapes him, but it was surely hard to wrest secrets when there were none to be found in the first place.

Yet to my mind the words which most profoundly resonate with those years went unmentioned by Duch. They prophesy a time of annihilation and unspeakable horrors:[1]

'A darkness will settle on the people of Cambodia. There will be houses but no people in them, roads with no travellers; the land will be ruled by barbarians with no religion; blood will run so deep as to touch the belly of the elephant. Only the deaf and the mute will survive.'

As a description of life under the Khmer Rouge, it could hardly be more apt.

---

1. Ian Harris, a scholar of Buddhism, believes this prophecy, known as the *Put Tumneay* or Predictions of the Buddha, was written in the 1860s. See *Buddhism in a Dark Age: Cambodian Monks under Pol Pot* (University of Hawai'i Press, 2012), p. 175, note 11.

COMRADE DUCH SITS in the air-conditioned comfort of the court-room under the sharp glare of fluorescent lamps, whose bone-coloured light reflects off his collared, white shirt. He is positioned on one side of the stage, a man apart, behind his defence lawyers. Above them the domed bulbs of the ceiling lamps stare down unblinking, the size and shape of upturned skulls.

Conjoined sheets of bulletproof glass run from floor to ceiling separating the 500-seat auditorium from the stage that holds Duch, his defence team, the judges and the prosecutors. This is justice set apart from the people whom it is here to represent, justice raised up and visible. On this side of the glass screen is the public seating, and it is from these blue-cushioned, cinema-style chairs that thousands of Cambodians, row after raised row, will watch the proceedings as the months roll by.

The VIP seats closest to the stage are reserved for Buddhist monks or nuns, swathed in orange and white robes respectively, and occasionally those diplomats whose countries are paying for proceedings. White, rectangular air-conditioning units, taller than a man, stand like pale sentries around the periphery and push cold air across the auditorium. The air drifts and mingles in the warmth of so many bodies, then rises to the ceiling while the seats fall away to the stage in measured steps.

From my media seat in the auditorium the scene is resonant of a fishbowl with the key players in this drama safely behind glass. Their words, translated into Khmer when the foreign nationals speak, are piped through speakers into the auditorium where they echo off pale-green tiles and pale-green walls, then vanish in the stale air. Like most foreigners, I listen through headphones to the simultaneous translation in English or French and, because the court has banned recording equipment, mobile phones and laptops from the auditorium, I capture those fleeting words in black ballpoint in an array of notebooks.[2]

The stage is dominated by a circular logo of blue on white, illustrating the tribunal's dual nature, and some of us wonder whether this mix of judicial cultures will work. The logo depicts a Cambodian god of justice sitting cross-legged on a dais, wielding a sword, and surrounded by the olive wreaths of the United Nations: this conjunction of a weapon amid the

---

2. Full transcripts of each day's proceedings were made available in each of the court's three languages, typically within the same week. They can be found on the tribunal's website: www.eccc. gov.kh/en/

foliage representing peace seems odd, but in a way the symbol reflects the opposing traits of the human character, and that complexity is partly what this process is about.

The cross-cultural design also conveys the tribunal's hybrid nature: the delivery of international law within the formal mechanism of Cambodia's judicial system. The court, which is known formally as the Extraordinary Chambers in the Courts of Cambodia, or ECCC, has had a protracted birth, the consequence of years of often ill-tempered negotiations between the UN and the government. It seeks to combine Cambodia's French-derived, civil law process with international law derived from the Nuremberg trials of the Nazis, topped up with precedent from subsequent tribunals including that of Rwanda, Sierra Leone and the former Yugoslavia.

The ECCC has set itself the Herculean task of delivering justice and the additional one of reconciliation. The latter, though unrealistic,[3] looms large in the tribunal's perception of itself.[4] One of the ECCC's founding pillars is that the truths uncovered here will promote reconciliation in much the same way as those that emanated from South Africa's Truth and Reconciliation Commission (TRC) did; for that we have the members of the UN General Assembly to thank: their resolution 57/228 of December 2002 explicitly linked reconciliation and justice when they called on then-Secretary General Kofi Annan to resume stalled negotiations with Phnom Penh to establish the ECCC. After decades of immobility the General Assembly had determined with no apparent irony that the events of 1975–79 were 'of vitally important concern to the international community as a whole'.

After much more bargaining between the Cambodian government and the UN, the agreement to establish the ECCC was finally signed in 2003.[5]

---

3. See, for instance, the thoughts of Duch's international lawyer, François Roux, who rightly noted that the judges' primary role is to achieve justice by handing down a judgment that accords with the law. Effecting national reconciliation can only ever be a by-product. The task of achieving national reconciliation is, on the other hand, unequivocally the responsibility of the government, and among the paths open to it are a truth and reconciliation commission. Taken from: 'Interview with Defense Counsel François Roux' by Michael Saliba, J.D., consultant to the Center for International Human Rights, Northwestern School of Law. It can be found on the Cambodia Tribunal Monitor website, September 21, 2009.

4. Ironically, most Cambodians do not see a link between justice and reconciliation, a topic that we will turn to later in the book.

5. Among the books providing in-depth coverage of the process of establishing the tribunal is *Hybrid Justice: The Extraordinary Chambers in the Courts of Cambodia*, John D. Ciorciari and Anne Heindel (University of Michigan Press, 2014). Another is *Getting Away With Genocide: Cambodia's Long Struggle Against the Khmer Rouge*, Tom Fawthrop and Helen Jarvis (Pluto Press, 2004).

Although the ECCC's goals are absurdly high, I would argue that reconciliation and post-atrocity justice are intimately connected. The two concepts are at the heart of British-American journalist Helena Cobban's book which examined the approaches used in three post-atrocity states: South Africa, Rwanda and Mozambique.[6] The idea was to see what worked. These nations used different processes in their efforts to seek closure or resolution for acts of political violence. My country, South Africa, established the TRC, which offered amnesty to those who told the truth provided their acts of criminality had been undertaken with a political motive.[7] The logic was that society would benefit from learning the truth behind how the apartheid system had been propped up or fought against, even if it meant that those who had committed acts of violence escaped prosecution.

'There are different kinds of justice,' TRC chair Desmond Tutu, the former Anglican Archbishop of Cape Town, told the *New Yorker* magazine in late 1996, midway through that process. 'Retributive justice is largely Western. The African understanding is far more restorative – not so much to punish as to redress or restore a balance that has been knocked askew. The justice we hope for is restorative of the dignity of the people.'[8]

For its part Rwanda, which saw 800,000 people murdered during three months in 1994, provided a case study of three types of judicial processes. The well-funded and ponderous UN tribunal held in neighbouring Tanzania prosecuted the leaders and the most egregious offenders, while two domestic processes between them tried more than a million other cases, most under the much-criticised village-level system. A fourth programme combines training, research and peace education in a bid to bring about reconciliation.

Mozambique took the most unusual route. After the end of its 15-year civil war, this former Portuguese colony decided there was no reason to have a judicial process or inquiry of any sort since what had happened was effectively beyond the realm of humans to adjudicate. It was felt that an evil spirit had descended upon the land during that time of conflict in which one million people had died, but now the spirit was gone and it would not benefit the nation to dig into the past. In Mozambique the approach was widely accepted by the government and the people as the best solution.

---

6. *Amnesty After Atrocity: Healing Nations after Genocide and War Crimes*, Helena Cobban (Paradigm, 2007).

7. Unless, that is, those acts were regarded as disproportionately egregious, in which case the door for prosecution could in theory be left open.

8. 'Recovering from Apartheid', by Tina Rosenberg, *New Yorker*, November 18, 1996, p. 90.

'A veil of silence and intentional forgetting was formally laid over all those deeds,' Cobban wrote. 'Mozambicans, who live in one of the world's very poorest countries, then turned their attentions to trying to build a new future for their nation.'[9]

A decade after the 1992 granting of amnesties, almost all of the Mozambicans to whom Cobban spoke supported that decision. The responses, she found, typically went like this: 'In war-time, everyone does bad things. But that was during the time of violence. Now we are in a time of peace. Our main concern now is to prevent any return to a time of war ... Besides, if you started prosecuting people for what they did during war there would be no end of it.'[10]

By 2015 Mozambique, despite recent stutters, was still at peace and, as development economists know, the longer a poor, post-conflict country remains peaceful, the lower its chance of relapsing into violence. Yet the fact that Mozambique eschewed a national process does not mean nothing was done. In villages and towns across the country, people found ways to deal with the consequences of the violence that had been unleashed. Cobban recounted the findings of a Mozambican anthropologist who studied how people traditionally cope in that country and in Angola, another former Portuguese colony that also saw decades of civil war. Survivors did not talk about what happened because that would 'be like opening a door for the harmful spirits to penetrate the communities'. Instead healing was achieved through symbolic rites.

Cobban cited a story from researcher and academic Carolyn Nordstrom of a ceremony performed in one Mozambican village for a young woman who had been enslaved for months at a military camp.[11] Mozambique's conservative views meant the woman's future prospects were bleak: she would likely never find a husband, would be compelled to live with her father and would be known within her community as a tainted person.

Her situation was shared by many and, in response to the need to mend society, traditional healers created purification ceremonies where previously none had existed. Nordstrom witnessed the days-long rite performed for this particular woman. On the last day the villagers prepared food, and the musicians gathered in a shaded compound of plants and cloth and lit by lanterns:

---

9. Cobban, op. cit.

10. Ibid.

11. Taken from the book *A Different Kind of War Story (The Ethnography of Political Violence)*, Carolyn Nordstrom (University of Pennsylvania Press, 1997), pp. 145–146.

The ceremony itself continued throughout the night, a mosaic of support and healing practices. Several high points included the ritual bath the woman received at dusk. Numerous women picked up the patient, and carefully gave her a complete bath – a cleansing of the soul as well as the body. The bathing was accompanied with songs and stories about healing, about dealing with trauma, about reclaiming a new life and being welcomed into the community. The patient was then dressed in her new clothing, and fed a nutritious meal. Shortly thereafter, the musicians began a new rhythm of music, and all the women gathered about the patient to carry her inside the hut … Throughout the ceremony, the woman was continually reassured with stories of ongoing support; of her need to place responsibility for her plight with war and not her own actions; and of *her own responsibility to heal war's wounds so she does not inflict the violence that she was subjected to on others.*[12]

The ceremony was not about reconciling this survivor with those who had perpetrated such cruelties against her; it was about welcoming her back into society's fold. In that context it links directly to the broader topic of reconciliation within her village: acceptance, reintegration and healing.

But bringing survivors back into the community is just one element of reconciliation, and the lack of a national process of accountability and truth-telling runs counter to related elements such as justice and the notion that society benefits from the public airing of a multitude of unpalatable truths. Mozambique's path meant every perpetrator escaped unpunished. That riled some, including those who had spent years documenting rapes, killings, mutilations and the use of child soldiers.

How best to deal with crimes against humanity varies between and within cultures, and short of turning back the clock there are no perfect answers. Cobban properly asks which approach is best suited to healing nations, and the answer naturally depends in part on the country concerned. It is a complicated topic that raises many issues including what the goals should be, how one goes about calculating the trade-offs that result, what works, how you measure the results, and who has the right to decide.

In Cambodia's case those questions were not asked of its people, although some NGO workers in the late 1990s did show videos of South Africa's TRC process and the 1961 trial in Jerusalem of the Nazi Adolf Eichmann and asked people which they preferred. Cambodians felt a TRC format – in which victims face their perpetrators – was too confrontational. And given

---

12. As cited in Cobban, op. cit., pp. 17–18. The emphasis is in Cobban's text.

that few Cambodians have faith in their corrupt judiciary, most of them favoured a court with international involvement. Although their opinion was not sought, the hybrid format of the ECCC, then, did partly match what these Cambodians felt was suitable.

WHILE SOME IN THE human rights community and elsewhere view the formation of war crimes tribunals like the ECCC as a success, American legal scholar Peter Maguire holds that such courts by their very existence constitute a failure to have acted in the first place. It might appear at first glance a contrary view, but Maguire is far from alone in holding it.

A trenchant critic of the practice (though not the theory) of international law, Maguire notes that the UN and its member states failed in the 1990s to act in wars as diverse as Sierra Leone, the former Yugoslavia and East Timor in which civilians were murdered with impunity.[13] Instead of intervening early on, the international community established war crimes courts after the event that delivered a form of justice he has described as 'selective, uneven and absurdly expensive'. The ECCC was similarly 'all about failure and three decades of cynicism'.[14]

Maguire is one of a number of academics and commentators who reject the notion that war crimes trials can deliver truth, reconciliation or healing; in his mind these are nebulous concepts touted by 'therapeutic legalists' that cannot be measured and that do not fall within the scope of a judicial process. At best, he holds that such trials 'can punish the guilty and exonerate the innocent'.

'The idea that war crimes trials can "re-educate" societies is based upon the assumption that the Nuremberg trials transformed Nazis into law-abiding democrats,' Maguire said. 'Neither assumption stands up to analysis.'[15]

This analysis is not widely known because 'the lines separating journalism, scholarship and advocacy grew extremely blurry during the 1990s,'

---

13. For a comprehensive rendering of his position, see *Law and War: International War & American History*, Peter Maguire (Columbia University Press, revised edition, 2010). For his criticisms of the ECCC itself, see *Facing Death in Cambodia*, Peter Maguire (Columbia University Press, 2005).

14. *Phnom Penh Post*, May 6, 2009. Maguire's comment on cynicism relates to the fact that for decades – before, during and after Democratic Kampuchea – the Cambodian people were sold short by, among others, China, the US, Thailand and the UN (which recognised the Khmer Rouge as the rightful holders of Cambodia's seat at the UN for more than a decade after 1979). In the same interview – 'Bridging ideals and realities' – Maguire also criticised the ECCC for its slow approach: 'This court has taken more time to indict a handful of geriatric Khmer Rouge leaders than it took to try every single (5,000 plus) German and Japanese war criminals [*sic*] after WWII.'

15. Ibid.

he added, around the time that war crimes courts became imprinted in the public's consciousness as a solution for serious breaches of international law. By then merely criticising the practice of international law, he said, 'was considered to be in bad taste in most academic circles', and that has helped drive a widespread and mistaken perception of war crimes courts and their function.

The solution, Maguire has written elsewhere, will not be found in adding more law to the international canon.

'Today, despite the most comprehensive set of laws governing war and international relations in human history, the oldest and most basic distinction, the one between soldier and civilian, is fast disappearing,' Maguire wrote in *Law and War*. 'Having just concluded the bloodiest century in the history of man, is it enough to seek salvation in new codes of international criminal law? More laws are not necessary; what is necessary if we are to avoid an even bloodier twenty-first century is the will to enforce the laws that exist.'[16]

Others go further. British academic Stephen Hopgood has long been an opponent of the practice of imposing what he regards as Western-driven (and often legally coded) concepts of human rights. Hopgood views war crimes courts as a relic of a failed effort by the West to impose a new imperialism on the world, and holds that this West-driven model is on the verge of collapse as US power declines and other nations such as China, India and Brazil rise.

Broadly, Hopgood reckons the answer lies in human rights being locally derived rather than externally imposed.[17] In this, it seems to me, Hopgood's view is not too removed from Cobban's, which is that solutions to atrocities should come from the affected communities themselves.

IN CONTRAST TO THE BLOOD, heat, thirst and violence of S-21, the courtroom of the ECCC is sanitised, comfortable and measured. There is bottled water, there are rules of conduct and there are regular breaks. Air-conditioners purr as the press beams to the world images from the trial of a key member of this once closed society. Even the threat of sentencing is civilised: because Cambodia outlawed capital punishment in 1989, the maximum tariff is life imprisonment. The ironies are legion and I doubt they are lost on Duch.

---

16. Maguire, *Law and War*, op. cit., p. 212.

17. For his complete treatment of this subject, see *The Endtimes of Human Rights*, Stephen Hopgood (Cornell University, 2013).

Beneath the hybrid logo is the raised wooden bench where, facing the spectators, the red-robed judges sit: three Cambodian, two international. The leading Cambodian judge, Nil Nonn, is the président of the Trial Chamber and it falls to him to maintain order and keep the process moving. Square-faced, Nil Nonn eases slowly into his role over the weeks, a focused, brooding and at times hectoring and insensitive presence.

His fellow Cambodian judges – Ya Sokhan and You Ottara – are less visible and will play only minor roles. It will be the international judges who most often make the running. New Zealand's former governor-general, Dame Silvia Cartwright, who was once a High Court judge, commonly leads when the five huddle to discuss questions of process, and is the sole judge to whom one could imagine Nil Nonn deferring. In court Cartwright is gravitas personified, issuing succinct, probing questions. Making up the quintet is the bespectacled Jean-Marc Lavergne, a French appeal court judge with school-boyish looks who seems most at ease when questioning Duch for hours on end.

Directly below the judges are the courtroom administration staff, a string of foreign and Cambodian nationals obscured from view behind flat-screen terminals. To the right of the bench and the left of the audience are the prosecution. Opposite them is the defence section where Duch usually sits behind his brace of lawyers, one foreign, one Cambodian. The authority of the tribunal is scripted in coloured gowns: judges in red, prosecution in purple, lawyers in black.

The French-influenced civil law system means that anyone whom the court recognises as having suffered from the crimes with which Duch has been charged – people such as Neary and Martine – are entitled to join in as civil parties. In a first for an international war crimes court, 93 civil parties are participating.[18] This enlightened approach adds humanity to what can become a dry legal process.

Nil Nonn opens proceedings 'in the name of the Cambodian people and the United Nations' to state that Duch is charged with crimes against humanity, war crimes and crimes under Cambodia's 1956 Penal Code including murder and torture.

He does not mention the remit of the ECCC, which is tasked with trying the 'surviving senior leaders' of the Khmer Rouge and those regarded as 'most responsible' for crimes committed during the movement's rule

18. Three civil parties later withdrew from the trial.

between April 17, 1975, and January 6, 1979. Those parameters are important: they cover the two categories of defendant and the dates between which the crimes must have taken place. Those dates bracket the day Phnom Penh fell to Pol Pot's forces and the final full day that the Khmer Rouge held the capital before it was wrested from them by a joint force of Vietnamese troops and Khmer Rouge defectors.

Also left unsaid are the limitations of politics, cash and time, which mean the court will not examine the involvement of nations such as the United States, China, Vietnam, Thailand, Australia or the United Kingdom. It will not examine the actions of Cambodian politicians like Sihanouk either. These are important exclusions, but international justice is a highly political process and there is limited appetite domestically or internationally for this tribunal.

Nearly two dozen lawyers are involved, from Duch's defence to the prosecution and the civil party groups, yet it is the international defence lawyer, French national François Roux, who will dominate this trial. Roux, a diminutive man with a shock of hair and an engaging smile, is referred to by the French legal custom of *maître* or master. He is adept at the sharp riposte, and through a mixture of courtroom theatrics and dramatic flair will prove the most memorable player on this stage. (With Roux, who somewhat resembles the 1970s TV detective Columbo, it does at times seem a stage.)

Roux's rhetorical skills were in evidence at an earlier hearing when he outlined his thoughts on the purpose of transitional justice. Citing French writer Pierre Hazan, he told the bench that a crime against humanity 'unbinds humans, but transitional justice seeks to accomplish the reverse journey' by uniting society once more. From there he segued into reconciliation, again quoting Hazan's words that the process required victims and perpetrators to 'manage to accept the past' and recognise 'the humanity of the other, that they accept each other and that they be capable of contemplating the possibility of constructing a positive relationship'.

It is little coincidence that this will prove a central plank of Roux's strategy, and that the audience, but really the judges, must seek to recognise the humanity in his client. There were glimpses too of Roux's style, a mix of the theatrical and the combative, when he ridiculed the prosecution's position in order to hammer home a point in emotive tones.

'Please keep in mind just this one major question,' Roux had chastised the prosecutors. 'Have you ever seen a child, who in his childhood or her childhood was dreaming of one day becoming an executioner?'

Understand the facts behind my client's decline, Roux was asking, and only then render judgment.

NIL NONN SUMMONS DUCH to the witness box where the defendant stands to answer the first question, a formality.

'My name is Kaing Guek Eav, alias Duch,' he replies.

It is shortly after 10am on Monday March 30, 2009, and these are Duch's first words at trial. Despite the extraordinariness of the crimes with which he is charged, there is much about Duch that is quite ordinary. He is of average height with bad teeth, jug ears, a small paunch and a flop of grey hair. A surfeit of prison time and regular meals have filled out the narrow face familiar from photographs of his time running S-21, but his eyes remain keen and alert.

For the rest of Duch's nine-month trial he will be constantly in the spotlight and, as it turns out, being the centre of attention is a position in which he revels. It allows him to watch hawk-eyed, assessing evidence, weighing up testimony, consulting documents, accepting this, rejecting that. As the defendant, Duch is not formally in control of proceedings but he is always heard and the bench seems to respect his opinion and recall.

Because his is the first trial of a former member of the Khmer Rouge it generates extraordinary media interest and a scrum descends on Phnom Penh. On opening day the big beasts of international rolling news – the BBC, CNN, Al-Jazeera and many others – jam the pressroom at the court building 15 kilometres from the city centre. Also crammed in are the locally based wire services such as Associated Press, Reuters, AFP, and my soon-to-be employer the German Press Agency dpa. There are reporters for foreign newspapers and radio stations, local newspapers, TV and radio, and there are numerous freelancers for whom Cambodia has long proved a fascinating place to work.

Not for me, though, the overcrowded hubbub of the pressroom. I choose to sit inside the court in one of the seats reserved for the media. The pressroom has a TV feed from a single vantage point but being inside the auditorium allows me to watch what I want. In the pressroom your line of sight is at the mercy of the camera technician, but inside the auditorium, once the huge white curtain sweeps away to reveal the stage, you can focus on whatever you choose until such time as the curtain is swooshed back. Being here lets me keep an eye on Duch, observing his movements, gestures and habits. Months later that freedom to view would answer one important question.

The first entry in my notebook lists Duch's age: 66. The third entry notes 'microphone problems' and after that the jottings build up a potted history of Duch's many names. He was born Kaing Chheav in 1942 but three months later his father nicknamed him Yin Keav on the advice of a bogus soothsayer. When he started school he called himself Kaing Keav and by 1957 the eager teenage student was Kaing Guek Eav, having largely reverted to his birth name and added the name 'Guek' with his father's permission. A decade later he recast himself in revolutionary mode with the moniker Duch, after a boy in a book who stood up straight in front of his teacher. Later still, when he was in China between 1986 and 1988, he renamed himself Hang Pin, the name he was using when Nic Dunlop found him. We hear too that Duch's father died in 1990 but that his mother is still alive. Duch's wife, by whom he had four children, died in 1995.

Then a court officer begins reading aloud the lengthy indictment, essentially the prosecution's case. It outlines the period of Khmer Rouge rule following its victory over Lon Nol's Khmer Republic: how it enslaved the population, evacuated the cities and tried to turn 'new' people into peasants; arrested, tortured and killed hundreds of thousands; and where Duch fitted into this regime.

'The old legal structures were replaced by re-education, interrogation and security centres where former Khmer Republic officials and supporters, as well as others accused of offences against the CPK [the Communist Party of Kampuchea], were detained and executed,' the court officer says. 'This network of security centres was supplemented by a programme of surveillance at all levels of the regime which aimed to identify, report and eliminate the potential enemies of those in control of the Party.'[19]

In that way, she continues, vast numbers of people connected to the Khmer Republic or who were believed linked to it or to the enemy classes were arrested and killed. Many were taken to S-21, which was 'unique in the network of security centres given its direct link to the Central Committee and its role in the detention and execution of CPK cadres'.

The Central Committee was the CPK's policymaking body. Real power rested in the smaller Standing Committee.

With that, S-21 heaves directly into view as the place where the CPK's policy of 'smashing enemies' was carried out.

---

19. ECCC trial transcript, March 30, 2009, p. 10.

'The primary role of S-21 was to implement "the Party political line regarding the enemy" according to which prisoners "absolutely had to be smashed",' she says, explaining that the term 'smash' meant 'kill'. 'Every prisoner who arrived at S-21 was destined for execution.'

The court officer outlines S-21's function and operation: summaries of how arrests were carried out, who was taken there, the circumstances of those imprisoned, the system of confessions, why detainees were photographed ('in the event they escaped,' Duch had told the investigating judges), and the medical experiments carried out on prisoners while they were still alive.

After more than an hour another officer takes over. The list continues, starting with S-21's interrogation procedures ('the end only came when the confessions were considered completed'), Duch's formulation for three methods of interrogation (cold, hot and chewing), and his instructions to interrogators ('break the prisoner by propaganda or break him by torture'). We hear too the vague boundaries of Duch's involvement: that he largely denied torturing prisoners but that he admitted ordering his subordinates to do so. On at least one occasion Duch permitted an interrogator to torture a prisoner to death, telling him he would not be punished for doing so.

We hear too how the final stage in the lives of most prisoners was to be taken to Chhoeung Ek, where the execution squad was told by Duch that 'hitting their necks with the steel bar would not kill them, so their throat had to be cut too'. The policy was to kill entire families, not just 'enemies', and to that end, the officer notes, on one day in July 1977 the executioners at Chhoeung Ek murdered 160 children. Other children were killed by being dropped from the third-floor walkway at S-21.

The clerk reads that 'no fewer than 1,000' prisoners died after all of their blood was drained, leaving them 'unconscious and gasping', with the blood bags sent to a government hospital for injured Khmer Rouge soldiers.

It takes more than two hours to read the indictment. By mid-afternoon the tribunal concludes its first session and we have been introduced to the savage world Duch helped to create just 15 kilometres from here.

IT WAS NIC DUNLOP'S OBSESSIVE QUEST to find Duch that saw the former commandant of S-21 eventually unmasked. Dunlop wrote that after the 1979 fall of Phnom Penh, Duch had disappeared 'into the murky world of secret camps' that populated the western border region before reuniting with his wife and two young children in Samlaut district, which was then under Pol Pot's control. Those were dangerous days for Duch. Brother Number Two Nuon Chea, the Khmer Rouge's chief ideologue and Duch's former boss, had destroyed his own archive and was livid that Duch had failed to do the same with S-21's documents. The fact that S-21's archives had fallen into the hands of the loathed Vietnamese had put Nuon Chea in a bad light.[20]

For his folly, Duch was given a demeaning job in logistics. Oddly he was not killed despite the amount of incriminating information he carried in his head. Dunlop believed Duch was protected by his former boss, the defence minister Son Sen, whose children Duch ended up teaching. The leaders might also have reasoned that Duch was more valuable alive, with his logical brain and hard-won knowledge of their enemies. Once the Khmer Rouge returned to power, as they believed they would, Duch could again prove himself useful weeding out those whose treachery had ensured a Vietnamese-backed victory.

Dunlop's pursuit took him across Cambodia on regular visits from his home in Bangkok, a creased photograph of Duch accompanying him on every trip. As the Khmer Rouge imploded, Dunlop visited places that for decades had been off-limits. It was on one of those trips in 1999, less than a year after the death of Pol Pot, that Dunlop ventured into Samlaut with a mine clearance organisation. Samlaut had been the site of the 1967 uprising that marked the start of the Khmer Rouge's road to victory and was among the last areas to return to government control in the late 1990s. While the mine clearance staff met local leaders, Dunlop went for a stroll. It was then that a man called Hang Pin, wearing an American Refugee Committee T-shirt, walked up to Dunlop and started talking to him in English about his camera. Dunlop was convinced that Hang Pin, with his bad teeth, gaunt face and prominent ears, was Duch, and surreptitiously snapped a photograph.

A few weeks later Dunlop returned to Samlaut with US journalist Nate Thayer. The two men confronted Duch, who told them he had converted to Christianity, an unusual path in this predominantly Buddhist nation. Thayer put it to Duch that he had been part of the Khmer Rouge's security services during Democratic Kampuchea. No, Duch replied, I translated textbooks for the education ministry. Thayer repeated the question and Duch again dissembled, but when Duch realised Thayer had the previous

---

20. Dunlop, *The Lost Executioner*, op. cit., p. 199.

year interviewed Pol Pot and *Ta* Mok[21] – the latter arguably the Khmer Rouge's most brutal commander – he knew the game was up.

'It is God's will that you are here,' he told them. 'Now my future is in God's hands.'[22]

Softly at first Duch began to talk of the 'very bad things' he had done and acknowledged it was time he faced the consequences. In the first half of his life, he said, he had served men and communism, believing that God was bad. Now he wanted to help his fellow man and do God's work.

In the article Dunlop and Thayer wrote for the *Far Eastern Economic Review*, they said Duch seemed genuinely sorry as he pored over documents that the two had brought from S-21 – confessions with his handwritten comments and notations from his two bosses, Nuon Chea and Son Sen.[23] Those who had died, Duch told the men, 'were good people'.[24]

'There were many men who were innocent,' he said. 'I have great difficulty in my life thinking that the people who died did nothing wrong.'

He spoke for two days with Dunlop and Thayer, and later for a further three days with UN rights worker Christophe Peschoux, whose notes run to nearly 30,000 words and which cover Duch's life before, during and after S-21. Duch told Peschoux of the difficulties he encountered after being appointed by Vorn Vet in 1971 to run M-13A, the precursor to S-21. M-13A's function, Duch said, was to interrogate prisoners who were suspected of spying for the Lon Nol regime. The experience with this first prisoner, as it turned out, defined Duch's subsequent approach.

'I would return a little later to interrogate him again,' Duch said of that initial interrogation, 'ensuring he understood that if he lied he would be killed, but if he confessed his life would be saved. He would confess.'[25]

After that, Duch wrote up the prisoner's confession and claimed he tried to have him released. Vorn Vet refused, asking Duch whether he was prepared to take responsibility for the prisoner and whether he would feel confident proposing him as a candidate for the CPK 'even after five years of

---

21. '*Ta*' is an honorific meaning 'grandfather'.

22. Dunlop, op. cit., p. 272.

23. 'Duch Confesses', Nic Dunlop and Nate Thayer, *Far Eastern Economic Review*, May 6, 1999, p. 76.

24. Dunlop, *The Lost Executioner*, p. 274.

25. 'Interview with Kaing Guek Eav, also known as Duch, Chairman of S-21', Christophe Peschoux, (unpublished manuscript), p. 6.

following his progress and re-educating him'.

'How will you be able to trust him since he has already once been a spy in the enemy's pay? Only people absolutely trustworthy and reliable can become members of the Party,' Vorn Vet told him.

In other words, said Duch, the choice he had been given was no choice at all: to risk his own life for the prisoner's. Since Duch would not do that, releasing the prisoner was out of the question. And so the modus operandi was established. In this war there could be no grey area and, Duch concluded, that set the parameters of his position.

'Once arrested, a spy or enemy could not be released,' Duch told Peschoux. 'We had to kill them.'[26]

Within days of Dunlop finding him, Duch was arrested by the Cambodian authorities. It was no coincidence that his luck ran out when it did. The end of the Cold War meant the past was about to catch up with a number of the ageing Khmer Rouge leaders as the movement stumbled towards its end, which fittingly was a violent internecine struggle. In this unfamiliar post-Cold War world the Khmer Rouge were an embarrassment to their former sponsors – China, the United States and Thailand among others – and besides, priorities had changed. Trade was replacing dirty wars and unholy alliances as the preferred means of exerting influence.

Ever so slowly the wheels of international justice, oiled by political expediencies on all sides, began to turn. Duch was an obvious candidate for trial, as were his former boss Nuon Chea and the movement's last leader *Ta Mok*, a man whose blood lust was extraordinary even by the Khmer Rouge's standards. By the time Duch was jailed at a military prison, Son Sen was dead, consumed in the movement's death throes, as was Pol Pot, who died in his sleep in 1998 as government forces closed in on his holdout near the Thai border.[27]

Four years after Duch's arrest, the Cambodian government and the UN signed the agreement that established the tribunal. Four years later, in July 2007, Duch was transferred from the military prison to the ECCC. A further 19 months came and went before he spoke his first words at trial, the phrase broadcast live across Cambodia.

'My name is Kaing Guek Eav, alias Duch.'

THE PROSECUTION OPENS ITS CASE on the morning of the

---

26. Peschoux, ibid., p. 6.

27. Short, op. cit., p. 442.

second day of Duch's trial describing S-21 as 'an integral and indeed a vital part of a widespread and systematic attack on the entire population'. Duch's crimes, says Cambodian co-prosecutor Chea Leang, were part of this attack.

'Their ultimate goal was the establishment of a "pure" communist society unlike any seen before,' she tells the bench, 'although the Stalinist, Chinese and Vietnamese models did influence the Khmer communists. To ensure the success of its revolution the CPK sought to eradicate all those it considered "enemies".'

With that the prosecution starts to lay out its case: the various charges that fall within international law, such as war crimes and crimes against humanity, as well as those that constitute breaches of Cambodian law. Chea Leang says the targeting of the regime's enemies began with immediate effect with the execution of Lon Nol politicians and senior military figures and was later extended to soldiers and bureaucrats of the defeated regime.

'The CPK also pursued an explicit policy of eliminating members of economic classes that were considered beyond redemption: the land owner, the shopkeeper, the merchant, the educated and all those tainted by association with those classes,' she says.

As the CPK pursued its revolution, she continues, the Khmer Rouge killed vast numbers of 'new people', as well as ethnic Vietnamese, Muslim Chams, Buddhist monks and intellectuals coaxed back from overseas; and 'the backbone of this persecution was a nationwide network of security centres which were created throughout Cambodia'. S-21, the prosecution contends, stood at its apex. While most people deemed enemies of the regime were brutalised and executed at prisons at the local level, those who were thought to be more significant were propelled up the chain.

'Eventually, certain prisoners would end up at S-21; the end of the line for anyone unfortunate enough to reach it,' says Chea Leang.

Next to take the floor is the international co-prosecutor Robert Petit, a Canadian, who lays out the use of torture to extract confessions.

'Victims were beaten with rattan sticks and whips, electrocuted, had toenails and fingernails pulled out, were suffocated with plastic bags forcibly held over their heads, and were stripped naked and had their genitals electrocuted,' says Petit.

It was Duch who taught these methods, Petit says, and it was Duch who encouraged the use of his favoured technique: beating prisoners with sticks.

Petit says Duch's position that he merely passed on orders from his superiors was 'implausible, unsupported by the evidence and cannot be believed'. The TV screens inside the court flash to pages of execution logs, of which there were 'hundreds and hundreds' with each line on each page comprising a life. Petit then turns to Duch's efforts to limit his responsibility, which will lie at the heart of the trial.

'The accused has also stated during the investigation and through his counsels' statements that he recognises his responsibility for those crimes,' says Petit. 'However, to what extent is that admission of responsibility as framed and argued by the accused and his counsel truly supported by the evidence?'

This, Petit tells the judges, is likely the most contentious issue they will have to consider, and yet, he feels, one that should not prove too taxing.

'The accused has attempted to describe his authority as limited and in name only; his participation in the crimes perfunctory, essentially relaying orders; and his commitment to the criminal policies of the CPK and of S-21 reluctant and made under duress,' he says. 'We submit however that the evidence examined as a whole will establish beyond any doubt that the accused had independent authority within the administration of S-21, that he used that authority knowingly and actively in the commission of the crimes, and that he was committed until the very end to the goals and success of S-21.'

The prosecution says it will prove Duch 'ordered, planned, supervised and participated' in arresting prisoners; that he devised S-21's 'inhumane conditions' and not only ordered but took part in torturing and executing prisoners; that he made no effort to improve conditions at S-21; and that he was not merely a facilitator, passing on instructions to torture and execute, but that documents bearing his handwriting showed he was actively involved in taking those decisions.

In mitigation, Petit adds, the prosecution acknowledges that Duch cooperated with the investigating judges, took part in reconstructions where he met victims, helped to authenticate documents and in so doing had helped to determine the truth.

'The accused alleges that his cooperation is rooted in a sense of contrition. He acknowledges the immorality of his past actions and indeed has asked forgiveness from his victims either directly during the reconstructions, or through his lawyer,' Petit says. 'I have no doubt that he will do so again before you at the first opportunity. But how genuine is that contrition?'

THE PROSECUTION IS FOLLOWED by the defence, and it is Duch's national lawyer, Kar Savuth, who opens. Kar Savuth is a heavy-faced man who can prove combative but who is used to winning with little effort. That is because he also acts for former Khmer Rouge soldier and Cambodian Prime Minister Hun Sen when the premier takes action in the domestic courts, which are firmly under the thumb of the executive. Having Hun Sen's lawyer representing Duch confirms for many their belief that the premier wants to control key elements of this tribunal to ensure that nothing will emerge to implicate or embarrass his ex-Khmer Rouge colleagues now in his government.

In Cambodia a great speech is by definition a long speech, with logic and substance less meaningful than word count and delivery. Kar Savuth shows us that he is an exponent of the great Cambodian speech and in his ramblings he provides the surprise of opening week with a string of arguments questioning the tribunal's jurisdiction. In summary: Duch ran one prison but there were nearly 200 others, so it is unfair to prosecute only him.[28]

He follows that with a comparison of killings at different prisons: while thousands of S-21's inmates were indeed murdered, another prison saw an estimated 150,000 people put to death.[29] By Kar Savuth's count S-21 ranked 10th in the numbers of murdered inmates, leading him to conclude that Duch is being prosecuted because he killed fewer inmates than other prison chiefs, and wondering what sort of lesson that conveys. He adds that he does not expect the tribunal to find any and all of these missing prison chiefs; his argument is merely to prove his stance that trying Duch is inherently unfair.

'I just don't want Duch to be a scapegoat,' he says unconvincingly.

Kar Savuth raises eyebrows further when he conflates the two potential classes of defendant – the 'senior leaders and those most responsible'. This, he says, is a single category, because the senior leaders are those who were most responsible. Therefore anyone who was not one of the Khmer Rouge's 14 senior leaders is by definition not most responsible and ought not to be on trial. Duch, he says, was not one of the 14 senior leaders.

'It's better not to try anyone rather than trying some but leaving the

---

28. With this argument Kar Savuth neatly ignored the fact that most other prison chiefs were either dead or had disappeared long before.

29. This figure was almost certainly hugely inflated, although many thousands were murdered at Chong Chruoy prison, which is the centre Kar Savuth referred to here. Today there is little left of the former prison, which lies in a rural area in Kampong Chhnang province some 60 kilometres north-west of Phnom Penh.

others at large,' Kar Savuth says, adding that to do otherwise would be unconstitutional and a breach of Cambodia's sovereignty.

His arguments draw an angry response from the prosecution, which says the defence must state unambiguously whether it plans to challenge the legality of the proceedings against their client. The time to raise such preliminary objections came and went two months earlier, and at that time the defence said only that it would object to the ECCC trying Duch for crimes committed under national law.[30] Petit suggests that Duch appears to be running two contradictory defence strategies, and that is unacceptable.

'I am, I must say, shocked that over two years into these proceedings, on the day that the substantive hearings start, after having heard on numerous occasions and quite eloquently ... how the accused wants the proceedings to go, wants to admit his culpability and wants to receive a fair trial and sentence ... rather he should walk out free because we don't have the jurisdiction to prosecute him,' says an exasperated Petit.

LATER ROUX ADDRESSES THE COURT, and where Kar Savuth's delivery was woolly and flawed, Roux's is fluid and precise. The judges will need to decide, Roux says, whether his client is sincere in his expressions of regret, and how much freedom Duch enjoyed when running S-21. And, he adds, the court will need to consider the realities of working for such a regime.

'All the experts agree that this dictatorship operated on the basis of the twin pillars of terror and secrecy,' Roux says. 'It was because of the terror that every link in the chain of command acted zealously to please superiors who were the ones who issued the orders, and this is the reason why Duch [said]: "I gave the orders to my subordinates – I assume responsibility."'

Roux agrees that following orders is no defence, but says the bench must consider the realities of the regime as a mitigating factor given that those who did not do so risked being killed. And, he adds, since the day he first met Duch, his client has acknowledged his guilt and wishes to make amends by telling what he knows. He agreed in 2008 to return to S-21 and to Chhoeung Ek to see the sites of his crimes, for example, and specifically asked to spend time alone there.

It was the first time Duch had been to either place since fleeing in

---

30. The defence objected to the Cambodian government's 2004 extension of the statute of limitations on serious crimes to 30 years in order to bring charges under national law.

1979, and, although the media were barred from the visit, he reportedly wept after seeing the tree against which babies and young children – the offspring of executed S-21 inmates – were beaten to death.

'During these proceedings you will see the film of this re-enactment and you will have the opportunity to see the tears he shed, the tears that were shed between the victims and Duch when he spoke to them,' Roux says. 'Who can say that at that time, none of them were honest?'

And, he adds, Duch's willingness to confront his past shows that he believes he can contribute positively to humanity.

'By asking for forgiveness from the victims, by addressing himself to his people, by addressing himself to young people,' Roux says. 'By telling them: "This is it, this is what we have done, this is what we fell into, this is what you should never repeat."'

Not that Roux is suggesting that his client is a model of probity; and yes, he admits there are some points about which Duch is still not entirely truthful, but who among us could not say we would be the same had we too committed such terrible deeds? Turning to the victims, Roux warns that although the civil party lawyers will get to question Duch, the victims should temper their hopes about the answers.

'Your main question, and I am aware of this, is: "Why all of this?"' he says. 'I am not sure that Duch on his own has the answer to this tragic question: "Why all of this?" Why these scenes – these unthinkable scenes, these unbearable scenes at S-21? Why these scenes that dehumanise the victims, but which also dehumanise at the same time those that perpetrated these atrocities?'

Over the coming months much of this will become familiar as vintage Roux: emphasising his client's contrition and victimhood, and asking us to concede that this man, while undoubtedly guilty of terrible crimes, has seen the error of his ways. It is a seductive message, and one that Roux returns to as he wraps up with a rhetorical flourish.

'Will we be able at the end of these hearings to … return to the victims all of their humanity?' he asks. 'But also to be able to allow … the one who had exited humanity to return to humanity?'

This, he concludes grandly, is what is at stake.

IT IS NOT UNTIL the following morning – Day 3, April 1, 2009 – that the bench asks Kar Savuth to explain his odd opening remarks. Did he merely want to highlight his thoughts or is he asking the ECCC to rule on issues of legality and responsibility? Kar Savuth replies that his words are merely food for the judges to consider. Four times in as many minutes he assures the bench that he will not challenge the court's jurisdiction and says he is 'quite aware' that it is too late to raise those as grounds for dispute. However, he does suggest the prosecution should draft a list of everyone it considers most responsible for crimes committed under Democratic Kampuchea and go after them too. In that way the court would treat all citizens equally.

With that the tribunal moves on. By now most of the foreign media have left, because although Duch's story fits the definition of news as 'man bites dog', the current affairs machine has a short attention span. By the end of the first week the media room holds only locally based journalists. It will fall to us to follow this increasingly Shakespearean tale.

NATIONAL ANTHEM OF DEMOCRATIC KAMPUCHEA

*Glittering red blood which blankets the towns and countryside
of the Kampuchean motherland!*

Blood of our splendid worker-peasants!

Blood of our revolutionary combatants, male and female!

Blood that was transmuted into seething fury, into fierce struggle,

On 17 April, under the revolutionary flag!

Blood that has liberated us from slavery!

Long live the dazzling victory of 17 April!

More grandiose, more meaningful than the Angkor era!

Let us all band together to build Kampuchea,

And a radiant new society,

Democratic, egalitarian and just,

Absolutely determined to rely only on our own forces!

Determined to defend our country at all costs!

Our wonderful land, our glorious Revolution!

Long live! Long live! Long live! New Kampuchea!

Democratic and gloriously prosperous!

*Let us be determined to wave always higher the red
banner of Revolution!*

Let us build our homeland to achieve a Great Leap Forward,

A gigantic, a glorious, a prodigious Leap Forward!

— The national anthem, which was purportedly written by Pol Pot

From *Pol Pot's Little Red Book,* by Henri Locard

CHAPTER EIGHT

LEARNING CURVE: 1971–75

IT IS MEN LIKE DUCH who make revolutions work. Leaders like Pol Pot, Nuon Chea, Son Sen and Hou Youn are the rare birds that soar in the thin revolutionary air, fabricating grand objectives, crafting seductive futures and laying out policies. People like Duch are the implementers. Without the Duchs of this world, without their convictions and passion, the leaders would be alone.

The tireless French academic Henri Locard, who has done extensive research on the prisons of the Khmer Rouge, explains Duch's unique place. We are standing outside the ECCC building during a break and I ask Locard to elaborate on Kar Savuth's point that it is grossly unfair that his client is on trial when the heads of nearly 200 other Khmer Rouge prisons are not.

'There are a number of reasons for that,' Locard replies, his eyes alive behind tinted glasses. 'First, S-21 was really special – very, very special because it was the prison of the centre. Second, Duch was really special. He did this job from 1971 to 1979, for eight years, and I am sure there was no director [at any other prison] who went on for so long.'

The Khmer Rouge's relentless purges were in large part to blame for the absence of prison directors in the dock.

'Every commune had three different leaders, more or less, over that period of three years, eight months and 20 days, and the same is true for prisons,' Locard tells me in his rapid-fire, French-accented English. 'Most of them were purged or killed by the Khmer Rouge themselves.'

Some who survived fled west in early 1979, where 'very naive and sentimental' NGO workers in the refugee camps inside Thailand did not distinguish between Cambodians who were victims and those who were perpetrators.

'So they passed themselves off as victims and now they are in America, Australia, Canada and France – quite a few of them, if they are still alive,' Locard concludes. 'But they would be very difficult to trace because we only have their revolutionary names.'

DUCH'S FIRST OPPORTUNITY to address the court comes on day two. It represents a chance to tell his side of the story but, more importantly, it is an occasion to impress the judges that the person on trial is a different man, contrite and willing – eager even – to face the consequences. He starts suitably wide. Between the mid-1960s until April 1975, all participants in the civil war committed terrible crimes, he says, but after victory it was the Communist Party of Kampuchea alone that was responsible for 'staggering' violations. As a CPK member, Duch acknowledges that he bears moral responsibility for what was wrought and expresses his 'regret and deepest sorrow' for the crimes of the Party.

Duch's focus then narrows as he turns to S-21. I was legally responsible for what happened there, he tells the bench, 'especially the acts of torture and the executions'.

'Now, I would like these people to know that I wish to apologise, and I would like you to consider my intentions,' he says. 'I do not ask that you forgive me here and now. I know that the crimes I committed against the lives of those people, including women and children, are intolerably and unforgivably serious crimes. My plea is that you leave the door open for me to seek forgiveness.'

It is a reasonable request. Let me prove myself to you, Duch is asking, and if at the end you are satisfied, then and only then consider whether my apologies and subsequent actions are sufficient atonement.

The benefit of hindsight has brought Duch deep pain, he continues, and today he feels wracked with remorse and appalled by what happened, not least by what he ordered his staff to do. Yet he did not perpetrate these unspeakable acts unbidden and with free will. They were committed under the terrifying aegis of *Angkar* in which he was 'a hostage, a mere puppet in the criminal regime'.

'I am sure that the general public now regards me as a cowardly and inhumane person,' Duch admits, asking that people consider that he acted to protect his life and those of his family for whom that period was also a matter of life and death, a risk that was amplified as S-21 took in growing numbers of Khmer Rouge.

'To challenge the order from the top, although I knew that the order was criminal, I never dared to even think about it,' he says.

Duch stresses too that he was a mere implementer of policy, his hands tied; that he tried to avoid being placed at M-13A and S-21, and that once there he sought to be transferred; that he had no right to release any prisoner sent to S-21; and that he did not torture or kill anyone but simply ordered others to do so. Only indirectly, he is saying, is there blood on my hands.

Duch's opening remarks are heavy on contrition yet they are leavened too by emphasising that he had no room for manoeuvre. In the coming months we will hear many more expressions of remorse, and the regrets that emerge from key moments in his life: joining the CPK, his appointment to run M-13A, and his time at S-21.

But words do not prove sincerity and many are sceptical of Duch's approach. Tactically Duch has little option because his signature appears on many thousands of execution orders. His obsession with paperwork has proved his undoing and the archives bear witness to his deep complicity in the torture and execution of more than 12,000 people. Duch's comments pepper the confessions, and instructions such as this leave no room to plead ignorance: 'If [the prisoner Ney Saran] continues to hide his treacherous linkages … he should be executed and not be allowed to play games with the Party any more.'

Duch's jottings are evidence of a casual brutality. One note states: 'Not yet confessed. To be tortured.' Others in his neat script demand that specific prisoners be killed, such as a document to *Angkar* in which he recommends that a batch of 115 people be 'smashed'. *Angkar* agreed. Or this notation relating to a group of 29 prisoners: 'Suggest interrogation of four persons and kill the rest.'

And then there is this three-word sentence in which Duch instructs his violent bodyguard Peng: 'Kill them all.'[1] It was May 1978 and he was referring to a group of 17 prisoners brought to S-21 from the Eastern Zone, which at the time was undergoing the most violent massacres of Democratic Kampuchea with cadres murdering tens of thousands of ordinary people. Of this batch of 17 peasants, two were boys aged 9 and two were girls aged 10. Five of the others were not yet 16 years old.[2]

---

1. Even in the savage environment of S-21, the 28-year-old Peng stood out for his murderous nature. Vann Nath, the artist, was terrified of Peng, whom he referred to as 'a brutal young butcher'. See Chandler, *Voices from S-21*, p. 23.

2. Kiernan, *The Pol Pot Regime*, op. cit., p. 394.

This mountain of evidence has left the defence with two options: dispute the court's legitimacy to try Duch, which was what Kar Savuth flirted with in his opening remarks, or plead mitigating circumstances in an effort to get a reduced sentence. Since there is no doubt that Duch falls within the court's remit – he is considered to be one of those 'most responsible' for the crimes of the period – it is little surprise to see Roux settle on the second approach. In doing so he will repeatedly emphasise his client's regret, his assistance to the tribunal, and his lack of room to manoeuvre.

Roux will also rely on one other plank: redemption. Here is a man, he tells the court, who recognises what he did, yet what is justice but a chance to reform? This man has done that already: Duch is apologetic, tearful in a video during his return in 2008 to the former prison, stricken with remorse. For Roux repentance and redemption are key constructs, and they underpin a compelling message that a man who committed such monstrous crimes has seen the error of his ways. Furthermore, says Roux, had Duch tried to flee then he and his family would almost certainly have been captured and executed. Surely one can understand that this system of fear, paranoia, torture and execution – a system Duch was admittedly instrumental in establishing – struck fear even into the hearts of those who had built it?

The prosecution, as expected, rejects much of this, saying Duch's claim to have been a facilitator who merely relayed instructions and documents is not credible. His involvement was far more insidious, says Petit, and the evidence will show he 'ordered, planned, supervised and participated' in arresting prisoners, and that although most such orders came from *Angkar*, some came about at Duch's behest through information he sent up the chain of command. It will also prove he 'devised the inhumane conditions of detention in S-21', that he took part in the interrogation and torture of prisoners, and that he ordered executions. Some witnesses will claim they saw him kill.

By way of showing how devoted the defendant was to his task, Petit reads a note written just a fortnight before the regime was driven from power in which Duch asks *Angkar* to allow him 'please' to arrest another person. It appears in the confession of one Kim Sok and shows Duch 'eagerly asking for another victim'. Taken as a whole, he says, the evidence will show a man who was in control of 'the entire S-21 criminal apparatus' who had the power to arrest, interrogate, torture and kill, and who used that power throughout his time in charge.

BEFORE EXAMINING S-21, the tribunal turns its judicial eye on M-13A, the jungle prison that Duch ran from mid-1971 and one of the places where the Khmer Rouge's perceived enemies were shackled before being interrogated, tortured and executed. M-13A is a natural focus since it was here that Duch spent four years honing his considerable skills.

Because the camp's existence largely pre-dates April 1975, almost none of the crimes committed there fall within the tribunal's remit. Yet examining M-13A does carry risks for the defence since any proof that Duch had killed or tortured at M-13A would colour perceptions of his actions at S-21.

The bench's questions are led by Judge Lavergne and broadly cover the camp's establishment, its function and its form. Duch explains that he was chosen to head M-13, the collective name for M-13A and its associated camp M-13B, because the Party knew he was 'a sincere person who dares not to hide anything', a man of meticulousness and attention to detail.

'In my entire life if I do something, I do it properly,' he says without irony.

M-13B fell somewhere between a transit station and a prison for lesser offenders and it seems its inmates would typically be freed after undergoing education sessions that would inculcate 'a firm class stance'. People taken to M-13A, on the other hand, had almost no chance of leaving. At M-13A, says Duch, 'they were to be tortured, interrogated and smashed, not to be released'.

Duch claims his first experience of inflicting torture came after a man was arrested for crossing into the liberated zone, the area controlled by the Khmer Rouge. When Duch questioned him 'humbly', the prisoner denied he was a Lon Nol spy and claimed he was merely looking to buy a chicken. Yet when two Vietnamese cadres beat him up, the man freely confessed. Duch was livid and later went to work on the prisoner with a whip. Some time after that, Duch tortured another prisoner, a poet, as a way of testing out what he had learned.

'I interrogated him for almost one month, and I beat up the person by myself,' he says. 'That's the truth.'

Duch, ever inquisitive, experimented with different torture techniques to see what worked best. At one point he and a deputy forced a woman prisoner called Sok to submerge herself in the river while clothed and then stand in the cold air. He says this was to avoid beating her to generate a confession but it comes across as a way for two men with limitless power to get a cheap sexual kick. Duch seems to worry the judges will see it that way.

'When she got soaked with water, you could feel the – you could see her physical condition, so I was afraid that we could not hold [back] our emotions, you know, like when we witness such things,' he says awkwardly, '[so] that's why we stopped.'

He also admits that – given the Khmer Rouge's unforgiving approach to sex outside marriage – he had feared that should he or his deputy act on their arousal they would have been killed. And besides, this method did not work: Sok continued to deny she was a spy for the Lon Nol regime. It made no difference, and she was eventually executed.

During these days Duch gives eager testimony. He thanks the judges for their questions, launches into detailed responses and repeatedly apologises. Inevitably this continual repetition of regret while taking some responsibility starts to jar, not least because he regularly couches his words in terms of carrying out orders, a soft blanket to cloak his acts, as one example will show: 'So the crimes in the smashing of the people, although the decision was made from the upper echelon, I was responsible at my level for every smashing order. So the burden still falls on me, it's my responsibility, and I would like to apologise to the souls of those who died. I still cannot forget their names and I would write their names in a book. I can never forget the crimes that fall on my head.'

Duch estimates that no more than 300 people were executed at M-13A, but that seems far too low given that there were between 15 and 30 prisoners there at any one time and that it was in operation for four years. What is clear is that, despite the lack of food, few prisoners starved because most were executed before long. None of his 30 or so staff died of hunger.

Duch says he instructed his interrogators how to do their work and also outsourced the bloody work of torture and execution down the chain of command. He trained the cadres on the preferred method of killing, which was a wooden stave to the back of the neck, but claims he never visited the execution site even though it was just 100 metres from his office through the forest.

When the questions turn to the veracity of the confessions, which after all was M-13A's purpose, Duch freely admits most were concocted. Speaking as a mathematician, he says, the confessions might be 40 per cent true, and perhaps one in five of those implicated in the confessions were actually guilty of working against the revolution. Later he halves that estimate. Yet it made no difference to the detainees. In four years of operation, just 10 were freed. Duch rightly considers his efforts on that front to be worth 'a drop of water against a large amount of water in a pond' when compared to the number who died.

Knowing it can hardly hold out Duch as a good man, the defence seeks to fix the boundaries of his behaviour. Kar Savuth asks Duch whether he is a killer. I passed on orders to execute, Duch replies, but, 'I never killed anyone with my own hands,' he says. 'Ever.'

With that line drawn, Roux takes over. He skirts the topic of torture and instead gets Duch to talk about the regime's unflinching stance on secrecy and on obeying orders ('that you yourself' carried out 'in a feeling of fear', Roux helpfully suggests). Duch talks about the self-criticism sessions – as important to the cadres as food – in which they learned the political lines, got rid of their personal stances and built a collective outlook as the Khmer Rouge subsumed the individual.

Duch says the killings at M-13A had disturbed him greatly, and that to cope he would recall stanzas of a French poem he had learned by heart at school.[3] He recites the lines to the court:

> *Complaining, weeping, praying – all this is in vain.*
> *Shoulder your lengthy and difficult task,*
> *The way that Destiny sees fit to ask,*
> *Then afterwards, as I have done, suffer and die without complaint.*

Judge Lavergne asks Duch whether he enjoyed this brutal work. No, he replies, but I had no choice.

'Probably it was my fate to do that job,' he says.

IF IT WAS DUCH'S FATE to run M-13A, then it was also the fate of a 30-year-old French anthropologist called François Bizot to be imprisoned there. In late 1971 during the civil war Bizot, a member of the École française d'Extrême-Orient, France's School for Oriental Studies, was researching Cambodian Buddhism with two Cambodian colleagues at a pagoda near Udong, the former royal capital near Phnom Penh, when the three men were captured by Khmer Rouge forces.

Bizot's book tells the story of how he survived being held by Duch for

---

3. The poem is 'La Mort du Loup', or 'The Death of the Wolf', by the nineteenth-century poet Alfred de Vigny.

three months, accused of being a CIA spy.[4] It also reveals Duch's fascination with this educated foreigner. Duch, nearly two years younger than Bizot, had met other foreigners in his youth. However, here in rural Cambodia, surrounded by imprisoned subsistence farmers and uneducated peasant boys whom he had selected to work at M-13A, his interest in Bizot is easy to fathom. Bizot's book is full of remembered conversations between the two men, Bizot shackled, Duch dangerous, on occasion charming, yet always diligent in his work and zealous in his beliefs.

Bizot is the first witness to testify at the tribunal and his experience is noteworthy because he is one of the few whom Duch worked to release. As a foreigner, Bizot is also the one who seems to have grown closest to his captor. He recalls asking Duch who would hit the prisoners. Duch said he sometimes did. He seemed embarrassed to admit that, Bizot remembers, but felt it was a necessary duty.

'He would hit the prisoners because they would lie and because their testimony would come up with contradictions and he hated lying,' the 69-year-old scholar tells the court. 'Lying was abhorrent to him and this kind of job was not at all to his liking but it was the responsibility that *Angkar* had entrusted to him; it was his job and the particular task was part of his duties.'

Bizot spent most of his time at M-13A shackled to a wooden post. Every so often Duch would question him, and over time was convinced that Bizot was not a CIA spy and was indeed a scholar of Cambodian Buddhism. Bizot speculates that the months of conversation humanised him in Duch's eyes, which made it possible for Duch to see 'the man behind the spy'. In their numerous conversations – interrogations really, since Bizot knew the objective was to see whether he would contradict himself – Bizot talked authoritatively on Cambodian Buddhism, on the conservation project at the 800-year-old temple of Angkor Wat, and on ancient manuscripts.

'And therefore sending me to my death became something more difficult than when you send people that you have dehumanised to their deaths, or in any case, people that you did not seek to humanise,' he says.

Releasing him was not a decision Duch could take unilaterally – his reports went up the Party ladder and orders were handed down – yet there is no doubt that Duch went out on a limb and, on Christmas Eve

---

4. *The Gate*, François Bizot (The Harvill Press, 2003). Originally published as *Le Portail* (Editions de la Table Ronde, 2000).

1971, he told Bizot he was to be freed. Bizot did not believe him yet he clung to the possibility that it might be true because 'hope never leaves a prisoner'.

That evening Duch ordered Bizot's chains removed and the two men sat by the campfire and talked. Bizot told Duch that he had left his two-year-old daughter with a family for a few hours at a village near the Buddhist pagoda on the day he was captured.

'And that fact was one of the most constant and deepest reasons for suffering,' Bizot says of that decision. 'Throughout my detention I did not know where my daughter was, what had happened to her.'

Duch's sincerity in his beliefs reminded Bizot of Marxist friends in France, some of whom were fervently in favour of Cambodia's revolution.

'[Duch] believed in this cause, and the ultimate goal of his commitment and his belief was the welfare and wellbeing of the inhabitants of Cambodia. He was fighting against injustice, inequity,' Bizot says.

Even though Duch's descriptions of the Khmer peasantry were clichéd Cambodian communist archetypes, 'there nevertheless was a measure of true sincerity, fundamental sincerity in his perceptions, as is the case with many revolutionaries'. The experience shattered Bizot's naive perception that the world was divided between humans and monsters. Duch, he realised, was both. The encounter affected him deeply and, four decades on, Bizot remains consumed with the contradictions. Here was a man who was the vector of 'state-institutionalised, massive killing'.

'I cannot imagine being in his shoes today with so much horror behind him,' Bizot tells the judges. 'And on the other hand, the recollection that I have of a young man who committed his life and his existence to a cause and to a purpose that was based on the idea that crime was not only legitimate but that it was deserved. I do not know what I can make of this, Your Honours.'

Bizot later revisits that theme, saying there is no purpose in labelling men as inhuman.

'If we turn these people into monsters, a category apart from human beings with which we can have no identification as human beings … then I think there is no way we can have any kind of grasp of what they have perpetrated,' he says.

We might be afraid to try to understand that such men are in many ways the same as us, and yet we must do so, and we must not pretend we are so different from those who kill.

'Unfortunately we seem to have a much more frightening understanding of the executioner, actually, when we look at the executioner as a truly human being,' he says, then adds: 'On the other hand, to seek to understand is not to condone.'

Even more so, he says, there is no possible forgiveness.

'On behalf of whom might we be able to forgive? On behalf of those who died? I don't think so,' Bizot says. 'And the sheer horror of what happened, what was done in Cambodia – and this is not exclusive, this does not belong only to this unfortunate country. The screams of victims must be heard and we must never allow ourselves to think that that scream is excessively loud. The harshest condemnations that we can have against the accused can never be harsh enough.'

In the same way that Duch saw the man behind the "spy", the firelight conversation allowed Bizot to see the man behind Duch and to see that Duch's humanity proved no barrier to his participation in mass killings.

'I had expected to encounter a monster, an inhumane person, but I realised then that things were much more tragic, much more frightening,' he says.

BEFORE HIS TESTIMONY CONCLUDES, Bizot recounts two stories that reveal the Duch of M-13A. The first took place shortly before Duch told Bizot he was to be freed. Duch had returned from a meeting with his superiors – a meeting where Bizot knew his case was to be discussed – and told Bizot in French that he had been unmasked as a spy and that Vorn Vet would not allow him to leave. After months of captivity and strain, Bizot fell to his knees in tears.

But wait, Duch told him as he pulled the trembling prisoner back to his feet, I am only joking. You have not really been unmasked as a spy. Later Duch played another of his cold jokes, a form of 'Sophie's Choice'. Bizot's two companions, Lay and Son, were by now unshackled and allowed to move around the camp. Bizot had known Lay for five years and the newly married Son for six months; understandably he was closer to Lay. Knowing this, Duch approached Son and told him that Bizot was permitted to take only one of the two men with him. He has chosen to take Lay, Duch said. Son remained quiet and Duch asked whether he believed him, whether Son thought that was possible?

'Yes,' Son replied in earshot of Bizot. 'I think this is possible.'

That reply, Bizot tells the court, was awful to hear but it amused Duch, who laughed saying: 'Oh, so at last here is somebody who believes me!'[5]

It was little short of miraculous that Bizot was freed after three months with a promise from Duch that his two Cambodian co-workers would be unshackled, but would have to remain at M-13A. While awaiting trial many years later, Duch told Bizot that the two men had in fact been executed – at another camp, Duch claimed, and on instruction from above. It is, Bizot says, a burden that has never left him.

AROUND A YEAR AFTER Bizot's release, a middle-aged farmer called Uch Sorn was arrested and taken to M-13A. It was 1973 and Sorn and two friends had crossed into the liberated zone to buy a pig for a Buddhist ceremony. They knew the Khmer Rouge were communist and would likely ban Buddhism when they came to power, so they decided to conduct a ceremony before that happened.

Sorn was shackled to five other detainees in a deep pit. Prisoners slept on their backs on the soil, were constantly thirsty, got wet when it rained, and were fed miserable rations. They were forced to urinate in bamboo receptacles, and if they needed to defecate they were taken, their wrists bound, by a guard to a stinking pit. Sorn spent the best part of a year there but Duch eventually concluded he was not a spy and put him to work growing rice.

The two friends who were arrested with Sorn died at M-13A, one of them from starvation. It reminds Sorn of the fate of a man called Kin, a fellow prisoner whom he met while shackled in the pit. After Kin was arrested, his father had come to M-13A to ask why his son was being held. The father was arrested too and both men starved to death; first the father, then Kin.

Sorn tells the court he witnessed torture, starvation, beatings, simulated drownings and prisoners dying every day. He buried numerous bodies in pits that were sometimes so shallow that stray dogs got at the corpses and left bones scattered in the dirt. On at least one occasion he witnessed five naked

---

5. Rithy Panh, the Cambodian film-maker who spent months interviewing Duch in 2008–09 while the latter was awaiting trial, tells of another chilling exchange: Duch would check the palms of M-13A's prisoners and was astonished each time he found an inmate whose palm had a long lifeline. When Panh asks whether such prisoners would later be executed, Duch laughs and says yes. *The Elimination: A Survivor of the Khmer Rouge Confronts His Past and the Commandant of the Killing Fields*, Rithy Panh with Christophe Bataille, translated by John Cullen (The Clerkenwell Press, 2013), p. 130.

prisoners tied to wooden posts. The one in the middle was shot in the head by one of Duch's deputies and then the others were taken back to the pits to await further interrogation. Sorn believes the execution was done to scare the four survivors. They were just ordinary people like me, he tells the court.

Sorn is asked whether he saw Duch hit prisoners.

'Yes, I did,' the 72-year-old witness replies, explaining that he watched Duch beat a female detainee with a whip the thickness of a man's thumb.

'After a while the young guards came and beat the girl – the woman,' he continues. 'After she became unconscious, Duch slapped his butt and he laughed because the girl was having a seizure on the ground.'

Sorn also cites an instance of execution. It happened after he was ordered to dig a pit to which one man and one woman were brought, chained by their necks. The teenage guards beat the man to death and then hit the woman until she became unconscious. After that they kicked her into the pit and buried her alive.

The Khmer Rouge, he says, treated their fellow Cambodians 'worse than animals'. At the time Sorn was terrified of Duch. And now, he is asked?

'Today I am not afraid of him because he is now a tiger with no teeth,' he replies.

Duch admits Sorn's testimony is fundamentally true but denies beating any female prisoners. In fact, he says, it is impossible that Sorn saw him with detainees since he would always make sure to interrogate prisoners out of sight. But Duch does concede that a prisoner was executed while tied to a pole. Sorn repeats his story about Duch beating the woman and laughing, and Duch looks on with a puzzled expression, stretching out his hands and shrugging his shoulders. Neither Roux nor Kar Savuth takes up the issue.

OFTEN WITH PEOPLE it is the small things that count, the seemingly insignificant acts that give an insight into personality or character and reveal more about a person than they might think possible. With Duch that can be found in the simplest act: pouring and drinking a glass of water.

By now those of us watching his trial know that Duch is a highly methodical man, as one would expect from a mathematician. Duch craves order above all and he loves the incontestable truths that mathematics can convey. In mathematics there are no grey areas: an answer is either right or it is wrong. It cannot be both.

It is a July day in court and Duch sits behind Roux and Kar Savuth as the prosecution addresses the bench. Duch takes a break from writing notes and reaches across his desk, a haven of order with a small stack of papers neatly squared away. At the back of the desk are a glass and a plastic bottle of drinking water. Duch reaches forward, takes the glass and places it in front of him. He holds the glass and slowly pours in the water, just as much as is needed. Then he replaces the top on the bottle, places it back at the rear of the desk. He lifts the glass and in one fluid motion he drains it. There is no pause and there is no half-glass, only precision and order. He holds the empty glass, flicks it twice on the floor to clear out any remaining drops, and then replaces it at the rear of the desk.

The only variation in this routine comes when Duch is in the dock in full view of the judges. Then he does not flick the drops on the floor. The rest is unchanged.

In all the times I watched him, the process never wavered. I wondered what had made him decide when he was a much younger man that a half glass of water on his desk was a danger. Had he knocked it across his papers and then resolved, immediately and without exception, that he would never make that mistake again?

It fits his character, as does another aspect of his behaviour that escapes no one: when dealing with people who have authority over him, Duch is deferential to the point of obsequiousness. In front of the judges, Duch is the obedient schoolboy and, like the boy in the story he so liked as a child, he stands up straight and talks respectfully.

Yet like a classroom bully, he is far less accommodating with those he considers beneath him, which in this court amounts to almost everyone else. It is as though Duch at times cannot help himself. In those moments the mask slips and we catch glimpses of that other as he turns on those whom he considers have erred in their testimony, for instance, or who ask him questions of which he disapproves. One CPK cadre, who met Duch around 1972, described the then-head of M-13A as 'ill-tempered, impatient and doctrinaire'.[6] When Duch snarls in court, even though constrained and powerless in this sanitised atmosphere, it is easy to see how terrifying he must have been.

The weeks of hearings also reveal Duch's prodigious memory and his capacity for recall decades after the event. Dates, names and events seem as clear to him in court as they were at the time. His knowledge of the case file

---

6. Chandler, *Tragedy,* op. cit., p. 359, note 77.

is astounding and he reels off the 8-digit reference numbers of documents without any trouble. His movements are precise, even delicate. Generally he sits upright, but as the months pass Duch gets ever more comfortable and allows himself to lean back in his chair during sessions. He has an imperious air exuding confidence, yet he finds it hard to sit still. His hands riffle through documents on his desk, an unending search for facts and the truths they convey. At these moments, with his glasses on and scribbling notes, Duch seems at his most relaxed.

More than anything Duch loves being the centre of attention, controlling the court and at times seeming to dictate its operation. This spotlight, after years in jail awaiting trial, fulfils him.

As the testimony surrounding M-13A closes out we have heard enough to know that Duch of the early 1970s was a bully and a sadist, a committed revolutionary for whom the ends justified the means, a survivor, a liar, a man with the capacity for the cold joke in the cruellest of circumstances, someone who wielded tremendous power and was prince of his dark domain. We have also seen his subtle efforts to slip the reins of responsibility, and will encounter that repeatedly in the coming months: admit responsibility, then deflect it; I had power, yet I was powerless; I ordered criminal acts, but I did not commit any.

All of that is true, yet none of it means the man on trial is not truly sorry.

Pol Pot (right), the leader of the Khmer Rouge, was also known as Brother Number One. Pol Pot and Nuon Chea co-wrote the Party magazine *Revolutionary Flag* (above), which was required reading for cadres and in which the two men laid out the Party line. (Photos courtesy of the Documentation Center of Cambodia Archives)

Brother Number Two Nuon Chea (second from right) seen here with Minister of Defence Son Sen (wearing glasses) and Foreign Affairs Minister Ieng Sary (gesturing). The man on the right is a Chinese adviser. (Photo courtesy of the Documentation Center of Cambodia Archives)

Pol Pot (centre), Ieng Sary (left) and Son Sen in an image taken after the fall of Democratic Kampuchea. (Photo courtesy of the Documentation Center of Cambodia Archives)

S-21 staff and their children (above). Duch is in the back row, second from right. Mam Nai, a feared S-21 torturer, is on the far left. The image on the right shows Duch with his S-21 messenger Sok. (Photos courtesy of the Documentation Center of Cambodia Archives)

One of the upper corridors at S-21. Prisoners were shackled together in the converted classrooms on the left. The barbed wire was installed to prevent desperate prisoners committing suicide. (Photo courtesy of Daniel Mehta)

A burial pit at Chhoeung Ek. Thousands of S-21's inmates were executed at this site, known to tourists as the Killing Fields, after Duch had reviewed their confessions and deemed them acceptable. (Photo courtesy of Rachel Foo)

A page from the execution register (above) dated December 9, 1977. On that day, 301 prisoners were sent by Duch to their deaths at Chhoeung Ek. Ket's name is the ninth from the top. (Author photo)

The final page (right) in the S-21 confession of Kol Dorathy, a friend of Ket's. Dorathy was executed on March 13, 1978. (Author photo)

With the population enslaved, millions were forced into work gangs, known as *chalat*, labouring without respite as *Angkar* sought to build a new country. At the centre of that were irrigation projects (top and centre) to grow rice, seen being bagged (above). (Photos courtesy of the Documentation Center of Cambodia Archives)

Days after Pol Pot's regime was driven from power, Cambodians began to rebuild their shattered lives. Here people arrive back in Phnom Penh in January 1979. (Photo courtesy of the Documentation Center of Cambodia Archives)

Villagers in Kandal province hold a ceremony in 1984 to install a new Buddha statue in their pagoda, which the Khmer Rouge had destroyed when they outlawed religion. Bringing back their religious beliefs was central, one Kandal villager said, 'to remind people what was right and wrong'. (Photo courtesy of FoundCambodia Project)

In this 1989 image villagers take religious statues to a Buddhist pagoda near Chhoeung Ek, the infamous killing field where thousands of S-21's victims were executed. (© John Vink)

A wooden elephant laden with incense sticks stands in a spirit house next to Pol Pot's grave on the Dangrek Hills near Anlong Veng in Cambodia's north-west. (Author photo)

UNCONTESTED FACTS ABOUT S-21

Paragraph 139. Prisoners were generally blindfolded and handcuffed when brought inside S-21.

Paragraph 143. Persons who were arrested and imprisoned at S-21 were usually not informed of the reason for their arrest.

Paragraph 144. Prisoners at S-21 were kept in restraints nearly 24 hours a day.

Paragraph 150. Prisoners at S-21 were not permitted to speak to one another or to the guards.

Paragraph 151. When prisoners first arrived at S-21 they were often stripped of their clothes, leaving just their underwear.

Paragraph 153. The majority of S-21 detainees were provided with no bedding and slept on the concrete floor. A few privileged prisoners were provided with old mats or mattresses to sleep on.

Paragraph 156. There were no washing facilities at S-21. Prisoners remained shackled when bathed. Bathing consisted of guards spraying the cell with a hose from the doorway. The primary purpose of this hosing was to clean the cells, not the prisoners.

Paragraph 157. Prisoners were not permitted to leave their cells to use the toilet and were forced to urinate in jerry cans and defecate in ammunition boxes.

Paragraph 158. Prisoners were typically fed twice a day with poor quality gruel.

Paragraph 159. S-21 detainees only received starvation rations of food. As a result, many suffered substantial weight loss and physical deterioration and some died.

Paragraph 160. Starvation of prisoners was a deliberate policy of the CPK.

Paragraph 163. Medical services at S-21 were provided by a team of three to five medics who had not studied medicine. Some of those medics were children and they worked without the supervision of medical doctors.

Paragraph 167. S-21 medics understood that the purpose of medical treatment for prisoners was to keep them alive long enough that their interrogations could be completed.

Paragraph 168. S-21 personnel performed medical experiments on prisoners.

Paragraph 168A. Research of the effects of poisons [on prisoners] was carried out upon the orders of the Central Committee provided to Duch by Nuon Chea.

Paragraph 168B. Autopsies were practised on living persons.

Paragraph 168C. Blood was taken from prisoners.

— Extract from the list of agreed facts between the defence and the prosecution at Duch's trial, April 1, 2009

CHAPTER NINE

DEAD ALREADY: 1975-79

IN JULY 1975 the two camps that comprised M-13 were closed, and the following month the leaders decided to establish a central prison for the regime's enemies. S-21 was one of a large number of interrogation centres set up across the country after victory and was by far the most important. Although these prisons in many ways echoed M-13A, they were different in one key aspect: where the Khmer Rouge had used centres such as M-13A largely to identify Lon Nol spies – in other words, seeking out external enemies – this new breed of security centre would soon be turned against the Party's internal enemies.

First, though, *Angkar* would unleash its vengeance on the remnants of Lon Nol's Khmer Republic. In the months following victory, Duch was tasked with ferreting through the abandoned ministries in Phnom Penh and collating and reviewing the intelligence archives of the defeated regime. Such work was essential and one can reasonably assume that he found hundreds of names. Once the new rulers had determined who had worked for Lon Nol's government as intelligence officers and who within their own ranks had fed intelligence to the defeated Khmer Republic, many (and probably most) would have been hunted down.

Duch was particularly well suited to trawling such a vast database, said US academic Craig Etcheson, who worked for the ECCC prosecution as an investigator between 2006 and 2012 and who also appeared as an expert witness. Etcheson noted that Duch's skills were very much in evidence at his trial.

'One of my strongest impressions of the whole trial is how when [Duch] would take the floor and essentially seize control of the Trial Chamber

– correcting the interpreters in real time in all three languages, summoning supporting evidence from the case file by memory without notes, citing the [case file reference] numbers of the pages he was referring to in all three languages from memory,' Etcheson told me in 2012.

Duch's was a stellar performance, Etcheson said, picking his words carefully as he cast his mind back to the trial.

'You have the impression that he not only has a photographic memory but he's got an indexing system in his brain that is not normal. There are very, very few human beings who can do something like that,' he said. '[He has] an extraordinary intellect in terms of his pure recall and ability to process and analyse factual information.'

In other words, Duch was just the kind of person *Angkar* needed for such a data-heavy task. He was also loyal, ruthless and keen to pass on his knowledge to his subordinates. Having proven his skills at M-13A, and armed with a firm grip of the defeated regime's intelligence apparatus, later in 1975 Duch was appointed as deputy chairman of S-21. By then, *Angkar* was in full pursuit of its enemies in the Khmer Republic.

When the prosecution asks Duch whether he knew that the named people in those intelligence lists would be executed, he says the thought did not cross his mind. By now the court is dealing with acts that fall within its timeframe for prosecution and Duch is under no obligation to incriminate himself, but it would take some stretch of the imagination to believe that. By 1975 Duch was hardly naive in the ways of the Khmer Rouge.

S-21 WAS THE SECRET HEART of *Angkar's* security apparatus, a network of nearly 200 interrogation centres that covered the country. If Cambodia was a prison without walls, then this network was the unyielding web through which *Angkar* crushed any effort, real or imagined, to subvert the revolution. S-21 was its dark keep, the only centre with direct daily access to the leaders.

Duch explains that the 'S' in the prison's code comes from the term *santebal*, a contraction of the words '*santisuk nokorbal*' meaning 'secret police', or as he rather grandly puts it, those who 'preserve the peace in the country'. The number '21' was Duch's communication code. The prison, he says, was Pol Pot's idea.

On taking power the Khmer Rouge had divided the country into a number of zones and autonomous regions. Those were further divided into sectors and districts, with a three-person Party committee wielding power at each level. Below the district level was the commune level where the villages were organised into brutal collectives. The district level centres were key to this network since it was here that the decision was taken to execute enemies or to send them up the ladder.

S-21's operations were on a different scale to the rest. Take torture, for example. While the lower-level centres used beatings, electrocution, whippings and suffocation, the violence inflicted on prisoners at S-21 was more varied, presumably because Duch had decided these additional methods were desirable and effective. And although many centres extracted confessions, S-21 was unique in this respect because some of its prisoners were veteran revolutionaries, and generating confessions from them was a far more rigorous and lengthy undertaking than interrogating the lower ranks.[1] Furthermore, while lower-level centres could take in prisoners only from their area, S-21's reach was nationwide. It was, Duch tells the court, 'a tool exclusively for the use of the Central Committee'.

All of this effort meant S-21 required numerous workers. While district security centres typically had a dozen staff, those at the sector level had twice that. Zone security centres were larger still, with 50 or more staff. But S-21, as Etcheson testifies, 'was in a category all by itself'. In March 1977, a year after Duch took over as chairman, S-21 and its associated camp S-24 had hundreds of employees, some of whom had followed Duch from M-13A.

Their skills varied. Interrogators needed to be literate, as did those who handled documents. But simpler tasks such as guarding prisoners required no such ability and, as he had done at M-13A, Duch selected those workers from the poorest class of peasants, favouring those who were young, some just children. The logic was simple, as he told the investigating judges: the young and uneducated were 'of pure origin' like 'a blank piece of paper on which one could write whatever one wanted'.[2] They were more malleable and in terms of class-consciousness they were the flower of the revolution.[3]

---

1. According to DC-Cam's Youk Chhang, records have been found in only two of Democratic Kampuchea's 197 prisons: one in Takeo province and the other in Svay Rieng province. This general absence of documents makes S-21's archive of significant historical value.

2. ECCC document 'Co-Prosecutors' Rule 66 Final Submission', August 16, 2010, p. 124, note 349. Duch's statement echoes Chairman Mao's wording about the young.

3. Or, as Duch put it to Rithy Panh, the closest followers of Marxism were those who were illiterate. Panh, op. cit., p. 22.

Choosing peasants also reinforced the Party's trust in Duch and chimed with Article 1 of the CPK's statutes, which laid out the 'purity' requirement for anyone wishing to join the Party. Such people 'must have good and clean life morals and be good and clean politically, never having been involved with the enemy'. Peasant boys from the poorest areas were the least likely to have been corrupted by the feudalist or capitalist classes, and choosing them burnished Duch's credentials despite his revolutionary shortcomings as an intellectual of Chinese heritage.

IN MARCH 1976, DUCH, who had been S-21 deputy since August the previous year, was appointed chairman after his boss, Nat, was promoted to a different office. Duch was a better interrogator, and besides, he tells the judges, the Party did not trust Nat, who was 'full of tricks' whereas Duch was loyal 'like a dog', the 'eyes and nose of the Party'. Son Sen, the defence minister who had responsibility for internal security and who was therefore Duch's boss, trusted him more than Nat.[4]

At the time S-21 was located in a cluster of houses near the Chao Ponhea Yat High School, but the following month Duch was granted permission to move the facility into the school grounds where it remained for the duration of Democratic Kampuchea.

He ordered that the abandoned homes in the nearby streets be used as interrogation rooms as well as premises ranging from housing and mess halls to execution sites and mass graves. Using a school for such work, the former teacher says, seemed of no consequence at the time although he now realises it represented a denial of culture and humanity.

This was an important time for another reason too. By the time of Duch's promotion *Angkar* had been in power nearly a year and had exterminated most of its enemies outside the Party. Now it began the savage turning in on itself. In a document dated March 30, 1976, *Angkar* formalised precisely who was allowed to order the smashing of the enemies that lurked 'within and outside the ranks'.

The document – 'Decisions of the Central Committee Regarding a Number of Matters' – was ascribed to the CPK's Central Committee, in theory the highest decision-making body in the Party. In all likelihood it was the product of the Standing Committee, a smaller, elite group that

---

4. Nat later fell under suspicion and, ironically, was taken to S-21 in 1978 where he was tortured and executed shortly before the regime fell. Nat's wife was also arrested at that time, according to Duch's testimony to the tribunal (ECCC document E1_29.1_TR001, June 9, 2009, p. 45).

included Pol Pot, Nuon Chea, Son Sen, Ieng Sary and *Ta* Mok, and which operated as the executive body of the Central Committee.

The power to order an arrest was limited strictly to four groups of the most senior Party members, including the Standing Committee and the secretaries of the seven zones. Duch was not one of those permitted to arrest, but his job did regularly involve ensuring those arrests were carried out. Historian David Chandler says this document is as close as one can get to a smoking gun that the policy of executing enemies was authorised from the top.

Although the Decisions document in some ways merely formalised existing execution practices, it is hard to overemphasise its consequences. With the messianic application of its message, the Khmer Rouge underwrote the destruction of vast numbers of their own, and from April 1976 the Party largely targeted the enemy within. Nearly half of S-21's victims came from Democratic Kampuchea's military, the Revolutionary Army of Kampuchea. The army was the guardian of external and internal security, and the message to focus on internal enemies was propounded vocally by Son Sen. At a meeting of military commanders in August 1976, for example, Son Sen ordered them to begin purging their units.

'In carrying out the duty of defending the country it is imperative to think in terms of fending off enemies both external and internal, but it is especially important to pay attention to fending off the enemy that is boring from within,' Son Sen said. 'This means it is imperative to pay attention to purging "no-good" elements completely from the Party, the core organisations, and our male and female combatants within the revolutionary army.'[5]

The order rang out across the country through every channel: in meetings, via telegrams, through radio broadcasts and in *Revolutionary Flag* magazine. Untold numbers of enemies lurked within the movement and were trying to destroy the revolution. They must be stopped. From March 1976, the executions at S-21 were driven by the need to unmask and smash this hidden foe.

The numbers prove the effectiveness of that message: by the time the regime collapsed, some 10,000 military and Party cadres had been executed at S-21 alone, more than half the total number of prisoners known to have been killed there. S-21 took in people from across the country and from nearly every government institution. The year Ket was imprisoned, 1977, saw more arrests and executions at the centre than 1976 and 1978 combined.

---

5. As quoted by Craig Etcheson at Duch's trial. ECCC trial transcript, May 18, 2009, p. 90.

The purges caused chaos within government: the Ministry of Public Works lost more than 500 staff to S-21; nearly 400 were sent from the Ministry of Commerce; and more than 250 came from each of the energy ministry and the railways ministry.

Among S-21's victims were 200 of its own staff. Those who overstepped the mark, who failed to do what they were told or who talked back to Duch or his deputy Comrade Hor would be executed. It was unavoidable, Duch says, because if he did not act then he too would fall under suspicion.

'So if [S-21 staff] were perceived to be confronting us, then they would be in trouble,' he says with some understatement.

Suspicion was rife in the increasingly paranoid atmosphere that stifled Democratic Kampuchea, and woe betide those whose superiors were arrested, as Duch illustrates with the story of Sok, a senior official who was executed.

'Then … his subordinates were monitored and traced by the upper echelon,' says Duch. 'People who were followed or monitored, they would not be able to escape from being purged as well. So when the superior was arrested, it was just a matter of time before his subordinates were also arrested. It is the principle.'

Once they arrived at S-21 ('not a prison [but] the place to store people before killing [them],' as Duch describes it) detainees were to be interrogated to extract their confessions, and then – in conformity with the Party line on enemies – they were, without exception, to be smashed. No prisoner could be released even if taken to S-21 by mistake. In a regime obsessed with secrecy, nobody could know it existed.[6]

'Anyone who was arrested and sent to S-21 [was] presumed dead already. S-21 did not dare release anyone otherwise we would be beheaded,' Duch explains. 'So these crimes [with which I am accused] were committed on people who were perceived as dead already.'[7]

---

6. Based on its assessment of 'release lists' found in the archives, DC-Cam estimated in 2011 that at least 179 prisoners were in fact freed during S-21's existence. Most were Khmer Rouge soldiers. See 'Analysis: Surviving the Khmer Rouge', by Dacil Q Keo and Nean Yin (*Phnom Penh Post*, January 7, 2011). However, during his trial in 2009, Duch said the lists were false, and insisted that those named as being freed 'were all killed'. (ECCC trial transcript, June 23, 2009, pp. 31–33.) The previous week Duch explained that his predecessor, Nat, had falsified one such list, for instance, to cover up the fact that he (Nat) had illegally arrested people of his own accord – a crime of 'individualism' (ECCC trial transcript, June 15, 2009, pp. 70-71). That said, DC-Cam stands by its assessment, with its director Youk Chhang noting in an email to me (August 2013) that one of these released prisoners became a civil party in Case 002 – the trial of the ex-leaders. Moreover, it would have been in Duch's interest to lie, as the ability to release prisoners would have undermined his defence that he had no latitude to free anyone.

7. This dehumanisation was central to S-21. One former staffer told Rithy Panh that prisoners 'were

THROUGH THESE DRAWN-OUT DAYS, with every document laboriously referred to by each of its three case file reference numbers in Khmer, English and French, we learn how S-21 was established, how it operated and who did what. The Standing Committee sent lists of people whom Duch was to arrest, or ordered people under suspicion to be sent to S-21. The lanky, pale Mam Nai interrogated the Vietnamese prisoners, and was Duch's secretary and right-hand man. Comrade Pon's sole responsibility was to interrogate the most important prisoners. Comrade Hor ran S-21's day-to-day operations and was, in Duch's words, 'always occupied'. By way of example, Duch rattles through Comrade Hor's daily tasks.

'Those included inspecting the work of the guards, inspecting the receiving of the prisoners who were sent to S-21, inspecting the people who were taken out to Chhoeung Ek. When there was any mishap or any event then an order would be immediately issued before he reported to me,' Duch says. 'At the same time there were also other tasks; for instance for the production, for [providing] supplies to the units, the work on the health care unit and the implementation of orders and discipline for the entire unit.'

Duch masks the inhumane realities behind these tasks with soft words. 'Inspecting' prisoners sent to Chhoeung Ek referred to the process by which they were taken for execution. Talk of the 'health care unit' is absurd – the sole task of the typically illiterate teenagers who worked as medics was to keep the prisoners alive until they had completed a satisfactory confession, after which Duch signed their execution warrants; besides, there were no medicines to speak of. A 'mishap' or 'event' might mean a prisoner had been beaten to death by an over-zealous interrogator or had managed to commit suicide, or it could refer to this 'incident', which Duch maintains was an aberration, when a male interrogator 'inserted a stick into the vagina of that female detainee'.[8] The woman had been Duch's primary school teacher.[9]

There were other tasks that kept Comrade Hor busy. Helping to arrest

---

like pieces of wood'. Another described them as 'half human and half corpse. They're not humans, and they're not corpses. They're soulless, like animals. You're not afraid to hurt them. We weren't worried about our karma.' Panh, op. cit., p. 2.

8. There were many instances of rape at S-21, wrote Rithy Panh, ibid, p. 114.) It would indeed be surprising if rape and sexual assault were not more common – despite Duch's statements to the contrary – given the prevalence of young male interrogators and their near-unlimited power over the prisoners.

9. In response, Duch created a female interrogation team drawn from the wives of S-21 staff. Two of these interrogators were later executed after their husbands were arrested. As Duch put it at trial: 'When the husband is smashed, the wife would end up the same.'

cadres who had been told to report to Duch's home on spurious grounds, or digging up the corpses of important prisoners in order to photograph them and reassure *Angkar* that its foes had been dealt with. Duch's manipulation of language to disguise the underlying realities is a constant feature, yet given how repugnant those acts were, that is perhaps not surprising.

As for Duch, his most important role was to analyse the confessions that were the raison d'être of S-21. He would read each one, annotate it and send the most important to his boss.[10] He was looking for links that proved *Angkar*'s fervent belief: that the USSR and the US viewed Cambodia as the jewel in their contest for global domination. That was why the interrogators were ordered to find evidence of KGB or CIA links, of which there was usually none.[11]

In that quest prisoners would be taken from their cell to an interrogation room where they were shackled to a table. Detainees who, like Ket, were literate were told first to write their biographies and then their confessions, which were typically a concoction, a rewriting of their lives. One of the most insidious aspects of this process was the express aim that ultimately *the victims themselves must believe their confessions to be true.*[12] In this open-ended system, those who tried to hold out would be broken through torture – most commonly by being beaten – and, once their confession met with Duch's satisfaction (and in the cases of the most important prisoners, to the satisfaction of Son Sen or Nuon Chea), the prisoner would be executed. The confessions often led to more arrests, which saw further people brought in. The cycle continued, a bleak canvas that stretched across the years.

Confessions had to be sufficiently detailed and they had to list strings of traitors. Extracting names was vital and Duch freely admits that confessions would be 'sharpened' by *Angkar*. In this sharpening process, references to men such as Son Sen and *Ta* Mok would be deleted ('I was frequently asked to remove names' from the confessions of important people, Duch told the investigating judges the previous year) and confessions would be 'aimed'

---

10. Until mid-1977 his boss was Son Sen, but Nuon Chea then took over that role after Son Sen was sent to eastern Cambodia to lead the fight against the Vietnamese.

11. In his book, Rithy Panh quotes Prak Khan instructing other interrogators that, as with any good story, the confession must have a beginning and an end. 'And the enemy must be working for the KGB or the CIA, or he must be a Vietnamese agent bent on swallowing up our country.' Panh, op. cit., p. 164.

12. Panh, ibid., p. 249, citing the contents of an exercise book (Duch's '*Black Book*') found at S-21. The notes, which were written down by an interrogator, are from training sessions given by Duch.

in a particular direction to ensure that suspected enemies were implicated.[13] As Duch had phrased it, the purpose of such confessions was 'about finding excuses to eliminate those who represented obstacles'.[14]

Aside from assessing confessions, Duch's other key role was to train and indoctrinate the interrogators, to make them 'absolute' in their work so that they would not be afraid to harm detainees. It was designed to turn the innocent into cruel people, he admits, to fill them with class anger and ensure that they were unafraid to arrest, to interrogate and to kill. Yet it was also important to rein them in, for fear that they would beat prisoners to death as they showed off 'their strong stance'. Such overzealousness, which he believes happened just twice, cost confessions – and that was not permitted.

Despite being an enthusiastic proponent of torture and killing, Duch says he found its blood-soaked reality unsettling. He tells the bench that he stayed away from S-21's cells, and claims he was nauseated by the 1975 execution of two cadres who were knifed in the neck. He had been ordered to watch the killings; their visceral nature, he says, repelled him.

Plausibly, Duch recalls with disgust Son Sen ordering him to exhume the three days' old corpse of a prisoner who had been executed at S-21, presumably so that it could be photographed. Digging up the body and cleaning it angered Duch – the dirty work would have been done by Duch's underlings but overseen by him – as did the instruction to go three times to Chhoeung Ek to watch executions. Duch says he went just once[15] and, in typically analytical fashion, wonders why Son Sen ordered him to undertake these unpleasant tasks when he did not ask the same of his then-boss Nat. This, he concludes, was evidence that Son Sen trusted him more.

Duch also claims that he took part in only one interrogation, that of Koy Thuon, one of the most senior leaders in the Party, in 1977. It was Koy Thuon who had named Minister of Information Hu Nim as a traitor, and

---

13. 'Written Record of Interview of Charged Person,' Office of the Co-Investigating Judges, dated April 10, 2008, p. 6. (Document No. 00178058.)

14. Ibid., dated April 8, 2008, p. 4. (Document No. 00177635.)

15. A lie, if what Duch previously told Rithy Panh can be believed (see *The Elimination*, op. cit., p. 241). In addition, two S-21 torturers told Panh that Duch had visited Chhoeung Ek more than once, which given his obsession with ensuring that his S-21 machine functioned smoothly from entry to execution is certainly plausible. And Him Huy, who eventually headed S-21's Unit to Receive Detainees (see Chapter 10), testified that he saw Duch at Chhoeung Ek twice, telling the judges that Duch 'stayed there until all detainees were executed. Then he left.' (See Him Huy's testimony, ECCC trial transcript, July 16, 2009, p. 78.)

it was the confession of Hu Nim, who was executed in July 1977, that had so scared Martine when she read it in France two years later, the words of a broken man: 'I am not a human being, I am an animal.'

It was at that point, as we saw earlier, that Martine realised something terrible had happened to Ket.

THE DAYS PASS in a whirl of names, many long dead; army division numbers and document references; and with regular spats between the defence and the prosecution on points of procedure that bore the dwindling audience. But bit by bit, between ongoing translation problems, breaks for procedural rulings and sundry diversions, the picture of S-21 as a total institution is constructed from hours of testimony.

There is an interesting exchange when the prosecution wonders whether Duch, who claims this work revolted him, asked to be moved. Yes, Duch replies. Yet when the prosecution probes repeatedly for specifics, it turns out that Duch did not actually say that he wanted to be transferred. I would not have dared say such a thing, he says, but my bosses knew full well I wanted out. It was obvious enough, he says, using a Khmer proverb: 'Is it necessary for somebody to peel the crap to show the shit inside the crap?'

His testiness draws a response from the prosecution, which concludes wryly that 'you hated your work but you did not specifically tell anyone that you hated your work'. Therefore is it fair to say that he was fascinated by it? Duch's rambling, evasive response includes Pol Pot's name and those of executed senior Khmer Rouge and ends with a comment that S-21 was 'just an instrument of the proletarian class of the Party'.

'I am just the absolute dictatorial instrument of the Party and this is why I bow myself before the chamber and before the nation, to accept my guilt,' Duch concludes.

When the question is repeated, Duch says that no, he was not interested in this sort of work. He had only wanted to be a teacher and had come to the capital in 1975 hoping to find teacher-training materials. Instead he found a book on intelligence and another on torture but had no time to read them and gave them away. Besides by then he had learned all he needed at M-13A, inspired by the writings of Chairman Mao quoting the sixth century BCE warlord Sun Tzu that if you know your enemy as you know yourself, then you will never be defeated. In this, he tells the prosecutor, I am a self-taught man.

The line leads naturally enough to a conversation about different types of torture. Where Nat favoured electric shocks to induce confessions, Duch preferred whips. Waterboarding was used later too. His patron at M-13A, Vorn Vet, was a fan of two other techniques, which Duch claims he rejected on practical grounds: plastic bags ('very dangerous' because the prisoner might suffocate and then 'we lost a confession', although he admitted bags were used when necessary) and watching an artery on the neck to see if it pulsed rapidly during questioning – a sure sign of guilt, Vorn Vet reckoned. Duch was less certain, and felt it was 'not effective'.[16]

For expert witness Craig Etcheson, Duch was 'very much an innovator, a creator, a developer and an institutionaliser' of this method of extracting detailed confessions that resulted in 'a nearly exponential growth' of victims.

'In part, it is the zeal with which the accused person pursued this project that caused this methodology to result in such a large number of victims,' Etcheson tells Roux during a testy examination by the defence.

In this, says Etcheson, Duch was applying the Khmer Rouge concept of 'independence mastery', which meant using one's own skills and innovative methods to ensure that the result obtained was in line with the Party's policies and needs. Roux's suggestion that Duch was a passive victim draws a dry response: 'Counsel, one always has choices in life.'

It also elicits an interruption from the prosecution that the defence's argument – that cadres had only two options, duty or death – be modified to add a third: escape.

WHAT TO MAKE OF ALL THIS? Neary has no time for what she regards as Duch's convenient and cowardly evasions, yet is shocked that some in the audience are buying into them. At the end of one afternoon session, an Asian-American visitor to the tribunal turns to Neary unprompted and asks: 'So, what do you think? Guilty or not guilty?'

Instead of answering, Neary instead turns the question on him, hoping, she tells me later, that he would say: 'Of course guilty'.

'Hmmm. I think,' he starts, then pauses. 'Not guilty.'

Neary, astonished, asks him why.

'Not enough proof,' he answers.

Neary turns away, seething that this casual visitor has concluded after a mere half-day that Duch is innocent, the consequence, as she sees it, of the

16. In late 1978, Vorn Vet was arrested and brought to S-21, where he was tortured and executed. On his arrival, he told Duch that he was nothing more than a 'filthy killer'. As was the practice, Vorn Vet's wife was also arrested at the same time, Duch told the tribunal (ECCC document E1_29.1_TR001, June 9, 2009, p. 45).

passing years and the man's obvious lack of knowledge. To her it constitutes a victory for Duch ('who looks so sure of himself behind the court's bullet-proof glass') and validates the defence's strategy to deny everything except that which is undeniable.

'Duch could make him believe in half a day that he wasn't someone who could find pleasure in cruelty,' she says with disbelief.

Yet, she continues, this fits the pattern of how Duch wants to be viewed in what she sees as his strange quest for fame: Duch as prison chief; Duch as the instrument of the Standing Committee, a passive object and, in that way, Duch implies, less accountable; and Duch as victim, a man who viewed his actions as part of an unfortunate but necessary journey: unfortunate in the cost to others, but necessary in that this ensured that Duch and his family survived.

Neary finds Duch's toned-down character sketches wholly unconvincing, created as they are by a man whose eyes, she says, 'are full of dark emptiness'. Yet the encounter with the sightseer in the auditorium shows an unsettled Neary that, on some levels at least, Duch looks to be winning.

BY THE TIME HISTORIAN David Chandler takes the stand in August 2009, the tribunal has heard from five civil parties, nine former S-21 staff, two expert witnesses and four of the prison's survivors. It had concluded its questioning of Duch in late June and from that point on the defendant's role is largely confined to responding to the testimony of others.

The two great internal purges of the regime are clearly visible in S-21's confessions, says Chandler. Included in the first purge were diplomats because they had experienced life outside Democratic Kampuchea and were therefore not trusted. Also targeted in 1977 were intellectuals, which in practice meant anyone with an education in French. They were not targeted because they were intellectuals per se, Chandler says, but because by then Koy Thuon, a member of the Standing Committee, had fallen under suspicion. Given that Koy Thuon was an intellectual, and given that many of his associates were intellectuals, everyone of that ilk was automatically suspect.

This shift was compounded by the agricultural failings in the north-west, an area that was largely administered by intellectual CPK members but populated by urban evictees – among them Ket's family – who had no experience of farming. The centre refused to believe its policies were at fault, preferring to blame wreckers.

'And these [wreckers] had to be the people in charge, these had to be their cadres, and in the north-west these people happened to fall into the category of intellectuals,' Chandler explains.

The North-west Zone was heavily purged in 1977. The following year the Party moved against the East Zone and against groups of able-bodied men such as railway workers and factory workers on the grounds that they could be mobilised to fight the regime. Chandler says it is impossible to know how many prisoners were tortured but believes that interrogators preferred 'doing politics' to torture when trying to elicit confessions since the former was more efficient. 'Doing politics' amounted to any non-violent method to generate a confession and included undermining the prisoner, befriending him or her, and contradicting them.

What strikes me about Chandler's comments is that Duch's preference for 'doing politics' over crueller, physical tortures had nothing to do with behaving more humanely; it was simply because experience had proven that this was the most efficient method.

As Chandler tells the court, S-21 itself was a dehumanised universe and all but the highest-ranking prisoners were treated with contempt.

'They were mistreated physically and mentally, psychologically, from the moment they arrived,' he says. 'They were considered, from the moment they arrived, to have departed from the human world.'

One of the anomalies of S-21 was that, in 'doing politics', interrogators held out the promise that prisoners could repent and return to society. That pledge was common enough in other communist systems, but in S-21's case it was a lie. Instead of confessions laying the path for prisoners to rebuild themselves 'into better citizens by having admitted what they had done, they were re-educating themselves in order to be killed', says Chandler.

Many confessions contained hundreds of names, the 'strings of traitors' with whom the prisoner had allegedly conspired. The presence of such a vast number of enemies simply confirmed what the paranoid leaders felt they already knew: Democratic Kampuchea was overflowing with people who could not be trusted. Chandler says it is likely that many simply reeled off the names of everyone they knew, but it is also likely that the Party paid much more attention to the strings of traitors in the confessions of senior members than it did to similar numbers of names given by those who were junior.

He tells the bench that the leaders would have approved the executions of only the most senior detainees, not the majority of the prisoners.

'Son Sen [and] Nuon Chea certainly didn't sign off on individual deaths because … the dehumanisation process had already set in. These people were of no importance whatsoever to those upper leaders. They had departed from the revolution; they had departed from Khmer society … they're as good as dead … the minute they came in,' he says, adding that Duch's mandate was to ensure that every detainee was eventually executed.

'That was never withdrawn by a higher authority and therefore I don't think [Duch] had to seek higher authority to supervise a system in which he had no choice about who got killed and who didn't,' he says. 'Everybody got killed, no matter what they'd done or who they were.'

Did Duch have a choice? Perhaps not, says Chandler, given the context of the period. But equally he made no effort to free the hundreds of children who were executed along with their parents, for instance, or to ameliorate the suffering of the prisoners. Those who harmed so many in such terrible ways knew exactly what they were doing, 'and almost worse, did not seem to suffer themselves from what was happening'.

Chandler is asked whether he found written proof in the archives that Duch was against what was happening. No, he replies, and to have generated such evidence would have been 'suicidal'.

'You do find some places where he suggests that maybe less torture might be used, that maybe more "doing politics" should be employed,' he says. 'And of the statements that I have read from the tribunal and elsewhere, he was quite happy about some of the confessions that could be extracted without torture.'

Yet there is no evidence for Duch's claim that he would have been happier running S-21 as a place where torture was not necessary to get confessions. Duch's subsequent remorse seems to be just that – after the fact. Chandler does subscribe to the defence's contention that Duch's 'enthusiasm' was what the Party required, but says Duch had 'absolutely no trouble accepting' that either.

'It suited his own inclinations and his own abilities, and he was a revolutionary Party person,' he says. 'He was doing not only what was accepted but what he wanted to do. They coincided because you're not independent from the Party. You and the Party are one force.'

By mid-1978, as we know, Duch had become fearful for his own safety. A number of his former mentors had been arrested and executed, and Son Sen might well have followed them had the regime remained in power much longer. As Chandler points out, Pol Pot seems to have lost his reason, and his paranoia now extended to envisioning clashes involving Warsaw Pact forces in the rice fields of Cambodia. Duch's regrets at that point might well have been authentic yet he still chose to remain with the Khmer Rouge for a further two decades after the regime was ousted.

FOR HIS BOOK ON S-21, Chandler read around 1,000 confessions, and in consequence his testimony proves to be one of the high points of the trial. He is sober, level-headed and reflective and, as arguably the leading scholar on S-21, his analysis is hard to counter.

He is also unwilling to caricature Duch as a monster and like Bizot, prefers to try and understand the reality of the situation he was in, with the obvious caveat that Duch had played a significant role in creating that environment.

Unsurprisingly, Roux seizes on that element and brings up the famous Milgram experiment, which Chandler cites in his book, asking him to explain it. The Milgram experiment, which was conducted in the US in the 1960s, was a sociological study to test obedience. A volunteer was seated with an instructor in front of various dials, and told to ask questions of a third person who was out of sight behind a wall. Every time this third person gave a wrong answer, the volunteer was told to press a button and deliver an electric shock as punishment. Although the instructor knew the third person was an actor and that there was no electric shock being delivered, the volunteer did not. As the questions went on, the instructor encouraged the volunteer to deliver ever stronger shocks. Most complied, despite knowing that they were pushing the voltage past the danger sign and despite hearing the victim screaming and pleading for them to stop.

'And it seems to me that this gets very close to the culture, not just of S-21, but the culture of Democratic Kampuchea, where the people who gave the orders were accustomed to giving them [and] the people who received the orders were accustomed to obeying,' Chandler replies. 'There is no culture in Cambodia of questioning commands by someone who is in authority – in other words, questioning a military leader, a teacher, and so on.'

Obedience, says Chandler, was central to the horror of S-21.

One of Chandler's most intriguing answers comes when he is asked about the archive, which runs to hundreds of thousands of pages: more than 4,000 confessions, as well as prisoner lists, execution lists, administrative papers, study session documents and self-criticism material. What, he is asked, was its value?

'It seems to me that one purpose of assembling this archive was to demonstrate to the Party leadership that S-21 was thoroughly responsible [and] efficient – a modern and productive body inside the government, inside a country where conditions were in many places, as wide evidence suggests, completely chaotic from day to day,' he replies.

Duch was running an organisation so well that it would come to be regarded as a model of efficiency in the years to come and one of which 'he, as its administrator, could be justly proud'.[17]

'I think he wanted to excel in this job, and indeed in other things earlier in his career,' Chandler says. 'He wanted to excel as a student. He wanted to excel as an apprentice revolutionary. And throughout his professional life I think he was interested in not just serving those above him – that wasn't that hard really – but to serve them with enthusiasm and skill that he could be proud of himself.'

But as 1977 became 1978 and Duch's former mentors started appearing at the gates of S-21 as prisoners, his enthusiasm began to wane. Of that, says Chandler, there is no doubt.

Weeks earlier Duch had told the court about those days and of his fear as he realised the revolution was going off the rails. When Son Sen ordered the purging of the North Zone, Duch was shocked as hundreds of loyal Khmer Rouge were brought to S-21. It was then that he knew he was trapped in a system that could consume him and his family. His revolutionary dream had been a socialist society that followed the precept: 'From each according to his abilities, and to each according to his needs', yet he was now enmeshed in a murderous security state.

As a result Duch trained his subordinates to have the right class stance, to smash the enemies of the revolution and to keep the machine turning in the hope that he and his family would be spared.

CHANDLER'S MEASURED WORDS provide some relief for Roux, coming as they do after testimony that has proved damaging for his client

17. At trial, Duch referred to himself and to S-21 on several occasions as being 'instruments' of the Party (see, for example, trial document E1_17.1_EN, April 28, 2009, p. 46). Rithy Panh points out that, when he interviewed Duch three decades later, the former commandant of S-21 was still annoyed that his creation had not been awarded Democratic Kampuchea's most prestigious title of 'pure instrument of the revolution'. Panh, op. cit., p. 72.

and that has provided easy pickings for the prosecution: evidence given by the four living survivors of S-21, by several civil parties and by some of Duch's former staff. The weeks ahead also hold little promise for the defence with 16 civil parties scheduled to appear. Among them will be Martine and Neary.

We have been able to sweep cleanly away more than 99 per cent of the contemptible major concealed enemies boring from within. Things throughout the country must be examined like this. Each sector must be examined like this. Each district must be examined like this. Each cooperative must be examined like this. The army and ministries and offices must be examined like this.

— Extract from November 1977 issue of *Revolutionary Flag* magazine

We must see as key the duties of attacking the domestic enemy, that this is related to every one of all our other duties. Every Party level must therefore adopt the role of leading the army and the people to attack all such enemies. Sweep them cleanly away. Sweep and sweep and sweep again and again, ceaselessly, so that our Party forces are pure, our leading forces at every level and every sphere are clean at all times.

— Extract from May 1978 issue of *Revolutionary Flag* magazine

You must destroy the visible enemy, and the hidden one, too – the enemy in the mind!

— Khmer Rouge slogan

CHAPTER TEN

AN INEXCUSABLE MURDER

LESS THAN A WEEK AFTER leaving his wife and children in France, Ket was shackled in a small brick cell at S-21. The date was June 15, 1977 and, although we do not know exactly what had happened in the few days after he landed in Phnom Penh, it seems likely that he was taken either to a camp for intellectuals in the capital or held at the Ministry of Foreign Affairs while the Khmer Rouge decided what to do with him. In any event, the testimony of a man called Him Huy means we know enough about how the process worked to determine what happened next.

You would not guess Him Huy's fearsome reputation from the slightly built man in his fifties who takes the stand in July 2009. The few survivors of S-21 recall him as particularly brutal. By his own admission he is a killer, although he claims implausibly that he murdered only one prisoner. Him Huy was stationed at the Unit to Receive Detainees, the guardhouse positioned a block away from S-21. People destined for S-21 would be dropped off at the guardhouse and his unit would escort them up the road and through the main gate. Given the timelines, it is a near certainty that Him Huy brought Ket to S-21 and later transported him to Chhoeung Ek for execution.

In the early 1970s, as a teenager, Him Huy fought as an infantryman in the Khmer Rouge army and in April 1975 was involved in the capture of Phnom Penh. The following year he was assigned to work as a guard at S-21 and after that he was posted to the Unit to Receive Detainees. The perennial internal purges of 1976–78 provided opportunities for advancement and by 1977 Him Huy was in charge of the unit. He tells the court that promotion worked much the same way in S-21's other sections too: the interrogation unit, the economics unit, the kitchen unit, the medical unit. As the months went by, their members fell under suspicion and were taken away and killed.

'In the end, there were only a few left,' he says.

The procedure for arresting prisoners varied, but not by much. Those detained in other parts of the country – like the artist Vann Nath, for instance – would be handcuffed and blindfolded at source before being trucked to Him Huy's guardhouse and unloaded. If there were just a few dozen detainees, Him Huy's men would rope them together and march them along the rough, unpaved road and through S-21's front gate. A delivery of hundreds was different: in order to preserve S-21's secret status, the drivers and guards would get out and Him Huy's group of up to 10 men would drive the vehicles the final few hundred yards.

In the case of returnees from France, a Khmer Rouge messenger would come to the guardhouse and tell them to expect new arrivals.

'Then they would transport those people to the house where we were stationed and we prepared our forces to arrest them,' Him Huy says.

Earlier that day Ket would likely have been told in deceptive, reassuring terms that he was being taken to a new location for work ('Brother, you must come with us. *Angkar* has a position for you elsewhere').[1]

With perhaps two or three others, he would have been driven through Phnom Penh's once familiar streets, now deserted, across silent intersections and through a city almost devoid of life.

The jeep would have pulled up outside the guardhouse on Street 360 and the cadres would have escorted them inside. Ket and those with him would have been ordered to sit at a table and wait. At this point they were likely not blindfolded or handcuffed – after all, they had been told they were going somewhere new for work – so even now Ket would have had no idea of what was to come. Everything was done in secret, all soft words and duplicity. The escort would have left and, after a short time and a secret signal, Him Huy's men would have arrested Ket.

Him Huy is not asked, and he does not volunteer, how the atmosphere changed as the arrests were made but it is easy to conclude that violence would be threatened and used. After all, as Him Huy explains, they were

---

1. In his testimony, Him Huy said deception was commonly practised, and agreed that there were two types of arrest: either people were told they had been assigned to work elsewhere, and were subsequently arrested when they arrived at his unit, or they were arrested, handcuffed and blindfolded at source before being delivered to his unit. See Him Huy's testimony, ECCC trial transcript, July 16, 2009, p. 23.

trained to respect *Angkar's* discipline and to be 'absolute toward the enemies' during a time when 'absolute' meant being serious about smashing the foes of the revolution.

'Those who can follow the so-called wheel of history would be spared,' he tells the bench. 'Those who could not follow would be dead.'[2]

Ket might well have protested his innocence – since he had done nothing wrong – but to do so would have carried no weight. The guards were not trained to listen; they were uneducated peasants, devotees of the revolution, automatons who did what they were told.

At this point Ket and the others would have been handcuffed, blindfolded and roped together, then marched the few hundred yards up the road and into the compound of S-21. A guard at the front held the rope and others flanked the detainees until they had passed safely through the gates and been handed over.

It is only now that Ket re-enters our sight, although just briefly. Five days earlier he had sent the postcard from Beijing telling his family of his love for them. Now he is in S-21, his name is entered in the register, and he is ordered to recount his biography: his name and family background, his schooling and training and his work history. All of these, like his subsequent confession, have long since disappeared. Ket's blindfold is removed. He is photographed and assigned a cell.

In the image, the one that Martine and Neary found in 2009 that they identified as him, Ket looks reprovingly at the young photographer. Ket's jaw is clenched, his body tilted slightly to the left, his eyes hold firm with the camera. A metal tag with the number 238 stencilled across its narrow width is pinned to a worn, black, long-sleeved collared shirt, nothing like the elegant clothes in which he left Paris. Ket's arms are by his side and look to be handcuffed behind his back. The harsh flash has bleached his face and thrown a deep shadow on to the pale wall behind him, mimicking his head and shoulders, the negative unable to cope with the extremes of white and black and the shades of grey in between.

The image shows a fresh wound to his face, a thin diagonal welt that starts above his right eye and runs across his nose and under his left eye. It is the mark of a whip or a bamboo switch, probably inflicted by someone

---

2. As Locard points out, this was a common phrase during Democratic Kampuchea: 'He who does not move forward fast enough will be crushed by the wheel of history.' *Pol Pot's Little Red Book*, op. cit., p. 213.

in Him Huy's unit while Ket was seated at the table as he was told of his arrest. Perhaps he protested or perhaps someone decided that this educated, unsuspecting man warranted a beating.

In any event, Neary tells me, paraphrasing the Auschwitz survivor Jean Améry, that first blow partially destroys your trust in the world and makes you understand that what is to come will outdo everything you have experienced. For Primo Levi, who also survived Auschwitz and became one of the most compelling voices of the Holocaust, the first time he was beaten – as he and others were loaded onto transport trains – generated no pain: 'Only a profound amazement: how can one hit a man without anger?'[3]

It is a question, Neary believes, that Duch can answer. S-21 survivor Chum Mey told her that he witnessed Duch several times hitting prisoners across the face with a wooden stick when they arrived.

'I can't help thinking that in Duch's case, the first hit was just *fun*,' Neary told me later.

Regardless of who first hit him and why, Ket must surely have known that by now he was in desperate trouble. Yet he must surely have assumed too – for who would not hold such common logic? – that once the prison authorities learned that he was innocent of any crimes against the revolution they would release him. How could it be any other way? But in this machine the only logic was the certainty of suffering and death, and all that stood between those certainties and the beaten man in the photograph was time.

Once again, after the briefest of views, Ouk Ket disappears from our sight, this time into the void of S-21. He will reappear six months later when, on December 9, 1977, he was sent for execution. Twenty-five weeks had passed between that Wednesday in June when he was taken here and the Friday in December when he was driven out of the gate to his death. We know he was held in a tiny room on the ground floor of Building C – cell number 23 in room 2 – and we know he spent 177 nights in S-21. Other than that we know almost nothing, because Ket's file has disappeared.

ON AUGUST 17, 2009, Martine takes the stand. It is day 59 of the 78-day trial and she is the eighth civil party to testify. Another 15 will follow her. Allowing civil parties to tell the court how these crimes affected them makes for powerful testimony. For the defence it marks a dangerous time. Unlike

3. *Survival in Auschwitz: The Nazi Assault on Humanity*, Primo Levi, translated Stuart Woolf (Simon & Schuster, 1996), p. 16.

the evidence given by experts or former S-21 staff, it would be disastrous for Duch to attack the civil parties or query them. His best course is to acknowledge what they tell the court and keep his head down, to apologise and be contrite.

On this day, a Monday, the tribunal's outreach office has bussed in dozens of Cham Muslims, an ethnic group that suffered disproportionately under the Khmer Rouge, to watch proceedings. I have secured a front-row seat in the auditorium and the rows behind me are filled with men wearing white *chhnut* skullcaps and women in coloured headscarves.

Martine, in a black suit, crosses the floor to the wooden witness box, then turns to the audience and greets them with the traditional Khmer *sampeah*, her hands clasped together. She acknowledges the judges in the same way, then sits in her chair facing the bench, straight-backed, Duch to her right. To her left on the stage are some of the other civil parties, including Neary.

When I had met them the previous evening – she and Neary had flown back to Cambodia from France to testify – Martine had told us she would remove her headphones to avoid hearing Duch's apologies that follow each civil party's statement. She felt they were weasel words. Neary smiled at Martine and told her there was no harm in listening to Duch, but her mother was adamant. This was Martine's way of determining the discourse, and I wondered whether she would follow through.

On the stand it takes just a few minutes to outline the seven years the couple shared prior to Ket's disappearance. She tells how she had met Ket in 1970, how they were married in October 1971, and how in January 1972 she had followed him to his diplomatic posting in Senegal where their two children were born. She explains that, after the recall letter from the foreign ministry, they had returned to France in May 1977. Weeks later Ket left for home. From Karachi and Beijing he sent two postcards, which she received in June, 'where he told of his love for me, my children and my family'.

'After this I didn't receive any more news from my husband,' she says.

Martine speaks of how her efforts to track down Ket were repeatedly frustrated, starting with her visit in September 1977 to the Chinese embassy in Paris, and noting that she later learned Ket was still alive at this juncture and 'something could have been done to prevent his death'. She reached out to Amnesty International and to the International Red Cross to see whether they could help and she feverishly followed the trickle of news emanating from Cambodia.

In early 1979, Martine had received the duplicitous letter from Chan Youran, the former Cambodian ambassador to Senegal and Ket's boss, in which he told her, 'I know [Ket] was fine before the Vietnamese invasion'. She recounts her failed trip to Geneva when Chan Youran proved unable to provide any details, leaving her convinced that he had lied.

Duch, in a white shirt, watches attentively, his left hand cupping his chin and his elbows on his desk.

In France in 1979, Martine met several of Ket's acquaintances who had survived Democratic Kampuchea. Some had been held in the camp for intellectuals 'and their accounts were horrific', she said. One handed her the confession of Hu Nim, the information minister who was tortured and executed at S-21. It struck terror in her heart.

Given the trauma she is recounting, Martine is astonishingly composed, her words measured, her voice fixed. By now I have met her several times during her and Neary's two visits to Cambodia and I have some idea of what this was costing her. I know her composure here today is a brittle facade. Every few seconds Martine's eyes look to the ceiling as though to drain the tears she is disguising.

Just before Christmas 1979, she continues, she headed to the refugee camps in Thailand to try and learn more. It was there that she met Ong Thong Hoeung, who told her he had seen the line in the ledger stating that Ket had been murdered at S-21. Learning what had happened to Ket enraged and saddened Martine in equal measure. Shortly afterwards she returned to France, the worst realised.

'I must organise my life without my husband and I must explain to my children what happened to their father and how they will have to grow up without their daddy,' she says.

But how to tell them? The children were so young, and even for Martine, just 27, 'it is already very difficult to accept this reality'.

Only now does her voice crack as she tells the court through sobs how, after she returned, her children asked every day whether she had seen their father and when they would see him again. They were the same pleading questions she had heard for more than two years, and so, one week after coming back from Thailand, Martine hugged Mackara and Neary close and told them what had happened.

ELEVEN YEARS LATER, IN 1991, Martine, Mackara and Neary had

saved enough money to come to Phnom Penh, returning, as Martine says, in Ket's footsteps. The four surviving members of Ket's 11-strong family – his mother and her three youngest children – were living in poverty with no running water or electricity.

Two days after landing, Martine and the children went to the former prison where, among the faces on the walls, she recognised friends from their Paris days. But Ket's photo was not there.

'The three of us are profoundly saddened and very, very angry,' she says. 'And I have great difficulty convincing my children to stay, with their fists clenched and their teeth gritted in the face of so much horror.'

It was no better the following day when they visited Chhoeung Ek, a place that left them 'completely revolted'. Bones, rags of clothing and white teeth, like the grim seeds of a bitter harvest, pushed up through the earth. They were convinced Ket's skull was one of the thousands stacked in the mausoleum.

During their few weeks in Cambodia, Martine and the children returned to the archives of S-21 to try and find some record of Ket. His name came up just twice in those dusty records: once in an entry list for June 15, 1977 and once on a typed execution list of 301 names dated December 9, 1977. Ket's name was on line 43. Other friends, she tells the court, also appeared on this document.

Aware that her mind could not take in all of this horror, Martine photographed as much as possible, including images of some of the senior staff at S-21. Among them were Duch and Mam Nai, the head interrogator and Duch's right-hand man.

'And just by looking at their faces, I told myself that Ket must have had a rough time,' she says. 'I knew these people had had something to do with the death of my husband, and as I looked at their terrifying faces, I could picture how he himself was terrified.'

In the years since, Martine has conjured suitably apocalyptic visions of Ket's time at S-21: chained like a slave to a metal bar in a cramped, dirty cell, stripped of his rights and unaware of why he was 'in this hell'.

'He was deprived of the most fundamental needs – no food, no medical care, no hygiene, psychological solitude, torture by henchmen using Nazi methods. Six relentless months of this, and I am certain that Ket resisted and that he did everything he could to hold on so that one day he could see us again,' she says. 'We were like the fingers of one hand.'

By now Martine has been talking for 35 minutes, an unbroken monologue of heartbreaking testimony that transfixes the court.

'So now I understand his physical and psychological degradation,' she says. 'He died a slow death at S-21 in the most complete secrecy, in solitude, and on the 9th of December 1977, murderers broke his skull at Chhoeung Ek and then they cut his throat in a pit. That is an inexcusable murder.'

The court is silent as Martine sips water from a plastic cup before continuing.

'Ket's suffering was and still is our suffering,' she says, 'and, far from diminishing with time, I can tell you that the suffering is in fact more and more intense. It is like having a big screen too close to one's face.'

Even today there is no body, no grave, no restitution, Martine says, not even a document from the Cambodian government.

'And the result for me is total human failure,' she says. 'And so I came before this court to demand justice – justice for this barbaric crime so that the suffering experienced by Ket and all other Cambodians can at last be recognised, whether they were in S-21 or anywhere else in the country, and that our suffering as survivors is also acknowledged.'

For Martine the tribunal is more than an opportunity to see some form of justice exacted.

'I also came here before you in order to restore Ket's dignity, which was trampled at S-21, and the dignity of our French and Cambodian family,' she says.

As for Duch's protestations that he was trapped in a system, these strike Martine as worthless. In her view, Duch, responsible for so many thousands of deaths, should have committed suicide years ago.

'There's an imbalance between the fear of dying oneself and the number of people who were killed, and for me that is unacceptable,' Martine says, as Duch looks on, his arms crossed on the desk. 'Instead I will speak of vengeance and zeal. Had this mathematics teacher forgotten to think, so that he could gorge on blood, on the screams of the tortured, on corpses for nine years? If one can't call this revelling in a dirty job, then tell me: What does it look like?'

The deaths of others, she concludes, were Duch's 'daily food' for nearly a decade, and for that he deserves a life sentence. And once that is handed down, she would like Duch to be forgotten and this time instead be spent remembering the victims of the Khmer Rouge and those they left behind, among them Ket's five grandchildren in France: Neary's son and Mackara's four children.

'[They] need to be reconciled with the Khmer part of our family history and that won't be possible in S-21 nor in Chhoeung Ek. These places are the shame of humanity. We need a peaceful place here in Cambodia, open to the public,' Martine says. 'We thought of a media library, bearing the name of Ouk Ket, that would operate in both the Khmer and French languages in the neighbourhood where Ket lived for the first 23 years of his life.'

In that way, by investing in education and culture, her family's sorrow might diminish, and the dignity of Ket and other Cambodians could be restored.

With that, Martine closes her address.

'I would like to conclude by stating that Ket is today more present than ever in our hearts and that we love him and that we will always love him,' Martine says, her voice breaking again. 'His face is here before us.'

ON DECEMBER 9, 1977, Duch ordered Ket and 300 other prisoners to be executed. The purges that *Ta* Mok was carrying out in the East Zone with tens of thousands killed meant S-21 had to make room for new arrivals.[4] The cadres in the East were accused of having Cambodian bodies and Vietnamese minds, a charge that was both unprovable and, for those unfortunate enough to have it levelled against them, indefensible.[5]

The precision of record-keeping at S-21 makes it easy enough to recreate Ket's last day. Months of starvation rations – two tiny bowls of watery rice soup per day – would have left his bones pushing hard against the skin. His body would have been beaten and tortured to a near broken state and by now he must have confessed to whatever crimes *Angkar* sought, most likely to being CIA and having feudalist tendencies. By early December, with his confession deemed suitable, Duch would have ordered Ket moved to Building D, the holding pen for those to be transported to Chhoeung Ek.

As the sun went down behind S-21, casting the evening sky with the orange of a monk's robes, Him Huy's unit drove its trucks to the gates, the

---

4. The execution register at S-21's archives lists 776 names of prisoners murdered in 11 batches during November and December 1977 alone. Ket's name is one of those.

5. It is worth noting that Pol Pot was by now rattled by a recent, ongoing invasion of Vietnamese troops, a warning from Hanoi that it was tired of cross-border Khmer Rouge raids that had left hundreds dead inside Vietnam. The Vietnamese withdrew on January 6, 1978, but invaded again in late 1978 and drove out the Khmer Rouge.

diesel engines rattling in the air. The prisoners were taken, their hands tied behind their backs, blindfolded. The guards, who were instructed to use deception to ensure that their charges remained passive, told the condemned: 'We are moving you to a new home, brother.'

A chair was placed behind each truck and the detainees ordered to use it to climb on board. Once the convoy was ready, it set off through empty streets, snaking south and west through a near-lifeless city.

While it is impossible to know what Ket was thinking, it is impossible too not to wonder. Did he believe his hell was over and that he would now be allowed to return to society? Or was he convinced that he was going to his death, and after 177 days of suffering did that much matter? The prospect of death might well have seemed a relief,[6] even as the thought of never seeing his family must have been a final agony.

And so Ket would have been packed in with dozens of others on the metal floor of a Chinese-made military truck, flanked by hard-faced guards, Him Huy among them, bumping along the rutted roads out of Phnom Penh. They crossed a small bridge into the open expanse of rice fields where the rattle of the engines no longer reverberated off empty buildings but filtered out into the widening gloom, rippling and disappearing into the night. Half an hour after leaving S-21, the trucks turned left down a dirt road and into a compound where they parked next to a stilted house with a walled pen on its ground floor.

The guards climbed down, opened the rear door panel and told the prisoners to dismount. Still handcuffed, still blindfolded, this broken mass was shuffled into a holding pen. Outside, a diesel generator beat out its regular rhythm and a dozen fluorescent lights cast their clinical glow as Him Huy began the process of checking the prisoners against the list of names.

Earlier in the day another team based at Chhoeung Ek had dug deep holes in the sandy soil. Now, with the names crosschecked, the prisoners, still handcuffed, still blindfolded, are led out of the holding pen one at a time, pinioned between the guards. At some point, with the moon just a pale sliver in the sky, it would have been Ket's turn to be walked into the darkness. He was number 43 on the list; it is likely he was the 43rd to die.

---

6. Not a phrase I use lightly, but as Hannah Arendt noted: 'There exist many things considerably worse than death.' Arendt was referring to the months of torture endured by 430 Dutch Jews as a reprisal for an attack on German forces in 1941. The prisoners were eventually killed. *Eichmann in Jerusalem: A Report on the Banality of Evil*, Hannah Arendt (first published by Viking Press, 1963; this edition by Penguin Books, 2006), p. 12.

The process was the same for all. Ket was taken 50 metres to the edge of a pit, the smell of earth and fresh blood filling the air. Now, surely, there could be no doubt of what was to come, but to cry out would be futile – even if he had the strength, the diesel generator would drown out the warning, which was indeed part of its function: to ensure that any noise would be swallowed by its thuds and pushed into the inky blackness that reaches out across this land, beyond the pale fringe where the lamps cast their weak glow.

Ouk Ket is 31. He is married with a young wife, Martine, and two small children, Mackara and Neary, who are waiting for him halfway across the world, and in whose small garden the arum lilies' pale petals have been crushed by winter's shroud. He is a family man with an excellent education. He is a person of culture who loves volleyball and cooking and playing the guitar, and who talks in Khmer-accented French to his children. He has come back to help rebuild his nation and to teach, because he believes there is nothing worse than ignorance.

Ket is pushed to his knees at the side of the pit, his hands still tied behind his back, his eyes still blindfolded, the heavy thud of the generator pulsing through the cooling air, as behind him the moths and insects throw themselves against the ghostly glow of the fluorescent bulbs.

And then, the end. With a practised swing, the executioner smashes the axle of an oxcart against the base of Ket's skull. His body slumps forward into the mass grave where another cadre wielding a knife slashes Ket's throat. As his blood mixes with the dust of his homeland, Ket's life leaves him. Only now are his handcuffs removed. Last of all, Ket is stripped of his clothes, and his body is pushed into the anonymity of this common grave.

With 301 prisoners, it is well into the early hours before the executioners finish their assignment, covering the pit before the sun casts long fingers of soft light across the flat plain, drawing colour from the dawn's grey gradients and marking out the lines of a new day over the fresh red earth.

ANY TALK OF FORGIVENESS is premature, Martine tells the court. It first requires finding the guilty parties, seeing them judged, and after that reparations.

'At this moment, no,' she says in reply to her civil party lawyer. 'It is a process. Maybe in 30 years – maybe it will take as much time to forgive as the time that we have taken to uncover the truth.'

As the surviving parent, Martine's life became a complex balancing act of mourning her husband, not weeping in front of Mackara and Neary, avoiding the temptation of suicide, and realigning her life to provide for her children who cried daily for their father.

'We weren't able to mourn properly – there was no body, no restitution of a body, no tomb. Ket, he is dust in Chhoeung Ek just like millions of Cambodians. This is a daily suffering. There isn't a single day that I don't think of it,' she tells the court. 'They destroyed our life, and that is unforgivable, inexcusable.'

After returning from the refugee camps, Martine trained as a nurse and then worked in the emergency department. Neary believes Martine chose that path 'to help my dad – it's like you want to help but it's too late, so you've got to help everyone'.

Eventually Martine transferred to work in a psychiatric ward. The sight of blood bags in the emergency department made her vomit; the injuries of the patients and the condition of the poorest – their ragged clothes, gauntness and lank, dirty hair – only served to remind her of what had happened to Ket.

Martine does not wish to ask Duch any questions, but her lawyer puts a question to him on her behalf: How were the returning intellectuals brought to S-21?

Duch stands up, his hands squared on the desktop and addresses himself to Martine. Initially, he replies, the returning intellectuals from the FUNK were taken to re-education camps where they were watched by the Party. Some intellectuals were sent to S-21, he continues, where they were tortured for their confessions and then smashed. Those numbers increased through 1976 and 1977. That is all he has to say.

Neither the prosecution nor the defence has any questions for Martine and the floor is given over to Duch to comment on her testimony. Martine looks resolutely away from him, to the left and high into the court's ceiling, as Duch tells her that her testimony will be 'forever true' and will be of use to people looking to research the crimes of the Khmer Rouge. His is a remarkably clumsy response and I wonder whether Duch's mind is forever locked into the value of archiving above all else, and that he is unable to link to personal suffering.

Unlike a flower, he continues, 'the truth can never change'.

It is now that Martine, true to her word, removes her headphones and for part of Duch's speech at least, closes her eyes, blocking him entirely.

It unnerves Duch. His head flicks three times to the side as he pauses to gather his thoughts, before stating that what happened to 'your loved one' – he does not use Ket's name – and to other Cambodians should never be forgotten.

'And I would like to state further that – in particular to Madame Lefeuvre and to the chamber – that I will not run away from the crimes I have committed. It is inexcusable. The nation of Cambodia can point their finger to me. They can curse me. They can punish me, whatever they would wish to do so,' Duch says. 'And the court is here and I am before the court and responsible for all the crimes committed at S-21 legally and psychologically, and I do not intend to deny any crimes committed at S-21, and I would like to seek forgiveness from Madame Lefeuvre and other people who have lost their loved ones during the regime. That's all.'

Hey you, evil informer … you lowest of things
You are an enemy lackey;
And even if you are a relative, we are not deluded;
We take a strong stance of smashing every single one of you.

— Song broadcast in villages during Khmer Rouge rallies

From interview of Duch by the tribunal's investigating judges

CHAPTER ELEVEN

TO KEEP YOU IS NO BENEFIT, TO DESTROY YOU IS NO LOSS

EVEN BY THE BRUTAL STANDARDS of the Khmer Rouge, the story seemed implausible. It was the middle of the rainy season, when the monsoon funnels in from the south-west soaking the land, swelling the rivers and painting the countryside in vivid greens. As I headed north-west from Phnom Penh along Route 5 to the city of Battambang, the fields were busy with people bent double replanting the rice seedlings on which their livelihoods depend.

It was 2011 and I was travelling with a friend, Dar Seng, a gregarious Cambodian-American lawyer in his thirties. As a child growing up in Democratic Kampuchea, he and his siblings had been orphaned; after 1979 they had been fortunate enough to reach the United States. After graduating, he had returned to Cambodia and spent the intervening decade working in a number of different areas including, when I first met him, running a NGO whose focus was reconciliation. Dar's former colleagues had heard a strange story about a factory near Battambang, and he knew I was planning to write a book about the Khmer Rouge. He felt I might want to look into it.

A decade earlier Route 5 was a pot-holed mess, like nearly every other road, but donor funds saw many of them rebuilt. The work was often shoddy, because the government typically awarded the contracts to the military or dodgy front companies that skimmed much of the cash. Route 5 retained that schizophrenic aspect – part good, part terrible – and the car lurched as we bounded along the southern edge of the Tonle Sap Lake.

Over the years Battambang has managed to retain its charm, in part because it was not bombed by the Americans in the 1970s and more recently because It attracts few tourists. This region is Cambodia's rice basket, the hub of the agricultural sector that underpins the economy. Run-down but functioning rice mills stand every few hundred yards along the main road into town, huge sheds of clanking, inefficient machinery.

We started our search for the factory 15 kilometres from Battambang. All we had was a photograph showing a redbrick building that looked to be two storeys high and with distinctive chimneys. The style was unusual, with some of the brickwork inset in herringbone giving it a faintly colonial air.

We turned off Route 5 at O Taki village and drove down a dirt road across the derelict railway track that links Poipet on the Thai border with Phnom Penh. At a roadside stall we showed the photograph to a group of men and women, who were standing with a cluster of children. A teenage girl pointed back the way we had come.

'It's further along the main road,' she said.

Dar asked her what she knew about the building.

'It's where the Khmer Rouge took people to turn them into fertiliser,' she replied with a nervous giggle. 'My parents and the old people living here talk about it.'

As we left, a man in his twenties with a Chelsea football shirt chipped in: 'That place is haunted.'

I HAD ASSUMED that processing human corpses into fertiliser was extreme even by the standards of the twentieth century's most utilitarian (for want of a better word) political movement. I was wrong. US academic Craig Etcheson said the perceived wisdom among the Khmer Rouge was to bury half a corpse under a young coconut palm. A full body provided too much nutrition and would kill the sapling.

Once I started looking, the evidence kept coming. In 2012 villagers in Siem Reap province uncovered a mass grave containing several dozen skulls. The deputy village chief told reporters from the *Phnom Penh Post* that he had not known about this site, but said that in 1980 he had paid villagers five cans of rice a day to dig through a nearby furnace pit and recover the bones of victims. He said the Khmer Rouge had thrown both the dead and the living into the 15-metre by 25-metre pit and burned them to make fertiliser.

There are other accounts. An elderly woman told researchers from DC-Cam that people in her area were executed, thrown into pits, then doused in rice husks and fuel and their bodies set alight. The cremated remains were turned out as ash for the rice fields to improve production.

In 1979 a man called Kung Saray told interviewers that all 10 members of his family had been imprisoned after they were accused of being lazy. One day the Khmer Rouge took away the rest of Saray's family, but left him behind in jail. He knew his parents and siblings had been murdered when he saw the Khmer Rouge dividing up their clothing. Villagers told him that bodies were burned in nearby pits for fertiliser. Several days later Saray was ordered to mend a fence just yards from those pits and watched as men moved among stacks of bones. The next day, trucks brought 60 people to the site and he witnessed them being beaten to death and dumped into the flames.

The Khmer Rouge did not always burn the dead before using them to enrich the soil. A tailor in Siem Reap province told investigators that she was regularly forced to dig up human bones, mix them with urine and grind them up for fertiliser. Another survivor, Youkimny Chan, told other researchers that cadres had thrown the body parts of a boy they had hacked to pieces into the rice fields, telling the workers it was fertiliser.

Yet another survivor, an old woman called Chhay Rin, had headed an all-women unit in north-western Banteay Meanchey province whose role was to turn human remains into fertiliser. The unit sought out mass graves, exhumed the bodies, stripped the flesh then burned the bones to ash. She did that for more than a year, watched over constantly by four Khmer Rouge soldiers.

'In the beginning, I could not stand the smell of corpses, but as time passed it would not really matter to me,' she told staff from DC-Cam. 'I did not try to remove the flesh from the corpses immediately after I excavated them, because it smelled too bad. No matter how bad the smell was, I never had any objections since the Khmer Rouge constantly kept their eyes on me.'

By 1978 the killings in her area had reached such a scale that only a few families were left alive. Half of the women in her unit had been executed or had died of starvation or illness. Twenty-six people in her family were killed, including her children, nephews, nieces, her brothers and sisters.

It is hard to comprehend viewing people in such a manner but the sayings of the time make it clear that people had no value other than their labour. Among the many phrases that dehumanised was this one: 'To keep you is no benefit, to destroy you is no loss.' If people were not trusted or if they committed some minor infraction then, in some regions at least, their worth was limited to their flesh and bones, a barbarically utilitarian view of human life.

Even Duch, ensconced in S-21, was aware of the practice. At Duch's trial, the S-21 survivor Vann Nath told how in 1978 his fellow painter Bou Meng was taken away. At the time Vann Nath wrongly assumed Bou Meng had been freed, but one day he reappeared looking pale and drawn, chains on his neck and legs. Bou Meng was forced to his knees to apologise. Duch turned to Vann Nath and asked, 'whether contemptible Meng could be used any longer or could he be used to make fertiliser?'

Vann Nath assumed Duch meant Bou Meng should be put to work making fertiliser, which he felt was a waste of his artistic talents so he asked Duch to let Bou Meng come back and paint. It was only much later that Vann Nath realised what Duch had really suggested.

WE FOUND THE BUILDING a few kilometres further along the main road where it backed on to rice fields. Out front where the rains had turned the earth to mud was a stand of heavy-fronded banana trees. A date in Khmer script fashioned from clay bricks showed it was built in 1976, and while this might once have been a small factory it was now home to several impoverished families. The rear portion of the roof had collapsed, the walls were punctured by gaping holes and the floor was an uneven run of hard earth pecked over by chickens. Washing lines held clothes faded and greyed. A bedstead stood in the middle of the left-hand room.

We talked to Chan, a wiry man in his early fifties. He wore a *krama* around his waist, and his bare chest sported the faded tattoos common to ex-soldiers who once needed protection from bullets. Chan's family had lived in the area for generations, and he spent 'the Pol Pot time' in a nearby village. Nowadays, he said, he farmed rice and on occasion helped the commune chief organise functions.

Chan had an odd manner, speaking through the left side of his mouth and repeatedly stressing that he was telling the truth. The stories about people being turned into fertiliser were true, he told us. Well, sort of. He would explain.

Chan's great-uncle had been a village leader during Democratic Kampuchea and it was from him that he had learned the building's history: those who had built it were later lured away and executed by *Ta* Mok's

South-west Zone troops in one of the purges of that time. Its original purpose was to act as a centralised system for storing natural fertiliser – nitrates, cow dung, potash – in the concrete tanks outside. However, a woman who claimed she had been an engineer during Democratic Kampuchea told Chan that the factory was refitted to process people instead. It seems the grinding machines were moved in – they stood here and here, Chan said, pointing to concrete posts set in the ground, with pipes connected under the floor to the holding tanks outside – but before the process began there was a power struggle between this district and neighbouring Mong district. Mong district won and took the machines.

Dar and I looked around. The bricks were poorly laid but the herringbone decorative elements in the upper quadrants were dangerously bourgeois. Whoever had laid those bricks during Democratic Kampuchea had taken an obvious, perhaps dangerous, pride in their handiwork, though the building's crumbling condition meant it was unlikely that it would stand for another three decades. Our amiable guide clearly had no means of improving it.

'Just a handful of people come each year to see the building,' he said. 'My neighbours suggested that I have a contribution box for tourists to donate but I dare not do that in case people accuse me of misusing the money.'

Chan told us that just three people had died here, all of them Khmer Rouge cadres killed by embittered villagers in 1979 as the movement's remaining supporters fled. During Democratic Kampuchea the villagers had been warned to keep their distance from the building so Chan had seen nothing that could shed further light on its function, but he insisted it was not used to turn people into fertiliser even though the means were in place.

I asked whether he was worried about the spirits of the dead. No, he said. Even though there are ghosts, those who killed them were not from here.

'So the spirits don't haunt us,' he told me. 'They live peacefully.'

In the end it was impossible to be certain about what happened here. Although the Khmer Rouge committed crimes on an industrial scale, there was no proof they had turned people into fertiliser in this building despite the apparent intention to do so. With the human fertiliser factory, as with so much else, it was difficult to know where the truth began and where it ended. The most terrifying aspect was that, between 1975 and 1979, human life was so cheap that it was wholly plausible.

MOST CAMBODIANS CANNOT UNDERSTAND why their fellow Khmers unleashed such cruelties on them. In 1992 that also puzzled a US graduate student called Alexander Hinton. Back then the Khmer Rouge were still a military force to be reckoned with and Hinton, who had planned to study cultural aspects of the Khmer language, instead explored what motivated the countless brutalities of their rule. His book *Why Did They Kill?* was the result.[1]

Hinton looks to identify what was unique about Cambodia's experience and what it had in common with other mass killings. It is a complex topic, he writes, with numerous causes and significant variations depending on local circumstances. Moreover, while it is individuals who carry out mass killings, each perpetrator melds their national picture with their own experiences. That said, Hinton believes there are notable factors and in this context he highlights Cambodian society's stress on obligation. The classic example is towards one's parents: although you can never repay your parents' good deeds, you are expected to try to do so throughout your life. The same moral obligation holds true for the help given by teachers, relatives or patrons.

Such debts create a disproportionate obligation towards those who assist you and, crucially for these purposes, that imbalance also holds true for those who wrong you. Broadly speaking, wrongdoing in the West requires a rough equality in compensation. That is not the case in Cambodia, Hinton says, where a grudge is thought of as 'packaged anger' that burns inside the wronged party. When revenge is taken, it should be greater than the harm suffered.

Hinton believes there is a connection with the concept of 'face', inasmuch as the person who inflicted the wrong has undermined the honour of the other. Revenge – in Khmer, *kar sang soek*, which literally means 'to pay back the enemy' – requires a disproportionate response that diminishes the person who wronged you and in so doing restores your honour. To repay an eye for an eye would simply level the land between the two parties.

What counts in Khmer culture, Hinton contends, is both to regain face and to destroy your enemy. To kill him removes the chance that he can take revenge. Only in that way will you recover your honour and show the rest of society that you are not to be mistreated. And there is no hurry when repaying a grudge or *kum*, which is stored, white-hot in the head or the heart

---

1. *Why Did They Kill? Cambodia in the Shadow of Genocide*, Alexander Laban Hinton (University of California Press, 2005).

and that upsets the essential balance between hot and cold that the body requires. This process of revenge can take years.

The risk of killing your enemy, however, is that their relatives might become seized with *kum* and look to exact disproportionate revenge against you, which is why in extreme cases the solution is to extinguish the family line. But that can only be done by those with the power to enforce such acts of disproportionate revenge. The nineteenth-century narrative poem *Tum Teav*, which every Cambodian knows, is a rough equivalent of *Romeo and Juliet* but with a far more violent ending. Near its conclusion, Tum, a handsome young man with a fine singing voice, is murdered by the son of a local governor over the affections of Teav, a beautiful young woman. Teav commits suicide over Tum's body. The enraged king, for whom Tum had worked, orders seven generations of the governor's family obliterated in revenge. They are buried up to their necks and decapitated by a plough.

Tum Teav is an extreme example of disproportionate revenge. Most slights do not end so drastically because Cambodian society, like any other, exerts significant pressure on people to avoid seeking revenge. Buddhism contains religious and moral precepts that help to contain or channel conflict, and there are other ways to overcome anger, including avoiding the person concerned or taking out one's rage by hitting an animal.

The Khmer Rouge made good use of these cultural understandings of revenge and anger in their indoctrination sessions. They were helped by the corruption and poverty that afflicted most, the dismissive attitude of the rich to the poor, and the relentless US bombing. Cadres were told to 'maintain a burning rage toward the enemy', and the movement motivated them by dividing society into two groups: the oppressed (us) and the oppressors (them). Once the youth understood how they had been wronged, they would take disproportionate revenge. Moreover, they had an obligation to do so. With *Angkar* as their patron providing the power, the exploited masses would regain their honour.

Part of the challenge for the Khmer Rouge was how to frame the complex, alien concepts of Marxism-Leninism and Maoism for an uneducated peasant class. In this, says Hinton, they sweetened the foreign language of revolution with concepts that were Buddhist and culturally Cambodian, a mixed approach that is common to genocidal regimes. This combined the concept of disproportionate revenge with the Marxist-Leninist requirement to kill class enemies, as one peasant recalled the indoctrination sessions.

'The Khmer Rouge "told us that the poor were poor because of the rich, and the rich were rich because of the poor. They wanted us to become seized with painful anger about this exploitation, to hate and fight bravely against the capitalist, feudal and landlord classes, the rich big people who harmed the poor",' one of them told Hinton.[2]

It tapped into societal notions of slights and revenge and, Hinton says, made sense to many. He believes class hatred was a powerful motivator for much of the violence that the Khmer Rouge meted out: abstract concepts of 'bad deeds' unleashed the rebalancing violence seen as necessary to remove the heat of anger within their heads and hearts. It was one reason the Khmer Rouge killed so many Lon Nol officials and their families after taking control.

Angkar made sure to keep the anger alive well after victory. By 1977, *Revolutionary Flag* magazine was still ordering cadres to maintain 'a constantly burning rage' against their enemies but by then the enemy was no longer only those who had worked for the Lon Nol regime. By now, everyone was suspect and the movement was seeking the traitors within. As Nuon Chea told Duch: 'In the whole of Cambodia, all are enemies except for me and Brother Pol [Pot].'[3]

IF HINTON'S NARRATIVE WITH ITS FOCUS on certain cultural elements is shared to a greater or lesser degree by a number of other writers and researchers, it is rejected outright by celebrated Cambodian film- and documentary-maker Rithy Panh. In Panh's eyes, these attempts to divine a cultural element for the killings and cruelties of Democratic Kampuchea are wrongheaded, the stuff of academic necessity.

Panh was 13 when he and his family were ordered to leave Phnom Penh in 1975. One of nine children, nearly half of Panh's immediate family died during Democratic Kampuchea.[4] After 1979, Panh joined relatives in France where he finished his schooling and then studied film-making.

---

2. Ibid., p. 75.

3. Testimony of Duch at the ECCC, April 3, 2012 (Document E1/58.1, p. 56). By now Duch was appearing as a witness at the trial of the four surviving leaders of the Khmer Rouge: Nuon Chea, Khieu Samphan, Ieng Sary and Ieng Thirith.

4. Four of Panh's brothers were studying overseas when the Khmer Rouge took power. They chose to stay away, and lived. One of his sisters survived Democratic Kampuchea, but Panh's parents, older brother and three sisters perished. One of Panh's uncles – who, like Ket, had chosen to return from abroad and help to rebuild the country – was tortured at S-21 and executed.

Decades later he is one of Cambodia's most significant creative talents whose work, particularly over the past fifteen years, has been dominated by his unflinching examination of the Khmer Rouge period. Among his most important works are the 2003 documentary *S-21, The Khmer Rouge Killing Machine*, the 2012 documentary *Duch: Master of the Forges of Hell*, and his 2013 Cannes Film Festival award-winning biopic *The Missing Picture*, a portrayal of his family's time during Democratic Kampuchea that was filmed used clay figurines and interspersed with documentary footage. *The Missing Picture* was nominated for an Academy Award in 2014, a first for Cambodia.

We met in Panh's office at Phnom Penh's Bophana Center, a film and audio archive that he helped to found in 2006 and which is dedicated to preserving the country's fractured memory. Books and papers lay scattered on the table where we talked, along with a cluster of painkillers and an ashtray. Behind him, the shelves of a tall bookcase held a compact hi-fi set, more books and DVDs.

As Panh, tousle-haired and with his trademark goatee, lit up a cigar, he testily explained his contempt for efforts to explain the violence of that period through a cultural framework.

'Of course, I am not saying we have no responsibility,' the usually amiable Panh said. 'But saying that our culture kills – first you say nothing about the responsibility of the others: the Khmer Rouge, the US, China, everybody. Because [you can say] it's culture. So the one who bombed us during the Khmer Rouge [revolution] can sleep well, no problem. The one who gave guns and money to the Khmer Rouge can sleep well also – because [you can blame] culture.'

Another danger is that this avenue taints all Cambodians 'because it's our culture', which means that ultimately 'it's useless to be Cambodian'.[5] And as for Hinton's identification of *kar sang soek* as a causal element, Panh countered, the concept of paying back one's enemy is hardly specific to Cambodia.

---

5. Much later, Hinton and I exchange emails in which he tells me that Panh has misconstrued his point. Cambodian culture per se did not 'cause' the mass killings of that period, Hinton writes, and indeed such events 'always take place in a context of upheaval that involves the factors' that Panh talks about. But, Hinton adds, culture 'does structure the violence and give it shape and form – just as it does in all local contexts, including the U.S. genocide of indigenous peoples'. In short, Hinton says, cultural dimensions – while insufficient on their own to explain mass killings and genocide – cannot be ignored, 'and, indeed, [Rithy's] films draw heavily on elements of Cambodian culture'. (From email exchange with Alexander Hinton, March 6, 2019.)

'You have the same words in French? In Chinese? In English?' he asked rhetorically. 'Yes. If you have the way to say *kar sang soek* in your language then it means that this feeling, this sentiment, this act exists in your culture also. [What happened] is more complex than *kar sang soek*.'

Years of fierce contemplation have led Panh to conclude the violence was political and ideological, 'a disease of purity' by men and women who claimed to be Marxists but who were incapable of understanding Marx. ('Marxism is philosophy, it's reflection,' he said.) Instead they followed the unflinching ideology of Mao, whose dogmatism they mixed with Khmer nationalism and pilfered elements of the Enlightenment. The resultant 'Polpotism' unleashed hatred and murder against a class whom the Khmer Rouge regarded as their political enemy – people like Panh and his middle-class parents, like Ket's parents and siblings, and like hundreds of thousands of urban Cambodians, 'new people' who by definition were unworthy. And that, he said, is before even seeking causes among other elements of that time such as the Cold War and the region's instability.

'Yet now scholars say Khmer killed Khmer [and] they say culture kills,' Panh told me, exasperated. 'But I was there. It was Khmer Rouge killing "new people".'

Those post-victory days in 1975 also saw the elimination of moderate Khmer Rouge leaders, men like Hou Youn who spoke out against the movement's extremist policies such as evacuating cities and banning markets. The Khmer Rouge revolution was to outshine even Mao's and nothing would be allowed to stand in the way of that unyielding vision. It bred a simplistic, brutal rationale even among educated believers such as Duch and Khieu Samphan, men who enjoyed positions at or near the apex of Democratic Kampuchea.

'They blocked everything, including their education, their culture, their reflection, their human dignity, morality and ethics – everything,' said Panh. 'Instead, we believe in *Angkar* and revolution and ideology, in one thing. So, if we have to kill, we kill; if we have to denounce, we denounce; if we have to falsify a report, we do that. If [the enemy] were CIA, we will find out.'

And as we know from the workings of M-13A, this rigid approach had permeated the country long before April 1975.

'It's barbarism,' Panh summed up through a swirl of smoke. 'War introduces something very animalistic, and that is common to all humans.'

You might think Panh's experiences have made him a pessimist about the human condition. Far from it. He takes the example of Hou Youn, whom he believes knew the fatal consequences of standing his ground against Pol Pot, yet who chose not to flee.

'Maybe this death will remind us that at that time somebody said: "No",' said Panh, whose father, a government official in the education department, also chose to stay in Cambodia believing his presence would help the country, a decision that cost him his life.

To further his point, Panh brought up another example, this one from outside Cambodia. It is a well-known photograph taken in Nazi Germany in 1936 of shipyard workers in Hamburg. All of them are giving the Nazi salute except for one man who stands with his arms crossed.

'Only one has the courage to say no. And because of this man, I know that there were Germans who resisted,' said Panh. 'There's always someone who says no – like Hou Youn, like this guy, like my father. And this one guy makes civilisation, he makes what we can call culture. This is the real guy. But when people say that [the barbarism of the Khmer Rouge] is our culture, they deny the existence of this "no".'

IN THOSE EARLY DAYS of Khmer Rouge rule, Sady and her family were among the millions engaged in a struggle to survive. After being forced out of Phnom Penh, they had made it as far as the ferry crossing at Neak Leung where they swapped their two dogs for a boat ride across the river and headed for an area called Ba Phnom in south-eastern Prey Veng province. Sady's father had worked in Ba Phnom a decade earlier and knew people there. When villagers visited the capital in the late 1960s and early 1970s, Sady's father had put them up at his home.

He felt those relationships would prove important, and he was right. The Khmer Rouge constantly checked the backgrounds of new people, and within weeks they found out that Sady's father had worked at T3 prison in Phnom Penh. They wanted to arrest the family, which would have meant execution. Friendly villagers warned them to leave.

'The villagers said that wherever we end up, we must not tell people our real background – that my father had worked with the government,' said Sady, who was 21 at the time. 'If you tell them that, then the Pol Pot staff will arrest you.'

In fear for their lives, they left Ba Phnom and walked 10 kilometres south to another district called Preah Sdach (meaning 'Sacred Prince'), which bordered Vietnam. In those disorganised weeks and months, huge numbers of people were on the move and although in theory it was risky to leave Ba Phnom without permission, in practice it was easy enough. Once they reached Preah Sdach they told the local Khmer Rouge they had worked as manual labourers in Phnom Penh. Because their hands and bodies had been toughened by weeks of ploughing and planting rice in Ba Phnom, the ruse worked.

They spent the next two years in Preah Sdach. Difficult though those years were, their lives were rendered even harder in September 1977 when the cadres ordered them to move to the western province of Pursat. So many people had been killed there, Sady said, that the only way to harvest the fields was to draft in outsiders like her family. It was a torrid time. The work in Pursat was much more difficult, there was less food, and the cadres, operating under the baleful glare of the commune chief *Ta* Out – 'a very cruel man', red-eyed, with a taste for human livers and gallbladders – took people away en masse to their deaths.

'It wasn't like that in Prey Veng,' she said of the group executions. 'There if you did something wrong, then the cadres would kill only you. But in Pursat they killed many people at a time.'

All the while *Angkar* was focused on agriculture. The economic plan envisioned rice harvests calculated with unrealistic simplicity and backed by the belief that because Cambodians had built the temples of Angkor there was nothing beyond their grasp. With two million hectares of land under cultivation, and with three tons per hectare deemed achievable as the annual harvest, the country would grow six million tons of rice. As with everything else, the Khmer Rouge had a slogan propounding success through violent, martial imagery: 'Strike, crush and win absolutely the production goal of three tons per hectare!'

By 1978 the ambitions were even grander. In *Revolutionary Flag* the Party congratulated itself on having achieved 'mastery' over irrigation, with vast numbers of dams and canals built to service the fields.[6] Since the key elements of agriculture were water and tamed land, and since Cambodia now had plenty of both, there was every reason to do better.

'Modern agriculture means having our rice paddies yield at the eight tons per year and up level … Can we do this within ten to fifteen years, or

---

6. 'The *Angkar* is master of the waters, master of the earth.' Locard, op. cit., p. 53.

not?' the journal asked rhetorically, before following up with the unsurprising answer: 'The Party Centre has discussed this and has decided that it can be fully done within ten to fifteen years throughout the country.'

Even today many countries struggle to harvest eight tons of rice per hectare. To achieve that requires intensive irrigation, excellent soil and high-quality seeds. Cambodia, with its limited irrigation and generally poor-quality soil, is still not close to that figure: in 2010 the country harvested an average of just 3.1 tons per hectare, according to the World Bank. Twenty years earlier that figure had been just 1.3 tons per hectare.

No matter the reality: *Angkar* was always right, so there could be no question of the goal being wrong. *Revolutionary Flag* did however warn that the revolution's foes would try to subvert this majestic target.

'It is not like there are no enemies destroying,' they wrote. 'The enemy destroys, beginning with transplanting. They fold the plants, they do not transplant the roots at all, they transplant destructively, they harvest destructively, they transport destructively, they thresh destructively.'

The Party crowed that its success in meeting its agricultural goals had made it the envy of the world. The Romanians said so, the Yugoslavs said so, and the Chinese particularly had said so – the Politburo member who had visited from Beijing told Pol Pot that, yes, these were first steps 'but that step was forward, forward, that it was pioneering forward and was correct'.[7]

The Party's fantastical line extended to how it would deal with its perennial enemy Vietnam, the *Yuon*, to use the pejorative colloquial term still current today. By April 1978 Vietnam and Cambodia had clashed extensively along their common border, and in that month's issue of *Revolutionary Flag* the leaders asked how the Cambodian army with only 100,000 troops could defeat nearly one million Vietnamese forces. Vietnam, as any good Khmer Rouge knew, had always desired to 'swallow' Cambodia.[8] In the same way that it used primary school mathematics and a can-do attitude to set the harvest target, the Communist Party of Kampuchea had calculated how to

7. Left unmentioned by Pol Pot and Nuon Chea was China's bewilderment that Cambodia's communists refused to use 200 donated tractors, preferring to let them rust. In 1979, a former member of the Chinese embassy in Phnom Penh said Cambodia's leaders felt human labour, not 'iron buffaloes', was what counted. See Locard, ibid., pp. 68–69.

8. Vietnam was largely responding to the aggression of Khmer Rouge forces who were massacring Vietnamese civilians in night-time cross-border raids. Vietnam had hoped an internal coup against Pol Pot would see a more reasonable government installed in Phnom Penh. When that failed to materialise, its forces invaded in December 1978.

achieve the impossible on the battlefield. The solution, it determined, was 'to fight and smash large numbers of the enemy's life forces and to protect our forces to the maximum'.

'Looking at the numbers, one of us must fight 30 *Yuon*,' the magazine exhorted. 'If we can implement this slogan, we win. No matter how many *Yuon* there are, we should be able to fight them and win. When any country commits aggression against Kampuchea we will use this slogan and we will fight them and win. Up until today we have implemented 1 against 30, meaning we lose 1, the *Yuon* lose 30. So then our losses are 30 times fewer than those of the *Yuon*.'

Given that the population of Vietnam was around 50 million, the article continued, Cambodia could afford to lose two million on a ratio of 30:1 and still have several million citizens to spare. And while some might manage to kill only five enemy soldiers, others would compensate by killing 100. To better the odds, one should attack when the enemy was having tea, not when he was on guard. This was 'the science of people's war' by dividing into small groups and 'attacking like sheet lightning, not just occasional strokes of lightning'. As with all enemies, it was imperative that the Vietnamese be 'smashed'.

'If we do not smash them, they will not fear us. But just upon hearing they are going to [be attacked by] the Kampuchean troops they tremble like a skinned frog being salted. They fear Kampuchean troops. They have gone from looking down on us to fearing us, and from fear to running away, not daring to fight,' the leaders wrote. 'It is imperative to attack them until they tremble even more, so even more of them will run away. And we attack them without expending large numbers of forces or equal numbers of forces, we expend 1 to their 30. In fact, our seizing this victory is huge. The world is in awe.'

The world was not in awe and *Angkar*'s reasoning was delusional. The Vietnamese had recently defeated the US, and in 1979 Hanoi would repel an invasion by China, which sought to punish Vietnam for its late-1978 invasion of Cambodia. For its part, *Angkar* had decimated its own military with repeated purges. A November 1978 document from the Stasi archives of East Germany, a staunch ally of Vietnam, presciently noted that, in the opinion of the Vietnamese, although the Cambodian army had 21 of its 24 divisions ranged along its border with Vietnam, '[it] is on the verge of falling apart'. Furthermore, it stated, anti-Pol Pot forces in Cambodia had requested Vietnam's help, and Hanoi would 'fulfil its internationalist duty and do everything for the revolution in Kampuchea'.[9]

In the end it took the combined force of Vietnamese troops and Khmer Rouge defectors less than two weeks to compel Pol Pot's forces to retreat west towards the Thai border. Although Vietnam was concerned that China might send troops to help Pol Pot, in the end Beijing did not do so. German scholar Bernd Schaefer argues that Deng Xiaoping, who was soon to take control in China, was unable to help Pol Pot for at least two key reasons: first, the Chinese Communist Party was to hold its 'crucial and hard-fought plenum' in December 1978 during which Deng would outmanoeuvre his political opponents and secure his own position; second, Deng was scheduled to make an official visit to the US in January 1979 to establish official diplomatic relations.

'[So] the last thing Deng Xiaoping would have wanted was Chinese forces fighting protracted battles on Cambodian territory on behalf of a controversial and unpopular regime and against a probably superior Vietnamese army on the ground,' Schaefer said.[10]

Even in his last days in control of Phnom Penh, Pol Pot believed he would be victorious. In early January 1979, days before he fled, Pol Pot sent for Sihanouk, who had been removed as head of state in 1976 but who had been barred from leaving Phnom Penh. Now Pol Pot needed Sihanouk's international standing and he briefed the prince before sending him off to address the United Nations.

At the time, Sihanouk's wife and his mother-in-law were also effectively imprisoned in the capital with him. When they heard Pol Pot wanted to see the prince they feared he would be killed, but when Sihanouk saw the size of the car – a large Mercedes – that Pol Pot had sent, he knew he would be safe. In the meeting, Sihanouk wrote later, Pol Pot ranted about destroying Vietnam even as his remaining troops were being crushed just miles away.

'Our Kampuchea will not be at peace as long as we Kampucheans have not overcome the evil *Yuon* race,' Pol Pot told Sihanouk at that meeting. 'I started by sending our army to Kampuchea Krom[11] with the mission to kill as many men, women and children as possible of the evil race. However, it

---

9. Document from East German Ministry of Defence dated November 20, 1978. Courtesy Bernd Schaefer.

10. Email correspondence with Bernd Schaefer, March 2014.

11. An area in southern Vietnam that was once part of the Khmer empire and where several hundred thousand ethnic Khmers still live.

was not possible to kill them all in their territory. In Annam and Tonkin, tens of millions of them are still alive and kicking.'

For that reason, Pol Pot continued, he had altered his approach 'entirely', which was why Vietnamese troops were now inside Cambodia.

'It is to lure them to our country, give them the impression that they have won military victory. And once they are inside Democratic Kampuchea, we the men and women of Kampuchea will hack them to pieces,' Pol Pot went on. 'We will chop them up. Back home in Vietnam, when they realise that their soldiers are not returning, they will send us more divisions. We the people of Kampuchea will continue to chop them up. And, in the final phase, we will enter their territory, Annam and Tonkin, after liberating our Kampuchea Krom, and kill their women and children (boys, girls and infants). That way, the evil *Yuon* race will be wiped off the face of the earth'.[12]

By any measure this was deranged. As David Chandler put it, by January 1979 there was little doubt that Pol Pot had gone 'off the rails'.[13]

THIS DISCONNECT WITH REALITY disseminated through the ranks of the Khmer Rouge too, as Sady and her family found when they moved to Preah Sdach in 1975. There the cadres felt they could do better than three tons per hectare; they demanded six. What rice people did manage to grow seldom stayed long in the village; no sooner was it harvested than trucks arrived and took it to unknown destinations. As Cambodians starved under Khmer Rouge rule, the regime sent rice to China in exchange for military supplies, diesel and cloth for garments. Other ships set out for China filled with dried geckoes, tiger skins, animal bones and pangolins, all used as ingredients in traditional medicine by Democratic Kampuchea's most important backer.

Because each area had been ordered to deliver a certain quantity of rice to the centre, and because the local leaders knew the punishment for failure, their priority was to ensure that they sent their quota come collection time.

---

12. As cited in the Closing Order for Case 002, p. 203. 'Letter from Sihanouk to the ECCC' (footnote 3490 in the Closing Order, September 15, 2010). The letter was taken from Sihanouk's unpublished book, *Histoire: Les derniers jours du Regime Polpotien et moi*.

13. Author's interview with David Chandler, Phnom Penh, July 23, 2012. Pol Pot's paranoia was evident from Vorn Vet's comment to Duch after the former's arrest and imprisonment at S-21 in late 1978. Duch said that Vorn Vet – his mentor and former boss – had told him Pol Pot 'took many precautions "like a sleeping bird raising its legs to prevent the sky falling on its head".' (See 'Written Record of Interview of Charged Person', Office of the Co-Investigating Judges, dated April 8, 2008, p. 7. (Document No. 00177635).)

Not doing so would be seen as counter-revolutionary. Since three tons per hectare was achievable – after all, *Angkar* had said it was – then the only reason an area might miss that target was because of the undetected presence of saboteurs, wreckers and no-good elements.

Inevitably that meant less rice for those doing the work, and rations were cut. Even in the 1975 harvest season, which was bountiful in Preah Sdach, there was not enough to eat. There was even less in the planting season, yet the cadres there insisted on six tons per hectare. To compensate for the poor quality of the soil, Sady said, they ordered them to use natural fertiliser: human excrement, leaves and even the corpses of the dead.

Sady spent those years in a *chalat*, a mobile work team of young people tasked with ploughing, planting rice and building irrigation canals, the self-same work that would torment and ultimately kill her cousins on the other side of the country. Mostly Sady worked in the fields. It was not uncommon to find feet, hands or assorted bones.

'People who died or who were taken away to be executed would some-times be buried in the rice fields,' she said. 'I remember one day after taking a break from ploughing, I went to look for snails to eat and I saw a person's skull.'

That was in Borei village, home to the district security office, and an area of excellent fertility because cadres dumped the bodies of murdered prisoners in its fields.

When there was no work to be done growing rice, Sady's *chalat* was sent to dig canals. Each person had to fulfil the daily quota of shifting two cubic metres of earth and if they failed, 'we would get in trouble'. The danger of failure meant that the men in the work group often helped the women to reach their target.

For Sady, as for Cambodians enslaved across the country, the daily routine was as constant as the midday heat. There were no days off. At 4am the bell would ring to start the working day. There was no breakfast so Sady and her *chalat* would labour until 11 before taking a two-hour break for lunch, which was a small bowl of thin rice porridge, before resuming work until 5pm. That was followed by a compulsory two-hour meeting to discuss the work done by their *chalat* and other groups. People who did not work well would get less rice.

Although some villagers were implacably hostile to 'new people' such as Sady, others were sympathetic and helped her to meet her planting targets.

'They took pity on me because they knew I came from Phnom Penh and was not an expert on working in the rice field, so sometimes they would help me to plant the rice seedlings,' she said.

Every tenth day the villagers came together for a much bigger meeting where people thought to be harbouring counter-revolutionary thoughts would be accused of being CIA. The villagers were encouraged to follow the example of the good revolutionaries and were warned against emulating the bad. The Khmer Rouge would throw out slogans taken from *Angkar*, in the violent phrases of the time cursing people as enemies, spies or no-good elements.

'At every meeting they would tell us that those who were CIA would be taken away and destroyed,' Sady said. 'They didn't say "we will kill them" or "we will shoot them", they said *komtech*, or "we will smash them". We understood that *komtech* meant "to kill".'

These sessions were terrifying because you ran the risk that someone else would criticise your work. Yet no one had any choice: you had to point out flaws in yourself and in others.

'For instance, I might tell them that today I did something wrong, because when I was planting the rice I reached down and grabbed a snail because I was so hungry. If we had a fault and we criticised ourselves then that was a big mistake, but they might not mind it,' she explained.

But should you fail to report the error of your ways and somebody else informed on you, your workload could be doubled as punishment: instead of planting 50 bunches of seedlings a day you would be told to plant 100.

'And if you don't reach that target, then they might kill you the next day,' she said. 'That happened a lot to my group.'

ONG THONG HOEUNG RECALLED the terrifying precision of these self-criticism sessions whose mission of 'attack[ing] the illness to save the sufferer' was worthy of Orwell. He noted:

> The leader would open the session and invite N. to take the floor. N. would start with the words: 'My respects to my comrades and the leader.' Then he would say that he had done both positive and negative things since the last meeting. N. would then ask the others to help him. He would solemnly confirm that he was at the disposal of the collective. The leader would then intervene, thanking him for placing himself in the hands of the collective. Next, he would encourage the other participants to share their opinions in order to 'construct' N. The statements would vary from one person to the

next. Everything was admissible. N. was not disciplined. N. did not work actively. N. was not punctual. N. talked too much, or did not talk enough. N. ate too fast. N. looked sad: he was clearly missing the old society. N. had a confused spirit.[14]

Throughout these proceedings, which in Hoeung's group took place every few days, the person being criticised had to accept these faults laid upon him wholeheartedly, even if they were false. Furthermore:

> Under no circumstances could he show indignation. On the contrary, he had to show how happy he was to receive 'constructive ideas'. At the end, he would thank the participants for their kindness in helping him to progress in the right direction. He would promise to try to apply the recommendations, as these were evidence of the collective's love for him, and express the hope that the group would follow him even more closely to ensure that he progressed along the correct path chosen by *Angkar*.

FOR SADY, THE BENEFIT of these meetings was that they allowed her to see her parents and siblings, all of whom had been sent to work elsewhere. Although they were forbidden to talk and although everyone had to leave afterwards, it was at least a chance for loved ones to glimpse one another and know they were still alive. The other advantage was that everyone received better rations: a larger portion of rice and a serving of Khmer soup with fish or pork. Yet there was never enough food and many of her co-workers starved to death.

'At work we would talk carefully to each other, and someone would whisper that a colleague had died last night from starvation,' Sady said. 'I was always very hungry and I would grab the water lilies and eat them with salt, but there weren't many lilies because so many people were doing that.'

Eating anything other than the meagre food allotment dished out for lunch and dinner was frowned upon but the women got around that by telling the cadres they needed the plants to make medicine. When it came to supplementing food, some Khmer Rouge were sympathetic and turned a blind eye. There was less flexibility when it came to meeting work targets.

'For instance, they might order us to harvest 100 metres of rice and they would give us until 8 o'clock. If you finished early then you could take

---

14. *J'ai cru aux Khmers rouges: Retour sur une Illusion* ('I believed in the Khmer Rouge: Return to an Illusion'), Ong Thong Hoeung (Buchet-Chastel, 2003). This extract is taken from an unpublished English translation provided by Hoeung.

a break, but if you missed it then they would order you to work until it was done, and then the next day you would get new tasks that would be even harder,' she said. 'And if you couldn't complete that, then within a few days they would take you away and kill you.'

The executioners came at night when the villagers were confined to their shelters. In Sady's case, she shared a small room two metres square with three other young women.

'Some nights we heard the sounds of the dogs barking or the horses making a noise and that was the sign that the Khmer Rouge had taken people away to kill them,' she said. 'We lost our co-workers one, one, one.'

Men and women were kept apart even if they were married. In this dystopia the only family was *Angkar*, and sexual relations between married couples were, at its instruction, solely for the purpose of breeding a new generation of revolutionaries. Falling in love was punishable by death and you could lose your life for any one of the innumerable and unknowable breaches. Sady remembered what happened to one young woman.

'That girl was very beautiful but she worked very slowly. She was put to work in the water and when the leeches got on her she screamed,' she said. 'The cadres got upset with that and took her away to kill her, because she worked slowly and because she screamed about the leeches. They killed her family too.'

Overseeing their lives was the commune chief helped by teenage spies known as *chhlop*. Their main job was to watch the 'new people' in the mobile work brigades day and night. They also arrested anyone who fell under suspicion and executed those deemed guilty of transgressions. Sady was careful never to look at the faces of the two most brutal men, Teang and Vong.

'The villagers were very careful of the *chhlop*. During the day things were normally safe, but at night they would watch everything we did, and even when we went out to urinate we would see them sitting there, watching,' she said. 'The *chhlop* might order someone to dig a grave saying they were going to kill a prisoner; then they would kill the person who had done the digging.'

Sady escaped the clutches of the *chhlop* but her 15-year-old brother Kanyang did not. Kanyang's first job in Preah Sdach was looking after the water buffaloes, which are used to plough the fields. After that he was put in a *chalat*, building irrigation canals and dams. As fate would have it, he was in the same *chalat* as Lim Sophon, who later became Sady's husband.

'Kanyang never got enough food to eat,' Sady said, 'and he always liked his food. He ate like a horse when we lived in Phnom Penh.'

By 1977 Kanyang and four other youngsters had had enough and decided to escape across the nearby border. Kanyang hoped to find somewhere for the family to live, and said he would return for them. The five youngsters stole a small boat and rowed to Vietnam, but as they crossed the border they were stopped by a group of Vietnamese civilians who demanded money. Had they run into Vietnamese soldiers, Sady said, they might have had better luck. Kanyang and his friends had nothing, no gold, no possessions, not even a chicken with which to bargain.

'And so after they had nothing to exchange, the Victnamese called across to the Pol Pot staff to take them back,' she said. 'First they tied them up, then they told the cadres that these guys want to escape.'

The Khmer Rouge beat Kanyang with wooden staves then summoned his family to watch as they punished him further.

'And they said if one of us cries then they will torture that person,' Sady said, her actions animated by this remembrance. 'They ordered my mother to hit my younger brother and then they told her to warn the other villagers: "Don't do what my son did, because he is a traitor."'

The words come like bullets from Sady, her voice hardened with the injustice.

'They said he had betrayed the nation and they beat him so many times around the head,' she said, her hand to her head. 'Then they took him away.'

Days later the family learned Kanyang was dead. Their neighbours' son was Khmer Rouge and, by way of warning his family not to flee, told his parents that the five escapees had been executed. One of the parents told Sady's family that her brother was dead.

'But we were not allowed to cry or to feel pity for him. We had to pretend that we were happy, that we worked for the community, that we loved the regime. We could cry only at night,' she said. 'Kanyang would be in his fifties now. He couldn't stay because they forced him to work and never gave him enough food and so he tried to escape. I know if he had had a chicken or a duck or a pig or some gold then he would have been allowed to stay in Vietnam, but he had nothing.'

APRIL 1978

In the name of the Party Central Committee and in the name of the Government of Democratic Kampuchea, I wish to express our extreme happiness along with the entire Party, the entire Revolutionary Army, the entire people, our happiness with the magnificently successful results during this past year.

And along with this, our entire Party, entire Revolutionary Army, and entire people:

— Remain in monolithic solidarity and unity to go on offensives to absolutely defend the country and defend the Kampuchean race;

— Remain in monolithic solidarity and unity to build the country in the rhythm of great magnificent leaps following the 1978 annual plan;

— Remain in monolithic solidarity and unity to go on offensives to raise the livelihood of all our people to make constant and rapid progress.

Finally, I wish to send best wishes to all you Comrade Representatives attending this meeting. May you all have good health and prosperity during this year and future years, and may you fulfil the revolutionary missions delegated to you by the Party 100 per cent successfully, or even more than 100 per cent successfully.

Cheers! The Communist Party of Kampuchea, current, clear-sighted, magnificent!

Cheers! The Kampuchean Revolution, mighty and magnificent!

Cheers! The Kampuchean people, huge and magnificent!

Cheers! The Revolutionary Army of Kampuchea, brave, skilled, and magnificent!

Cheers! The Third Anniversary of the Great Magnificent Victory of 17 April and the founding of Democratic Kampuchea, great and glorious.

— Taken from *Revolutionary Flag* magazine on the third anniversary of Khmer Rouge rule, by which time more than a million people were dead. Nine months later the regime was driven from power.

CHAPTER TWELVE

'WE ARE LEAVING'

AFTER MARTINE FINISHES her testimony on that August morning in 2009, Neary takes her place in the witness box. This is her opportunity to tell the judges and those who are following the trial on television and radio how her father's disappearance and murder affected her. Neary is elegantly dressed in a black trouser suit and is wearing a pair of silver drop-earrings. Her charcoal hair is pulled back under the headphones that carry the translator's words rendering her French into Khmer and English. On the stand she appears calm but inside she is a whirl of emotions.

A month earlier Neary had no idea she would get to testify – after all, the court did not have time to hear more than a handful of the more than 90 civil parties – and had returned to Cambodia solely to support Martine. And, she added, not only was she unaware that she would be invited to address the court in front of Duch, initially she did not want to.

'Not because I was afraid of him,' she explained later, 'but because I didn't want him to touch me with his eyes. I thought maybe my dad would disagree with that.'

Eventually she reasoned that the opportunity to speak would provide a unique chance to remember her father publicly and to tell the court how his absence and her subsequent knowledge of the circumstances of his murder had caused her such distress. In this way, her words will give the judges a different view of the impact Ket's killing had on his family than the picture painted by Martine. Where by 1980, for instance, Martine knew enough to understand the reality of what had happened, Neary's was a slow rolling-back of a curtain over years revealing a scene that burned itself ever deeper into her growing mind.

After greeting the bench and the audience in the gallery with the *sampeah* greeting, Neary opens her testimony with a few words she has written especially for her father, a man about whom she has the briefest of memories, as fragile as tissue, yet to which she has clung with a fierce intensity.

'About my father, the first memory I have is of his hand,' she says.

Translation issues have dogged the tribunal from its first day, in part because there is no direct Khmer-French translation. Words spoken in Khmer are rendered first into English and then into French, and vice versa.[1] In this case the translator mixes up the French word *main*, meaning 'hand', with *mort* meaning 'death', so what we hear, and what the official transcript of Neary's testimony wrongly states in English, is that her first memory of Ket is his death.

Her next sentence makes clear her words.

'I remember we were hiding for a birthday surprise for friends,' she says. 'I can still hear the crinkle of wrapping paper and see the amused look on his face and him indicating to me not to make any noise, and he's holding my hand while I look up at him.'

This is the hand, she tells the court, as anger now seeps into her words, that wrote elegantly in the refined Cambodian script, that coaxed Beatles' songs from a guitar, that passed on to Neary's French mother his knowledge of Cambodian cuisine, and that shook the hands of foreign diplomats without judging by race or culture or religion. Her words are a paean to a man barely remembered by a two-year-old girl, now a woman of 34.

'And a hand that was never without the immense smile that lit up your face. When I see the faces of the temples of Angkor, I recall the only person through whom I saw them open their eyes and smile, and I admire them even more. You will forever remain a wonderful page to be discovered, a page that we continue to pass on tirelessly.'

NEARY HAD SEEN DUCH several times before she entered the witness box. The first time she watched him in court she had drawn his image as a way to maintain her distance from him. On another occasion, Neary and I had been watching proceedings from the auditorium and, at the end of the session as we walked towards the exit, she looked up and saw Duch just yards away behind the bulletproof screen.

---

1. French is not taught in Cambodian schools, and has not been an official language of the country since 1975.

'He looked at me and he was very sure of himself,' she told me later. 'Maybe on the outside I didn't show, but inside I was petrified.'

Then there was the time when Neary was standing outside the court building in an area off-limits to the public and media, but open to civil parties. After each trial session, a white UN four-wheel drive vehicle would ferry Duch 100 yards from court to the detention centre he shared with the four defendants in Case 002 – Nuon Chea, Khieu Samphan, Ieng Sary and Ieng Thirith.[2]

'He was in the car and I was all alone,' she recalled, her words slowing as she continued. 'He looked at me from the head to the feet and, you know, the look was very different from who he was inside the court. And I told myself: this is the guy my dad saw.'

I asked Neary how that look had differed.

'Inside the court, it's like he is the pupil, you know: "I'm listening and I'm very obedient,"' she replied. 'Outside it's the chief [of S-21]. He's the guy everyone speaks about – when he was walking in Phnom Penh's streets and he was feeling free and he was proud because he was the only one who could move, he was the only one who had a microphone, he was the only one who had a motorbike. He had this *laissez-passer* [permit] that allowed him to go everywhere. He was the chief, and that was the look of the guy. "I am the only one in this city who can move and who is allowed to do so. I have the power."'

Neary paused, and her dark eyes flashed reflecting on that encounter.

'"I am the chief and I have the right to let you live or die,"' she said of Duch's look.

She paused again and then, with slow phrasing, painted in words the question she had seen in Duch's eyes: '"What am I going to do with you?"'

A SERIES OF PHOTOGRAPHS OF KET appears on the television screens in the court, putting a face to the name of just one of the two million people who died under the Khmer Rouge's rule. The pictures were taken during Ket's time outside Cambodia and show the handsome young

---

2. Ieng Sary died in Phnom Penh in 2013 aged 87 while on trial for genocide, war crimes and crimes against humanity. In late 2011 the ECCC ruled that dementia had left Ieng Sary's wife, Ieng Thirith, unfit for trial. That left just Nuon Chea and Khieu Samphan on trial. In 2018, both men were convicted of genocide and jailed for life. The tribunal had previously handed down the same sentence to Nuon Chea and Khieu Samphan after finding them guilty of crimes against humanity – that was in 2014 at the conclusion of an earlier portion of their lengthy trial.

diplomat as a family man. Among the images is the final photograph taken with Martine, Mackara and Neary in the garden in Le Mans on that summer's day when he left.

Neary tells her story: that she was born on July 16, 1975, in Dakar, Senegal; that before she turned two, her father was ordered by Cambodia's foreign ministry to return and help to rebuild the country; and that as a consequence she grew up without him. Cambodia's strong identity, as explained to her by Martine, meant that her childhood in France saw her wearing sarongs, eating Khmer dishes and learning the Khmer language.

When she was six Neary heard talk of a prison where people had been held and tortured. Although she did not understand what that meant, it marked the beginning of a realisation – too early and too personally – of the acts that men such as Duch are capable.

From his position behind his lawyers, Duch watches Neary intently as she speaks. She moves swiftly through the years and we soon reach the day in 1990 when the letter arrived from Cambodia written in Khmer, containing Ket's photograph and addressed to 'My beloved son'. She tells the bench how, for a few moments, hopes had flared – that what Martine had learned in the refugee camp was wrong, that Ket had not been murdered at S-21, that he had finally managed to get in touch – but were then extinguished.

'It was his mother who was speaking to my father,' Neary recalls, 'which is why I can tell you that she was not aware that her son had returned to his country, and so we were the ones who told her that my father was not with us but that he had gone back when I was two.'

Their trip the following year – when Neary turned 16 – was a phenomenal shock 'because I grew up in a country where we are free in our choices'. S-21 and her imagined experiences of Ket's time there have consumed her since: photographs of bodies on stretchers, shackled limbs and broken skulls, and the mass graves at Chhoeung Ek. Metal bars, torture implements and reams of confessions saw a former school whose function was creativity and learning replaced by a machine 'to crush human beings'.

It takes Neary almost 10 minutes to tell the bench about her first visit to Duch's domain, the day, she says, that 'a seed of poison' entered her body.

'Since that day I have never stopped trying to find out what happened.'

DURING HER STUDIES in France, Neary had chosen to write her English Masters thesis about Yale University's project to microfilm S-21's archive. The US university had started a genocide research project that eventually became the Documentation Center of Cambodia. As Neary worked on her thesis in the 1990s, Cambodia's civil war rumbled on, with the Khmer Rouge still fighting. Eventually she shelved her thesis after reading the vitriolic, threatening comments that this charged subject elicited online. By then she had determined that anyone deemed too successful or too cultured in the eyes of the Khmer Rouge risked death.

Yet although she stepped back from a career in academia, Neary did not stop trying to find Ket's file. As the years went by and it failed to materialise, and as the possibilities of locating it diminished, Neary became convinced it had been deliberately hidden.

'Why?' I asked her.

Because even though Ket was a junior diplomat, she told me, he might well have named people in his confession who were still politically significant.

We discussed the topic of the missing file on several occasions yet I was not convinced Ket's file had been deliberately targeted. After all, the confession of Hu Nim, the former information minister, was found as were the files of other senior people killed at S-21. Many documents went missing after 1979 and Ket's could easily have been among them.[3]

If the file had not been destroyed, though, it was logical to wonder where it might be.[4] Here, too, Neary had suggestions: perhaps it had been moved to

---

3. Ket's circle of Cambodian friends in Paris returned to the country before or during Democratic Kampuchea, and seem to have shared a similar fate: four of them appear in S-21's records (Loeung Hong Sour, who returned to Democratic Kampuchea with Ket; Kol Dorathy; Khuon Davith; and Ching Kok Huor). Ching Kok Huor, a junior diplomat, was beaten so severely that he died of his injuries on October 29, 1976, less than a week after his arrest. Neary believes three others were also taken there (Huor Someth; Van Sang Sambath; and Yem Yok San), although I could find no record of them in the archives. All three do, however, appear in Ong Thong Hoeung's list of returnees taken to S-21. Ket's remaining five friends disappeared after coming back to Democratic Kampuchea and, Neary told me, were almost certainly killed.

4. In S-21's archives I was able to find the confession of just one of Ket's friends from his Paris days: Kol Dorathy, 32, who was arrested in November 1977. He later confessed to being a spy who had worked against the Khmer Rouge throughout the 1960s and 1970s, and who after returning to Cambodia had conspired with other 'traitors' to undermine *Angkar* by destroying rice stocks and salt supplies, uprooting coconut trees, manufacturing sub-standard farm tools and damaging irrigation works. His 26-page confession, dated March 7, 1978, took one month to extract, and was written up by interrogator Chea Kak. Ironically the 21-year-old Chea Kak was himself arrested that month and later executed, consumed by the machine of S-21. In his confession, Chea Kak echoed a range of similar crimes: working with others to 'destroy equipment' and recruiting people to join him. Chea Kak at least knew what awaited him; prisoners like Kol Dorathy were often told that *Angkar* would forgive them once they had confessed their supposed crimes. Lastly, it is of course highly unlikely that most of what was in Kol Dorathy's confession – including the list of 69 names that he gave as his 'strings' of fellow traitors – was true. He was executed on March 13, 1978.

Vietnamese archives in Hanoi or possibly it was in a box in some Cambodian ministry. It might have been taken home by one of the staff at S-21 when the site was in the process of becoming the genocide museum and could be languishing in a cupboard. This last possibility is less outlandish than it sounds: in 2012, more than 1,000 previously unknown photographs of S-21 prisoners were handed over to DC-Cam by a civil servant in Phnom Penh.

I had long assumed that Neary wanted Ket's file to get answers about his time inside S-21, some precision beyond the guesswork. It was partly that, Neary told me, but she had by now done so much research about prisoner conditions that she could easily imagine his experience.

'[So in his file] he might tell me that he was lacking sleep, he can tell me that he was beaten in one way or another,' she said of the file's expected contents. 'I know six months is long. I've read a lot. I can imagine that after torture, you don't know where you are any more and you try to remember the date, but it quickly disappears. I want to know for how long he was conscious and …'

Neary paused for a long time. When she resumed, she told me that what had happened to Ket was 'obvious'. The reason for wanting his file was far more profound. To understand that, she said, we had to return to the day that she and Martine had testified. They were followed on the stand by a third civil party, New Zealander Rob Hamill, whose older brother Kerry had been taken by the Khmer Rouge in August 1978 from his yacht after it strayed into Cambodian waters. Kerry's Canadian crewmate, Stuart Glass, was shot dead when the Khmer Rouge attacked the yacht. Kerry and the third crewmember, British national John Dewhirst, were taken to S-21 and accused of being CIA spies. There they were tortured and executed and their bodies burned.

In his testimony Rob Hamill, whose broad shoulders mark out his past as an Olympic and trans-Atlantic oarsman, gave an unrestrained account of the damage Kerry's death had done to his family and spoke frankly of the tortures he had long dreamed of inflicting on Duch. In such circumstances it seems bizarre to talk of luck but in one event the Hamill family were more fortunate than Martine and Neary: Kerry's confession was found in the archives of S-21. This document, which Rob Hamill stressed was a work of fiction, contained a series of hidden messages from Kerry to his family, written despite the fact that he could never have known they would read his words.

Kerry was accused of being a CIA operative and Duch's men demanded to know his 'strings'. Showing astonishing composure and even humour in the face of torture, Kerry used the family's home phone number as his supposed CIA operative number, named a number of family friends as fellow spies and told the interrogator about one officer called 'Major Ruse'. He also stated that a Colonel Sanders (of KFC fame) was one of his superior officers.

'Perhaps the most poignant comment in my brother's confession was the mention of the public speaking instructor, a Mr S. Tarr. The instructor's family name was spelled Tarr – T-A-R-R. Only the initial of the instructor's first name was given as S. "S. Tarr",' Hamill told the court, in tears. 'It is in fact the name of my adoring mother, Esther – Esther Hamill. That's my mother's name. He was sending a message to our mother, a message of love and hope. It was as if, whatever the final outcome, he would have the last say. And he has.'

Kerry Hamill clearly believed his confession was his final opportunity to say goodbye. Neary was convinced Ket would also have tried to reach out to Martine and their children, and that was why she would never stop looking for his file. She was certain that, by the time of his last confession, Ket would have known he was going to die and would not have passed up this opportunity.

'So I want to read this moment when [Ket] was trying to tell us something,' she said. 'I'm interested in the names he mentioned – did he speak about us in another way? How he probably created a story to last. That's what I want to know.'

BACK IN COURT, NEARY mentions a brief phone conversation from 1993. The year was an important one for Cambodia, with the UN overseeing elections in a process that largely ended the violence that had plagued the country for years. Even the Khmer Rouge entered the democratic process, albeit briefly. Among those who had stayed faithful to the cause for all those years was Ket's old boss Chan Youran, who by now was a senior figure in the movement.[5]

On that day in 1993, Neary was on her own at home in France when the phone rang. After mistaking Neary for Martine, Chan Youran introduced himself as 'a great friend of your father', a phrase she found highly offensive coming from the man who had written to Martine 14 years earlier saying that Ket, to his knowledge, 'was fine'.

---

5. Chan Youran, a born survivor, had been a school friend of the Khmer Rouge's foreign minister Ieng Sary, who had protected some people in his ministry – among them, clearly, Chan Youran himself.

As it turned out, Chan Youran had been on television the previous day, one face in a news clip about a visiting Khmer Rouge delegation. An astonished Martine had pointed him out to Neary. So when Chan Youran explained that he was 'passing through' France, Neary replied that she already knew he was in the country because she had seen him on television. Her comment, she said later, seemed to make him uneasy.

Neary, at the time a teenager, was herself so surprised at the call that she failed to ask any questions about Ket, something she still regrets. In the end the entire exchange took less than a minute. Martine was out and Chan Youran did not call back.

His name had come up several times in my conversations with Martine and Neary. Martine had heard that Chan Youran was now a devout Buddhist and was memorising sacred texts during regular visits to Phnom Penh's Wat Tuol Tumpoung, which stands just a few hundred metres from the Tuol Sleng Genocide Museum. In Cambodia, devoting the final years of one's life in Buddhist reflection is a way to accumulate merit before death.

In May 2012 I went to Wat Tuol Tumpoung with my translator Sina. A chubby, chain-smoking monk confirmed that Chan Youran was a regular visitor but was not here that day. He suggested we return the following week. An old man at the same table said Chan Youran came to the pagoda every full moon to seek advice from the monks on the Buddhist scriptures and travelled regularly to Udong outside Phnom Penh to meditate. Chan Youran was a gentleman, they told us, kind and friendly to young and old.

We returned the following week and, after learning that Chan Youran was again absent, we talked to some of the elderly civilians, or *achar*, who help out at the pagoda. A man in his eighties told us how to reach Chan Youran's house – go straight out of the pagoda and turn right, go past the school, across one or maybe two more roads and you will see his house on the corner – but it was all a bit vague so Sina persuaded the *achar* to get on the back of his motorbike.

Minutes later we were outside a modern three-storey house that sported pink paint, gleaming stainless steel balcony railings, a high green gate and 10-foot-high wall. Through a crack between the gate's doors we could see a brace of four-wheel-drive vehicles. Sina rang the bell, and someone came into the driveway to ask what we wanted. The high gate and high wall meant we could not see her, but Sina asked the disembodied voice whether Chan Youran was home. The voice went back inside and Sina chose that moment to take our geriatric guide back to the pagoda. It looked unpromising but then again I was not expecting much. Martine and Neary both felt Chan Youran was unlikely to talk.

While I waited I stepped into the road to take in the neighbourhood. The houses were packed in along the narrow street, grills and barbed wire preventing entrance from the street level other than through locked gates. A few houses up was a metal-cutting shop. A flyer jammed under Chan Youran's doorbell advertised broadband internet. Nearby was a cluster of pot plants too heavy to steal. I looked up to see an old man peering down from one of the balconies, vetting this unusual visitor. I recognised Chan Youran from photographs and waved. By the time the latch on the metal gate clunked a few minutes later, my iPhone was recording surreptitiously. The green gate swung open and he emerged in a long-sleeved white shirt, liver spots on his face below a balding pate. A young woman, presumably his granddaughter, stood and watched.

There was much I wanted to know: what Chan Youran remembered of Ket; whether he could explain Ket's fate, particularly the fact that both he and Ket were royalists yet Chan Youran had survived; why he had sent Martine that letter in 1979 saying Ket was well; how he had managed to escape the *santebal*'s noose, despite being named (no doubt falsely) as a CIA spy several times in Hu Nim's 1976 confession; and not least why he had remained within the Khmer Rouge into the late 1990s. Chan Youran was among the very last to quit the movement.

Chan Youran eyed my motorbike suspiciously.

'*Bonjour* – Mr Chan Youran?' I asked him by way of confirming it was actually him. My eyes followed his gaze. 'The *moto* is mine.'

'What are you?' he asked in English in monotone.

'I am a writer. Are you Mr Chan Youran?'

There was a long pause and he walked the few yards along the narrow, cracked concrete pavement towards the potted plants. It put distance between him and his granddaughter, who chose that moment to slip away behind the gate.

'I am now almost a monk,' he told me. 'A monk, you see. I have no intention to meet anybody since more than 10 years. As you can see. So excuse me. I could not say anything. Thank you.'

At this point Sina returned and Chan Youran told him in Khmer that he did not wish to talk.

'But I haven't even asked anything,' I said. 'OK, let me at least explain…'

Chan Youran started walking back to the sanctuary of his gate. My window of opportunity was slipping rapidly away so I told him I was writing a book about Ouk Ket and about Duch. Chan Youran paused then looked down, his eyes baggy. His lower lip moved a little.

'How do you know Ouk Ket?' he asked Sina in Khmer, pointing his finger at me but keeping his eyes fixed on Sina.

'I know Martine and I know Neary,' I replied, explaining that I had first met them in 2009 ahead of Duch's trial. Chan Youran stared fixedly at the road. 'I am now writing a book about Duch and about Ouk Ket, about what happened to him and about what happened to Ouk Ket's family in Cambodia as well.'

Chan Youran shook his head.

'So I wanted to ask you – because you were his boss in Senegal – I wanted to ask you about Ouk Ket and what you remember of him and what happened to him.'

Chan Youran continued to stare at the road.

'I could…' he paused. 'I could not tell anything about Ket, because I am now practising Buddhism.'

That was so transparent an excuse that I pressed on.

'But you can still talk,' I replied.

Chan Youran turned and looked at me and wagged his finger. He had lost none of his ability to try and intimidate.

'Because you are coming here, don't be confused,' he admonished me, his tone growing menacing. 'Because you are here in my house, so I have to be friendly to you.'

I declined to point out that we were standing on the pavement and that he had not invited us in.

'OK, but you remember Ouk Ket?' I replied.

'He is my best friend,' Chan Youran said.

'Your best friend,' I repeated.

'My best friend. I can just say that.'

'But I'd like to ask you some questions about him.'

'Thank you,' he said with a half-grimace, half-smile and, as he moved to walk back behind his steel gate, asked: 'Do you know what is a best friend?'

His hand chopped down in a guillotine motion as he completed his question.

'Yes I do – this is why I want to ask you about him.'

But Chan Youran had no interest in talking as he turned to disappear behind the 8-foot-high gate. With my mind on Neary and Martine, I asked him about the letter he had sent decades earlier.

'Do you remember in 1979 you sent a letter to Martine saying Ket was well and she came to Geneva to see you? Do you remember that?' I asked him. 'Why did you send the letter?'

'Thank you,' he said, shaking his head and shutting the green gate. The bolt slid back, metal grinding on metal.

'Mr Chan Youran, why did you send the letter?'

No answer.

'Why did you send the letter if you knew he wasn't fine?'

The only sound was the shuffling of Chan Youran's feet as he slipped back into his large, cool house on this backstreet of Phnom Penh behind the safety of his gate.

'I think he is angry with us,' Sina said to me.

Sina had interviewed many former Khmer Rouge and, like many Cambodians, some of his extended family had once been part of the movement. He reckoned efforts might be more successful without my presence, and told me he would come back alone in a few weeks. He did but it made no difference. Chan Youran's wife scolded him, saying her husband was old and could not remember much. She was even angrier than Chan Youran had been, Sina said.

'Who knows where Ouk Ket died and when,' she snapped at him. 'My husband doesn't want to talk about anything, so if you are doing a book on Duch then please go and ask Duch. Don't ask my husband!'

As for why Chan Youran had written letters encouraging intellectuals to return to Cambodia – which was not a question I had asked – well, she said, he was ordered to do so.

'So if you want to know, then go and ask [former] deputy prime minister Khieu Samphan,' she said. 'He is on trial at the ECCC.'

With that she slammed the gate and walked back inside, muttering: 'Boring, boring, boring boy. Go away!'

In July 1998 the Associated Press had interviewed Chan Youran for a brief article on that year's pending election. By then Chan Youran, who had been the Khmer Rouge's ambassador to China in the 1980s, had quit the movement. Describing himself as 'not a communist, not at all – I am 100 per cent nationalist', he told AP he had had nothing to do with the mass killings under the Khmer Rouge and 'never condoned the class struggle and violation of human rights'. Given that Chan Youran had survived, he surely kept those beliefs to himself while working in the foreign ministry in Democratic Kampuchea, assuming, that is, he held them in the first place.

In November 2009, staff from the ECCC had visited Chan Youran, then aged 75, at his house in Phnom Penh to ask him – as a witness – about his former boss, Ieng Sary, who was by now a defendant in Case 002. It is clear from the nine-page transcript that Chan Youran was little inclined to be helpful.[6] In his opening remarks he told the investigator that he was 'tired and bored of my life, which has been a life of pain' (many of his family had died during the Democratic Kampuchea period) and was 'prepared to leave this world in supreme peace and quiet'.

That quiet is much in evidence in most of his replies. He sketches a brief description of his life prior to the March 1970 coup, first as a junior diplomat in the embassy in Paris in the late 1950s and early 1960s, then eventually as ambassador to Senegal, which was where he was working when Sihanouk was overthrown. Chan Youran aligned himself with Sihanouk (and by default, with the Khmer Rouge) and for the next five years worked against the Lon Nol regime. It wasn't until late 1975 that he came back to Phnom Penh ('I was very happy to return'), a place that 'had been transformed into a silent city'. Despite the significance of that day, he could not recall who met him at the airport.

Before long Chan Youran was placed at the Foreign Ministry, known as B-1, and tasked with growing vegetables and listening to foreign radio broadcasts, the latter being something for which his fluency in French and English made him particularly suitable. Those three years, he claimed, went by in a virtual vacuum. He had never heard of S-21, he replied when asked about Duch's prison, and while, yes, some staff did disappear from the ministry 'once in a while … and it was heard that this was because of documents about [them]', he did not know why staff had left or how their disappearance was effected.

He insisted too that he was 'oblivious' to any mention by Ieng Sary of internal enemies, and when asked why Ieng Sary had protected him after he was named in confessions from S-21, Chan Youran replied that he didn't know.

---

6. 'Written Record of Witness Chan Youran', ECCC [Record number in English: 00410252–00410260]. November 27, 2009.

'This is the first time I've heard of this matter,' he said.

By and large, in the three years between 1976 and 1979, Chan Youran saw nothing, heard nothing and as a result had little to offer. Back then he didn't want to know how B-1 was organised, so he couldn't help the investigators with that part of their inquiry; he wasn't a member of the Party (something he insisted the investigator underline in the transcript) and so he had nothing to say about meetings, documents or confession sessions; he had been to the countryside just 'once or twice' with Ieng Sary 'to watch rice farming' or to accompany foreign visitors, yet saw nothing out of the ordinary; his boss and old school friend Ieng Sary was rarely around and, even when he was, he never told Chan Youran about *Angkar*, so he couldn't help with questions about that; and although Chan Youran had gone with Ieng Sary to the United Nations in late 1977 (his presence on the Democratic Kampuchea delegation indicating that he wasn't quite the ministry nobody that he professed to be), he offered no information whatsoever about the trip and insisted he had no recollection of the meetings they had held while in New York.

The transcript of the interview leaves little doubt that Chan Youran was unwilling to provide anything more than the bare minimum, and sometimes not even that. His reticence applied equally to questions about Ket. Near the end of the interview, the investigator asked whether he knew during Democratic Kampuchea that Ket had been arrested. Interestingly, Chan Youran didn't actually answer the question, and the investigator unfortunately did not repeat it. Instead Chan Youran offered this about the man whom he later claimed had been his 'best friend': some incontestable facts and two assertions.

'Ouk Ket was a diplomat along with me in Senegal. He had a French wife and two children. I [last saw] him in 1975. We were very close friends,' he said. 'I do not know when Ouk Ket returned to Cambodia.'

LATER I WENT TO SEE Youk Chhang, the director of DC-Cam, to ask if he could explain why Chan Youran had written to Martine telling her Ket was fine when at best he could not have known that, and at worst he was aware his former staffer had been taken to S-21. The latter was by no means impossible; after all, Chan Youran's brother was killed at S-21 and, despite his protestations, Chan Youran was well placed within the foreign ministry.

Sitting in his office, with neat piles of bound documents, books and papers covering most of the floor space, Youk Chhang said the reason was simple enough: to keep Martine quiet. In 1979 the Khmer Rouge, having been forced from their murderous reign, were desperately trying to drum up diplomatic support.[7] A number of other foreigners whose loved ones had returned to Cambodia and disappeared, and whom we now know were by then dead, had received similar letters.

Why write to foreigners? Because they might be listened to by their governments, he replied, in ways that Cambodian nationals would not. The obvious solution was to lie to people like Martine. Ieng Sary doubtless told Chan Youran to write a letter stating that Ket was fine, Youk Chhang told me.

In that way this was nothing personal, just politics of the most cynical sort waged at the lowest level by a movement that had never believed in the value of the individual. People were objects to be used for whatever purpose the leaders decreed and Ket's murder was a minor but potential bump in the Khmer Rouge's road to international political redemption.[8]

NEARY TELLS THE JUDGES of a day in Paris in 2004 when she watched the screening of Rithy Panh's documentary about S-21.[9] By then she was well aware of S-21 and much of what was in the documentary was familiar – though not everything. Three elements in particular appalled her. One was the practice of draining the blood from prisoners in order to send it to the hospital where wounded Khmer Rouge soldiers were treated. In the documentary, Prak Khan, whom I later interviewed, recalled the dying prisoners, their eyes rolled back, their last breaths rattling in their bodies 'like crickets'. The violence tormented Neary for years, not knowing whether this was what had happened to Ket, dehumanised and dying on a concrete floor as his full complement of blood was drained into a bag.

'I wonder how two people … can hold down a man or a woman who is already weak in order to cut into a vein, making them believe that it's going to be for a blood test, and enjoying it probably, preventing that person from defending themselves,' she says.

Or perhaps Ket had been murdered in another brutal fashion outlined

---

7. As Chan Youran put it in his March 1979 letter to Martine: 'You are right that we need to have friends. Indeed it is our duty to make many friends [at this time].'

8. The letter's wording led Neary to believe that Chan Youran knew that something had happened to Ket, and was warning Martine not to visit Cambodia to find out more. Neary says Chan Youran's motives in doing so might even have been partly positive, but his refusal to speak means that is impossible to know.

9. *S-21, The Khmer Rouge Killing Machine*. Directed by Rithy Panh (2003).

in the documentary, with 'medical staff' learning surgery by tying living prisoners to a pole, slicing them open without anaesthetic, since there was none in Democratic Kampuchea, and pulling out their organs? The third element that shocked her was the suicide of a young woman prisoner at S-21 'because she wanted to escape what she was being subjected to, and of course I could identify with that'.

All of this violence, death and destruction, and Neary's efforts to understand what had happened, left her battling for her sanity – in her words, 'an invisible disability, a psychological agony, a journey into hell', even driving her to contemplate suicide. Learning about S-21 forced her to confront how humans are wired to obey and submit, how regimes of terror use that to function, and how in Cambodia's case 'a few individuals with such evil intentions' had taken the lives of so many.

It was not until February 2009, when Martine and Neary came back to Cambodia to attend the start of Duch's trial, that they were handed the photograph of Ket taken on his arrival at S-21. For Neary this image 'confirmed that he had been there and is no longer alive'. The two women went back to Chhoeung Ek, 'the worst place I've ever been in the world', with its mass graves and the killing tree grown into a tortured shape and against whose trunk the youngest victims were smashed.

'That baby could have been me,' says Neary, turning to look at Duch, the first time she has done so during her testimony. 'I could have been grabbed by the foot and had my skull crushed against the tree that was used to destroy all of the children. And sometimes I feel that I'm the only survivor amongst all of them.

'What happened in Chhoeung Ek, and that is only one example of what happened throughout the country, is unforgivable. In the bone dust of Chhoeung Ek, where the grass grew, fed by the bodies of children, an earthquake underneath me opened the silent earth that has seen all this blood spilled,' she says.

As Neary continues, after 45 minutes of testimony, her poise finally crumbles and the tears flow as, in a cracked voice, she recites Articles 1, 3 and 5 of the Universal Declaration of Human Rights: that all people are born free and equal in dignity and rights; that everyone has the right to life, liberty and personal safety; and that no one shall be subjected to torture or to cruel, inhuman or degrading treatment. Yet the reality for Ket and for countless others was that those rights were too easily snatched away.

'And I don't remember now what I was taught in school about human rights; Chhoeung Ek...' she pauses, fighting to keep her composure on the stand, 'has eroded my self-confidence.'

Now Neary turns her head and again faces Duch. He has spent the session watching her intently, his hands clasped together resting on a blue folder on the desk, his head tilted to the right. Much of what follows she says directly to him rather than to the five judges in front of her.

'I must conclude by saying that I spent my entire life trying to come closer to the truth, the truth which the accused thinks he owns and which I was deprived of, and what was uncovered in 1991 is something that I never stopped trying to learn more because I wanted to know – to know my history, to know what the truth was, and this quest is something I undertook on my own and I owe it only to myself,' she says. 'I've managed to make the link with the accused, who is nothing but the nerve centre of a crime industry which took place in S-21.

'I must specify that from the outset ... witnesses are asked whether or not they know the accused, and I wish to state that the accused is the one who does not know me, but I have come to know him – because I've been observing you for several months,' she says to Duch. 'However, I know enough at this point to tell the accused that I have no interest in him and that, whether or not I come into possession of the confession of my father, I give it back to him and I hope he will sink with it.

'As a Cambodian, his obsequiousness cannot hide from my eyes the cynical and bloodthirsty brute whom I know. As a Frenchwoman, I see the accused took on responsibilities without ever getting his hands dirty by evoking his agreement in principle, he says, but he neglects to clarify that at that time he didn't have a job as an objective, but rather dirty work, dirtily fed by others. As far as I'm concerned, this is the shame of the human race.'

None of the judges has any questions for Neary. Duch's defence chooses not to query her either, so after a few questions from her civil party lawyer she closes out her testimony under the bright lights and in the cold air of the court with a message of personal responsibility for healing.

'To those Cambodians who perhaps struggle to talk about it,' she says, 'the only way to go forward is to dissect what happened and to construct your own explanation. Because when you break down what happened and then reassemble that puzzle in the right way, as it really happened, that can obviously improve things. We cannot stay permanently in solitude and submission.

'Moreover, one should not believe that S-21 stops at the gates of S-21; the prison without walls has walls that keep in their memory what happened,' she continues. 'The walls are shouting. Borders do not stop what happened at S-21 and Cambodia is not alone. The whole world is watching it.'

WITH HER TESTIMONY FINISHED, Neary remains seated in the witness chair, her back to the audience, facing the bench. The presiding judge asks Duch whether he wishes to say anything. He does. He stands and addresses Neary directly, using the Cambodian custom of putting her family name – Ouk – first.

'I would like to bow my mind and my body to acknowledge the testimony of this Ouk Neary as an orphan who lost her father at S-21. This testimony is valuable. It is an historical document for the next generation not to forget the tragedy and not to allow mankind to repeat such crimes,' Duch says. 'In the future we could hear the testimonies of other orphans who lost their fathers, and I am ready to receive those testimonies.'

Of the crimes committed at S-21 and on the country as a whole, of these things, says Duch, I have spoken extensively.

'My personal crimes on the people who were alive, on those offences, I do not deny them. I am responsible both legally and emotionally,' he says. 'I am entirely responsible.'

ONE ELEMENT OF NEARY'S testimony I did not understand came when she turned to Duch and told him he could sink with Ket's confession. The image of Duch the archivist disappearing into a watery void, weighed down by reams of paper from his creation, was a powerful one, and I wanted to know: was this a welcome release for her and was she gladly getting rid of the file that she felt she would never find? Or was this a surrender – had she given up on finding it? Neither, she replied.

'I'm not saying I'm quitting looking for it and that I'm not interested in it,' she told me. 'I said that [in court] because I don't like Duch and I have no reason to like him. But I've never said I was quitting on it.'

THAT EVENING MARTINE STAYED in their hotel after what had been an emotional day and I met Neary to talk. She told me she was going back to the former prison the following morning.

'Mum doesn't want to come,' she said. 'I wondered if you'd like to?'

After the family's 1991 visit to Cambodia, the International Red Cross had written to Martine to tell her that their records showed Ket had been held in Cell 23 on the ground floor of Building C. Neary wanted to go back and see Cell 23 for a final time before leaving the country.

The next morning we entered the compound through the same gate that Ket had been taken 32 years earlier, crossing the courtyard under the shadows of the thin-ribbed coconut palms and up the worn steps into the ground-level coolness of Building C. Cell 23 is as gaunt, anonymous and cramped as the dozens of others hewn from these classrooms: roughly erected, 6-foot-high brick walls laid directly onto tiles of beige and dirty-white. A crumbling rectangular ammunition box, the toilet, sat in one corner next to a rusting shackle that would have clamped one of Ket's legs to a bolt fused to the floor.

Half of a barred and glassless window let in the sun, and its harsh rays highlighted the cracked floor and the cement that bled between the walls' red bricks. There was no bed and nor would there have been. The cell's dimensions, a metre across and little more than that in length, left just enough room for Ket to lie on the floor. This was Ket's solitary home for months.

As occasional tourists drifted by recording their digital memories, it struck me that so much of what Ket had experienced was missing. Of the five senses, we can share only what he would have seen and touched and even then only partially and in the most fleeting way. The smells, the sounds, the tastes – to say nothing of the pain and the visceral fear that permeated each day – are absent.

As we stood silently in the cell, Neary pulled a permanent marker pen from her bag and started writing, thick, black capital letters one-inch tall taking slow shape on the plastered wall next to the barred window.

First the letter 'W' appeared, then the letter 'E'.

'What are you doing?' I asked in an alarmed whisper.

'I'm writing something for Ket,' she replied calmly.

Her arm shifted along the wall and left a space before the letter 'A' began to take shape. I found myself looking around nervously. My mind was churning: what if one of the museum staff walked past and saw this? Or if another visitor reported that a tourist was graffiti-ing on the wall? It was not graffiti, of course, and Neary was hardly a tourist, and if anyone had the right to scrawl a message on this wall then surely she did, but it still made me uncomfortable. As she obviously had no intention of stopping, I decided to let her be and left the cell.

By now the letter 'L' had followed the letters 'R' and 'E' on to the wall. These were Neary's final moments with her father and, feeling conflicted, I made my apologies and walked over to Building D whose ground floor contained yet more monochrome images of the condemned, the life stories of the few survivors, plaster busts of Pol Pot, ranks of rusted shackles and boards of enlarged images of forced labour.

Twenty minutes later we met up on the other side of the courtyard near a souvenir shop selling tourist trinkets. Neary looked tired yet relieved and flashed me her magnetic smile. I asked her how she was feeling.

'Fine,' she said. 'I'm fine.'

We went back to Cell 23. There on the wall was the message, written in English, for Ket.

'**WE ARE LEAVING**.'

LATER NEARY TOLD ME she had asked the genocide museum for permission to place a plaque in Cell 23 with an inscription in Khmer and French. The museum had refused but she decided to leave her father a message regardless.

But why not write in French, I asked? After all, you are French, Ket was Cambodian and fluent in French, and he adored France. So why English?

'Because in English you can have this play on words, but in French you cannot,' she explained. 'My message was not only saying goodbye to Ket, but it's like, OK, come on now. We are leaving and we are not living in this cell any more. We are going out.'

A dozen letters, then, in thick, black ink to tell Ket that his wife and daughter were leaving Cambodia, and that it was time he left this place too.

'And obviously I arrived too late but I needed to do this,' she said.

There was a third meaning too, she told me, directed at the Khmer Rouge. 'We are alive, standing up and going, and you – Khmer Rouge – have failed [to eliminate us].'

WHEN NEARY WALKED OUT of Building C, she told me later, the harsh light and the stultifying heat of that August day had left her dizzy, as had been the case on her first visit in 1991. But on this day in 2009 there was more: the emotion of being in Ket's cell, the accumulated knowledge of the beatings and the electric shocks that had punished his body, the uncountable torments, and the pressure and release of her testimony the previous day.

All of that crashed upon her, and as the palm trees reached up into the searing sky, Neary felt the ground tremble and her tears flowed.

A tourist asked if she needed help. Neary shook her head, unable to answer. Any offer of help, she reflected, was decades too late.

'And I thought, if she had asked this 30 years before, the prisoners would have loved to hear those words,' she said. 'They would have been more than relieved to hear the sentence: "Can I help you?" And then I realised that in the end we all die. What we can do better is not to be like them.'

'Being like them' was what terrified Neary. Despite her gentle nature, as someone who was half Khmer she feared she had inherited whatever element she presumed it was that had led Khmer to kill so many Khmer.

'I was wondering about my own identity [and] when I was looking at myself in the mirror I was seeing the killer in me,' she said. 'It was not me – I was seeing what Duch had done – [but] it was like my blood was dirty. So I was someone bad, but I didn't know why because I had done nothing wrong. I am sure I'm not the only person to feel that, but I am the only one who spoke about that openly.'

BY THE TIME WE LEFT it was lunchtime and the wind had begun to pick up. Neary told me Ket used to fly kites when he was a boy living just a mile away. The best place to catch the breeze in Phnom Penh is by the river, so after lunch we bought a kite from a man whose bicycle was a mobile shop. We headed to the promenade where the ferries leave throughout the day for the short crossing to the Mekong's east bank.

This stretch of the river is known as Chaktomuk and it marks the confluence of the main rivers: where the Tonle Sap, which alternately fills and drains the great lake, meets the Bassac and the Mekong. The water was teak-coloured, thick with mud and so swollen by the wet season's rains that the two-deck wooden ferryboats rode nearly level with the promenade. Our kite was a two-foot wide red and blue design featuring a Chinese princess and a fiery bird of prey with a four-foot-long tail. Fishermen mended their nets nearby, while their children covetously watched us assemble the toy.

We managed to launch it, but flying kites was never my forte and Neary was little better. Besides, the wind soon dropped so eventually we gave the kite to the children and watched as they spent the next 15 minutes running up and down the promenade squealing with delight in their largely unsuccessful efforts to get it to fly. Before long it was snagged in a spiky tree, damaged beyond repair.

In a photograph of that day, Neary stands in the sun with the kite ready to launch and the Mekong stretching far behind her. She looks relaxed and happy and her radiant smile dominates. It would be impossible to guess that one day earlier she had confronted in court one of Cambodia's most reviled men. It was as if that short time by the river had washed away, albeit briefly, the stresses of a lifetime.

Much later, Neary and I were talking on Skype. Ket was seldom far from our conversations, whether directly or indirectly, and she brought up the picture of Ket in a Tuareg's tent in which he struggles to keep hold of a baby goat while the photographer lines up the shot. It is one of her favourite photographs of her father, a young man in his late twenties, a life full of promise, engaged with the world. Yet within a few years he was dead.

'How can such a shiny man finish in such a dark place?' she asked sadly. 'It's not possible.'

*In the world of torture, man exists only by ruining the other person who
stands before him.
The name of it was power, dominion over spirit and flesh,
orgy of unchecked self-expansion …
Amazed, the tortured person experienced that in this world
there can be the other as absolute sovereign,
and sovereignty revealed itself as the power
to inflict suffering and to destroy.*

— Auschwitz survivor Jean Améry (1912–78) on torture

*I will never become a healthy person again like I was before being
incarcerated in the torture prison S-21. The visible and invisible scars
remain forever and my body and mind [are] destroyed.*

— S-21 survivor and artist Bou Meng, who testified against Duch

CHAPTER THIRTEEN

'DUCH IS DEAD'

BY THE START OF THE FINAL WEEK of trial in November 2009, this much is obvious: Duch appears regretful, although it is not wholly clear what he regrets; he has admitted to crimes but typically only to those that were documented and undeniable; he has often been antagonistic towards witnesses whose testimony implicates him in torture and murder, yet he openly chastised his former deputy, the notorious Mam Nai, for claiming to remember nothing about M-13A and S-21 when Mam Nai took the stand.[1] Duch has given multiple apologies, is deferential to the bench and has shown an astounding grasp of detail.

Charged with war crimes, crimes against humanity, and crimes under Cambodia's 1956 Penal Code, the defence's strategy has been straightforward enough, revolving as it must around mitigation. Accept some responsibility, express remorse, apologise repeatedly. Although under civil law, Duch cannot technically enter a guilty plea, that is effectively what he has done. Those of us reporting on the tribunal feel Roux has outperformed everyone.

That said, you would need to look hard to find a Cambodian who believes Duch is genuinely sorry. Aware of the scepticism surrounding his client, Roux has lashed out repeatedly at the prosecution for denying Duch his chance at redemption. As the final week begins, I hope Roux is right. After all, as we shall see, Duch is no sociopath, and a man who has done so much damage can surely see the consequences of his actions. If that is the case, then how can he be anything but truly penitent?

---

1. Rithy Panh felt the exchange between Duch and Mam Nai was a charade designed to impress the judges. As he pointed out during our interview, by the time Mam Nai took the stand, he and Duch had been revolutionary brothers for more than 40 years – 'They understand each other ... and you cannot let [down] your brother-in-arms like that.'

And so, as this week commences, a predictable stroll to the finish looks certain. The schedule looks like this: on Monday the civil party lawyers will deliver their closing arguments and will surely ask for a sentence long enough to ensure that Duch can never live as a free man. The next day and a half are reserved for the prosecution, which will, we expect, acknowledge some mitigating factors but will push for a lengthy jail term. Then, on Wednesday, Duch is scheduled to take the stand and will doubtless deliver another apology. After that Kar Savuth will outline the first part of the defence's closing argument and, on Thursday, Roux will close out. The rest of the week is scheduled for final comments from the civil party lawyers, the prosecution and the defence. And that, we wrongly assume, will be that.

THE WEEKS FOLLOWING Martine's and Neary's appearances in mid-August heard an array of gripping testimony. Civil parties gave harrowing accounts of the deaths of their loved ones. Cambodia's leading psychologist explained the traumas endured by civil parties and survivors, and then two psychiatrists took the stand to discuss Duch's personality. They were followed by a scattering of other witnesses, among whom was Cambodian-American pastor Christopher LaPel, who had baptised Duch into the Christian faith.

LaPel's testimony is important for the defence because Duch converted to Christianity in January 1996, well before he was found and unmasked. In Roux's eyes, this indicates his client was aware of his past wrongs and eager to make amends. It should be said that LaPel is no wide-eyed naïf: his parents, siblings and friends died under the Khmer Rouge, some at S-21, but he has forgiven Duch for his actions because, 'I hate sin, not sinners'.

LaPel tells the bench that during the handful of days of Bible study before Duch converted – at the time Duch was using the alias Hang Pin – the former master of S-21 had said nothing of his past save that he had sinned so extensively he felt others could never forgive him. When LaPel finally learned of Duch's background three years later, his reaction was one of joy that God 'can change his life from the killer to the believer'. Before Duch converted, he was a man 'with sadness, no peace, no joy, no purpose in life'. LaPel thinks that was in part due to an attack at Duch's home in 1995 when his wife was murdered with a bayonet and he was injured by intruders.[2] Afterwards Duch

---

2. Duch told the court that he suspected Pol Pot had sent people to try and kill him (see ECCC document E1_70.1_TR001, August 27, 2009, p. 78).

became the most attentive of students, fervently curious about God, sin and salvation.

A fortnight after Duch was baptised, LaPel made him a minister 'with the right to preach, to teach and to baptise'. Duch returned to his village, built a Protestant church and converted his children and a dozen other families. A taut smile plays across Duch's face as LaPel tells the bench that these enthusiastic actions convinced him the conversion was genuine because Duch was not only baptised but acted on his new belief. Even now, LaPel tells the judges, Duch tells him he feels guilty and repentant for what he did. His conversion was sincere, he concludes, Duch is a 'man of God', and his spiritual rebirth was not an opportunistic attempt to game Christianity's exonerating nature.

The subject of Duch's conversion came up during his interviews in early 2008 with the court-appointed psychiatrist and psychologist who subsequently wrote a 70-page report for the tribunal. Duch explained that the role the Catholic Church – rather than capitalism – had played in the 1980s in the overthrow of Poland's communist government, an event that helped set in train the collapse of the Soviet Union, had inspired him. Duch saw that Christianity, not communism, had triumphed and that surely proved God was greater than the political ideology whose tenets had underpinned his adult life.

These two specialists felt that moment signified the end of the second of three dominant affiliations that had marked Duch's life, all of them driven by his need for certainty. The first was as a student who excelled in subjects that convey elemental truths, such as mathematics. The second was the 'logical, tangible and rational realm' of communism that handed Duch control of his destiny in the face of the injustices and uncertainties afflicting Cambodia in the 1960s. The third affiliation was Christianity, which provided the stability he felt was lacking.

'Communism … had been defeated,' the medical experts wrote. 'So he chose to join what he considered to be the safest community, the community of the victors. For that reason his conversion was not driven by spirituality, but mainly by pragmatic considerations relating to his deep-rooted desire for personal safety.'[3]

While they did not question Duch's decision to convert, they noted that he had made a 'safe choice' in doing so.

---

3. 'Psychological Assessment Report Concerning: Kaing Guek Eav alias Duch', Françoise Sironi-Guilbaud and Sunbaunat Ka (ECCC, 2008).

'It could also be argued that he converted to Christianity because of his responsibility for the many killings at S-21. The Buddhist faith could not protect him from reincarnation as an evil soul, due to the offences he has committed in this life,' they wrote. 'Also, he would require many "rewards" in order to earn reincarnation as a good soul. But there was no such hope in view of his past actions. Christianity offered a better "way out" for his "soul".'

Kong Pisey, a Cambodian civil party lawyer, later tells the judges that, had Duch stayed with Buddhism, 'his crimes would have deemed him to the 18th level of hell [from which] there is no return'.

Buddhism and Christianity both incorporate the concept of the immortality of the soul and both outline terrible punishments for wrongdoing. Yet only Christianity offers a way to save a soul so weighed down with sin. As a practical man there were clear benefits for Duch to discard Buddhism as he had discarded communism. In court LaPel was certain Duch's conversion was genuine. Yet it surely helped that Christianity offered a solution to an otherwise impossible dilemma.

THE LAST DAYS of evidentiary hearings see input from South African judge Richard Goldstone and Cambodia expert Raoul Marc Jennar. But most intriguing were the words of 91-year-old Stéphane Hessel, a French resistance fighter during the Second World War and later a prominent rights activist and writer.[4] During the war, Hessel had been captured by the Nazis, survived internment at two concentration camps despite being tortured and marked for execution, and escaped while being sent to a third. He witnessed the Nuremberg trials and helped to draft the Universal Declaration of Human Rights, three of whose articles Neary had cited in her testimony.

Hessel appears by video link from France in the final week, a patently decent man who has wrestled with some of the most complex issues of our time, and yet whose sparkling eyes have retained more than a tinge of mischief. As someone who worked towards restoring relations between Germany and France, Hessel is asked to discuss post-conflict reconciliation and forgiveness. In the same way that Nuremberg helped to rebuild bridges between Germany and the world by making known some of the crimes of the Nazis, he says, a fair trial of Duch could help promote reconciliation in Cambodia. This tribunal's purpose, as with any international criminal court, serves in part to let people know about the savageries it has investigated.

---

4. Hessel died in France in February 2013 aged 95.

'But beyond that, judicial proceedings should have an effect that might be comparable to what obtains in other countries where the truth and reconciliation commissions have been set up,' Hessel says. 'I will use the example of South Africa [and] by this I mean to enable the peoples who are victims of these horrors to continue to enjoy, or to contemplate the prospect of, a peaceful life within their countries.'

Having summed up his somewhat idealistic view of the court's possible reach, Hessel is asked to turn to the subject of forgiveness, something Duch has repeatedly sought, and tell the court what lessons life has taught him.

'I will begin by saying that the word "forgiveness" can apply only to those who have been the victims of the horrific acts, the trace of which remains in the history of Cambodia,' Hessel replies. 'It is for them, the victims, to undertake vis-à-vis those who are guilty following the judgment that will be handed down, to have an attitude which will either be to reject any type of forgiveness – which falls fully within their rights – or to consider that the judgment handed down enables them as victims to overcome their pain and to resume a friendly contact with all of their compatriots in the same manner that this was made possible after the Nuremberg Trial between the victors and the vanquished of the Second World War.'

Although Duch has recognised his guilt, Hessel says, that is not enough to secure forgiveness. And while Duch's efforts towards telling the truth – 'the *sine qua non* condition of reconciliation' – deserve credit, 'an accused who admits to his guilt cannot avoid being tried for the crimes that he admits he has committed'.

Continuing on that theme, Hessel is asked whether simply admitting guilt is sufficient to engender reconciliation, despite the fact that the civil parties believe Duch has kept the bulk of the facts hidden. Let us not even talk of forgiveness, says civil party lawyer Christine Martineau, since most civil parties are in no state for that. Does Hessel believe a mere admission of guilt could allow them to move forward?

In her question, Martineau cites the Nuremberg Trial of Albert Speer, the German armaments minister who pleaded not guilty and who was eventually jailed for 20 years. Many of his co-defendants were hanged and, although Speer's sentence was controversial, he had two elements in his favour: he could show he had worked against the Nazi regime in its final throes, and he accepted some responsibility for his actions.[5]

---

5. Today there is little doubt that Speer (d. 1981) knew much more about the Holocaust than he

On this important question, Hessel replies, the two of them 'could write volumes'. Speer's acts during the last days of the Third Reich – such as countermanding Hitler's orders to destroy Germany's infrastructure – had allowed the judges to treat him more leniently, he says, but clemency cannot apply to someone who admits their guilt yet who is unable to support their claim to have opposed criminal instructions. Turning to the civil parties, Hessel is determined not to be proscriptive. Certainly they could take into account the circumstances under which Duch was operating, but doing so need not mean they forgive him or even wish to reconcile.

As is the custom, the final word goes to the defence. Roux refers to one of the earliest days in the trial when Duch recited the last four lines of a well-known French poem called *La Mort du Loup*, or *The Death of the Wolf*. Written in the nineteenth century by Alfred de Vigny, the narrator, a hunter, tells how he and his colleagues tracked down a wolf, its mate and their two cubs and how the male stood his ground, dying at the hands of man so that the family could escape.

Duch, Roux tells Hessel as part of the preface to his question, is a stoic, and even when running M-13A found that task distasteful. Yet he had been assigned the role, and as a stoic, Roux is saying, had to shoulder his 'lengthy and difficult task' as the poem puts it. In order to help Duch get through those dark days he would recite the final verses. Roux commences with the hunter's reflection on the moment when the wolf, having killed the hunters' best dog, which is the tame version of itself, is mortally wounded by the men's daggers and guns. Now the hunter realises that the wolf is the superior being.

> *'Alas, I thought, in spite of the great name of Men,*
> *How ashamed I am, how weak we are.*
> *How should one leave life and all its ills?*
> *You know the secret, magnificent animals.*
> *To see what it was, and what is left behind on earth,*
> *Only the silence is great. Everything else is weakness.'*

---

admitted to at trial or, indeed, later in life. The repentance he expressed on the stand and afterwards has also been the subject of much speculation. His biographer, Gitta Sereny, believed Speer was aware of the plan to murder the Jews of occupied Europe from no later than October 1943 when Himmler delivered his infamous Posen speech. For more, see: *Albert Speer: His Battle with Truth*, Gitta Sereny (Alfred A. Knopf, 1995).

It is as dramatic as Roux's theatrical style requires. No doubt, he suggests rhetorically to Hessel, you were mentally reciting those verses in which the hunter relates to the wolf whose stoic demise so moves him?

Roux closes the poem, whose last lines tell of the hunter's connection with the wolf as its life spark – its fiery eyes – passes on a final message.

'O wild traveller, I understand you well,
Your final gaze went to my heart.
Saying: "If you can, you must strive with all your being,
Your strength and purpose and thought,
To gain that high degree of stoic pride
To which, though only a beast, I have aspired.
Complaining, weeping, praying – all this is in vain.
Shoulder your lengthy and difficult task,
The way that Destiny sees fit to ask,
Then afterwards, as I have done, suffer and die without complaint."'

Roux's image of Duch as a stoic victim makes for very uncomfortable viewing. No doubt Duch sees himself that way but it is extraordinary that Roux is portraying him like this to one of France's leading thinkers. It proves to be a rare error by Roux: Hessel finds the parallel unconvincing and quickly overturns the sentiment. De Vigny's poem is indeed a beautiful work, he replies, and is a call to 'men of honour' about the stance they ought to take despite the slings and arrows of life.

'If the accused, for instance, feels that he is in agreement with what is said in the poem, he will need to suffer through his possible sentence with the same strength and the same courage as the wolf,' Hessel says, adding that Duch cannot use those sentiments to escape responsibility for his actions.

Roux wades further into awkward territory when he asks whether a man can redeem himself. That, Hessel replies, is a difficult question.

'And it is an embarrassing question when we give thought to the pain of the victims; victims whose imagination cannot let go of the memory of what was accomplished in terrible fashion by the accused,' he continues.

Doubtless Duch will gain from what he has learned over the preceding months, Hessel says.

'This being said, I am not sure that a genuinely honourable and stoic man may wish for anything other than fair retribution for the crimes of which he knows he is guilty,' he concludes.

It is a none-too-subtle demolition of Roux's contrivances. As if to let his compatriot know that his responses are not personal, Hessel uses his final words to say how much he admires lawyers like Roux who appear on behalf of people such as Duch, 'a man who is difficult to defend'.

AND SO AFTER MONTHS OF TESTIMONY, countless documents, accusations and courtroom drama, we have reached the point – November 23, 2009 – where the participants will have their final say before the judges retire to consider their verdict. It starts predictably enough. On the Monday the court hears the final submissions from the lawyers representing the civil parties. As expected, they have little time for Duch.

British lawyer Karim Khan, who represents 37 civil parties, says that although the defendant should get some credit for helping the court, the evidence leads to one overriding conclusion: that Duch has downplayed his role, the 'awful reality' of S-21 and the agony visited upon the civil parties.

Khan's Cambodian colleague, Ty Srinna, reads a brief summary of each civil party in their group. Among the names: Neth Phally, whose brother Bunthy was executed at S-21; Man Saut, whose son Sim was taken there in December 1976; Suos Sarin, whose sister Sovann was a victim. The list goes on, and in this way each person is named and remembered.

Khan wraps up by attacking two of the defence's arguments: Duch's purported lack of autonomy – the fact that he allowed certain prisoners to survive proves otherwise – and that he had used what little freedom he enjoyed to alleviate suffering. Beyond the occasional example, he says, there is no sustained evidence of that.

'This is no individual that sought to minimise suffering. Rather we say that he was continuously dedicated to his job,' Khan says, adding that Duch's actions underpinned the layer of paranoia at the centre of the Party, creating a vicious cycle that saw more and more people swept up.

Even when he could have let prisoners leave – on January 7, 1979, as the Vietnamese-backed liberation forces closed in – he instead killed many of these last inmates. He had the option, yet chose not to exert it. And had he wanted to save lives, then during the preceding years he could have inserted the names of the dead into confessions, yet he did not. Even when there was an option to do the right thing – when S-21 had a surplus of rice that could have been used to add to the thin gruel served to the prisoners – Duch chose inhumanely.

'When he has the boon of having ample rice, what does he do? Does he feed it to these starving and emaciated people in his care? Your Honours, no, he does not. What he does: he gives it to his superiors and he says, very clearly, he wanted to promote the reputation of S-21,' he says.

Duch's relationship with the civil party lawyers has been consistently bad and for that he largely has himself to blame. On too many occasions he has come across as bullying, rude and insensitive to the representatives of those whom he ordered tortured and killed. As far as the civil party lawyers are concerned, those moments of trial were when his mask slipped, revealing the real Duch.

Indeed, at times Duch has proved his own worst enemy, his attitude drifting dangerously from the defence's portrayal of him as a contrite man. Towards the judges, the figures of authority and the arbiters of his fate, he was unfailingly amenable, typically thanking them for their questions and punctuating his answers by stressing 'the truth' of what he was saying. Yet he has been too often contemptuous and even hostile towards the civil party lawyers; during one exchange, the bench weighed in and warned Duch for laughing as a civil party lawyer put a question to him. He was told to behave himself and maintain a better attitude.

Civil party lawyer Kong Pisey rejects Duch's effort to portray himself as a cog in a machine, and explains why Duch has so vehemently objected to accusations that he took part in torture and killings: before the trial started, Duch believed criminal responsibility rested with those 'who have blood on their hands, and that orchestrating murder from behind a desk bears no, or at least less, criminal guilt'. Duch only changed his approach, Kong Pisey says, after Roux advised him to take responsibility for his crimes rather than blaming *Angkar*.[6]

'This shows clearly that he lacked any consciousness of wrongdoing at the time he committed the crimes. He was convinced of the policy of the Party line to smash the enemy,' Kong Pisey says, describing Duch's claims of contrition as 'crocodile tears … orchestrated and devoid of meaning'.

NEXT IS THE TURN OF the prosecution, and as its closing statements commence there is still no indication of the extraordinary reversal that we are about to witness. Prosecutor William Smith concedes, as expected, that

---

6. That much is clear, too, in Rithy Panh's book, where Duch admits that: 'In the past, I thought I was innocent.' *The Elimination*, op. cit., p. 160.

there are mitigating circumstances, such as Duch's taking responsibility, but insists that was driven by the sheer volume of documentary evidence.

'[Moreover] wherever possible, the accused has adamantly sought to minimise his role,' Smith says. 'He accepts responsibility only on his own terms where he attempts to paint a picture of himself as an unwilling participant caught up in a machine he could not escape; trapped by secrecy and terror. You must not allow him to hide behind these false claims. You must recall that he was not a victim of the system, but its loyal and dedicated agent.'

The bench must consider too that the crimes of which Duch is accused 'are rarely matched in modern history in terms of their combined barbarity, scope, duration, premeditation and callousness'. Turning next to Duch's character, Smith stresses that he was nothing like the uneducated peasant youth he employed.

'Particularly relevant [in determining the verdict] are his age and education at the time that he joined S-21,' Smith says. 'Unlike most of the staff he employed, the accused was highly educated, intelligent and exceptionally logical. It is clear that he had the ability to move towards the [Communist Party of Kampuchea] or away from it, and he made his choice.'

Smith says that Duch's contention that he acted out of fear for his own life could have been true in 1978 when he noticed that his mentors were being sent to S-21, but did not account for his earlier actions. No doubt there was a climate of terror but the defence had failed to show Duch was affected by it.

'[The evidence] demonstrates that he was not a victim of terror, but its cause,' he says. 'The evidence does not show a fearful man. To the contrary, it demonstrates a confident man who spreads terror across Cambodia through his work at S-21; a man who was irreplaceable in his position.'

Smith quotes the German-born political theorist Hannah Arendt, who wrote of totalitarian regimes: 'Terror turns not only against its enemies but against its friends and supporters as well. The climax of terror is reached when the police state begins to devour its own children; when yesterday's executioner becomes today's victim.'

The waves of fear that began to lap at Duch's feet in 1978 were therefore no more than one could expect from a regime that exerted control through the ruthless application of terror. It is hardly surprising that Duch and other key cadres grew worried towards the end.

'It would be far more surprising if they didn't,' Smith says. 'Ultimately, the fact that the accused may have felt fear in 1978 does not overshadow the fact that he freely and willingly designed a system of terror or that he was once an enthusiastic and willing participant in these crimes. Your Honours, the accused should not be able to hide behind the effects of the terror that he, in fact, created.'

Smith reminds the judges that, under international law, cruelties such as those practised at S-21 are an aggravating factor when determining a sentence. The acts, whether physical or psychological, must be of an extreme nature 'and display a particularly savage, sadistic or ruthless quality'. What happened at S-21 was 'truly grotesque'. There were also the conditions in which prisoners were held, the lack of food, medicine and sanitation, and the repeated disappearances of their fellow prisoners, an ongoing war of psychological cruelty.

'The terror, shock, fear and utter confusion endured by the prisoners is beyond our imagination,' he says. 'These prisoners were held in cells, aware of the torture and suffering that surrounded them, seeing wounds and [hearing] moans of the victims that foreshadowed their own fate ... From this distance, we cannot even begin to understand the extreme psychological effects of being subjected to multiple interrogation and torture sessions with the savage violence these prisoners endured.'

The final act in this litany of cruelty came at Chhoeung Ek.

Duch's crimes warrant a life term, Smith concludes, before conceding that his unlawful detention for nearly a decade before trial deserves a reduction to 45 years. Duch's cooperation with the court, his 'limited acceptance of responsibility, his conditional remorse and the possible effect it may have on national reconciliation' should earn a further five-year reduction.

Duch, he adds, has not been honest about the full extent of his criminal activities at S-21 and although he has broadly accepted his guilt, 'no one should make the mistake of believing that this case is equal to an unqualified guilty plea before an international tribunal'.

'We submit, therefore, that the sentence to be imposed by this Trial Chamber should be 40 years' imprisonment,' says Smith. 'Despite accepting general overall responsibility for the crimes he is, in effect, telling the court: "I did terrible things, but it's not really my fault. It's the fault of my superiors." It should also be recalled that he has mostly admitted crimes that are undoubtedly established by the documentary evidence and not more.'

IF THIS WERE NUREMBERG, the prosecution would surely have sought the death sentence and Duch would surely have been hanged. But this is a UN-backed court without that sanction, which has allowed the defence the latitude to operate in ways it otherwise would not have dared. Duch's next move is testament to that.

The first indication that things are going awry is when Duch, in a lilac shirt and beige trousers, takes to the stand to deliver his final address. Instead of another round of apologies Duch speaks for more than an hour listing dozens of names, dates and events that constitute a narrative history of the Communist Party of Kampuchea.

He plays down his influence, saying he had no power of arrest, and stresses that all those whom *Angkar* deemed enemies were to be smashed without exception. He had no right to object. All such decisions were handed down from on high and prisons such as S-21 were compelled to use torture.

During the first year of Khmer Rouge rule, he continues, Pol Pot, Nuon Chea, *Ta* Mok, Vorn Vet and a half-dozen other senior Party members 'enjoyed full power and were most responsible for crimes'. By the time the March 30, 1976 document was finalised, only 11 people – including Pol Pot, Nuon Chea, Son Sen and *Ta* Mok – were allowed to smash enemies. Not him.

As the internal purges hurtled towards their conclusion, the East Zone inhabitants were murdered in their tens of thousands. By mid-1978, S-21 was not even bothering to interrogate hundreds of prisoners sent from the East Zone and simply executed them in short order.

Each point in Duch's delivery is numbered and after nearly an hour he reaches number 64, which looks at the motives of Pol Pot. Brother Number One, 'a criminal person', was trying to construct a dynasty in which he would be de facto king with *Ta* Mok providing the military muscle.

By now the bench has twice told Duch to slow down to allow the translators to keep pace.

The internal purges and the other mass killings in which hundreds of thousands died was a 'monumental destruction … [that] is solely the crime committed by the Communist Party of Kampuchea' for which Duch says he is 'psychologically accountable'.

'I am deeply remorseful of and profoundly affected by destruction on such a mind-boggling scale,' he says, yet he fails to mention his role, before segueing into his inability to escape the regime. 'I was just like a cog in a running machine.'

'For the victims of S-21 and their families, I still claim that I am solely and individually liable for the loss of least 12,380 lives. These people, before their deaths, had endured a great and prolonged suffering and countless inhumane conditions. I still and forever wish to most respectfully and humbly apologise to the dead souls,' he says.[7]

'To the survivors, I stand by my acknowledgment of all crimes which were inflicted on you at S-21. I acknowledge them both in the legal and moral context,' Duch says. 'As for the families of the victims, my wish is that I will always maintain my humble and respectful behaviour by asking you to kindly leave your door open for me to make my apologies.'

Duch ends by reading 34 footnotes that accompany the text of his speech, a disjointed conclusion to a rambling address that leaves everyone puzzled. Oddly, he has used less than two minutes of his nearly 90-minute statement to address the victims of S-21 and their families. It is a mystifying break from the successful defence strategy that has run since March.

As DC-Cam legal adviser Anne Heindel said later, this academic potted history of the CPK 'seemed to be what he wanted people to understand. That was his truth of why things happened.'

These dates, these facts, these incontestable truths: these are what Duch wanted us to see all along. Were it up to Duch this is what he, if pushed, would have permitted the world to know.

AFTER DUCH'S STATEMENT, Kar Savuth stands to address the court and the proceedings take an even stranger turn. In a rambling rehash of his opening remarks months earlier, the bulky, bespectacled defence lawyer does what he had promised the bench in March that he would not do and questions the tribunal's legitimacy. Kar Savuth then goes further. He starts by asking the Cambodian people to understand that he can by no means defend Duch and do justice to the victims, before listing some of the facts of life under Democratic Kampuchea: hundreds of killing fields, 1.7 million dead and nearly 200 prisons that also practised torture and

---

7. Even at this late stage of the trial the Trial Chamber was using the figure of 12,380 as the number of documented victims of S-21 during Duch's tenure as deputy chairman and then chairman. In its ruling, the Trial Chamber later revised down the number of executed victims to 'no fewer than' 12,272 men, women and children, 'the majority of whom were also systematically tortured'. The true number, while certainly higher, can never be known.

executions. Some prisons had more victims than S-21, he says, yet his client alone is on trial.

'It's only Duch, by himself, who killed very few people, and he is brought for trial [in the manner] of a scapegoat,' says Kar Savuth. Is this justice, he asks?

Kar Savuth turns to the crimes prosecutable under Cambodian law, including murder, torture and rape, and says the country's 10-year statute of limitations on those expired in 1989. Extending the time allowed to prosecute such crimes by a further 30 years is illegal since it was applied retroactively.[8]

After this, Kar Savuth's arguments degenerate completely. Turning to the war crimes charge – or more properly, Grave Breaches of the Geneva Conventions of 1949, which criminalise mistreatment of the enemy – Kar Savuth says Duch only became aware that Democratic Kampuchea and Vietnam were in a state of war at the end of 1977, thereby ignoring the fact that many Vietnamese combatants were taken to S-21 after that date. Besides, he continues, it was not Duch who violated the provisions of the Geneva Conventions but the leaders and it is they who should be charged.

Kar Savuth provides more reasons why Duch, who is still on the stand and who spends these hours appearing alternately bored and worried, is not responsible: he was 'led, ordered and instructed by the Party' and merely obeyed orders.[9] He moves from points of law to contentions over jurisdiction, bringing up the court's mandate to try surviving senior leaders and those regarded as 'most responsible'.

Duch is not a senior leader, he rightly tells the court, then ponderously lists the names of those leaders. And since the CPK's Standing Committee was 'the sole mastermind' of the crimes, and since Duch was not one of them, he should not be prosecuted. The infamous document of March 30, 1976 granted the power to order arrests and executions to a few key people. They are the 'most responsible', Kar Savuth says in animated fashion, as he returns to his former argument that the two categories of potential defendant are in fact one.

'I therefore submit that Duch did not commit the crimes against humanity or the war crimes as charged,' he says.

Kar Savuth's submission, regularly punctuated with flourishes of his right hand and a jabbing index finger, is rambling, repetitive and riddled with

8. The tribunal eventually ruled in the defence's favour on this point.

9. Under international law, the defence of following orders can be at best a mitigating factor.

errors of law. Again he returns to the argument he wheeled out earlier: that there were nearly 200 other prisons, and S-21 ranked tenth in terms of the number of victims. Cambodia's constitution guarantees the equality of all citizens under the law, he concludes, and to punish only Duch would breach it.

'I therefore request for the exemption of such prosecution against my client, Kaing Guek Eav, alias Duch,' he says.

It is hard to imagine that Kar Savuth, a reasonable orator, believes much of his own submission and harder still to overstate the legal poverty of his arguments. Besides, as civil party lawyer Silke Studzinsky angrily points out the following day, the constitution covers citizens' equality in having and getting rights. It does not guarantee the right to equality in injustice.

FOR THOSE WITH THE ABILITY to concentrate through months of at times tedious proceedings, there had been hints that Kar Savuth and Roux were marching to different drums. Now that divide is revealed to all. Yet if we are surprised, Roux seems dumbfounded. It appears that Roux, like us, has not expected this and he sits stunned as his co-lawyer demolishes months of skilfully crafted defence.

As the white curtain sweeps closed on the court, none of us can work out what has happened. Why has Kar Savuth sabotaged his client's defence? Has he done so on Duch's instructions or perhaps on the orders of Prime Minister Hun Sen? Or is there some other reason?

The only way to try and fathom that is to be in the auditorium the following morning and to watch the body language between Duch and his two defence lawyers. As the curtain draws back it is clear that Duch, in a cream turtleneck jersey, approves of Kar Savuth's ransacking of his defence. The two men stand and chat, smiling broadly at each other.

As the judges file in and take their seats, a chastened Roux stands to speak. Gone are the swagger and bluster that dominated the courtroom during 77 days of hearings. This is his last case as a defence lawyer and it is by any stretch an ignominious end. Roux will shortly leave to run the defence office at the tribunal investigating the 2005 assassination of Rafik Hariri, Lebanon's former premier.

Roux starts with an apology to the interpreters who would normally have received a copy of his closing remarks in the three working languages of the court.

'For reasons that will be clear to legal practitioners, we have had to review the entire plan of our pleadings after Mr Kar Savuth's pleadings yesterday afternoon,' Roux tells the bench, an acknowledgement that his colleague's words have overturned what he had planned to say.

Roux turns to the civil parties, congratulates them for their participation and puts forward his hope that the trial will provide them with their first step on the road to healing.

'Let us celebrate, at this stage, the fact that this little drop of water will come to cool the suffering – the great suffering that has been endured,' he says.

Next Roux tackles Kar Savuth's submission, noting drily that 'our team has not laboured without disagreements'. He acknowledges that the prosecution will turn on the defence after Kar Savuth's arguments, some of which Roux agrees are inadmissible, but in that he will take no part. The task is Kar Savuth's alone. It also looks as though the two sides of Duch's defence team are no longer on speaking terms, as Roux implies when he adds: 'I can assume that my esteemed colleague has already begun preparing his rebuttal to the pleadings of the national prosecutor.'

Now, Roux sets aside months of his painstaking defence by telling the court that Duch cannot seek to enter two opposing pleas.

'This has been expressed publicly. The accused will not plead guilty,' Roux says.

With his carefully constructed defence in ruins, Roux is compelled to reach for the emotive moments of the trial that he feels convey sincerity: Duch's outpourings of sorrow.

'Who is in a position to dispute and challenge the tears that have been wept by the accused? Who is in a position to contest the apologies that have been made by the accused person during the re-enactment at S-21? Who is in a position to contest those moments of truth?' Roux asks, warming to his theme. 'Moments of truth that were experienced by an accused person who wept before the victims and wept before the co-investigating judges and who proclaims: "These are the words that I have been waiting to utter for the last 30 years."'

It is desperate stuff, and Roux now turns on the prosecution: had it not harped on for months about how Duch was refusing to tell all, had it not said time and again that Duch was a monster and could not be rehabilitated, then perhaps that could have precluded Kar Savuth's presentation.

'[The prosecution] said: "He is not saying everything. What he is saying will aid reconciliation but little." This is what I heard. What a waste,' Roux says. 'As long as the prosecutor's submissions will focus on this man as a scapegoat, you will not advance by so much as a millimetre in the development of humanity. No, Duch does not have to bear on his head all the horrors of the Cambodian tragedy.'

Roux is right to assert that 'we must go further [than the cliché of the monster], we must try to understand the mechanisms that lead a man, who is a decent man by all accounts, to become a torturer'. But he is broadly wrong in his other areas and he surely knows his client is mostly to blame. Other arguments also fail to impress. Roux disputes that Duch 'enjoyed converting human beings into torturers', but surely his former passion for that is self-evident? He disagrees too that Duch was 'at the origin of the network of terror' that struck the country, a position that he says will not promote reconciliation.

I am struck by how fiercely Roux continues to fight for a client who has so humiliatingly discarded him.

'Has Duch become Pol Pot?' Roux asks, castigating the prosecution. 'I apologise in advance to the victims for what I am about to say, but how many people died in S-21? 12,380? We know it's 12,380 too many; that's all right. How many in Cambodia? One-point-seven million, we're told. That means that S-21 is responsible for less than one per cent of the deaths in Cambodia, and you're telling the chamber that Duch was the start – or started the network of terror – that bathed Cambodia in blood. How dare you?'

Roux moves to the issue of contrition, saying his client is 'full of remorse' as witnessed when he returned in February 2008 to Chhoeung Ek and the Tuol Sleng Genocide Museum in the company of the court's investigating judges and other court officials, as well as four of his former subordinates. At the time tribunal spokesmen and the defence had said that when Duch reached the tree against which babies and young children were killed, he fell to his knees and wept. This decision to return, says Roux, is testament to his client's inner journey, and to back that up he quotes from Duch's testimony of September 2009.

'"When I went to Chhoeung Ek ... I thought about the memory of the children who were executed and who were killed in the most atrocious manner when they were smashed against tree trunks and, at that point, I was determined to return to that place so that I could go fall on my knees and honour the souls of those who perished,"' Roux says.

So much for the public utterances, Roux continues. As his defence lawyer, I have a significant advantage over the prosecution in that I get to see the accused in private moments, not only in court. In his cell, Duch 'is able to speak freely from the heart'.

'We see what you, Mr and Ms Prosecutor, are unable to see. We see an accused person who tries to hide himself discreetly and when he collapses in tears there is no one other than his own lawyers who are able to witness the tears that he sheds on the graves of the children who died,' Roux says. 'That is what we bear witness to. And that is what I testify to today.'

(Nearly three years after the trial ends we will get another insight into Duch when the court reclassifies and releases papers that show that – regardless of how he might have behaved in the privacy of his cell in front of his lawyers – overt displays of contrition were seemingly not part of Duch's visit to Chhoeung Ek. The documents make no mention of him kneeling and weeping, which chimes with earlier comments made by two senior tribunal officials who said they had not noticed any such displays of remorse.[10] What the document does state are Duch's matter-of-fact observations about the killing of children: yes, they were killed at Chhoeung Ek, and yes it was 'plausible' they were murdered by being smashed against the trees, but he had not given orders that they be executed in that manner.)

Roux is on stronger ground when he quotes David Chandler, who had agreed in court that Duch's acknowledgement of responsibility was of service to history, and had noted that it was unique among the key Khmer Rouge figures still alive. Also valid are Roux's observations on the climate of the time: terror was the pervasive characteristic of a regime whose watchwords were secrecy and obedience. Again he turns to Chandler, in this case the historian's thoughts from his book on S-21: that one should pause before judging the interrogators, torturers and guards too harshly, for we have not walked in their shoes. Who can say they would not have done the same?

As Roux enters the home straight he turns to the bigger picture: what this trial will mean to humanity. It is too comfortable to see Duch as a monster and besides, for a man in his late sixties, a 40-year term is effectively a life sentence. What we must learn, he rightly notes, is the lesson about the crime of obedience, for it is this that turns a normal man into an executioner.

'"Be resolute to no longer serve and then you will be free",' says Roux

---

10. KR PRISON CHIEF WANTED PERSONAL PSYCHOLOGIST FOR TRIAL, Julia Wallace, the *Cambodia Daily*, September 20, 2012.

quoting the sixteenth-century philosopher Étienne de La Boétie, who wrote about the dangers of obedience. He reminds the court of the Milgram experiment, which showed that most of us will obey an order even to the point of inflicting potentially lethal amounts of pain on others.

The television camera switches to the defendant as Roux recalls how witnesses told the court that, prior to the revolution, Duch was 'a humble man, a simple man, a generous man, a respectful man … an honest man … a calm man … a sweet man … a nice man', and suggests his failure to tell the full truth of what he knows might be down to post-traumatic stress disorder. And yet, Roux continues, I believe my client has told 'the essence regarding most of the crimes'.

As Roux moves to close, he quotes a Cambodian proverb in which a wise man asks his followers: 'How do we know that we are moving from night to day, from the shadows to the light?' The answers come: 'When we begin to distinguish the colour of the mango leaves,' says one. 'When you begin to see the Cardamom [Mountains] in the distance,' offers another. A third disciple replies: 'When you can recognise your brother in another's eyes.'

Roux turns to Duch and tells him that all of those whom he ordered killed were his brothers and sisters, and for that the people of Cambodia will never forgive him. Roux then addresses the bench.

'But what about us, Your Honours? Are we prepared to look Duch in the eye and see him for the fellow human that he is? … Through your ruling will you bring back Duch into the fold of humanity?'

He closes with a rhetorical flourish.

'One last word, one final word,' Roux tells the court. 'Duch is dead! Today his name is Kaing Guek Eav. He is no longer the Duch of the revolution.'

THE ANGER OF THE CIVIL PARTY LAWYERS at Duch's switch is palpable. Karim Khan, whose carefully chosen words evince a love of court-room rhetoric, says Roux's attempt to introduce Duch's behind-closed-doors-tears 'was eloquent, was riveting, [but] is legally irrelevant'.

'The same applies to his hypothesis of post-traumatic stress disorder,' he says. 'There's been no evidence that I've seen on the issue of post-traumatic stress disorder. This is a court of law, not a forum for unsupported hypotheses to be brought like the conjurer's rabbit out of the hat at the last moment.'

It is, says Khan, 'unacceptable from every angle that we are left in this chaotic state of affairs where we do not know actually what has been said'.

'Mr Roux states that the accused is not pleading guilty but he's accepting contrition,' he says. 'His co-national lawyer says release him, he's absolutely not guilty.'

Khan's words are echoed by the other civil party groups who condemn Duch's 'two-horse' strategy. Civil party lawyer Hong Kimsuon, a survivor of the regime, apologises as he breaks down in tears saying Duch's position that he was a mere cog in a machine is 'a false argument … a lie'.

When the prosecution stands to speak, they call on the judges to determine whether Duch has instructed Kar Savuth to plead as he did. If so, then the bench must ignore any mitigating circumstances. On the other hand if Kar Savuth has acted on his own initiative then that needs to be cleared up too because Duch could appeal on the grounds that his Cambodian defence lawyer had acted contrary to his instructions.

'The fact of this change of approach by the defence on the second-to-last day of the trial – this is unacceptable in any court and it should be unacceptable in this court,' says Smith, adding that 40 years is the minimum tariff the court should hand down.

'Remember the victims,' he tells the bench.

WE NOW ENTER THE FINAL MOMENTS of Duch's trial and, despite the bench's call for the defence to clarify its dual strategy, neither Kar Savuth nor Roux does so as they wrap up their rebuttals. Instead they broadly outline once more their respective positions, leading Smith to query the judges.

'The defence have evaded your question in relation to why this change of plea,' says Smith. 'On the one hand, we have the defence saying mitigate his sentence and on the other hand they're saying acquit him for all of those jurisdictional grounds that were raised, and I think it's very important to find out why they are running these two defences.'

It is remarkable that, with nine months gone and with less than an hour left of Duch's trial, there is still no clarity. Smith tells the judges they must ask Duch whether he has instructed his lawyers to enter an effective plea for acquittal.

'Otherwise you will leave this courtroom with two defences: I'm not guilty and then, if I am, mitigate me,' says Smith.

Roux stands to respond and, as this trial of epic tragedy teeters on the edge of farce, tells the bench that the rules do not allow the prosecution to speak further, before continuing in mocking tone.

'However, if we have not been clear enough on this point, I am sorry. I am sorry the prosecutor was not listening to us closely enough. Acquittal was not used this morning – this word was not used,' says Roux. 'Both defence lawyers asked that the accused's sentence, were he to be found guilty, should be reduced and that he should be freed as soon as possible. It is not an acquittal. My learned friend, if this is not clear for you, then I'm sorry. He should be freed after being imprisoned for 10 years and after fully recognising his responsibility for the crimes in S-21. There is no change.'

The bench disagrees and chastises the defence for failing to answer the question. If the lawyers will not do so, then Duch must.

So Duch stands and lists his cooperation with the court, his apologies and admissions of guilt, his responsibility for the deaths of the prisoners at S-21, his desire to make amends, the responsibility of the leaders, and the fact that he has not challenged the crimes committed at S-21.

'From the 8th of May 1999 until now it has been 10 years already – 10 years, six months, 18 days,' he concludes. 'So during the course of my detention I cooperated with the chamber and I do not really challenge such detention as illegal. I will leave it to the court to decide. So I would ask the chamber to release me. I'm very grateful, Your Honours.'

Duch has pointedly not answered the question, and the judges are as bemused as the rest of us. Nil Nonn tells Duch to explain why he is seeking release? Does he want to be acquitted of all charges? Or is he seeking a reduced sentence?

I've said what I wanted to say, Duch replies. I wish to be released and if you want to know more then please ask Kar Savuth.

Once again Kar Savuth rises, running through his array of arguments.

'He was not the senior leader of Democratic Kampuchea and he was not among those who were most responsible for the crimes,' Kar Savuth says. 'So he only obeyed the [Communist Party of Kampuchea]. So the CPK was the culprit, was the criminal behind all the crimes. That's why my client asked that he be released.'

Even now the defence has failed to clarify. Judge Cartwright moves to close down this strange charade.

'Counsel Kar Savuth, do I infer from your last comments that the accused is seeking an acquittal?' she asks.

'I'm grateful to you, Your Honour,' he replies. 'I did say that, because to release means to acquit.'

Blood debts must be paid in blood.

— Khmer Rouge slogan

CHAPTER FOURTEEN

TOTALITARIAN PSEUDO-HERO

AND SO ENDED the first trial of any member of the Khmer Rouge at a court recognised as capable of delivering an international standard of justice. In mid-1979 the Vietnamese-backed government in Phnom Penh had held a genocide trial in absentia of the 'Pol Pot-Ieng Sary clique', which was both cathartic and highly political but which has long been criticised as a show trial.

For this reason, the ECCC's trial of Duch was a milestone. But it was important in other ways too, most obviously because each international war crimes trial lays down precedent from which subsequent tribunals can draw, and in so doing causes this relatively new field of law to move forward in incremental fashion.

The ECCC's trial of Duch was also groundbreaking in allowing civil parties to join proceedings, although that was a mixed success. Critics complained that allowing civil parties to participate had dragged out proceedings, thereby delaying the start of Case 002, the trial of the surviving leaders. For their part, civil party lawyers complained the court had failed to treat their clients with sufficient respect. When civil parties testified, the bench typically declined to ask questions, leaving the impression 'that the Trial Chamber was rather uninterested in their stories', as lawyer Silke Studzinsky put it during the last week of hearings. The bench's warning that civil parties should keep their emotions in check on the grounds that the court had no time to reschedule hearing the parties was seen as both heartless and threatening.

Duch's decision to seek an acquittal on bogus grounds was also a milestone, albeit of the bizarre sort, and puzzled me for months. What was his intention? Did his incongruous action provide an insight into the man?

Civil party lawyer Karim Khan felt that 'to peer into [Duch's] soul ... is simply not possible', but I am not so sure. The Russian writer Nadezhda Mandelstam might well have agreed with Khan: when reflecting on the cruelties inflicted in Stalin's gulags on the prisoners, of whom her husband, the poet Osip Mandelstam, was one, she wrote: 'The only really strange thing is that all of this was done by people, the most ordinary sort of people ... How can we understand it or explain it?'

Neary fears that focusing on trying to comprehend Duch detracts from his victims, which is a fair point. ('We please them when we shine a light on them,' she told me on one occasion.) Yet I feel it is important to try. Duch's testimony manipulated the truth and was of varying reliability, but there were other areas I could turn to. The most useful was the ECCC's 70-page psychological report, which was written by Cambodia's leading psychiatrist, Professor Ka Sunbaunat, and French psychologist, Dr Françoise Sironi-Guilbaud, an expert on mental disorders linked to torture. They spent 40 hours with Duch in the year before his trial. During those 13 interviews, they noted, Duch was an enthusiastic participant.

Among the report's findings were that: Duch has an overwhelming need to please his superiors; he is 'passionate about imparting knowledge'; he has an obsessive personality; he loathes lying; he is unable to speak about his emotions; and he is intelligent yet possesses a limited imagination. He also lacks empathy but that in part is because of the Khmer Rouge's demand that cadres strip themselves of emotion. This means he cannot put himself in the shoes of others, but instead 'projects his vision on the world and does not see it as it actually is, but rather as it should be'.

Unusually, the profile did not examine Duch's sexuality, which is a standard topic in this type of assessment. The two experts felt that to do so in a group setting would have been culturally taboo, while Sironi-Guilbaud felt it would have been inappropriate for her to bring that up during her one-on-one sessions. Sunbaunat simply 'did not discuss the subject' when he met alone with Duch. That despite the two experts' recognition that 'there is usually a correlation between problems relating to sexuality and the exercise of power (pursuit of absolute power and recognition from male superiors in powerful positions)'. Martine, with her background in nursing and psychiatry, felt this was a significant omission.

Sunbaunat and Sironi-Guilbaud determined that Duch's personality was damaged by four key traumas: the greed of a usurious uncle when Duch was young caused the family great distress and led to disillusionment with blood relatives; the girl of his dreams rejected his advances when he was 19, which caused disillusionment with love; the injustice and poverty that characterised Cambodia in the 1950s and 1960s meant he was disillusioned with society; and lastly the consequences of the Khmer Rouge's totalitarian methods of control, revolving as they did around terror, mistrust, obedience, and the ever-increasing gap between the theory of Communism and its practice.

Also important were Duch's defence mechanisms of avoidance ('I did not want to see' what was happening) and his rationalisation for his actions ('I had no choice'). They also highlighted two other defence mechanisms he has used throughout his life: denial and splitting. The latter is a subconscious way of dealing with a dangerous environment in which you replace the 'real you' with another. The result is effectively a new person – in Duch's case, the person running M-13A and S-21 concludes that torturing and killing people is the correct course of action. Even though part of him understood that this new person was bogus, Duch perpetuated the fraud in part because to do otherwise would have undermined his beliefs.

DUCH'S PSYCHOLOGICAL REPORT made for interesting reading, and to help me interpret it I spoke to Tanja Schunert, a German psychiatrist and psychotherapist.

Schunert was halfway through a two-year posting in Cambodia where she was lecturing on psychology, psychotherapy and trauma therapy. She was also working with the German development agency *Deutsche Entwick-lungsdienst* (DED), the German Development Service, on psychological issues emanating from the Khmer Rouge period.

We met at her house opposite one of the capital's oldest pagodas, Wat Botum Vaddei and there, on the balcony under a large umbrella to block the midday sun, Schunert – who had not met Duch – told me what stood out for her in the report.

The first was Duch's Chinese ancestry and his usurious uncle. Yes, the Khmers looked down on the Chinese, she said, but many others shared his background and did not go on to behave as he did. The second was his story of frustrated love, which was something he had brought up at trial as one of his greatest regrets. After finishing school, Duch wanted this young woman to study mathematics with him. Despite his pleas to reconsider, she insisted on French literature and that was the end of the relationship. Schunert felt

Duch's depiction of lost love as a traumatic event in the context of what he had done to others was both insensitive and horrific.

'It is strange that he thought he could only marry this person if she chose the same subjects. It stands out that he is very rigid and depends so much on reducing differences between people,' she said.

Such narrow-mindedness, which the teenage Duch had exhibited years before he joined the CPK, is common in conflicts in many countries because it promotes and accentuates differences between one side and another.

'So you oppose "the others" and cannot tolerate difference,' she said. 'There is only one permitted way to think, and that is the totalitarian factor that makes regimes like the Khmer Rouge possible.'

Duch's lack of empathy, though, was less surprising since it allowed him to cope. Developing empathy 'would have been dangerous'.

'This is why he held on to things like mathematics that represent hard facts,' Schunert said. 'He continued to enlarge this part of his fact-ridden personality and looked at subordinated human beings as numbers only. And that again is something that the others, the leaders, must have brought to perfection as well: looking at people without noticing they are like you – feeling human beings – what is called dehumanising.'

Dehumanisation was an important element covered by South Africa's Truth and Reconciliation Commission, whose purpose was to promote healing and understanding among the divided communities. For two years the commission, headed by former Archbishop Desmond Tutu, travelled the country holding public hearings, listening to victims and perpetrators, and helping to underline apartheid's human cost. Again and again the testimony showed that dehumanising 'others' had been central to the white government's efforts to retain power.

Antjie Krog, a South African journalist and poet, covered every TRC hearing and wrote a remarkable book about it, which she dedicated to 'every victim who had an Afrikaner surname on her lips'.[1] (Krog is a white Afrikaner.) Those giving testimony day after day, she pointed out, were ordinary people who sought answers when often none was forthcoming.

'And everyone wants to know: Who? Why?' Krog wrote. 'Out of the sighing arises more than the need for facts or the longing to get closure on someone's life. The victims ask the hardest of all the questions: how is it possible that the person I loved so much lit no spark of humanity in you?'[2]

---

1. *Country of My Skull*, Antjie Krog (Vintage, 1999).

2. Ibid., p. 67.

One could just as easily ask that question of those who worked at S-21. Schunert felt the answer, in Duch's case at least, seemed to lie in splitting. Without that, perpetrators who were not sociopaths simply could not function.

'And that's the same with [Duch] and probably with quite a lot of persecutors,' she said. 'Human beings are not built for this. There is an in-built conscience that normally prevents these things, so you can only do them by getting rid of [that aspect]. In Duch's case this in-built conscience seemed to function from time to time.'

Most people see life largely as a gradient of grey, and even though they can discern differences between themselves and others, they tend not to characterise those 'others' as enemies. Rather they see them as 'in-between, neutral persons'. But people who see the world in black-and-white, as Duch does, are more prone to develop splitting.

Another key element in understanding Duch is his obsessive obedience. Schunert was appalled that Duch continued to regard this as a positive trait, a heroic part of his character, and yet that fits with a personality that takes his flaws and sells them as something worthy.

'Most people I know who have a split personality feel weak and ashamed … but Duch emphasises this as a super quality,' she said. 'He manages very well to disguise his disabilities and problems by selling them as something great – and again this is a coping strategy.'

On those occasions when the reality of Duch's actions seeped into his consciousness, fear would bubble to the surface and he would employ splitting to block those truths. Consequently, said Schunert, what stood out most prominently was Duch's pride in doing the best he could in a given situation, since this focus on perfection allowed him to suppress the emotional aspects of running S-21 and M-13A.

'It just doesn't count what that situation is,' she said of Duch's approach. 'It only counts how good you are. For him the content or the situation is irrelevant. The process is the only important element. Whether it is killing others or inventing a machine, it doesn't matter.'

There was something else in the psychological report: Duch's visceral hatred of lying. As François Bizot, the man whom Duch helped to release from M-13A in 1971, put it during his testimony: 'Lying was abhorrent to him.' Yet, as the report noted, Duch knew 'lies could exist alongside good intentions'. After all, Duch had been released from prison in 1970 through the intervention of his aunt, who knew Lon Nol, yet he kept this hidden from his Khmer Rouge colleagues because he knew it to be dangerous. Uncovering the lies of others became his obsession, and his 'aversion to lies [meant] he even improved on the methods for extracting confessions', Sunbaunat and Sironi-Guilbaud wrote.

For Schunert this was another in Duch's array of psychological fixes without which he would have been unable to run S-21.

'If you couldn't block out your conscience and focus only on the task of perfecting getting true confessions, it wouldn't be possible to treat people like that. It is a sort of self-dehumanising process,' she said. 'He was willing to self-dehumanise, taking that approach to himself and doing the same to others – training himself to function as a robot.'

This shift from being human to becoming a robot had other consequences too. Although Duch repeatedly denied witness testimony that he had killed prisoners at M-13A or S-21 or that he had tortured them at S-21, Schunert said such acts would have been relatively easy for him. They would also have fitted his desire 'to become the best robot possible'.

'You can't only order others to do it – you can do it yourself of course,' she said. 'It's just a tiny bit more difficult, but not a lot.'

The report also shed light on one of the elements that most impressed during Duch's trial: his grasp on facts and figures, and his intelligence.

'Only a very specific part of his brain is intelligent – as they discussed, he can only focus on one thing at a time. He can't discuss several topics at the same time,' she said. 'For me an intelligent person can interlink, yet that seems to be completely missing. His brain function seems to be split into different sectors as well – he functions like a robot. That's how he trained himself to be.'

For Schunert, this was more an intelligent solution for someone who wanted to take part in and survive such a society rather than evidence of intelligence per se. And it came at the cost of dehumanising himself.

As the fan on Schunert's balcony puffed tepid air across the table, I put three final questions to her.

The first was about Duch's strange closing statement to the tribunal when, instead of an expected final apology, he read a list of names, dates and events detailing the history of the Communist Party of Kampuchea. Schunert agreed with the assessment of DC-Cam lawyer Anne Heindel that this represented Duch's truth, yet she felt there was more. Duch, she said, wanted the judges and the watching world to *adopt* his truth, not merely to have it stand as one truth among many.

As for Duch's sporadic apologies at trial, they reminded Schunert of rays of sunlight emanating through the dark clouds of the robot part of his split personality.

'And then the clouds cover over and this insight into his own history and guilt and responsibility gets closed down again by this huge wall of denial,' she said. 'But still it's good to know that the sun is shining behind this wall of denial, that there is knowledge within him, because otherwise he wouldn't have written these apologies at all. That's the interesting part for a psychotherapist.'

The third question concerned Duch's change of direction in the final days of trial. How did that fit with the findings of the report?

'I think [the looming sentencing] created a lot of fear inside him which reactivated his splitting mechanisms,' she said. 'His psyche had to maintain this denial so as to protect himself from collapsing from the realisation of what he had done. Probably he could only function during this menacing situation of his trial with this robot part of himself, which denies everything and says: "I don't know why I am being tried here," and: "I am not guilty."'

It also showed that Duch has a long way to go.

'I think he is capable of some change, but not enough to become human enough to live in this society again, because he's so far off. That's the problem,' she said. 'There are some changes possible – like the sun coming through – but the danger that the clouds cover over again is very high.'

DUCH'S PSYCHOLOGICAL REPORT is, it turns out, littered with such cloud-coverings. For instance, when Sunbaunat and Sironi-Guilbaud asked Duch about the cold joke he played on Bizot, telling the French anthropologist that he could not be released.

'Duch still laughs about this,' they wrote. His response was 'indicative of his sadistic disposition' and taking pleasure in wielding absolute power.

In another instance Duch exhibited no emotion when talking about his primary school teacher Dim Saroeun. He claimed to have been fond of her but when she was brought to S-21, sexually assaulted with a stick, tortured and then later executed, Duch did nothing for her. Years later he merely tried to justify his inaction and 'appeared ill-at-ease'.

'He then rationalised the act,' they wrote, 'saying that he reprimanded the interrogator. However he did not have a kind word for his teacher or express any regrets.'

The report lists many other occasions of Duch's behaviour but I shall end with the execution of children, surely the least forgivable of his many crimes. When asked, Duch told them: 'I let go of my own conscience … I closed my eyes and ears but I knew that was wrong.' As Sunbaunat and Sironi-Guilbaud pointed out, we use our conscience to determine whether or not to obey orders. Yet when they asked Duch how he had come to terms with his conscience on the matter of murdering children, he 'stirred in his chair with unease and said that he did not understand the question; he appeared to be on the defensive.'[3]

The final element of their report required them to state whether Duch could be brought back into society's fold. From a purely psychological consideration, they said, he could although there would be numerous challenges. The moral consideration, they added, was not for them to make.

When considering the question of responsibility, however, they were unequivocal: 'Duch is responsible for all his acts from both the logical and psychological standpoints. He does not suffer from any mental disorders. The choices he made were the ones he considered to be the right ones at the time. He was a willing participant.'

THE MASTER OF S-21, then, is a disturbing and complicated man who combined extreme deference, the ability to split, an obsessive belief in a violent political system, uncritical acceptance that the revolution's enemies were trying to undermine it, and a certainty that everyone who came under suspicion must be smashed. In short, Duch subscribed to the totalitarian doctrine that the individual has no value and that the collective is all.

In Duch, *Angkar* found the perfect man to deal with its foes, a man who aligned himself with its paranoias and ingratiated himself, all the while calculating how best to stay alive. What counted for Duch and for *Angkar* was not whether there was an objective truth behind what he was pursuing, but how good he was at that chase. The process was everything and in

---

3. In short, it would be wrong to conclude that Duch lacks feelings. When UN rights worker Christophe Peschoux interviewed him in 1999, shortly after Nic Dunlop located Duch, he asked him whether even the children of prisoners were considered enemies. Duch replied: 'Yes, even the children.' In Peschoux's notes to the interview he wrote that Duch then 'averted his eyes, visibly affected, and plunged into his memories'. That said, it was one of just four occasions in Peschoux's three-day interview that Duch 'manifested an emotion that has seemed to overwhelm him'. ('Interview with Kaing Guek Eav, also known as Duch, Chairman of S-21', Christophe Peschoux, unpublished manuscript, p. 22 and note 80).

becoming its perfect implementer, he dehumanised himself and became, in Schunert's phrase, the best human-robot possible.

Duch fits the mould of what Bulgarian intellectual Tzvetan Todorov calls the 'totalitarian pseudo-hero', a term he coined to describe Himmler's SS men.[4] Where the traditional hero shoulders their task with sacrifice, fortitude and without complaint, the totalitarian system inverts and perverts that ideal. With totalitarian pseudo-heroes, it is their victims who bear the sacrifice while their killers steel themselves in their murderous duties and take pride in their resoluteness in carrying out this 'most difficult task'.[5] Duch's love for de Vigny's poem and his strange identification with the wolf reveals a man who matches Todorov's description.

At his trial, Duch spoke about the steady erosion of moral behaviour that began at M-13A. There, he said, 'my initial criminal acts were mild at the beginning and I tried to minimise the tortures'. That seems likely – after all, we know from the tribunal's psychological report that Duch is no sociopath, and that means he would have had to overcome the inherent boundaries we all share in order to beat, torture and execute. In important ways he is a normal man and that, as Bizot said, is perhaps the most disturbing aspect.

Bizot rightly asked us not to condemn Duch as a monster. Yet if Duch is like us in some ways, he differs sharply in others. Most of us are deferential to authority, but in Duch's case this was acute and without checks and balances to interpret instructions or how they were carried out. Though many people are capable of violence, Duch's consistency and his extraordinary dehumanisation of others places him at the outermost boundary.

Here was a man who believed fervently in totalitarianism; who obeyed orders not only because they were orders but because he needed to believe in something bigger than himself; who studiously avoided seeing what he did not wish to see; and who became a father several times while overseeing the murders of children and adults.

---

4. *Facing the Extreme: Moral Life in the Concentration Camps*, Tzvetan Todorov (Phoenix, 2000), p. 191.

5. From the notorious speech given by SS chief Heinrich Himmler's to SS officers at Posen on October 4, 1943, when he told those assembled, in reference to the murder of Jews: 'Most of you will know what it means when 100 bodies lie together, when there are 500, or when there are 1,000. And to have seen this through, and – with the exception of human weaknesses – to have remained decent, has made us hard and is a page of glory never mentioned and never to be mentioned... We have carried out this most difficult task for the love of our people. And we have taken on no defect within us, in our soul, or in our character.' Himmler's speech has appeared in numerous books over the years. See, for instance, *Countrymen*, Bo Lidegaard (Knopf, 2013).

'In the realm of political crime – everything being equal – this functioning mode is identical in all subjects who commit crimes against humanity,' Sunbaunat and Sironi-Guilbaud wrote. 'It is not dependent on culture and has appeared in identical form at various periods in history.'

Todorov noted that humans are seduced by the capacity to exert power over others, whether that is the power to bring happiness or the power to mete out misery. Yet while happiness has no upper limit and its achievement is at least in part down to the other person being made happy, inflicting suffering is different: the person being acted upon does not choose to be tortured, the exertion is one-sided, and there is a finality that culminates in the victim's death, 'irrefutable proof of my power over him'.[6]

This irrefutable proof is what Duch exerted for more than 1,000 days at S-21 and for even longer at M-13A. It is strange to think that for nearly a decade he was as close to being an omnipotent deity in those twin universes as a human can be. The fall, when it came in 1979, must have been a tremendous shock. Yet none of that makes Duch unique. He is merely one in a long line of people with a talent for destruction in the pursuit of an uncompromising ideology.

At trial, Roux tried to compare Duch with Albert Speer, the Nazi armaments minister jailed for 20 years at Nuremberg. A number of civil party lawyers preferred to draw the comparison with Adolf Eichmann, the SS bureaucrat who ensured that the Third Reich's machinery worked to deliver millions of Jews and other 'undesirables' to the death camps.

In her book on Eichmann's 1961 trial, Hannah Arendt wrote that the trouble with Eichmann and his fellow Nazis was that they were 'neither perverted nor sadistic, that they were, and still are, terribly and terrifyingly normal'.[7]

Although the scale of human misery that Duch and Eichmann inflicted was different, their trials contained some similarities. Duch claimed he had not killed anyone, but did admit to ordering the executions of thousands. Eichmann, who was eventually hanged, also claimed he was innocent of murder: 'I never killed a Jew or a non-Jew,' he said, admitting only to 'aiding and abetting' such crimes.[8]

Totalitarian regimes divide populations into two categories: the worthy

---

6. Todorov, op. cit., p. 180.

7. Arendt, *Eichmann in Jerusalem*, op. cit., p. 276.

8. Ibid., p. 22.

and the rest. In this, the Khmer Rouge and the Nazis shared common ground and in this Eichmann and Duch were similarly employed: both worked in senior roles tasked with disposing of 'the rest'. The two men were sane, they were absolute in following orders, and they ignored the practical and moral consequences of what they were instructed to do.

'Throughout my entire life, I'd been used to obeying … from earliest infancy … an obedience that had become unconditional,' Eichmann told the court in Israel, having been abducted from Argentina the previous year by agents of Israel's intelligence agency Mossad. 'My guilt lies in my obedience, in my respect for discipline, for my military obligations in wartime, for my oath of loyalty.'[9]

As Todorov points out, these are qualities that we typically admire in others. What counts, of course, are the ends to which they are put.

Eichmann said he deliberately did not take decisions, a stance which provided no legal cover but that in his mind gave him moral protection. Had he not done this work, he said, others would have and the result would have been no different. When Eichmann was asked why he had not refused to obey orders, he was shocked that he could be considered culpable of something so base as disobedience. In his strange moral universe that really would have been a serious crime.

Duch too said he simply did what he was told and, as a means of survival, left decision-making to his superiors. He did not contest his appointment as deputy chairman of S-21 in August 1975 on the grounds that 'my duty is my duty' (although he did claim he had instead asked for a job in a ministry, and that this request had been refused). He steered a successful course by being neither rightist (too lax) nor leftist (too enthusiastic), and he acknowledged that he was seen as a good leader, someone who, in his own words, 'did not do surplus things, but did not miss or did not fail to complete what had been assigned'. Duch's psychological report notes: 'Obedience was not the motivation for his acts, but a consequence thereof, because he needed something in which to believe,'[10] a state that, the authors noted, is common to those who commit crimes against humanity.[11]

Both defendants claimed to be repelled by the act of killing. Duch

9. Todorov, op. cit., p. 172.

10. 'Psychological Assessment Report', op. cit., p. 30.

11. As are, the authors go on to point out, the defence mechanisms Duch exhibits including splitting, repression and denial. Ibid., p. 38.

maintained he had gone to Chhoeung Ek just once, smoked a cigarette and left.[12] Eichmann said he was profoundly troubled in 1941 after watching Jews being gassed in mobile trucks at Chelmno in Poland. Shortly after that he saw the final throes of a massacre of Jews in Minsk ('my knees went weak') and then a 'horrible sight' at the aftermath of another mass killing of Jews, this time in Lwow in Poland where blood flowed 'like a fountain' from a mass grave.[13] After that, Eichmann claimed during his trial, he did his best to avoid the realities of his job.[14]

The two men also saw themselves as idealists. Both were talented administrators, took pride in a job well done, had an obsessive interest in how efficiently their respective operations performed and gave no thought as to the human cost of the task in which they were engaged. Both tried to minimise their roles in these atrocities and by so doing their responsibility. Both claimed that they did not view themselves as guilty in any legal sense even though they accepted they had crossed a moral boundary.[15] They saw themselves in equally inanimate terms: while Duch claimed to be a cog in a machine, Eichmann saw himself as a pawn on a chessboard.

What Duch, Eichmann and Speer had in common is that they were idealists, yet their idealism was of a type that negated the worth of their fellow humans. In the end, only Speer seems to have recognised that, and even then only far too late.

Hinton's book notes that preparation for genocide or mass killings requires this negation, and that one of the hallmarks is dividing people into politically defined categories.[16] In Cambodia's case, they were either 'new' or 'old' people: the former being the capitalist/landowner class; the latter being the worker-peasant class. In this way the individual is subsumed within the collective, which means yesterday's human is today's merely abstract, and therefore less valuable, component of a larger group. It is then an easy step to devalue that group. In Cambodia's case, most 'new' people were seen as

---

12. This testimony was undermined and contradicted by several other witnesses, as mentioned earlier.

13. Arendt, op. cit., pp. 88–89.

14. It is impossible to know whether that was true. Eichmann was, after all, on trial for his life.

15. Arendt, op. cit., p. 21, referencing Eichmann's lawyer Robert Servatius, who told a press conference that his client felt guilty before God, but did not regard himself as guilty before the law.

16. Hinton, *Why Did They Kill?* op. cit.

not truly human, which made killing them far easier.

Next Hinton addressed the varied motives and actions of the killers. Frequently such murders are accompanied by violence and degradation that go well beyond the order to kill, such as torture or, as in Cambodia, eating the livers, hearts and gallbladders of victims. Motivations are complex and range from pleasing one's superiors to taking revenge. Other factors include the degree of freedom perpetrators have in which to operate – Duch's under-lings, for instance, had little opportunity to refuse an order to kill – as well as the historical and cultural context in which such killings take place.

This kind of divide-and-eliminate strategy is far easier in totalitarian systems yet such criminality can never be completely hidden. Hannah Arendt wrote that the Nazis sought to create 'holes of oblivion' which would swallow the evidence through cremation pits, flame-throwers and machinery to crush the bones of the dead. It did not work, she said. Indeed it could not work since humans are incapable of creating a perfect system.

'[T]here are simply too many people in the world to make oblivion possible,' she wrote. 'One man will always be left alive to tell the story.'[17]

In 2007, the film *Eichmann* was released, its script drawn from the lengthy interviews that Eichmann's interrogator, Captain Avner Less, had conducted in Jerusalem before the trial. The real Avner Less, a German-born Jew, appeared at the end of the film to warn that Eichmanns are all around and that it is political systems that propel men like him – and, for our purposes, Duch – to the forefront of such destruction. He felt that strong democratic structures are the best way to prevent such people from com-mitting those heinous acts. Authoritarian systems of the left or the right are inherently dangerous.

In a way, then, Less was saying there is something unique to humans about inflicting pain and suffering on others. The fact that soldiers can learn to love the intensity and the destructiveness of what they do, down to the close-quarters murder of individuals, has been written about so extensively that this capacity is clearly innate. And so the responsibility we all share is to ensure that the political systems in which our societies function are accountable. The mass of people likely would not let such things happen, Less reasoned, and a vibrant democracy was the best way to ensure they could exercise that restraint.

---

17. Arendt, op. cit., p. 233.

Antjie Krog used her skills as a poet and journalist to communicate a message of humanity, guilt and reparation from South Africa's TRC. At one point, she recalled how a radio piece she had written on the guilt of the white minority – both English-speakers and Afrikaans-speakers – had sparked a torrent of responses. Afrikaners wrote in to say they had not known what had been done in their name and rejected any responsibility; the people who had carried out those deeds, they told her, were psychopaths. They are not us. English-speakers held that they had done their bit to undermine the apartheid regime.

The experience prompted Krog to follow that piece with another on the four categories of guilt drafted after the Second World War by religious scholars in Germany. First was criminal guilt, which applies to those who carried out the tortures and killings. In this category we would include Duch and his staff. Then there was political guilt, which fell on those who had drafted policy and, in Germany's case, on those who had voted for Hitler. Third was moral guilt, which applied to those who had failed to do enough to overturn the system and who might have benefited from it. Finally there was metaphysical guilt, the guilt of the victims who had survived. Krog ended her piece with a quote by Karl Jaspers, the German psychiatrist and philosopher, who was in his mid-fifties when the war started. Jaspers wrote that Germans did not seek to topple the regime and did not protest when their Jewish neighbours were led away.

'We did not scream until we too were destroyed,' Jaspers wrote. 'We preferred to stay alive, on the feeble, if logical ground, that our death could not have helped anyone. We are guilty of being alive.'[18]

In our century, where digital communications mean we can choose to know what is happening anywhere in near real time, the conclusion surely is that we have a common responsibility to prevent such crimes, to take the initiative as soon as we know of them. There can be no meaningful justice for the anonymous dead in mass graves, and so we must stand up – scream, as Jaspers wrote – and compel our leaders to act. Or to paraphrase Roux's closing remarks, we must recognise our brothers in the eyes of others.

That was what Duch had proved singularly unable to do when running S-21, yet in Roux's final flourish he tried to convince us his client had changed, that the communist security chief Duch was dead. But in some significant ways Kaing Guek Eav in 2009 was no different from Duch: he was still a

---

18. Krog, op. cit., p. 146.

coward, he lacked empathy, he was unable to choose the moral path over the expedient. In so doing, he continued to place himself above his victims.

Craig Etcheson, the academic who worked for the prosecution, was not surprised. From the start, he said, Duch had seen his trial differently from Roux and played it for the long-term. In legal terms, Duch knew it was over, so this 'strange' and 'fundamentally deceptive' defendant had his eye firmly on history. By way of example, Etcheson referred to the S-21 prisoner list that the prosecutor's office drafted for the period when Duch ran the prison. The list contained nearly 12,500 names.

'[Duch] insisted that that number was about right, perhaps a few more,' Etcheson said. 'Well I doubted that very much, because I knew how that list was constructed. My subsequent research turned up thousands more names. It's clear there were many thousands of prisoners whose names were never recorded. Most of the children for example were not entered into the records.'

Etcheson reckoned the true toll was substantially higher, and that Duch knows that. So why avoid that truth? Was it partly embarrassment?

'There may be some element of embarrassment, but this is where you get back to the fascinating psychological aspect of what's going on in his head. He's trying to minimise his exposure in history. Not so much legally – he knew his fate. Notwithstanding that spectacular final week,' Etcheson paused and chuckled wryly, 'he surely realised that you don't do this and just walk away.'

Duch's lies, in other words, were partly a conscious decision, such as his strategy of admitting only what was documented, and partly an unconscious reaction to 'the horror' of what he had done.

'There are some places his brain just won't go,' Etcheson said.

FOR THE SURVIVORS OF Cambodia's experience, whether they are Cambodian or not, there is no getting over the damage done and, as the pioneering work of Cambodian-American sociologist Leakhena Nou has shown, the psychological harm afflicts the next generation too.

For Martine's family in France, who had adored Ket like a son, his murder pierced like an arrow.

'We have a very loving family who doesn't speak at all any more,' Neary told me. 'Everyone was hurt by Ket's disappearance. It was never possible to laugh again all together after that.'

Martine tried her best, particularly at occasional family events, but Ket's absence and the circumstances around it made matters impossible.

'There would come a time when you had to think: what do you want us to speak about?' Neary recalled. 'Because we can't pretend someone is not there. And these days it would be: "There is so much to speak about – it would take too long to explain."'

Ket and Martine (centre) on their wedding day in France. (Photo courtesy of Neary Ouk)

Ket (left) in a Tuareg tent in North Africa in the early 1970s, and (above) in more formal attire. (Photos courtesy of Neary Ouk)

Sam Sady (back left) with her husband and young family in Phnom Penh in 1991. (Photo courtesy of Neary Ouk)

Ong Thong Hoeung, who was a friend of Ket's in Paris, and Hoeung's wife Bounnie. Unlike most returnees, they survived. (Author photo)

A visitor to S-21, now known as the Tuol Sleng Genocide Museum, looks at mugshots of prisoners taken on their arrival at the prison. This was the first part of a process which would see them tortured and then executed. (Author photo)

Cell 23 in Building C at S-21, the cell in which Ket was held. Neary's message to her father can be made out at the top left of the rear wall. (Author photo)

Cambodians visiting the Tuol Sleng Genocide Museum view images of murdered prisoners. (Author photo)

Buildings C, left, and D at S-21, the torture centre run by Duch. (Author photo)

Duch, right, confers with his international lawyer François Roux during a pre-trial meeting at the war crimes tribunal in January 2009. (Photo: ECCC)

Duch listens as the verdict is read out at the conclusion of his trial on July 26, 2010. He would later appeal his 35-year sentence. (Photo: ECCC/Mark Peters)

Martine (left) and Neary on one of the many trips they made to Cambodia to follow Duch's trial. (Photo courtesy Neary Ouk)

Neary testifies at Duch's trial, August 17, 2009. Earlier that day Martine told the court about the impact Ket's disappearance had on their lives. (Photo from ECCC video)

Film-maker Rithy Panh, whose creative output has been deeply influenced by his experiences during 1975–79. (Author photo)

S-21 survivor Vann Nath shows at Duch's trial how he was shackled by the ankle to other prisoners. (Author photo)

July 25, 2010: the Buddhist ceremony at S-21 for relatives of the dead. Neary and Martine are in the centre; Rob Hamill is in black to their right. (Author photo)

Your Honour, I have thought [about this] from the beginning – that was after 1979. I never imagined that I would be able to sit in this courtroom today to describe my plight [and] experiences to the younger generation and the general public to understand what happened to me, and now I have the ability to testify before this chamber in public. This is my privilege. This is my honour. I do not want anything more than that [for myself].

What I want is something that is intangible, that is justice for those who already died. Whatever way justice could be done – [this] is my only hope that can be achieved by this chamber. And I hope by the end of the tribunal that justice can be tangible, can be seen by everybody, and that is something that I expect as a result, as an outcome of this chamber [and] of this tribunal, and this is what I want, Your Honour.

— Vann Nath, the artist and S-21 survivor, when asked by the ECCC's Judge Lavergne during his testimony on June 29, 2009 what he wanted from the trial of Duch. Vann Nath died on September 5, 2011.

CHAPTER FIFTEEN

FROM BITTERNESS TO SWEETNESS

ONE OF THE CHALLENGES of writing this book was processing the deluge of heartbreaking stories. Nearly every Cambodian I interviewed had appalling tales of life under the Khmer Rouge. Take Roth Marany, for example, whom I met in 2010 when she was living out her final years, impoverished and in failing health, in a small, bright room in a pagoda in Phnom Penh. Through the tears, in a mixture of Khmer and French, she told me how her three children had starved to death in her arms.

In 1975 they were forced to leave their two-storey villa in Phnom Penh, and they spent the following four years in a remote area of Pursat province amid an excess of fear and a dearth of food. Hunger so ravaged her children that they ate the indigestible husks of rice simply to fill their stomachs. One by one the hungry seasons took them: the eldest, a 14-year-old boy, in 1976; the middle child, a 13-year-old girl called Malina, in 1977; and finally, one year later, her last, a 12-year-old boy. Each time she wept for her children the Khmer Rouge would beat her with sticks for daring to have feelings for anything beyond *Angkar* and the revolution.

Perhaps the biggest tragedy of those years is simply this: Marany's story of truly profound agony during 'the Pol Pot time' is, in the Cambodian context, unremarkable. Uplifting stories are few and are rarely heard, because most people spent those days trying to survive.

Yet, despite the risks, there must have been countless occasions where people helped others, and indeed there are glimpses, small acts of lifesaving value, such as those Sady spoke about when the men of her *chalat*, or work group, helped the women to shift earth, because to miss today's target meant the Khmer Rouge would add more to tomorrow's and that would be fatal.

Helping others could be exceedingly dangerous, but acts of quiet heroism did take place.

Some, it turns out, were extraordinary, and in 2012 the *Phnom Penh Post* carried one such story about a man called Van Chhuon. In 1977, he had been appointed group leader, the rough equivalent of village chief, of Kuok Snuol, which is near the city of Siem Reap and just a few kilometres from Angkor Wat. Although I was unable to meet Van Chhuon – he refused to talk to any journalists after the Khmer-language edition of the newspaper conflated his name with those of Pol Pot and Ieng Sary in a headline, causing him problems – I did interview a man whose life he had saved.

The saved man's name was Nai Kong and he is by coincidence these days the village chief of Kuok Snuol. We met at his humble home on the edge of this village of 230 families, where rice fields of deepest green stretched away under a sky of mixed greys to a stand of trees. Kong is a 59-year-old farmer whose diminutive, wiry body betrays a life of toil. He was hospitable, as so many Cambodians are, to these strangers who arrived unannounced at his stilted home. We sat under a lean-to roof as chickens pecked in the dirt. Pigeon cages hung from the outside walls, and a dovecote stood along one side of the house.

Kong and his wife were born in Kuok Snuol and married in the early 1970s before Pol Pot's forces took control. In the days after April 1975, the Khmer Rouge rounded up all the males except for the very young and the very old. The men, around 100 of them, were told their labour was needed for an orchard at a place called Chambok Sar several miles away, but Kong recalls there was no work for weeks once they arrived.[1] There was no food either and the men survived by scavenging.

After two months, the Khmer Rouge called a meeting: Sihanouk was coming to Angkor Wat, they said, and all of the 'true patriots' who had served the Lon Nol regime were to go and meet him. There were not enough vehicles to take everyone so the several dozen men who had admitted to working for the defeated regime were to go first.

'But don't worry,' the others were told, 'you will all get to see Sihanouk.'

As Kong talked, the sky shed its shades of grey and turned uniformly dark. The rain began to fall, pinging off the corrugated iron roof and slowly filling the depressions in the beaten earth. The chickens clustered under the shelter of the house and a skinny dog slipped under the stilts away from the wet.

---

1. Just five of the 100 men survived the Democratic Kampuchea period.

I had heard this type of story before so I asked whether the men truly believed they were going to meet Sihanouk.

'Yes, and they were very happy to have the opportunity,' Kong said. 'They were cheering and clapping.'

It was a trap. All of those men were executed at a killing pit near the grove of trees in the distance across from these rice fields. Kong knew that something bad had happened when the Khmer Rouge returned a few days later with clothing they had recovered from *khmang* – enemies – whom they said they had encountered. Some pieces belonged to his father-in-law, others to friends. The practice of stripping victims before execution was a common one; the Khmer Rouge called it 'peeling the clothes'.

Kong fled a few days later and lived off the land, hiding out, scavenging cassava from the fields. He worked his way back to Kuok Snuol village, and concealed himself nearby for months. He was fortunate that his sister had been tasked with taking the collective's cows to graze and bringing them back to the village each evening. Every day their mother would cook rice porridge with banana stalks and his sister would deliver it to him.

Eventually word got out that Kong was hiding near the village, and he was forced to turn himself in. By then the villagers had vouched for him to the group leader, Prak. When Kong arrived, Prak asked whether he had worked for the Lon Nol regime. Kong had, but he knew what admitting that would entail. Besides, his skills as a handyman able to fashion fishing traps and shrimp baskets were in short supply. Prak, whom he called *Ta* ('Grandfather') Prak, let him stay. It was a tense time.

'*Ta* Prak would sit and watch, observing the quality of my craftsmanship to see whether I was merely going through the motions or was committed,' he said.

It took months but Prak was finally convinced and wrote Kong's name in the village registry book. Soon afterwards, Prak was replaced as group leader by *Ta* Lem, a vicious man who ordered the deaths of many villagers. Kong was nearly killed too and he told me how it happened: in his spare time he would cut bamboo, make traps and hide out catching fish and raising shrimp. By the standards of the time this individualism was, he noted with understatement, 'a bit naughty'.

'This time, when I went to check on the shrimp and thought I was alone, a bomb went off with a "boom!" and that reminded me of the years under Lon Nol [when there was regular shelling],' he said. 'I was grumbling to myself saying that our present situation was even worse than those bad days, because at least then we had plenty to eat, and now all I have is a bowl of porridge with banana stems.'

His mutterings were overheard. Such talk was counter-revolutionary. Kong was arrested, taken to Siem Reap prison and accused of being an enemy. He spent nine months in jail and was interrogated every day, his captors varying the methods of torture as they saw fit.

'One way was to put a plastic bag over my head and try to suffocate me. Another was to get a bottle and fill it with salty water and force it down my throat. They used pliers to stretch out my tongue, and they threw hot water on me. Yet another way was to tie my legs and ankles with rope' – here Kong, bare-chested, leaned his sinewy body forward on the low bamboo table we were sitting on and put his arms behind him – 'and bind my hands behind my back and attach me to a pulley and I would be hung upside down. The guys would kick and hit and push me and I would be a swinging pendulum between them.'

When he passed out, the guards took him back to the cells. Sometimes he was shackled on his own; more often he was shackled to a metal bar with other men.

'And if, in the middle of the night, one of the prisoners moved and their ankle shackle made a sound, then we knew they would be in trouble. The guards would come in and yell: "Who moved?" And that guy would most likely disappear,' he said.

By now it was late 1977 and the internal purges that were to sow the Khmer Rouge's destruction were well underway. Units from *Ta* Mok's south-west region arrived, killing the old cadres and local leaders and replacing them with their own. *Ta* Lem was executed.

It is now that the heroic Van Chhuon re-enters the picture. Chhuon had spent the previous two years leading a team that chased the birds from the rice fields, a lowly task that, in the Khmer Rouge's inversion of society, meant he was of the right revolutionary cloth. So when the new cadres asked the villagers who was the poorest among them, that being the class requirement for *Ta* Lem's replacement, they gave the name of the bird man. That was how, while Kong languished in prison, Chhuon was made group leader.

Before the war, the two men's families had been close, and when Chhuon heard Kong was still alive he pleaded with his superiors for his release. Kong is no enemy, he told them; he is an important part of the village team. It was a significant risk.

A few months before Vietnam's December 1978 invasion, the guards took Kong to the prison courtyard. He thought he was going to his death.

'I was terrified, but when I got there I saw Chhuon standing there smiling at me and I asked him: "Where are you going?" And he told me: "I'm not going anywhere – I just came to fetch you,"' Kong says. 'I nearly passed out from joy.'

Chhuon brought Kong back to the village, to his overjoyed wife and family, and made sure he was fed duck eggs until he regained his health. Yet even now his tribulations were not over.

'The spies were everywhere,' Kong said. 'Not long afterwards the men came back to the village to arrest me, accusing me of various crimes. During the night Chhuon came and told me about it.'

Chhuon managed to keep the Khmer Rouge at bay by vouching for Kong, insisting he had done nothing wrong. They left empty-handed but returned a few weeks later and then again after that. By now Chhuon feared he would not be able to protect Kong much longer. Fortunately for both men, Vietnam invaded and routed the Khmer Rouge.

'That is what saved me,' Kong said. 'Otherwise I would certainly have been killed.'

Chhuon saved other lives in similar fashion. Each time the Khmer Rouge came with a list of names, he would tell them that this person is already dead, this one ran away, that one has never lived here. For more than a year as group leader he fended off the killers, and no villagers were executed. Had Chhuon fallen under suspicion then he and his family would certainly have perished.

After 1979, Chhuon moved back to his home village in Siem Reap province and the residents of Kuok Snuol lost contact with him. Then in 1992 Chhuon returned to ask two men whether they could spare some time to help him build a new home. Of course, they replied. On the appointed day, dozens of Kuok Snuol's villagers turned up with food and their labour to thank Chhuon for his extraordinary efforts years before.

THE STORY OF THE GOOD VILLAGE CHIEF, though uplifting, is unusual. Most people did not behave as Van Chhuon did. Even today many Cambodian survivors live near the people who murdered their loved ones, and that proximity causes tremendous inner conflict, as noted in a 2011 study by the University of California Berkeley's Human Rights Center.[2] It found two-thirds of Cambodians wanted to see the perpetrators 'hurt or miserable' yet only one-third would seek personal revenge if they could.

Buddhism dictates that 'those who do good will receive good; those who do bad will receive bad', and it reserves extraordinary punishments for the latter group after they die. The belief that those who killed, raped and tortured will not get away scot-free is an important comfort. Yet seeing perpetrators living freely among those they once terrorised is a constant torment for many.

Reconciliation is one solution, but there is little interest from the government or donors to fund it. The tribunal can effect only the most basic form of reconciliation at the national level, if that, and it cannot resolve matters between the hundreds of thousands of victims and perpetrators in villages across the country.

By 2012 one of the few groups working on reconciliation was Kdei Karuna, the local offshoot of US-based non-profit The International Center for Conciliation. Kdei Karuna, which occupies an office on the upper floor of a crumbling villa in Phnom Penh, roughly translates as 'Compassionate Action to Heal'. Its goal is to restore society. It works at the village level to help victims and perpetrators come to terms with their past experiences. With around a dozen staff, however, there is only so much it can do.

That is only the start of the organisation's challenges. Most victims want perpetrators to apologise, but that is a surprisingly difficult act in Cambodia where to seek forgiveness runs up against issues of losing face, to say nothing of perpetrators' fears of being prosecuted by the tribunal – which they would not be – or of being killed in revenge attacks. Adding to the complication is that many ex-Khmer Rouge see themselves as victims too. After all, they say, had they not done what they were told, they would have been killed.

It seems an insurmountable divide: victims who want apologies from perpetrators who cannot or will not provide them. The solution is the 'Victim-Former Khmer Rouge' dialogue project, which the group runs in conjunction with a highly respected mental health organisation called the Transcultural Psychosocial Organisation Cambodia (TPO).

---

2. *After The First Trial: A Population-Based Survey on Knowledge and Perceptions of Justice and the Extraordinary Chambers in the Courts of Cambodia*, Pham PN, Vinck P, Balthazard M, Hean S; Human Rights Center, University of California, Berkeley (2011).

The first step is to get people talking about what happened. The next is to get the former Khmer Rouge cadre to acknowledge what he or she did while in return recognising their situation at that time. In this way the standard black-and-white markers of victim and perpetrator are graded more subtly. The third is to build links within these communities to ensure that children are not cast in the same light as their parents. In that way a healed society becomes possible.

That, at least, is the theory. In 2011 Kdei Karuna and TPO put it into practice with a pilot project in the southern province of Kampot. Although some people have reconciled of their own accord, this was the first project to study the dynamics around victims reconciling with perpetrators. The NGOs chose two adjacent villages, one richer and one poorer, each home to 100 families. When the Khmer Rouge inverted society, those in the richer village were deemed to belong to the wrong political class while those in the poorer village, now elevated to the apex of the social hierarchy, took out their frustrations. Many in the richer village died.

The project did not divulge the names of the villages nor those of the participants. 'Grandma' had lost her husband to the Khmer Rouge, while her neighbour 'Aunt' had lost her father. The person both women blame lives in the neighbouring poorer village, and he was referred to as 'Grandpa'. Unable to forgive Grandpa for his role in the killings, the women and their fellow villagers had shunned him for decades. In a society that actively avoids confrontation, shutting people out in this way is common.

The women said they wanted Grandpa to apologise for arresting the two men and taking them for execution. Using video initially rather than face-to-face meetings, Kdei Karuna filmed Grandma and Aunt telling their stories. The staff then went to Grandpa's village where he watched what they had filmed. Over several weeks the video diary shuttled back and forth with each encounter recorded, edited and presented. It built up a rapport of sorts, and in the end Grandpa acknowledged he had harmed both women but insisted he had been given no choice. He denied the killings but felt regret for his actions and asked the women 'Please don't be angry at me'.

'They ordered me to do these things,' he said of the arrests. 'I'm not a smart person and I didn't know what to do.'

It was not quite an apology but it came close enough. Eventually the three agreed to meet at a pagoda. Face to face, Grandpa again spoke of his regret and promised to pray for the souls of their loved ones during Pchum

Ben, the annual festival of the dead, and on other holy days. Veneration of one's deceased relatives is an important element of Cambodian culture and for Grandma and Aunt this proved particularly powerful.

By now Kdei Karuna had also spent months working on reconciliation between the two communities. One element is memorialisation, which can be something as simple as villagers writing down their experiences in a book for the younger generation, or the process can have a religious bent. The residents chose the latter: to build a stupa, a small, dome-roofed, sacred structure, as a memorial for the dead and to act as a reminder never to repeat those dark days. They also planted a Bodhi tree, which is the tree under which the Buddha attained enlightenment, as a way to help the spirits find peace. Of his own volition Grandpa, who is very poor, bought a set of electric lights to ensure the stupa could be seen at night.

The head of Kdei Karuna is Tim Minea, a Cambodian sociologist and anthropologist who, when I met him in 2012, had spent six years working on reconciliation issues. Grandpa's actions, he explained, had shown the victims that 'he feels regret and he tries to repair what he did in the past'. Before the process started, the women 'did not even want to see his footprints'. Now they knew he had spent 30 years terrified of retribution, and that back then he had been young and uneducated and drawn into an unyielding system. In the end the women even felt sorry for him. Talking had allowed both sides to see the humanity and the suffering in the other.

These days Grandpa goes to the market, a key hub of village life that he avoided for decades. He takes on transport jobs in the village that was once out of bounds and he attends Buddhist ceremonies and community events such as weddings, which he never did before. When he sees Aunt, Grandma and others who took part in the project, he stops and talks to them. Other residents of Grandpa's village have asked Kdei Karuna to do more to promote reconciliation. And although not everyone in Grandma's village felt he had told the truth, many were sufficiently satisfied with his words and actions.

This, then, is reconciliation in action: messy, time-consuming, difficult and like reconciliation everywhere undertaken with an uncertain outcome. But it fits Cambodia's cultural context. As Tim Minea put it, reconciliation here means 'living together in peace' and that begins with people in the villages talking to each other, exchanging their stories and recognising each other's situations.

'That's the first step for Cambodia,' Minea said. 'Then maybe they can go deeper and deeper.'

This single act required a vast amount of work. Kdei Karuna sent staff to the villages every few weeks. TPO despatched mental health therapists, and a videographer was present to record and edit what happened. Yet although the outcome was positive, as I watched the two short videos that Kdei Karuna had compiled, I felt some elements seemed forced. In one scene, the adviser sitting next to Aunt eggs her on to accept Grandpa's statements of regret.

I asked Kdei Karuna's Cambodian-American adviser Rothany Srun about that: surely this was overstepping the boundary? She agreed that it came across that way but said the villagers simply had not known how to deal with reconciliation. The entire process was so unusual yet so important to them that they had sought guidance throughout. Srun said she was struck by how the villagers accepted outcomes significantly different to those they had articulated at the start.

'I asked the victims: what do you expect from the project, what do you want to get? And it was that [they] wanted him to admit everything that he had done and wanted him to apologise,' she said. 'But by the end of the project I doubt he was able to say everything that he did, and I think the victims knew that, but they forgave him anyway because they saw how scared he was. Whether or not he told the whole truth, I guess they stopped expecting it – and then it was more about living together again.'

That concept – 'living together' – encompasses what the term reconciliation means for more than half of the Cambodian people, as UC Berkeley found in its 2011 study, a follow-up to an earlier survey.[3] In both cases 1,000 adults in the same 250 villages from across the country were questioned; in both cases 70 per cent of interviewees had survived Democratic Kampuchea. While some were ex-Khmer Rouge, most were not.

The two studies, which bookended the start and end of Duch's trial, show that reconciliation is as slippery a concept here as anywhere. More than half of the respondents in the earlier study described reconciliation as 'the absence of violence and conflict'. Two years later just 15 per cent saw it that way, while a majority felt it meant 'unity and living together'. Nearly two in five defined it as 'communicating and understanding each other' and a quarter as 'compassion'.[4] Forgiveness barely featured.

3. *So We Will Never Forget: A Population-Based Survey on Attitudes About Social Reconstruction and the Extraordinary Chambers in the Courts of Cambodia*, Pham PN, Vinck P, Balthazard M, Hean S, Stover E; Human Rights Center, University of California, Berkeley (2009).

4. People could give more than one definition.

More than 80 per cent told the interviewers that they still feel hatred towards the Khmer Rouge, and indeed they have much to be angry about. Of those who survived Pol Pot's rule, most experienced food shortages or starvation (82 per cent), lack of shelter (71 per cent) and forced evacuation (69 per cent). Nearly a third witnessed torture, a quarter had been tortured, and one in five saw people murdered.[5] Survivors 'were significantly more likely to have been exposed to violent events', the study noted. It is not surprising to learn that Cambodia has more people suffering from post-traumatic stress disorder (PTSD) than any other.[6] The global rate is less than 0.4 per cent, but estimates among Cambodian survivors range from 14 per cent to 33 per cent.[7]

The studies also show how far Cambodia has to go in meeting its own idea of reconciliation. Half of the respondents said they would be uncomfortable living in the same community as a former Khmer Rouge member or having their child marry the son or daughter of ex-Khmer Rouge.

Having a meal or a drink or even working together was similarly unappealing. One-third were unhappy at the prospect of their children attending school with the sons and daughters of former Khmer Rouge and the same number disliked the idea of going to the same *wat*. In two years those numbers barely budged.

PUTTING SOCIETIES BACK TOGETHER seems an impossible task, but an important place to start is allowing people to share their stories – as Kdei Karuna did with Grandma, Aunt and Grandpa.

---

5. To say nothing of forced marriage, another odious practice that, for reasons of space, did not make it into this book. Briefly, *Angkar* would order men and women to wed in a joyless ceremony, and spies would be stationed for several nights under the stilted huts in which the newlyweds were forced to spend time. The role of the spies was to ensure that the couple, who were often strangers, were having sex. Couples who refused to do so risked execution. An estimated 250,000 couples were forcibly married during Democratic Kampuchea. The practice stands as yet another indicator of the Khmer Rouge's belief that the value of the individual was limited to their utility – in this case, their ability to produce a new generation of revolutionaries and to meet Pol Pot's goal of boosting the population from 8 million to 20 million between 1977 and 1987. Forced marriage was recognised as a crime against humanity by the ECCC. For more, see the 2012 documentary *Red Wedding* by Lida Chan and Guillaume Suon. See also *Love and Dread in Cambodia: Weddings, Births and Ritual Harm under the Khmer Rouge* by Peg LeVine (NUS Press, 2010). LeVine is a clinical psychologist and medical anthropologist who spent a decade researching the effects of the Khmer Rouge on Cambodian traditions, including marriage.

6. *Mental Health and Human Rights in Cambodia*, McLaughlin D and Wickeri E; Leitner Center for International Law and Justice, Fordham Law School (2012).

7. A 2012 study of more than 2,600 people by the Royal University of Phnom Penh's Psychology Department found 2.7 per cent of the general population has PTSD – that in a country where some 70 per cent of the population was born after 1979. The rate is twice as high among women.

That requirement is hardly unique to Cambodia: while he was still imprisoned at Auschwitz, Italian chemist Primo Levi had a recurring dream in which he kept trying to tell people what had happened yet nobody was listening, as Tzvetan Todorov noted:

> They are talking to one another. In fact, they hardly notice he's there. Worse, they get up and leave without saying a word. After his liberation he continues to have this dream and discovers he is far from unique; other survivors tell them they have dreamed the same dream.[8]

Levi, however, had returned to a place where few had personal knowledge of what he had gone through. Cambodia is different. Most of the population experienced similar degradations and terror, and almost everyone over 40 views themselves as a victim of the Khmer Rouge – even former cadres – as I learned in 2010 when I attended a reconciliation meeting in Anlong Veng, a former Khmer Rouge stronghold in north-western Cambodia. The event was organised by an NGO called the Center for Justice and Reconciliation, which my Cambodian-American friend Dar Seng was running at the time, and it was held at the former compound of *Ta* Mok, the last leader of the Khmer Rouge who had died in prison in 2006. Dar wanted to hear from the late leader's followers just what reconciliation meant to them.

To reach *Ta* Mok's home you pass over a concrete ford just outside Anlong Veng town. On the right is a Tolkienesque wasteland: a lake with dead trees, debarked and leafless, burned black and stunted in the shallow waters. A hundred yards on, a jarring track juts right from the road past two huge boulders and into the wide, flat compound.

If you had never heard of *Ta* Mok you could infer much about him by visiting this place, several hectares of beaten earth extending into the lake and providing a near 360-degree vista. This is a place positioned for defence. There is plenty of shade but the trees – mangos, jackfruits and mangosteens – are here for their function. This is nature with a purpose, bent to the austere needs of its former owner. The concrete buildings, whose walls carry rough murals of Cambodia's greatest temples, are square and reflect a man for whom comfort was unnecessary. It is the home of a stringent nationalist and an ascetic. It might not surprise you to learn that *Ta* Mok trained as a monk before joining the anti-French Issarak movement in 1949 and later the Khmer Rouge.

---

8. Todorov, op. cit., p. 256.

His real name was Chhit Choeun, and across much of the country he is loathed, the one-legged commander with the blood of tens of thousands on his hands. In Anlong Veng he is respected and even loved. Like some Cambodian Moses, people say, he brought these ragged remnants out of their wandering life of jungle and malaria and suffering, and provided them with a refuge. This wasteland lake of spectral trees? *Ta* Mok built that for the people as a fish farm. He set up schools and a health clinic and he improved the roads. Through a long history of being ignored or let down, Cambodians have learned to expect little, and those who do provide for them are worthy of a fierce loyalty.

Anlong Veng is still a place of believers and killers but it is also a place of hope.

'Life is changing from bitterness to sweetness – and this is very important,' one university student told dozens of her fellow residents at the event. 'During the war we were always on the move, unable to stay together or even eat a meal together. But after the war ended we could gather at the same table and have a meal.'

Their lives have improved in many ways. Today their children attend school, an institution the Khmer Rouge destroyed, the residents practise Buddhism, which the Khmer Rouge banned, and they enjoy contact with the outside world, which was once impossible. Anlong Veng is a place of stark contradictions whose people, most of whom are former Khmer Rouge – a term they loathe since it stigmatises them – are trying to get by in a country which largely does not want them.

This event provided some of the grey that is missing from perceptions of the Khmer Rouge, both inside and outside Cambodia. These are tough, impoverished people who endured the most difficult of times and who lost. Their movement had inflicted untold hardships on the country, but these survivors had suffered mightily too. They also see themselves as victims, which in an important sense they are. The main lesson from the day was that now they want to be accepted back into society, to be known simply as Cambodians.

Later that afternoon the microphone was passed from person to person and the participants were encouraged to speak freely. An older man stood and sang a haunting song, one of suffering, words from a mother to her child about the difficulties that the youngster would never know. It shone a light on a traumatic past.

O my child, my dove, come close to me,
Your parents have something to tell you.
Child, remember, remember for the rest of your life,
To be mindful of our traditions and our nation's history.
My child, before we reached this place
– This new society with its revived culture –
Our people, our countrymen, endured the flames of hardship.
Our friends faced many difficulties,
Living in remote mountainous areas and bearing all forms of hardship.
The enemy was in constant pursuit, and we, without a moment's rest,
Were separated from our families. We never saw their faces.
During the day, my child, we hid in huts or in the open.
At night we lacked everything.
We ate yet were never full; we could not sleep;
And as the years passed our health worsened.
We had just one pair of clothes, worn and tattered and torn.
Each time we washed them we had to sit and shiver
Until our clothes were dry and we could return to our village and work.
When the enemy surrounded our fishing holes,
We ate banana shoots and leaves instead of rice porridge.
Exhausted, hungry and malaria-ridden,
We became thin and pale and deathly white.
And yet we persevered.
My child, this was the fate of your elders.
So many years have passed since they paved the way.
The revolution, red, pure and true, secured this present state of peace.
And this is why you, my child, can live as you wish.
Yet you must be careful, be wary of opening your chest [to foreign influences].
My child: maintain our customs and keep them red.
This is not a heavy burden, but one even a child can carry.
My child, my love, come close to me.
When you eat a meal, think of the past.
When life is going well, think of the blood that we spilled.
When you smile, think of your orphaned friends.

The afternoon drew on and a worn-looking man in his sixties got to his feet. Dressed in his best, a battered grey suit, he walked awkwardly to the microphone, his false leg a reminder of a distant day when he had stepped on a land mine. The wind picked up from the north and rattled the banner above the stage, kicked up the dust and scurried under the chairs.

Amid all this talk of justice, he asked the representatives of the tribunal who had travelled from Phnom Penh for today's event, what kind of justice do I deserve?

'I joined the Khmer Rouge when I was 17 years old, so I fought for three decades and I am also a victim because I sacrificed and lost my leg,' he said. 'The Khmer Rouge cost maybe three million lives. What is the cause of that tragedy? What makes our people so stupid that we followed orders all the time?'

He spoke as a foot soldier and a survivor, bitter about the losses that litter his life and about the tribunal's limited concept of justice. What about the US planes that flew overhead dropping bombs, he asked? What of the other events that preceded the Khmer Rouge's takeover of Cambodia? Why do you not investigate those too?

'We all sacrificed our lives, our economy was ruined, there was nothing left. Everything was utterly destroyed. And for what?' he asked angrily.

Fifteen years after the movement to which he gave himself had collapsed, his fury remained undimmed. And who could blame him, after a life spent in pursuit of a failed dream, and one that had surely cost the lives of people he loved? Among these revolutionary remnants, the surviving members of this unwanted tribe in Anlong Veng and elsewhere, his questions and his resentments are widely shared.

I've evoked the world of yesterday so that the bad part of it may not come back again. Let it live in our memories and in books, in the flesh of the survivors, in the monuments to the lost; and let it remain there.

— Rithy Panh, *The Elimination*

CHAPTER SIXTEEN

VERDICT AND REMEMBRANCE

EIGHT MONTHS AFTER the evidentiary hearings concluded, Neary and Martine came back to Cambodia to hear the court's verdict. It was scheduled for July 26, 2010. On the previous day, a Sunday, I met them for breakfast. Martine was on the verge of tears after reading one story in a newspaper that speculated Duch might be jailed for as little as five years once deductions were made for various mitigating factors: 11 years already served, his cooperation and professed remorse, and compensation for being detained for years prior to trial.

'It is not possible, surely?' she asked me, wide-eyed, her voice taut with decades of stress and pain. 'After everything he did, to get just five years?'

For people like Martine and Neary, deep in the emotional abyss of this case, the law's dispassionate nature can generate unseemly ironies – in Duch's case that the man who imprisoned thousands could benefit from provisions governing unlawful detention.

I told Martine that it was highly unlikely Duch would walk out of prison in five years. My guess was that he would get a total of 25 years in jail and I explained why. First, he had effectively pleaded not guilty at the end of his trial, which would have angered the bench. Second, politics had never been far from the ECCC, and the ruling party needed to be able to boast to the voting public that not only had it brought peace in 1979 and then dismantled the Khmer Rouge in the 1990s, but that it had also jailed this man. Third, the four defendants in Case 002 were elderly and some, and perhaps all, were unlikely to survive a lengthy trial, which meant Duch could yet be the only former Khmer Rouge to be convicted. And fourth, Duch had no friends in the political establishment.

And so, I told her, for reasons of law, morality and political expediency, I doubted he would ever leave jail. But as I was well aware this was merely informed guesswork on my part; there was no way to know.

That evening I met Martine and Neary for dinner. It was an edgy affair and Martine was particularly tense, and understandably so having spent most of her life swamped with the stresses and heartbreak of Ket's disappearance and all that had entailed. For both women, years of limbo were finally on the cusp of some sort of resolution.

THE AUDITORIUM STARTS FILLING UP well ahead of the 10am start. In the front rows at the centre are several dozen Buddhist monks in orange robes; nearby are Buddhist nuns in white. Behind them sit diplomats and some government officials. The rest of the rows running up to the back of the room are filled with an array of villagers – among them a group of Cham Muslims – as well as NGO workers, civil parties and some of their lawyers, and dozens of uniformed schoolchildren.

S-21 survivor Vann Nath arrives looking drawn after falling sick earlier in the year, a time many feared he would not survive. His illness has sparked debate and bitterness from victims that the defendants at the ECCC receive free healthcare while people like Vann Nath are forced to rely on donations for life-prolonging medical treatment.

Two other survivors from S-21 have also come: fellow artist Bou Meng and Chum Mey, the typewriter repairman. Martine and Neary are seated with some of the civil parties on the stage, determined to be on the same level as Duch.

The TV screens carry a looping 10-minute video that summarises Duch's trial including his final words: 'I would ask the court to release me.' That phrase echoes around the auditorium over and over as we wait for proceedings to start. Most of the audience are Cambodian and most of those are over 50, which means they carry vivid recollections of Democratic Kampuchea. Many have the rough hands and worn clothes of people who have spent a lifetime on the land.

At a few minutes to ten, the vast white curtain sweeps back and the audience can see the players on this stage. All eyes are on Duch, who is dressed in his favourite shirt – a lilac long-sleeved fake Ralph Lauren brand with a buttoned-down collar – over a white T-shirt, both tucked into grey pleated trousers. One obvious absence is François Roux. Three weeks earlier,

Duch fired Roux on the grounds that he had lost confidence in him. The feeling was surely mutual.

As the clock reaches ten, we stand and the red-robed judges glide in and take their places. Nil Nonn instructs Duch to cross to the dock to hear the judgment. This time Duch does not greet the audience with the traditional *sampeah*.

When the court first read out the long charge sheet more than a year ago, the crimes of which Duch stood accused seemed dangerously abstract, words on a page that lacked emotional resonance. No longer. The charges carry true poignancy, the abstract has become concrete, and we know something of the toll on the dead and the living. While it remains impossible to conceive the fullness of the horrors, observers like me are much closer than we were.

Nil Nonn notes that today's hearing will be a summary judgment of this 'historic trial' and that it follows 72 days of testimony from 24 witnesses, 22 civil parties and nine experts.

There is an early victory for Duch when Nil Nonn says the ECCC could not decide whether the 30-year extension of the statute of limitations for the crimes of murder, torture and other serious acts under Cambodia's 1956 Penal Code was valid. The lack of a decision means Duch will not face prosecution for crimes committed under Cambodian law.

But for Duch, the good news ends there. Next the court strips out one of the planks of Kar Savuth's argument by finding that Duch was 'one of those most responsible' for crimes committed under Democratic Kampuchea.

Nil Nonn runs through the historical background to the regime, the Standing Committee's overarching control and the policy of 'smashing' enemies, 'the most critical aspect of Communist Party of Kampuchea policy in relation to this trial'.

At least 12,273 people were detained at S-21, the court finds, but it qualifies that by stating 'the actual number of detainees is likely to have been considerably greater'. One of Duch's key tasks was training his subordinates, including instructing the interrogators 'to use physical and psychological violence' on the proviso that prisoners were killed only after Duch had approved their confessions. That approval would not come until confessions had sufficient detail and had named other people.

When it came to arresting people, the judges find Duch had a larger role than that to which he admitted, and his superiors 'sought and acted upon' his views when determining some arrests.

Duch also had authority over S-24, the satellite prison that was used not only as a re-education facility for the families or subordinates of people being held and tortured at S-21 but also as a detention centre for military and ministry staff.

For the next half hour, Nil Nonn continues the judges' summary, a litany of crimes whose reality the printed word could never convey: the destruction of thousands of men, women and children held in appalling conditions on largely bogus grounds, denied their rights, subjected to fear and torture, persecuted and given insufficient food before being murdered in the cruellest manner.

It takes the court little over an hour to find Duch guilty of war crimes and crimes against humanity. Although there was insufficient evidence to determine whether Duch had himself engaged in torture or other inhumane acts, the court rules that his participation in 'this criminal system' means that he bears individual responsibility for what happened at S-21.

As expected, another plank falls from Kar Savuth's defence when the court rules that Duch is criminally responsible, even though he claimed he was merely following orders. The bench also rejects Duch's claim that he acted under duress even though it accepts that in late 1978 he might well have feared for his safety and that of his family.

'Duress cannot be invoked when the perceived threat results from the implementation of a policy of terror in which he himself has willingly and actively participated,' Nil Nonn says. 'Indeed, the accused's conduct in carrying out these functions evidenced a high degree of efficiency and zeal.'

'The chamber has thus found the accused individually criminally responsible … for the following offences as crimes against humanity: murder, extermination, enslavement, imprisonment, torture (including one instance of rape), persecution on political grounds, and other inhumane acts; as well as for the following grave breaches of the Geneva Conventions of 1949: wilful killing, torture and inhumane treatment, wilfully causing great suffering or serious injury to body or health, wilfully depriving a prisoner of war or civilian of the rights of fair and regular trial, and unlawful confinement of a civilian.'

Before handing down the sentence for these crimes which he warns 'unambiguously mandate a substantial term of imprisonment', Nil Nonn reads a list of names: those whom the court has decided do meet the criteria needed to be recognised as civil parties – in other words, people who have provided enough proof that they or a loved one suffered harm as a result of these crimes. It is one of the most insensitive acts of this tribunal that it has chosen to wait until judgment day before excluding 24 of the 90 remaining civil parties.

As the list is read, I wait to hear whether Martine and Neary will be on it, and it is with some relief that I hear their names among the final three.

'Martine Lefeuvre and Ouk Neary, for the loss respectively of their husband and father Ouk Ket,' Nil Nonn reads.

The last name to be read is Rob Hamill's.

In another controversial decision, the judges rule that they have no authority to instruct the Cambodian government on reparations that civil parties have requested – such as building a monument to the dead at the Tuol Sleng Genocide Museum. The sum total of reparations: they will include the names of the civil parties in the final judgment, and they will compile all of Duch's apologies and post them on the tribunal's website. They will do nothing more. Although it is true that the judges could not order the government to build a memorial, they could easily have added their moral weight by merely stating that such a tribute would be fitting. Many feel this constitutes an abject failure by the bench.

WHEN THE TRIBUNAL RELEASED THE 19-page compilation of Duch's apologies – which it posted only on its website in this largely offline, impoverished nation – most of the pages had nothing to do with apologies per se. Some revolved around Duch's numerous comments in court when he told the bench that he accepted responsibility for what had happened; other paragraphs dealt with historical facts or elements that had emerged at trial.

By way of example, here is the full text of what the judges felt constituted Duch's apology to Martine:

'Mr President, first of all, allow me to speak to Mrs Lefeuvre as follows: I would like to acknowledge your family's biography as historical fact. When I say it is historical fact I mean it remains lasting forever. This means that whenever someone wants to conduct research on the suffering of the Cambodian people they will surely go to Mrs Lefeuvre for her testimony. In that sense, the truth differs from the flower. The flower has its life span; it blooms then dies, but the historical truth remains. It does not blossom or die. The truth lasts forever. The suffering of the Cambodian people, including that of Mrs Lefeuvre and her children, is historical fact that cannot be forgotten. I would like to acknowledge that.

'I wish Mrs Lefeuvre, the Trial Chamber, and the entire Cambodian people to know that I will not abscond. I stand before this court to be tried. The crimes being tried are intolerable. The Cambodian people can point their fingers at my face. If they want to lay the blame on me, they can. If they want to condemn me, they can do so. And here we have the court. I entrust myself to the court. I would like to confirm that I am morally and legally responsible for the crimes committed at S-21 and I am also morally answerable for the crimes committed throughout the country. I will not make any denial, not a word. *And right here before me, I would like to apologise to Mrs Lefeuvre and her daughter who is present here. In so doing, I would like to apologise to all the widows in Cambodia and to all the fatherless children.*' (Italics added.)

Just 40 of nearly 300 words listed actually amounted to an apology. When it came to Duch's comments to Neary, which were also reproduced in the apology document, there was nothing. For the other civil parties, much of this document was similarly barren. By one calculation compiling all of the sentences that actually comprised apologies filled just a page, yet the message to the world was that Duch had apologised so often as to fill 19. Not so, one civil party lawyer told me later. The rest constituted acknowledgements of his guilt, which given the overwhelming evidence against him was of limited value to the civil parties, and sundry comments by Duch about himself, such as one where he told the bench he would accept being stoned to death by the Cambodian people 'like St Stephen'.

Neary felt the Cambodian government should have issued an apology to all those affected by the Khmer Rouge's rule, yet it had uttered not a word. Nor for that matter, she said, did any of the other parties to the trial.

'In the end, Ket has been killed, there is no place where we know he is, and there is hardly any trace of him,' she told me later. 'Absolutely no honour has been given back to him, and neither to our family.'

IT IS 11.08AM on July 26, 2010, and we have been listening to Nil Nonn for an hour. Duch is ordered to stand for the verdict and does so, arms to his side, rigid, like the obedient schoolboy in the story who stands before his teacher.

Duch is told that he has been found guilty of crimes against humanity and war crimes.

Nil Nonn turns to sentencing and stresses the aggravating factors such as 'the shocking and heinous' crimes against no fewer than 12,273 people over a period of several years. On the other hand, he continues, mitigating factors that mandate against a life sentence include Duch's cooperation, his admission of responsibility, limited expressions of remorse, and the environment of Democratic Kampuchea.

The sentence is 35 years.

After deducting 11 years for time served and five more as compensation for the near-decade of his pre-trial detention, Duch will serve a further 19 years. It means he will be in his mid-eighties before he is released, assuming he lives that long. Some civil parties are angry at the apparent brevity of Duch's sentence, but Martine and Neary are relieved that today at least an internationally backed court has handed down a guilty verdict. That said, it constitutes 'so few years in terms of the context' of his crimes, as Neary later put it. They too would have preferred a longer jail term.

Later that day David Chandler sums up his thoughts on the defendant, a man he has followed with interest for years. Chandler believes Duch does regret his past actions but, crucially, does not regard himself as guilty.

'And there's a difference,' Chandler says. 'He feels sorry ... because what he did is what he did at the time, and he probably knows it was a terrible thing to do, but he wasn't conflicted at the time.'

LITTLE MORE THAN A YEAR AFTER the verdict, on September 5, 2011, as a tremendous thunderstorm burst across Phnom Penh, Vann Nath died. He had lived long enough to see the jailing of his tormentor, who was ironically also his liberator. Vann Nath's family sent a text message to his many friends: 'Nath just left us this morning. A big rain pours when he dies.'

Vann Nath was a humble and noble man. He would not bend for others and, in a country where deference is the custom, that was unusual. In his final years he had become a softly spoken, powerful moral voice on the crimes of the Khmer Rouge and by extension on the crimes of obedience. When he testified at the tribunal, he had said his fervent wish was that the country's youth would learn about what had happened in those years. Only then could he be certain it would not happen again.

In Rithy Panh's documentary about S-21, Vann Nath returned to the prison and to the room in which he had been shackled for weeks. There in his gentle tone he asked his former guards and torturers: when and how did you lose your humanity? It is a question that he of all people was qualified to ask. They had no answer.

Vann Nath's death came up in my next conversation with Neary. She wanted to know whether he would appear in this book. Perhaps, I said, although I was leaning more towards his fellow artist Bou Meng on the grounds that so many people had already interviewed Vann Nath.

'Yes, but not everyone talks to Vann Nath,' Neary replied. 'Vann Nath is talking to us for many years but no one is talking to him, because the way he speaks, he communicates with painting. And did someone do a painting for him? No. But this is the way he communicates … and no one is talking to him properly. We are just taking and taking.'

On her visit to Phnom Penh for Duch's verdict the previous year, Neary had planned to remedy that and so she brought with her pencils, brushes and pots of orange, yellow and red paint. She had decided she would sit down with Vann Nath, to be near him and, she said, to paint something as a gift for him – an image she would construct on canvas in sunny colours 'because we need more light'. But in the end her trip was too brief and, before she could arrange to see Vann Nath, it was time to return to France. The pencils, brushes and paints, unused, remained behind in her hotel room, and her intention to give back to Vann Nath in the universal language of art remained unfulfilled.

THERE WERE TWO MORE EVENTS that related to Duch. The first was that, despite his promise at trial that he would not appeal, he did. Few were surprised.

It proved a poor decision. On February 3, 2012 – nearly a year after three days of appeal hearings during which Kar Savuth once more wheeled out his bankrupt arguments – the seven-judge bench of the Supreme Chamber affirmed Duch's guilt and added further convictions including extermination encompassing murder, enslavement, imprisonment, torture and other inhumane acts.

Controversially, the Supreme Chamber also ruled in a majority decision that Duch's pre-trial detention was not the tribunal's responsibility since he had been held at a Cambodian military prison from the time of his arrest in 1999 until he was transferred to the court in 2006. For that reason Duch could not benefit from any remedy. With that removed, it ruled that the severity of Duch's crimes warranted a life sentence.

Two of the three foreign judges dissented, arguing in a minority opinion that, although Duch's crimes justified life, his lengthy pre-trial detention had breached international law and therefore his final sentence should have been less than life. But no further appeal was possible, and in 2013 Duch was transferred from the tribunal's detention facility to serve out his life term in a cell at a jail outside Phnom Penh.

The second event revolved around my efforts to interview Duch. At trial he had made much of his offer that his door would always be open to the victims of his crimes. By mid-2011, I had decided to write this book and sent two letters requesting the opportunity to interview him. The decision was Duch's alone to make, and on both occasions he declined. It was not unexpected: Duch had also refused to meet Rob Hamill, who wanted to know whether his brother Kerry had been burned alive at S-21.

With Duch terminating any possibility of an interview, I went to see documentary-maker Rithy Panh who had been far more fortunate in gaining access. It was 2013 and Panh, now 50, had enjoyed an artistically fruitful year: his biopic about the destruction of his family under the Khmer Rouge, filmed using clay images and interspersed with footage from the period, had won a leading award at the Cannes Film Festival and was nominated for a 2014 Academy Award, the first Cambodian film to be so honoured.[1] But it was Panh's experience when making a previous documentary – *Duch, Master of the Forges of Hell* – that I was there to discuss. This earlier work had been released in 2012, and was the product of hundreds of hours of interviews between the two men over the course of 2008 and 2009, conducted prior to Duch's trial.

Panh said that getting his subject to talk had proved close to impossible until one morning Duch announced that he had had a revelation while praying.

'God told me I have to talk to you,' Duch said.

And with that, the interviews began. From early on, Panh was puzzled by Duch's wholehearted belief that people would forgive him once he accepted responsibility and apologised for what he had done.

'I told him that people will not forgive easily but that the most important thing to do is to come back to humanity,' Panh told me as an overhead fan dispersed the drifts of cigar smoke to the four corners of his small first-floor

---

1. *The Missing Picture*, Rithy Panh, 2013. It won the *Un Certain Regard* award at Cannes, topping the category for innovative films. It missed out on the Oscar for best foreign language film to Italy's *The Great Beauty*.

office at the Bophana Center. 'We don't want you lost to this crime; we want you to come back. It hurts. It's very hard for us but we must do this, so come back to us. Don't stay with the killing.'

There were even times during the weeks and months of filming when Panh found himself in favour of seeing Duch freed by the tribunal, provided he returned to the fold.

'But you don't have 300 different ways to do that,' he told Duch. 'You have only one way, one road and that is telling the truth. I don't know another way.'

Interviewing Duch proved to be 'a real confrontation', with the two men on occasion shouting at each other. For weeks at a time Duch would refuse to see Panh, while during other sessions he cut short the filming after an hour. But often enough they managed to get on and Duch would sit through a day's three-hour session. The result was not just a gripping documentary; many of their exchanges also comprise a substantial part of Panh's book *The Elimination*, which is in part a recounting of his life under the Khmer Rouge.

Time and again, in the documentary and the book, Duch's fundamental strangeness shines through. Among the most peculiar mannerisms, given the topics they discussed, was that every interview Panh conducted – and there were dozens – concluded with Duch laughing or smiling. Then there was the former mathematics teacher's numerical obsession: Duch adores the perfection of numbers whose sum totals nine, so he was profoundly dissatisfied that the digits in M-13 added up to only 4, and even less pleased that those in S-21 gave a sum of just 3, because that represented an even lower 'score'.

And what was the reason, Duch wondered aloud to Panh, behind this apparent slight: S-21 had just two digits when the most prestigious offices in Democratic Kampuchea had either a single number such as the Ministry of Foreign Affairs, known as B-1, or three such as Office 870, which was the cabinet for the Central Committee?

'"Why did the security service have fewer digits than the others?"' Duch mused three decades later. '"My feelings were hurt."'[2]

One of the most significant exchanges between the two men took place when Panh handed Duch a sheaf of 50 pages, each containing a slogan from Democratic Kampuchea. Go on, he told Duch, pick one. Duch, his glasses on, riffled through the pages then stopped at the phrase that, as it happens, leads one of the chapters in this book: 'To keep you is no benefit,

2. Panh, *The Elimination*, op. cit., p. 129.

to destroy you is no loss.' That one, Duch told the film-maker, was 'very profound' not least because it had emanated from the Central Committee.

Duch then returned to the papers, and having examined them all told Panh that the most important slogan was missing: that blood debts must be paid in blood. Puzzled, Panh pointed out that the 'blood debts' slogan lacks the ideology inherent in many of the sayings of that period. Why, then, was it so important? Duch looked directly at him, saying: 'Mr Rithy, the Khmer Rouge were all about elimination.'[3]

These outbursts of honesty, though at times bizarre, were overshadowed by Duch's deceits, some small, many large. Panh concluded that Duch, talkative to the end, was using words to construct a bogus history. His comment reminded me of S-21's confessions.

As the interviews went on, Panh found himself becoming increasingly unsettled, but it was not the subject matter that made him ill at ease. After all, with all of the work Panh has done on S-21 – hundreds of hours spent interviewing survivors, torturers, guards and drivers for his documentary about S-21, and having spent countless hours in its archives – he is without question one of those most knowledgeable about the workings of Duch's prison and about Duch himself.[4] As he neared the end of his filming, it dawned on Panh that Duch had used this experience as not only a way to write his version of history but as a practice run for his trial.

'It was terrible for me, terrible,' Panh said of that sickening realisation.

The insights that Panh gleaned from the interviews meant that much of Duch's behaviour at trial came as little surprise, not the least of which was his *volte-face* in its final days. Not only did Panh know it was coming, he even warned François Roux to expect it. (Panh said that Roux did not believe him.) Early on Panh drew up a 'humanity scale', a rule-of-thumb measure to assess how truthful he reckoned Duch was being during filming. During the earlier interviews Panh felt Duch was telling the truth around 20 per cent of the time and, although he did not expect Duch to reach 100 per cent truth-telling, he did feel that attaining 80 per cent would be 'very good for all of us, because it means that he tells much more truth and in that way gets back his humanity and his dignity'.

That goal, as it happened, chimed with Roux's approach, which centred on trying to restore Duch's human dignity.

---

3. Ibid., p. 73.

4. *S-21, The Khmer Rouge Killing Machine*, Rithy Panh (2003).

'It's a very good idea from François — he's a good lawyer,' Panh said approvingly of Roux's method. 'Because by doing that you learn more truths, and the civil parties can also gain dignity from the trial. You cannot win dignity on one side if the other side loses. Either you both win or you both lose.'

As the months passed Panh kept careful watch while Duch's position ebbed and flowed along his humanity scale. Before the trial began, Panh had noticed a worrying trend: a sullen evasiveness when he produced incontrovertible evidence to counter specific denials from Duch; or antagonism when Panh appeared to favour the story of, for instance, a survivor from M-13A rather than Duch's version of events at his former jungle execution centre. On one occasion, for instance, an unnerved Duch rounded on Panh for believing 'this idiot' survivor and threatened to halt the interview.

'If you agree with Duch, you are intelligent,' Panh concluded of his subject's attitude. 'If you do not agree with him, you are naive.'

On other occasions Duch claimed he had never heard prisoners' screams even though the route from his home to S-21 took him past the interrogation rooms that lined the narrow street. Duch also denied seeing prisoners being taken in or out of S-21, one more example in a litany of implausibilities.

'So one day I am having lunch with François, and I say: you know, François, we have a big problem. Now on my scale,' Panh said, tapping the table twice with his finger, 'he has only five per cent of humanity.'

But Roux did not accept his client was backsliding, drifting ever further from his pledge to tell the truth. Roux also did not believe Panh's contention – prescient, as it turned out – that Duch would eventually sack him.

'I told him you will be fired and that Duch will also refuse to see me [any longer for interviews],' Panh said of these two other outcomes, both of which later transpired. 'That was because Duch had two strategies. If the people forgave him, he would continue to say that: "I did it because of the terror that was upon me but I accept the responsibility." But he will not tell the truth. And if people did not forgive him because they didn't accept that he acted because of this terror, then he would change his strategy and, with Kar Savuth, he would ask for release.'

When that played out in the closing days of Duch's trial, Panh was one of the very few who had seen it coming all along.

As our conversation about Duch wrapped up, I asked Panh what he thought of this man with whom he had spent so many hours cloistered in close conditions. Panh replied that he views Duch as he does many of the senior Khmer Rouge who survived: like them, he is afflicted with 'a disease of purity' that caused him to eliminate his innate humanity as he strove for revolution; and like them, to this day, he refuses to analyse his actions. This obsession with purity, he added, could be seen in Duch's love of French grammar, which, when the language is spoken well, constitutes something 'very special, very complex, very precise, very pure – a pure beauty'.

For Panh, the turning point at Duch's trial came not in the events of the final week but much earlier when Duch told the tribunal that although humans could condemn him, God would forgive him, and that he would bow to what the judges decided.

'The most important thing is God,' Panh concluded from Duch's statement. 'And for us, it was finished at that point.'

When I looked back later on our interview, what stood out for me was Panh's genuine disappointment that the man with whom he had quizzed, fought and even laughed during hundreds of hours of intense debate was in the end unable to return to society. The responsibility for the truth to emerge was wholly Duch's, but Panh was still saddened that he had not proven equal to the task. Instead Duch chose, as he put it, 'to stay with the killing'.

'He had an opportunity to get back his humanity,' said Panh, 'and he failed.'

DURING OUR INTERVIEW the conversation had also turned to the broader subject of the tribunal itself, with Panh convinced that it had erred in ignoring ideology and focusing solely on facts. After all, how could the tribunal hope to learn the truth without investigating what had motivated the very crimes it was adjudicating?

'I understand that the tribunal must judge only facts, that they don't judge ideology,' he said. 'But the problem is that in the case of mass crimes or crimes against humanity or genocide, it's *always* ideology. And if you don't at least explain what this ideology is, then you will have confusion with some authors saying it's culture.'

From his long experience investigating Democratic Kampuchea, Panh holds no hope that we will learn much from the likes of Duch, Nuon Chea, Khieu Samphan or even from the educated ex-Khmer Rouge who live freely in Cambodia and who are at no risk of prosecution. Such people, some of whom Panh knows, believe sincerely in their ideology and instead of analysing what happened they merely rewrite history to suit themselves.

'Pol Pot told [journalist] Nate Thayer [in 1997]: "I am not a savage person. I am a nice man, a nice guy",' said Panh, by way of example.[5] 'And Nate filmed it, Pol Pot's last message, and we didn't learn anything.'

Similarly, Duch's trial had failed to add to the knowledge that Panh had gained years earlier when working with the artist Vann Nath to make the documentary about S-21.

'I have learned nothing more. You take S-21 and you spend 80 million dollars, and because the tribunal refused to go into the ideology field – it's just facts, facts, facts, facts – it's nothing,' he said. 'We know the facts. But why did they kill? Because they believed! They believed that they had the right to do that. They believed in the ideology. They believed that they could go very far with their new idea of communism.'

By way of example, Panh cited the Khmer Rouge's decision to plant Phnom Penh's pavements with stands of coconut trees, rice and vegetables.

'There's no logic. They bring the countryside to the city. That's what it means. It's absurd. Absurd!' he said, rapping the table with his knuckles, one, two, three times, his voice rising. 'For hundreds of years you have cities and you have countryside – it is human civilisation. The city is the centre of command, the centre of education, the centre of culture. Yet they want to bring rice fields and coconuts to the city!'

As Phnom Penh became a farm, the new regime banned money and, evoking the concept of the noble savage, sought to remove what it regarded as the corrupting effect of materialism. As Panh saw firsthand, the new rulers quickly scrapped the cooperatives that had at least allowed people to tend small pieces of land for themselves, and replaced them with collectives. By 1975 even China knew collectives were a disaster but the Khmer Rouge ignored that, determined to go further than Mao ever had.

'And collectivism means that you create nothing,' he said. 'Some people eat, some people cannot eat.'

All of this ideological lunacy and more contributed to the catastrophe that was the Khmer Rouge's rule yet it remained unexamined by the tribunal. That was a missed opportunity, said Panh, as was the broader failure to ensure work was carried out in parallel with the tribunal on memory: preserving the

---

5. In his 1997 interview with US journalist Nate Thayer, an 'unrepentant' Pol Pot told him: 'I came to carry out the struggle, not to kill people. Even now, and you can look at me, am I a savage person? My conscience is clear.' *Phnom Penh Post*, October 24, 1997, p. 1.

knowledge of the past for future generations, which has long been a focus of Panh's life.

Yet despite the tribunal's failings, Panh continues to support the court. His reasoning is simple enough.

'It is the first time that we have identified who is the victim,' he explained. 'Before, nobody wanted to do that. Nobody. But now we can say, for example, that Ouk Ket is a victim. For 30 years he was not a victim, and nobody recognised Ket as a victim.'

Now people like Ket have been named, their experience acknowledged and they are, finally, remembered.

'And that,' he concluded, 'is *very* important.'

LEAVING S-21 PRISON: JULY 25, 2010

WHEN THE KHMER ROUGE REGIME collapsed on January 7, 1979 thousands of surviving cadres fled west to escape the invading army of Vietnamese soldiers and Cambodian defectors. Among them, of course, was Duch whose escape through the gates of S-21 and along the capital's backstreets was where this story started.

As Duch and other loyalists headed west, millions who had survived the Khmer Rouge's rule began their own journeys leaving the rural collectives and returning to their villages or towns. Among them were Sady and her family, who headed back to the capital. The country was devastated and its people were traumatised, fearful that the Khmer Rouge would re-emerge to wreak havoc.

Slowly, Sady and her family rebuilt their lives, and throughout 1979 more survivors trickled back with terrible stories of loss. Among them was Ket's mother, Saray, but without her husband or most of her children.

Eventually the families learned that Ouk Saron, Ket's brother who had gone to Svay Rieng in 1975, had died too, as had his uncle. If there was any consolation, it was that everyone had a similar array of stories. In that traumatised confederation, the only thing to do was to push ahead slowly.

Sady's husband started a business making detergent at home, decanting the liquid into scavenged bottles and selling them in the market. They used the proceeds to buy food. Sady eventually became a teacher. They raised a family, and around them life returned to Cambodia, literally, as a baby boom saw the country generate one of the most unequal population distribution curves in the world.

While Sady was starting over in Phnom Penh, Neary was growing up in France. One of Neary's most significant memories was watching the Oscar-winning film *The Killing Fields*, which describes the experiences of photojournalist Dith Pran before and during Democratic Kampuchea. In the film, which was released in 1984, the role of Dith Pran is played by Haing Ngor, a Cambodian doctor and a survivor of Democratic Kampuchea.

The film was a landmark in raising awareness of Cambodia's torment, and watching it was a pivotal moment for Neary, who first saw it when she was 10. She still regards Haing Ngor, who was shot dead in Los Angeles in 1996 in murky circumstances, as a key figure, a man who brought the crimes of Democratic Kampuchea to a vast audience. Much later, after Neary had become a mother, she bought a DVD of the film. Among the bonus tracks was an interview with some of the women who later became civil parties at Duch's trial.

BY THE MID-1990s the Khmer Rouge movement was approaching its end as strongholds like Pailin defected to the government. Among the hardliners, mistrust and paranoia increased and Pol Pot began purging those within the ranks. In June 1997 Duch's old boss, Son Sen, was murdered along with his wife Yun Yat, the former information minister, and a dozen members of their families including children. Pulling out the grass by the roots was the Khmer Rouge way. Pol Pot ordered them all shot and trucks driven over their bodies.

The movement's death throes were played out in Anlong Veng. *Ta* Mok turned on Pol Pot, arresting Brother Number One after the latter tried to have him killed. Journalist Nate Thayer witnessed Pol Pot being put on trial by his own people, convicted of treason and sentenced to house arrest. The following year Pol Pot died – 'he is nothing more than cow dung,' *Ta* Mok boasted – and his body was torched on a makeshift pyre of furniture and car tyres. The *Phnom Penh Post* headlined the story: BURNED LIKE OLD RUBBISH.

In 1999, *Ta* Mok's faction collapsed and he was arrested. Intransigent to the end, he had refused to strike a deal with the government. His jailing marked the end of the Khmer Rouge, whose uncompromising political vendetta against the Cambodian people had caused the deaths of millions. *Ta* Mok died in 2006 while awaiting trial.

Four years after that I went to *Ta* Mok's compound in Anlong Veng for the reconciliation day event, and while the participants broke for lunch I headed the 15 kilometres or so to the Dangrek Hills that mark the boundary between Thailand and Cambodia. The word *dangrek* refers, appropriately enough in this agricultural nation, to a method of carrying a heavy load, in this case by using a pole slung across the shoulders. This long, low-lying range hugs the ground much as a *dangrek* pole would when laid down.

The paved road to the Dangrek Hills runs through a flat landscape of rice fields and scattered trees, before climbing gently. At the summit, after a few wrong turns, we found what we had come to see.

When the Khmer Rouge captured Phnom Penh in 1975, Pol Pot surely saw himself as a Mao-like figure who would refashion a corrupt Cambodia, forging it in the purifying flames of an unflinching ideology. His revolution would outshine all others, and he presumably envisaged being seen by future generations as the architect of this brilliance and treated accordingly with dazzling monuments in heroic revolutionary style.

We know that one such monument was planned because Vann Nath was tasked with working on a scale model of it at S-21. The pagoda at Wat Phnom, the highest landmass in Phnom Penh, was to be demolished and a huge copper and concrete statue put in its place. Its design would portray Pol Pot striding forward, his right hand raised, the constitution clutched in his left, while an anonymous mass of smaller figures clustered closely to him as he guided them into the bright future promised by Democratic Kampuchea.

Doubtless Pol Pot cannot have foreseen what I came to see. His grave near the crest of the Dangrek Hills stands near some open scrubland at the end of a sandy path a few hundred yards from the border crossing. Nearby are a few houses on stilts behind a cluster of trees. Opposite them is a corrugated iron fence marking out yet another division of private property in a land where, under Pol Pot's rule, no such capitalist tenure was permitted.

His is a squalid resting place: a 6-foot-long corrugated iron roof held up by small wooden posts two feet high. Soft-drink bottles are embedded upside down in the earth, nearly swallowed, to create a decorative glass perimeter around the grave. The corrugated iron is rusting, and the posts are tired. A scattering of litter lies near a small shrine of burned incense sticks and an energy drink that someone has left for his spirit. It is the case that some still come here to pray to Pol Pot for luck.

In a bid to attract tourists, the government has put up a signpost, a faded blue board atop a weathered pole telling the occasional visitor that: 'Pol Pot's [sic] Was Cremated Here. Please Help To Preserve This Historical Site.' There is no other information.

Pol Pot surely expected a better remembrance despite the revolutionary rhetoric that subsumed the individual to the cause. That, after all, was for the masses. We all dream, yet how many of us manage to kidnap a nation?

For such people, how much bigger must their dreams be? Pol Pot had met some of the giants of the socialist movement, including Mao and Kim Il Sung, and was familiar with the personality cults they had built.

Historian David Chandler reckoned that in 1977 the Chinese told Pol Pot it was time he emerged from the shadows and become the visible leader of the revolution; drop the faceless *Angkar* and create a cult of personality.

'This was the trade-off,' Chandler told me. 'You want our aid and you want to be an international communist, then you come out of the woodwork and say so and take charge of these people personally.'

Had the Khmer Rouge remained in power, then one might imagine a Democratic Kampuchea today peppered with grandiose marble and bronze monuments praising Pol Pot's achievements as the leader of the greatest movement in the history of communism, manufacturer of the purest and most perfect revolution, the one that outstripped all others.

This is not that tribute. Rusting corrugated iron, rickety posts, burned incense sticks and crumpled cigarette butts in a windswept setting, and all of this about as far from Phnom Penh as it is possible to get in Cambodia, his grave jammed on to wasteland on a low slab of hill with no view. For a man whose revolution crushed the lives of millions and the dreams of many more, the near nullity of his final resting place is apt. Here he is reduced, and what little remains of him has become a largely unvisited tourist site.

IT IS LATE JULY, the height of the planting season, and across this nation countless hands transplant millions of iridescent seedlings from tightly packed paddy nurseries, the vigorous jade stems shimmering with the promise of life, sustenance and regeneration. This is the wet season, the months of downpours when rain drifts thick like smoke, hammering tin roofs, scoring and soaking the land, flooding the fields and providing the bounty of rice that is this nation's staple.

The life-giving clouds roll slowly above the courtyard of an old school in Phnom Penh. For now the rains hold off – they will come later – and the breeze rustles the fronds of the coconut palms. In the pale shade, Neary and Martine join the slow-moving flow of dozens of people who file past a painted concrete memorial. It stands just yards inside S-21's entrance whose gateway condemned so many, and whose metal script today marks out the words 'GENOCIDE MUSEUM'. At the memorial's feet are devotions of incense, and flowers wrapped in black ribbon with white writing.

This day, Sunday the 25th, 2010, is the day before Duch's verdict, and dozens of civil parties are here at a Buddhist ceremony for the dead of S-21, their dead. For these numerous relatives and the few survivors, today is about remembering their loved ones, and that commemoration on this day of high emotion is surely their most basic need. A man with a loudhailer chants verses through his tears as the mourners lay their wreaths. Close by, with their backs to the room where the prison's photographers once captured thousands of monochrome images, five Buddhist monks sit impassively on mats, their orange robes lending a swatch of vivid colour. To one side next to Building C, just yards from Ket's cell, are a half-dozen white-clad Buddhist nuns.

Martine and Neary sit near the front, their legs tucked to one side in the Cambodian way, surrounded by dozens of other civil parties dressed in white and black, the colours of mourning. Martine, wearing dark glasses, is to the right of and just behind Neary, her head buried in her daughter's back. Emotions are raw, and hands clasp neighbours' arms in support as the tears fall. The Buddhist monks provide a stoic contrast, removed from these displays of worldly sentiment.

I have come today not as a journalist but to take photographs on behalf of Neary and Martine as a memento of their final farewell to Ket. The long lens on my camera allows me to keep my distance and as the ceremony begins I retreat to Building C, to the walkway of its second floor where black-clad guards once kept sullen watch over the shackled prisoners.

The monks begin chanting prayers for the dead.

Next to Neary is New Zealander Rob Hamill, whose brother Kerry was murdered at S-21. Since there was no way to bring Kerry's remains home, Rob Hamill had instead brought something of his home country: seawater and sand in recognition of Kerry's love of the ocean. He had asked Neary where she felt would be best to leave that reminder and she had suggested the entrance gate 'because everyone passed through it' at one time or another.

It was a year earlier that Neary had written her message to Ket on his cell wall – '**WE ARE LEAVING**' – her and Martine's call to him to go, and as the monotone prayers pierce the thick air, something catches her eye: a figure, white-lit, that emerges from the building then pauses yards from her in the shelter of the trees.

'I could really feel it,' she told me later. 'I know that no one saw it but me [and] it's not that I saw it technically with my eyes, but it was very clear in my mind.'

'I am not a believer,' she continued. 'And I don't believe in reincarnation or the afterlife, things like that, but I can tell you that I saw him out.'

As the sacred chants rise above this courtyard where screams and fear once reigned, as the prayers curl around the coconut palms and swirl into the steel sky, and with Martine weeping into her shoulder, Neary keeps her eyes fixed fiercely on Ket so that no one can interrupt his leaving.

'He wasn't happy or sad, only exhausted at the time he had spent waiting in this sordid place,' she said. 'The gate was safe and, without a word, my Dad slowly walked out.'

INDEX

ABOUT THE AUTHOR

South African journalist Robert Carmichael lived in Cambodia for ten years. He spent two years as the managing editor of the *Phnom Penh Post*, the country's oldest English-language newspaper. From 2009 to 2013 he was the country correspondent for the German Press Agency dpa. His work has appeared in or been broadcast by numerous outlets including Voice of America, Radio Australia, the BBC and *Foreign Policy*. He currently lives in Hungary. This is his first book.